DATE DUE

27 OCT 67

DANILEVSKY

A Russian Totalitarian Philosopher

Russian Research Center Studies

53

DANILEVSKY

A Russian Totalitarian Philosopher

By

Robert E. MacMaster

HARVARD UNIVERSITY PRESS

CAMBRIDGE, MASSACHUSETTS

1967

Distributed in Great Britain by Oxford University Press, London

The Russian Research Center of Harvard University is supported by a grant from the Ford Foundation. The Center carries out interdisciplinary study of Russian institutions and behavior and related subjects.

This volume was prepared in part under a grant from the Carnegie Corporation of New York. That Corporation is not, however, the author, owner, publisher or proprietor of this publication and is not to be understood as approving by virtue of its grant any of the statements made or views expressed therein.

Library of Congress Catalog Card Number 66-21340

Printed in the United States of America

TO ANN

PREFACE

Nicholas Iakovlevich Danilevsky (1822–1885) has been much discussed by scholars: now as a forerunner of Spengler and Toynbee; now as a major Panslavist theoretician; occasionally as a biologist, statistician, and Russian critic of Darwin; or as a utopian socialist in the Fourierist Petrashevsky circle. I have studied all these facets in detail and put them together to work out a picture of Danilevsky in himself and in his time. I have found that the earlier piecemeal study of him, while useful in many ways, has obscured much of the real meaning of his thought and his historical significance. He is best seen not as a typical Panslavist or as a forerunner of Spengler but as a would-be political prophet whose thought has some striking and interesting if only general similarities to Bolshevism. In his famous book, *Russia and Europe*, he prophesied the coming of a total and inevitable war between "Europe" and the Slavs, led by Russia. This war was envisioned by him — as was revolution later by Lenin — not as a practical if brutal means to worldly ends but as a kind of ritual action that would purge men's sins, cure their inadequacies, and usher in a socialist's (Danilevsky was ever that) heaven on earth.

My purpose has been larger than one of straightening out a piece of prerevolutionary Russian intellectual history, however. I have attempted a somewhat new kind of historical research, using comparative historical, social scientific, and philosophical-psychological (mainly phenomenological) concepts quite extensively in the analysis of biographical materials. Specifically I have accompanied a description of Danilevsky's whole intellectual development with a detailed analysis of that development's relationship — historical, psychological, and social — to his life history and to Russia's cultural and institutional problems with modernization. This has made for more than a study of one man. It is a biographical history of the modern Russian radical mind, both romantic (for Danilevsky went through such a phase in his youth) and totalitarian. I hope that the reader will gain some useful insight not only into Danilevsky but also into the human meanings of a historical change of worldwide significance.

This has not been an easy book to write and I could not have done so without the generous help of many people. The late Michael M. Karpovich taught me Russian history and suggested that I study Danilevsky, "squeezing the scanty data very hard and placing him in his time." Robert L. Wolff has given me invaluable advice and criticism; his understanding and trust brought me through many difficult stages. I. Bernard Cohen advised me on the history of science. I benefited from the criticism of H. Stuart Hughes. Authur P. Mendel got me some key microfilms from Helsinki. I wish also to thank for major financial support and for encouragement the Russian Research Center and its former directors, the late Clyde Kluckhohn, Merle Fainsod, and William L. Langer. Mrs. Helen W. Parsons of the Center and Mrs. Ruth E. Dubois of the Humanities Department of the Massachusetts Institute of Technology gave me the best possible administrative assistance. That Department and its former and present chairmen, Howard R. Bartlett and Richard M. Douglas, gave me financial support and encouragement.

The book is dedicated with love to my wife, Ann Elizabeth MacMaster.

The quotations from Max Scheler, *Ressentiment*, and from Pitirim A. Sorokin, *Modern Historical and Social Philosophies* (1963; formerly, *Social Philosophies of an Age of Crisis*, Beacon Press, 1950), are printed with the permission of the respective publishers, The Macmillan Company and Dover Publications. The frontispiece has been reproduced from the second volume of Danilevsky's *Darvinism* (St. Petersburg, 1889). The epigraph is from Roger Garaudy, *Le Marxisme et la personne humaine* (Paris, 1949), p. 17.

Neither *Russia and Europe* nor *Darwinism* has been translated; for the convenience of the reader I have, however, used the English translation of the titles in the text. The only edition of *Russia and Europe* continuously available to me during the research was the "first" or *Zariia* edition. George Ivask's excellent new edition (New York, 1966) unfortunately came out too late to be of use.

The transliteration system used throughout this volume is that of the Library of Congress.

R. E. M.

Massachusetts Institute of Technology
October 10, 1966

CONTENTS

"Marxism revolutionizes the very idea of philosophy: true philosophy is politics, that is, history in the making and life itself in creative evolution."

Roger Garaudy, *Le Marxisme et la personne humaine*

1

INTRODUCTION

THE word "totalitarian," properly used, refers to some unique types of government, political doctrine, and related behavior patterns, group and individual. These phenomena are peculiar to the twentieth century, totalitarianism having reached its full development only in Nazism and Bolshevism.[1] But facets of it have a history running back into the nineteenth century. Intellectual forerunners are fairly numerous in European history from at least 1850 onward. Living as they did without the support or influence of totalitarian political movements or systems, these forerunners can be studied with profit; for they allow the historian an opportunity to see the totalitarian mind and the formation of its doctrine in relation to more normal historical phenomena. Such study emphasizes the fact that this evil is as much the product of moral and spiritual failure as of the cultural and intellectual difficulties of modern times. We are reminded that totalitarianism as a form of thought and behavior might under certain circumstances be adopted by practically anyone.

This biography of Nicholas Iakovlevich Danilevsky (1822–1885) is intended to be a chapter in the intellectual history of nineteenth century Russia. Danilevsky's story has its natural center, however, in the totalitarian philosophy he set forth in *Russia and Europe*, published in 1869. Placing an intellectual figure in the history of totalitarianism rather than liberalism or conservatism or nationalism is not unprecedented.[2] Nevertheless, intellectual totalitarianism, in the present state of historiography, is by no means as well-known or conceptualized as these. It seems appropriate, therefore, to lay out some key concepts. We need to know, at a minimum, the characteristics of a totalitarian philosophy, its main types in European history, and the classification of Danilevsky's philosophy according to type.

A philosophy of this kind is at once in and out of the intellectual culture of the modern age. It is a pseudoreligious blend of reason and myth, iron and sentimentality, technology and mysticism, realism and romanticism. It advocates the planning of some great upheaval, a revolution or a war, in a social and cultural world which, however imperfect, does not seem to the outside observer to invite drastic action at all. One gets the impression that totalitarian thinkers advocate war, revolution, or dictatorship less as means to ends than as transitional existential states, ones that will somehow render men essentially (ontologically) human and thus prepare them for a state of earthly beatitude. Such a philosophy is appropriately and sneeringly critical of those intellectual and cultural patterns which modern men have frequently thought worthy — liberalism, for instance, or the ordinary kind of nationalism. Impassioned scorn, hatred, buckets of filth are dumped upon such thin, bourgeois philistinism. On the other hand, such doctrines invariably take, as their own, distorted versions of these same ordinary modern ideas and values. These are adopted because of their supposed currently existential relevance, for the sake of agitational appeal, and because of the conviction that men are inevitably trapped in their moment of history. The totalitarian philosopher, especially the type with whom we are concerned, insults and attempts to subvert modernity with a distorted version of that age's own language and aspirations.

A doctrine of this type makes vague, eschatological promises. Most important, it promises the angry, the bored, the anxiety-ridden both a return to a romanticized past and a fusion of that past with the best of the present. It promises "real," final, deep satisfaction, an end of confusion, tension, disorder, change. It holds out beatitude and directs men to war, revolution, oppression as though they were *rites de passage*. Culturally, intellectual totalitarianism is related to two contrary tendencies in modern history. On the one hand, modernity disrupts tradition and — with its secularism, functional rationalism, science, and technology — seems to many men to devaluate religion, metaphysics, poetry and other means for achieving a sense of meaning. On the other hand, modernity does not take away human feelings. Indeed, by weakening older, "softer" cultural patterns, it often leaves a feeling of disorientation and makes men hungrier than ever for some sense of order, aspiration, and direction. Culturally, psychologically, and spiritually, modernity both frustrates and enhances human longings. Totalitarianism is simultaneously an outgrowth of and a kind of existential answer to this problem. It urges men to think hard and to be hard, more up-to-date than modernity itself, while at the same time surrounding toughness, irresponsibility, and the ability to manipulate with a pseudosacred aura and a chiliastic promise. It provides some men with a comforting fantasy that seems to be utterly realistic and that nevertheless gives them a grand feeling of belonging, of having escaped the modern sense of freedom, responsibility, isolation.

Examining this intellectual phenomenon more closely, we find some unique and decisive structural characteristics. Failure to note these can be a source of confusion about intellectual totalitarianism. Its most peculiar characteristic centers round the doctrine of violent action. This is, in turn, logically and intimately related to the especially pervasive determinism that is also distinctive of all such theory.

A totalitarian philosophy is completely and proudly ideological. That is, it does not claim or logically lead its proponents to claim that it is a *theory about* the world, nature, history. Philosophers of this type do not think of themselves as scientific (or even poetic), detached, Cartesian observers. A totalitarian philosophy is rather supposed to be a reflection, an important, operating, organic part of the moving, developing, cosmic, natural-historical (sometimes divine-historical) situation. The philosophy is supposedly that situation's own logic and its functionally necessary self-consciousness. In Hegelian language, the philosophy is the objective form of a dynamic cosmic consciousness. It is self-consciously an ideology. History, nature, race, the proletariat, not mere human beings, are supposed to be doing the talking. Because of this, an intellectual totalitarianism does not provide its proponents with any logical sense of responsibility for the violent and terrible things — war, revolution, dictatorship — which their doctrine urges them to undertake. Provided in this way with an "absolutely absolute" sense of assurance and with a detailed vision of everything around him, the totalitarian thinker undertakes some now sadly familiar intellectual practices. He does not argue with his critics or opponents, nor listen to what they have to say. He rather asks what, in the light of *the* "system," is wrong with them that makes them say it, and then, on the basis of his diagnosis, locates them in his own developmental world historical pattern. Finally, as appropriate to the situation, he fulfills his own great mission, now by using, now by obliterating them. In his doctrine, this behavior is supposedly the objective form of the way in which things in general are working themselves out: the old cosmic consciousness is giving way to the new; "new" philosophies are but the latter's instruments.

These philosophies have very little to say about the future (though that little is of great importance). No detailed utopian doctrine can be specifically totalitarian, regardless of what it says. The theorist merely claims a vague glimpse of something wonderful ahead: freedom, equality, plenty, every man an artist, all races and classes and nations in their "proper" places, the archaic recaptured amid the best of the civilized, the human spirit rendered whole. This vagueness about the future stems from the key implicit assumption that the philosophy is situational, a self-conscious ideology. Appropriately, in regard to the future the doctrine provides few details, but only a sense of forward vision within a large, teleological, self-determining situation. It is a situation moving toward an end whose exact nature only that situation itself can determine. This relative lack of explicitness about ends makes it very difficult for totalitarians in action to be self-critical. Lacking more than an urge to violent, group action — to war, to revolution, to dictatorship — they need not compare their benign ends with their vicious and dehumanizing means. In their world, the end for men here and now is identification with, belonging in and helping to structure the Process. Philosophically minded totalitarians are like distorted worshipers: greatest importance is attached to participating in the "liturgy" that the cosmos has set down. The absurdity, unpleasantness, and martyrdom which may be involved only make the whole business seem more miraculous.

Seen from this perspective, the essential characteristic of an authentic totalitarian philosophy is that it is centrally a philosophy of the deed. It concentrates attention chiefly upon the technical problems attendant upon violent or oppressive group actions. These actions are not conceived as merely unfortunate, necessary means to some great ends. The actions themselves are all but the ends. They are the categorical imperatives of the philosophy. Participation in them has positive, philosophical-psychological, "liturgical" — not simply practical — significance. Thus war or revolution, and the preparations for them, are not regarded pragmatically or operationally. The real totalitarian would refuse to "pursue" the ultimate vague ends of the doctrine except through such means. These have a positive, doctrinal, pseudosacred meaning to him; they are "objectively" determined actions, which are specifically necessary to the future development of world history. No other actions will do. Totalitarian doctrines may thus be described as philosophies of war or revolution. Because of this characteristic, especially after a totalitarian movement or a regime

comes into being, there is a strong tendency in totalitarian thinking for armies, political parties, the dictatorial state to take on
an aura of Kafkaesque holiness.

The fact that such activity is central to this kind of intellectual
system may often be used profitably by the historian to identify
degrees of totalitarianism in a given tradition. For example, Marxism was originally only mildly and intermittently totalitarian, because Marx and Engels also sought to give, at length, rational,
empirical, and ethical (that is, responsibly conceived) reasons for
revolution; they did not consistently eschew the role of Cartesian observer. This large dimension of Marxism helped make
possible its complete or nearly complete detotalitarianization in
the hands of Orthodox Marxists and Revisionists. Lenin's key contribution was to enhance the importance of revolution, to make
it heretical to pursue the millennium in any other way, indeed, to
shift attention more and more from that millennium as an end to
the revolutionary process as an end. Bolshevism was thus centered
much more around violence and was more totalitarian than Marxism itself had been. Stalin, Lenin's self-styled heir and follower,
carried the same development even further. He stripped almost
the entire rational and ethical framework from the doctrine,
either by simply eliminating it or by subtly making it appear
mythical. Appropriately, integrating Marxism with the modern
dictatorial state and Soviet Russian national interest, he demanded
that attention be almost exclusively focused on revolutionary,
military, and state-power techniques. From Marx to Lenin to
Stalin it became increasingly heretical not to concentrate upon
the frightful tasks at hand, for History had laid them down.
Lenin and Stalin enhanced the totalitarianism or, to say the same
thing, the pseudoreligion in Marxism.[3] Nazism per se had a
shorter and less coherent intellectual history. But the differences
between the more humanistic forerunners and Hitler seem quite
understandable on a similar basis.[4]

It should be emphasized that there is a peculiar blend of voluntarism and determinism in totalitarian theory. Too much has

been made of the supposed logical contradiction between these in the thinking of Lenin and Stalin.[5] Voluntaristic political action (always restricted to the deeds of the moment and never directed to the millennium itself) is in the totalitarian mind simply the most crucial human correlative of the self-movement of the All toward a beatific equilibrium. Men, their wills, their analytical and manipulative abilities, their political actions, are but necessary, determined, integral parts of a big developmental process. At an advanced stage, it is believed, this process has developed the human being and the human mind as tools for dealing with the complexities of its own relative maturity. The historical development of man's ability to manipulate is supposedly just a part of the whole fantastic business. The voluntarism in totalitarianism concerns only functional not teleological reasoning, and even that has a deterministic rationale. It is a narrow voluntarism and one without a sense of responsibility. Similarly, a totalitarian philosophy frequently tenders great importance to aspects of modern technology and, in some cases, science. These, like the organizational techniques of modern politics, are regarded as creatures of the Great Development, as indispensable epiphenomena of a late stage of History. A totalitarian philosophy manages the unprecedented intellectual trick of incorporating the norms of modern organizational and technological behavior into a primitive, pseudoreligious mysticism. It makes the worst aspects of modern life into fantasy and ritual which render them hopeful, good, laden with meaning. It covers up its own romanticism by directing its followers' energies to the toughest kind of thought and action. Releasing and channeling enormous amounts of spiritual and emotional energy through its powerful existential appeals, it makes possible spectacular power politics and thus appears to prove, almost experimentally, its own claim to be the mind of history.

Totalitarian philosophy or "ideology," like totalitarian government (as an ideal type), is *sui generis*. It is misleading and wrong to regard any particular doctrine of this kind or this whole intellectual tendency as a "natural" or "logical" outgrowth of more normal historical or cultural traditions. Let me stress this. This kind of thought, generally or specifically, cannot be derived from Hegelianism, Rousseauism, science, positivism, Darwinism, nationalism, conservatism, liberalism, or democratic socialism, nor from any branches of the Judeo-Christian tradition. Totalitarian doctrines have been developed under all kinds of influences, of course. But they have always deviated from these. It is even quite conceivable that any given doctrine of this sort could be put together in a different way and thus become, if not moderate, at least not *prima facie* evil. It seems to be the specific relationship of the constituent elements that is decisive. When we view a totalitarian doctrine as a logical outgrowth of some cultural or philosophical tradition, we are rendering that tradition guilty by association. Though it is tempting to do this with traditions we do not like, it is an insidious practice. Though totalitarian theorists claim exactly the contrary, they are indeed responsible for their own thinking.

Historically in Europe there has been a variety of such intellectual systems. Few have incorporated all the aspects of the ideal type. In some cases the student gets an impression only of appropriate attitude and of some clear possibility of development in a totalitarian direction. At other times, as in the case of Marxism, a whole systematic doctrine may seem rather mildly totalitarian (which, let us remember, is like saying mildly murderous). Leaving aside these questions of relative completeness and moderation, it is useful for purposes of this study to distinguish two species of the genus. From a mid-twentieth century perspective, we can identify a Western European and a Russian type.

The Western European type is conservative or reactionary in its emphasis. Doctrines in this category have been relatively unsystematic, "poetic." Their values have been pseudoaristocratic (or pseudobourgeois), particularistic, individualist, aesthetic, relatively negative toward science. Their intellectual methods have been intuitional, blatantly irrational. Bizarre, paganized versions of Christianity and dubious sorts of nationalism have often been highly regarded. The vaguely delineated ultimate futures of the doctrines in this type have been, in quality, more archaic than modern. The thinkers here seem to have had more interest in a return to some highly romanticized, pseudomedieval or pseudo-classical past than in movement forward to a new heaven and a new earth; intentionally or not, such thinkers were more specifically pagan and antihistorical than their Russian counterparts. Alfred Rosenberg and Hitler incarnated this species of totalitarian philosophy. It includes also twentieth century fascist intellectuals, who were more moderate. Scholars have identified numerous forerunners: Carlyle, Houston Stewart Chamberlain, Gobineau, Barrès, Maurras, Treitschke, Julius Langbehn, and others.

The Russian type is progressive. Doctrines have been actually or potentially more systematic than in the Western type. Values have been pseudodemocratic, universalist, communal; intellectual methods have been rationalistic, scientistic. Western European totalitarianism is like a monstrous form of idealism; Russian, like one of materialism. One is transcendentalist; the other is immanentist. The greatest "philosopher" within the Russian species was Stalin, with Lenin running a close second. That is, Bolshevism and this kind of intellectual totalitarianism are practically congruent, though theoretically the type could also include doctrines varying considerably in detail. There were a number of less typical forerunners, some of whom actually influenced Lenin: N. G. Chernyshevsky, Dmitri Pisarev, Peter Tkachev, and other figures in the Jacobin strand of Populism. Bakunin at times seems to have belonged to this group. One of the more rounded forerunners, though without any influence on Bolshevism — indeed, a victim of shrinking coverage in successive editions of the *Bolshaya sovietskaya entsiklopedia* — was Danilevsky.

Russian totalitarianism is considerably more optimistic than Western. Despite its frequent antireligious bias, it belongs, in a strange way, to the Judeo-Christian tradition. The typical ideas of the redemptive part to be played in world history by the poor and the downtrodden, urban or rural; of an absolute goal of history, whose tensions are not regarded as integral to the human condition; of a Golden Age, which lies at the start and finish of history — such ideas are also central to that religious tradition. Western European totalitarianism is more like an invitation to collective suicide. The outlook, especially in its Nazi manifestations, recalls the catastrophic end of the world prophesied and expected by the ancient pagan Germans. This catastrophe included a gigantic combat between the gods and the demons, ending in the death of all the gods and all the heroes and a final regression of the world into chaos. After this, the world would be reborn, regenerated, to begin a new cosmic cycle, one also destined to catastrophe.[6] Such blind fatalism could hardly have been blended with rationalism, scientism, the ideas of progress or democracy. The more typical Russian philosophical aberration has appropriated what many Western Europeans have regarded as their most precious heritage; the most typical Western has damned that heritage unmercifully.

Of course, this geographical and cultural division of totalitarianism is but a matter of emphasis. Exceptional examples of each type may be found in both Western Europe and Russia. Marx, the German, who lived and worked in France and England, is the glaring example. In some ways, however, this, the greatest exception, really proves the rule. For in the West, Marxism as a totalitarian philosophy did not take very well. The Western Marxist movements usually took to Marx the social scientist and ethical protester, not to Marx the myth-maker. Had it not been for his Bolshevik followers, we should probably today be much less conscious of the important totalitarian dimension of his doctrine. Western men, even Marxologists, seem to be peculiarly insensitive to it.

Even if I were capable of making it, a full explanation as to why there is a tendency for the two species of totalitarianism to cluster in different cultural regions of Europe and of Western civilization, and even of the world at large, would be out of place in the present study. But some of my historical presuppositions about the problem will come up later, and it will be useful to mention them briefly now. In particular, let me identify several important factors that might be kept in mind concerning the tendency of Russian totalitarianism to be leftist, rationalistic, "scientific."

This sort of doctrine being pseudoreligious, totalitarianisms probably have affinities to the religious traditions of the areas in which they arise or "take." The study of the regional localization of the types of this philosophy can be enriched by reference to a comparative analysis of religions. Even a superficial glance at key differences of emphasis between Orthodoxy, on the one hand, and Catholicism and Protestantism, on the other, is instructive.

Orthodoxy cultivates a sense of the closeness of God to the world. It was and is a relatively immanentist version of Christianity, markedly more so even than Catholicism. One has only to leaf through the Byzantine-Slavonic and the Latin (pre–Vatican II) liturgies to be struck by this difference. Each has its own kind of magnificent beauty. But the crisp Latin invocations consist of only slightly varying formulas directed almost manipulatively, magically, repetitively at a rather distant, relatively mysterious, somewhat unresponsive Being. The looser, more varied Byzantine-Slavonic prayers suggest a dialogue with a closer, warmer, more earthlike Deity. Similarly, the relation between priest and congregation differs in emphasis. In the East the responses are more numerous. Looking at the missal, one comes to feel that the Liturgy, less so than the Latin Mass, would seem most strange without a large congregation actively participating. Orthodoxy is panentheistic not pantheistic, but the Western observer is easily inclined to make the error, especially if he thinks of the sparse, aristocratic, individualist Protestantism of the Calvinist variety. In a sense, too, Russian Orthodoxy is more populist, democratic, and communal than Western varieties of Christianity. And its proximate God, understanding and understood, separates religion from both romantic irrationalism and markedly analytical rationalism.[7]

It appears that the Eastern Christian and relatively immanentist mind can regard science — and along with it, more or less logically, the ideas of progress and perfectibility, the devaluation of class and ethnic particularisms, democracy — somewhat differently from the Western Christian transcendentalist mind. In both religious minds, science, to take a key phenomenon, is disturbing because of its cold exactitude, its secularism, the impression it creates that man can be the master of his own destiny. The Western mind, however, is bothered by more than the secular and Promethean nature of science and progressivism generally. It is concerned also with the implicit assumption that there is a knowable order in nature and the world. To the Western religious mind this seems sacrilegious, for it suggests that man is placing himself too close to the level of the awesome, mysterious Jehovah. Western man has typically seen a fundamental dichotomy between science and religion. He has acted upon this feeling in various ways: by attacking science, by engaging in it as something quite apart from faith, by attacking religion in its name. The Eastern religious mind, on the other hand, is less disturbed by the assumption of a knowable order. To that mind, God and His design have always been closer, more available than to the Catholic and especially the Protestant mind. Though Western men in modern times have done more with science, worked more with philosophical rationalism, practiced more democracy (perhaps for just the reasons under discussion), they have done these things self-consciously apart from, often with a sense of defiance toward, religion. A great debate between science and religion, reason and faith, has been a hallmark of postmedieval intellectual and cultural history. In Russia, later, there was a similar conflict, but its temper was different and it was not so intense. Darwinism, for instance, elicited surprisingly little adverse religious discussion.[8] With some notable but not decisive exceptions, modern

Russian religious thinkers did not reject or damn science and reason. Critical mainly of positivism, they even adopted many a scientific or at least progressive idea into their philosophies. I have in mind thinkers like Nicholas Fedorov, Dostoevsky, Vladimir Soloviev.[9] One looks long and hard for parallels to their evolutionary Christian spiritualist-materialism in the West (there are some in our time; Teilhard de Chardin thought like a Russian religious philosopher and was accused of naturalism and the like in Catholic circles). Western man can do more with science but he finds it harder to square its implications with his faith or to make a religion of it. Modern Western intellectuals have thought of religion as something more irrational, and of God's world as one of variety, individuality, poetic beauty. Or they have damned faith as a hopeless muddle.

Against this background, it is possible to suggest one important possible reason for the fake scientific, rationalist, democratic, and progressive qualities of Russian as compared to Western totalitarian doctrines. Russian totalitarianism may be a pathological aberration of the Eastern postreligious mind, the outlook of Eastern *homo religiosus* after he has lost the content but not the form of his belief. Science and related phenomena may be prominent in that kind of totalitarianism because, in the world of science, order is proximate, and a proximate order can be regarded as a surrogate for the kindly, rather predictable, trustworthy, almost female God of Orthodoxy. The lonely, disillusioned Russian seeking a new faith was not tempted to regress to an irrational, pessimistic fatalism — even the temper of Russian paganism was optimistic and naturalistic. He did not try to recapture a sense of meaning suitable to the worship of a relatively inscrutable and distant God. An absurd, experientially disorderly, pluralistic world was not spiritually meaningful to him. Reason, science, democracy, progress at once challenged his old sense of meaning and promised a new, still distinctly spiritual one. He had but to make them holy. He built his false, totalitarian religion by doing just that. In an unfortunate way he had discovered the potential of his Orthodox heritage, not for modernizing on its own, but for bringing about a spiritual integration with the modern age. Thus, too, his kind of totalitarianism continued to have more similarity to the Judeo-Christian tradition, itself Eastern in origin, than did that of his Western, often Teutonic counterpart.

The influence of Orthodoxy on the intellectual content and quality of Russian totalitarianism was reinforced by other important and unique aspects of Russian culture, society, and history — phenomena, in turn, sometimes closely related to the temper of Russian Christianity both as effects and as causes. National character studies by social scientists stress the passivity, the receptivity, the "orality," the recognizably Leskovian stamp of the modal Great Russian personality.[10] Individualist and particularist values, assertiveness, innovation, irrational methods, imitation of aristocratic behavior, aestheticism are not likely, it would seem, to appeal to such a communal, "other-directed," commonsensical, peasant-gentry mind. Science and the idea of progress (once started by somebody else) undoubtedly had peculiarly strong cultural-psychological as well as spiritual appeals in Russia. Some of the gentry, those who constituted the most important source of the intelligentsia and those who set the intellectual styles, were subjected to other influences. The bureaucratic social environment of the educated classes helped create a more pervasively rationalist social psychology than was usual in Western Europe. The government-sponsored educational system gave science in particular unusual emphasis. Russian totalitarianism may have been also an aberration of the bureaucratic conservative mind. The fact that nineteenth century Russia was an underdeveloped area trying to improve itself materially through selective borrowings probably served to enhance the awe of science and rationalism. Finally, Russian totalitarianism was a direct though perverted derivative of the dominant Russian intellectual tradition, the radical and Westernist of the nineteenth century. Its relative dominance, in terms of numbers of intellectuals and influence on public opinion, was chiefly the result of a cultural, psychological, and spiritual temper similar to that of Russian totalitarianism. Russian intellectuals seeking a sense of meaning and continuity in an age of rapid change were particularly attracted to rationalism, scientism, and the like — that is, to the idea that the solution to their problem of meaning was immanent in its causes. As I shall explain later, serfdom, social and cultural malaise, and tsarist political obscurantism shaped, but were not the main occasions for, Russian radicalism. The point to be made now is that utopian radicalism was so strong an intellectual phenomenon in nineteenth century Russia that it became a significant cultural force itself. A powerful myth of the left held sway over much of Russian intellectual life. Leftist politics had the force of an intellectual institution. The peculiar quality of Russian totalitarianism owed much to this situation.

Again it must be stressed that, in this discussion of cultures in general and totalitarianism in particular, only trends are indicated. Comparative study of modern Western European and Russian thought unearths many an atypical thinker. Russia, for instance, had its nonradical romantics, its conservative intellectuals, its particularists, its individualists, and its innovators. Nor were they simply strangers in their own land; on the contrary, historicist conservatives like the Slavophils or idealists like Tolstoi had enormous influence. In the history of totalitarianism, the Bolsheviks were epigones of Marx, while Rosenberg apparently picked up some of his ideas in Russia. Western European and Russian cultures in modern times are like two symphonies each of which is made up of two similar themes, one major, one minor. The difference between them, speaking quite generally, stems from the fact that the major theme of one is the minor theme of the other. Modern Western civilization as a whole, something like the Graeco-Roman one to which it is heir, is made up of a series of varying dualisms.

Now Danilevsky's was a totalitarian philosophy. Historically this is the most significant thing about him. Just as Marx was a philosopher of revolution and earthly fulfillment, Danilevsky was

a philosopher of war and a new divine dispensation. In the 1860's
he thought a huge war between Slavdom and Western Europe
inevitable. He thought he could see the hand of God at work in
a remarkable series of historical "synchronisms" that pointed to
the political unification of Slavdom and to war. The very process
of fighting the war, as important in itself to Danilevsky as the
unification, would have had some (only vaguely specified) theological-metaphysical effect upon the Slavic soul; it was even
hinted that the war might somehow spiritually unite Slavdom
and its enemy, "Europe," and inaugurate a new age of human
blessedness. Danilevsky might be compared to one of Dostoevsky's
characters. He associated the achievement of spiritual ends with
practical, material, and violent means. Power and violence were
for him both gods and ways to God. Dostoevsky's Raskolnikov
associated human fulfillment with murder, his Kirillov associated
it with suicide. Danilevsky thought war the liturgical solution to
the problem of man's (though mainly Slavic man's) inner and
outer divisions.

In saying this about him, however, I do not mean to suggest
either that this was all there was to Danilevsky or that he was a
major figure comparable in sophistication, complexity, or depth
to Marx, Dostoevsky, or Herzen. He had a utopian socialist intellectual period before he went sour, and he was coming into a
sort of Aristotelian phase at the time of his death. As to his historical stature, it must depend mostly on his *Russia and Europe*.
But even that was a distinctly amateurish work, full of loose
ends, weak in unity and coherence. A typical Russian intellectual
document of the time, his eccentric, ambiguous, and delusionary
book should not be thought of as "important." We are going to
be concerned with a minor figure like Tkachev (though without
his influence), not an Engels or even a Chernyshevsky. Yet he
is an interesting figure. Interest in him arises mainly from the fact
that he was a totalitarian of the Russian type. Studying him
against the background to which he is typologically related provides significant insight into the history of Russian totalitarianism.

way that belies his own characterization of Panslavism as a modern nationalist movement with limited, realistic goals. Realistic political Panslavism was to him a means to ends that were romantic; having served its purpose, tough-minded Panslavism would have faded away, leaving the Slavs (though for the most part only they) to an updated traditionalist, not a modern nationalist, existence. In his vision the future Slavdom would have been a leftist paradise, a haven for the tender-minded modernist. His Orthodoxy, as I have said, was flimsy and laden with deism, occasionalism, scientific naturalism, and eighteenth century rationalism. His monarchism skews this classification a little. But it must be remembered that, like the Slavophils, he favored the monarchy because he thought it a popular, democratic institution. Moreover, unlike the Slavophils, he liked the monarchy because it seemed to him progressive, a modifier as well as a preserver of traditional institutions and cultures. His view of Peter the Great was at times relatively favorable, and he idolized Catherine II. If Herzen, say, could have shared Danilevsky's view of the monarchy, he might have been a monarchist also and that without altering his most fundamental aims. In any case, Russian utopian radicalism was more a specific kind of action-oriented attitude toward modernity and traditionalism than a political movement in the usual sense. Most radicals, though anti-tsarist, were basically agnostic regarding specific political forms. Thus Danilevsky's thought in the sixties was chiefly totalitarian, populist, and radical (there was a tendency toward this in nontotalitarian form during his Petrashevsky period also) but with not insignificant affinities to Slavophilism or to the modernistic spirituality of Fedorov or Dostoevsky. It also bore some largely formal similarities to the bureaucratic conservatism of Pogodin or Katkov. The kaleidoscopic nature of his intellectuality was due to a number of factors: his hypocrisy, his curious personality, and the fact that he was a loner, without intellectual associates to challenge or discipline him.

Danilevsky believed in a vaguely Christian, monarchical (but democratic), utopian socialist paradise and panhuman civilization, ordained by God and History for Russia and the Slavs. Russia's mission in History was to realize the true potential of the contributions of all previous civilizations to the world, especially those of the West, that is, the potential of the modern age, which interested him most. The negative thrust of his doctrine was against what he thought the West's incurable egoism, imperialism (both cultural and political), capitalism, and class divisions, whether aristocratic-peasant or bourgeois-proletarian. On balance, he was more like a mad Herzen than a Pogodin or a Khomiakov. He was a Russian socialist but without (at least explicitly — he did hint otherwise) the universalist, messianic urge often characteristic of the Slavophil left. Because he was left and Russian in the more decisive aspects of his orientation in the sixties — and because at the same time, with its determinism and its mystique of power politics and war, his was a pretty full-blown totalitarian philosophy — the study of Danilevsky becomes rather naturally part of the study of the nature and origins of Russian totalitarianism. Bolshevism (and Marxism itself to a degree) being the most well-known and complete variety of this kind of totalitarianism, it will be useful here and there to compare his ideas in a general way with that doctrine, and to study Danilevsky's intellectual formation with an eye on Bolshevism's other forerunners (including Marx) and on the problem of the origins of the whole Russian species of the philosophical genus. It is neither useful nor accurate to study Danilevsky in conjunction with conservative or reactionary totalitarians.

This is the first analytical study that has ever been made of Danilevsky's thought and of his intellectual development. It will involve a rather drastic revision of much of the study that has hitherto been made of him. So far he has been noted as an important and influential figure in the Russian Panslav movement and as a philosopher of history anticipating and comparable to

Spengler and sometimes Toynbee.[16] Although neither of these interpretations of his historical significance is entirely wrong, each attaches him to a historical movement or a scholarly philosophical tradition to which he bears only an oblique relationship. Each fails to take account of his whole doctrine, his intellectual development, his self-image as a member of the intelligentsia, his place in his own time. His attitude toward realistic Panslavism, as I have mentioned, was most ambivalent. His influence on the Russian Panslav movement was very small. Though Danilevsky was a much smaller intellectual figure, comparison of him to people in the left Hegelian tradition (like Marx) provides the basis for more accurate insight than comparison to Spengler. Spengler, like Toynbee, does not have Danilevsky's important tendency to formulate programs. There are also crucial differences of detail between their philosophies of civilization. More important, Spengler lacks Danilevsky's ultimate claim that his thinking about history is tantamount to history's thinking about itself.

Danilevsky is a difficult figure with which to work. The available sources are scarce. Yet they are sufficient to reveal a most involved, cantankerous, disturbingly committed individual. Grappling with the documents about and by him, one is impressed by more than his moral and human failures. In many ways he was quite like his greater and more influential intellectual and artistic contemporaries: a "crazy" Russian, naïve, intense, absurd, and tragic, a most graphic witness to the human condition everywhere. Though I shall be making some harsh judgments upon him, I must confess that I have come to like him as a human being. This is not because his totalitarianism was a dud and harmed no one. I like his many-sidedness, his willingness to attempt so much intellectually, and the fact that he had the spiritual and moral stature to begin to change his warmongering views toward the end of his life. His failures were related to his not inconsiderable good potentialities, ones of a spacious kind that seem not to be common in our time whether in Russia or the West.

2

The problem of working out Danilevsky's biography is difficult because of the scarcity of good source material. It is compounded by the task of understanding the man himself. Some preliminary general discussion of his life therefore seems in order.

He was an ambiguous individual and a paradoxical one. On the basis of an excellent scientific education, he undertook a career as a practical scientist working for the Russian government and, though less frequently, for private scientific societies. He rose to high rank in the civil service. Yet he also gave his existence much the form of a philosophic quest. Along the way he worked out several intellectual positions: scientific naturalism and utopian socialism; an extremist political romantic-realism or totalitarianism that included a utilitarian theory about the course of world history and a curious version of Slavophilism; and, finally, under the influence of the biologist Karl Ernest von Baer, a neo-Aristotelian philosophy of science and of evolution. He was at once a professional man and one seeking a sense of spiritual and intellectual context, a universe of discourse in an age, at least in his milieu, of rapid change, secularization, modernization, Westernization — processes to which his own scientific work contributed.

The professional Danilevsky was rather consistently, from the middle of the 1840's onward, a moderate, practical, unideological, bureaucratic liberal. This attitude seems to have arisen from a combination of acceptance of the tsarist system and constructive opposition within it. That is, Danilevsky, the operative or nearly "objective" liberal, apparently approved of Petrine tsarism insofar as that system was one of enlightened and progressive despotism. But he had an understandable dislike of tsarist political and cultural obscurantism and a conviction that legitimist, traditionalist political doctrines and practices, too strictly construed, provided a meager and improbable frame of reference within which effective work could be done to modernize, rationalize, and generally improve Russian conditions. His writings on population, the fall of the paper ruble, the economy of the far north, and the extermination of vinicultural lice (phylloxera) attest beyond doubt to this liberal-conservative attitude. Danilevsky could have been and partly was simply a progressive tsarist bureaucrat — like his friends Dmitri Miliutin and Peter and Nicholas Semenov. Such a political attitude was by no means uncommon in nineteenth century Russia.

The other, the questing, Danilevsky did not, by and large, accept the Russian situation as it was or operate on assumptions appropriate even to constructive opposition within it. In the forties he was a leading member of the Petrashevsky circle, one of the first groups of intellectuals in Russia to discuss the more practical aspects of revolution. While superficially loyal to the autocracy in the sixties, even this was an ambivalent loyalty, and his deeper commitments were to a democratic monarchy in a socialist paradise. More obviously subversive were his social and cultural ideas. If the censor who passed *Russia and Europe* in 1869 had been more alert, he would have noticed, in the official language of the time, "free speculations not corresponding to the form of government . . . in Russia." [17] The more philosophic Danilevsky was a radical. The fact that the political side of this was muted or ambivalent should not be allowed to obscure the fact of his leftist extremism. Throughout most of his adult life he was a utopian socialist. In the sixties he was prepared violently to turn the world upside down on behalf of his ideas.

It should be emphasized that Danilevsky held contradictory attitudes simultaneously. There was a kind of schizoid quality to his mind. It is not only that he was a bureaucratic liberal at the same time that he was first a utopian socialist and then a totalitarian philosopher on the left. The doctrine in *Russia and Europe*, like all totalitarian philosophies, has this same quality; the disunity and incoherence of that book, which have nothing to do with the "logic" of the doctrine, and the ways, noted earlier, in which Danilevsky's outlook defies easy classification show it also. His ambiguity is so marked that it cannot be explained simply by reference to general historical circumstances. It was rooted in his personality; it owed something to his particular life situation; and some decisions he made, or failed to make, about himself also appear to have exaggerated his ambivalences in the middle phase of his life. But more general factors were involved too and were not unimportant. Some discussion of him in relation to the cultural and intellectual situation of his time will facilitate understanding of his paradoxical mind and behavior and of their relationship to Russian intellectual history in the nineteenth century.

In the first place, it cannot be said that his intellectual searching and his radicalism, ordinary or totalitarian, resulted chiefly from frustration under an oppressive regime — that is, from lack of a constructive, socially useful outlet. This sort of thing has been said repeatedly by historians about Russian radical thought in general. A dubious and academic theory at best, it makes hardly any sense at all in regard to Danilevsky. He had plenty of scope, including political, and more than enough socially useful activity, sponsored more often than not by the tsarist government. Educated in government-founded schools, he was a statistician and biologist. In the forties, on a grant from the Free Economic Society, he and a friend surveyed the soil conditions in the black earth provinces. In the early fifties, as a government employee, he voluntarily undertook population and weather studies in Vologda province. From the fifties to the eighties he had an outstanding career as a fisheries expert. He headed a series of expeditions that surveyed all the fisheries of European Russia. He personally wrote the new imperial fisheries legislation of the 1870's. In his last years he played a leading role in a government effort, initially undertaken at his own suggestion, to stamp out vinicultural lice in the Crimea. Immediate political circumstances were not an important cause of Danilevsky's questing, of his radicalism and utopianism, or of his totalitarianism. True, he said in *Russia and Europe*, with obvious reference to himself as well as others, that Russian thinkers of the forties and beyond had been Chichikovs and Don Quixotes because of the lack of practical outlet in a stifling bureaucratic atmosphere.[18] But such statements should not be taken at face value. His own story belies them. The daydreaming came first. The sense of frustration arose from a feeling of inability to work out schemes that would have been stifled in any society. They were unrealizable less because of the nature of tsarism than because of the nature of reality.

Danilevsky's questing seems to have originated more out of his spiritual, cultural, and intellectual responses to a modern age, secularism, and the beliefs, values, and emotional attitudes connected with the recently imported science and technology that were so prominent in his immediate environment. Both on his own and on his countrymen's behalf (Danilevsky was ever a public-minded intellectual), he was a man in search of several interrelated things: a sense of continuity with a romanticized version of his own and Russia's Orthodox, rural, traditionalist past; a sense of identity in the midst of spiritual, intellectual, and cultural flux; a sense of direction and of large purpose, one at once relevant to practical solution by modern methods of the pressing economic and social problems of his Russia, qualitatively "Russian," and permissive of a strong hope for spiritual and psychological fulfillment. His philosophic quest was to a certain extent a matter of behavioral, reflexive response to conditions of rapid cultural change. Here, it should be noted, he was more than just disturbed and disoriented in his values and his world view, made to feel uncomfortable and threatened with despair by modern life. The consistently progressive temper of this thought indicates also that science and technical rationalism, together with some of the standard mythology that were all but inseparable from them in his time, stimulated him greatly and led him, as they did many other sensitive people in Russia, to think the whole situation of mankind could be rendered utterly different in kind: prosperous, stable, happy, and free. The modern age rendered Danilevsky, as it were, manic as well as depressive. His quest, however, was a matter too of purposive-rational (as distinguished from technical-rational) response to change. That is, Danilevsky's intellectual writings indicate that he reacted to cultural changes both because they affected his feelings and habits of mind and because he thought about, interpreted, and made intellectual decisions regarding those changes. And he reacted not as an individual in and for himself, but always as a public-minded man, seeking a solution for his countrymen at large.

This amounts to saying that Danilevsky's philosophizing, radical though it was in intention and implication, was not primarily related to the practical problems of obscurantist, monarchical despotism, the serious economic and social or the in some senses very real cultural backwardness of his Russia. Now, it is easy to imagine that a sensitive educated man might have been deeply concerned with these problems. It is almost as easy to imagine that their magnitude and the fact that the problems themselves tended to frustrate attempts at their practical solution could have led such a man into daydreaming and utopian radicalism. Indeed, in Danilevsky's own writings one can find evidence of serious interest in the enlightenment of the Russian public and in practical economic and social reform. There are also criticisms of stagnant bureaucracy, demands for a free press, approval of some guarantees (the jury system, for instance) of civil liberties. It would be falsifying the evidence to assert that he had no immediate societal interests beyond those more or less directly connected with his professional life, or to deny that the nature of the situation in which these interests developed contributed to their being discussed in very big, perhaps fantastically big, intellectual contexts. However, Danilevsky's writings and his behavior — to the limited extent the scanty data let us see it — indicate beyond doubt that this kind of immediate, practical interest, and the situation in which he developed it, constituted only a marginal (though not entirely unimportant) element in and influence upon his development into a speculative thinker. The focus of Danilevsky's more intellectual interests was intentionally humanistic, spiritual, and teleological. Cultural change and confusion were the occasions for and the immediate stimuli to his thinking, not the problems of social, educational, economic, administrative, or political reform in Russia. His quest for meaning was genuinely philosophical in its ultimate roots. He was a speculative thinker not a politician or a social reformer *manqué*. Consequently, it may be said that, on the whole, he became radical or radical-totalitarian at those times when he thought he had found a solution to the problem of the meaning of Russia's (and his own) Westernization and when he attempted to follow out the existential, social, and sometimes, especially in regard to the international relations of Russia, the political implications. The bad political and social conditions in Russia helped to focus his thought in a societal direction, to deepen his felt need for a sense of meaning, to encourage him to think that the human situation could be drastically improved; but those conditions were not the chief occasion for that thought.

His lifelong pattern of ambiguous intellectual and existential behavior was not inappropriate to the situation in Russia in the mid-nineteenth century. It should rather be regarded as an understandable, though eccentric, mode of adjustment and search for a mode of adjustment to difficult cultural circumstances. The modern age, first in the form of science, technology, and organizational skills, military and bureaucratic, then as new world views and value systems, had burst on the Russian scene with unusual rapidity, intensity, and disruptiveness. It was not, by and large, the result of maturation (at least in a technical direction) of the native culture; it was taken from abroad in rather fully developed form. Moreover, the powerful Russian government was the continuing sponsor of its practical aspects, and these, in turn, became an all too efficient vehicle (though contrary to the tsars' intention) for the rapid importation of broader intellectual and spiritual influences. By Danilevsky's time Westernism, official and unofficial, had driven such a wide breach into native traditions that Russian culture had become permanently dualistic. Cultural dualism was most marked in the overly sharp cleavage between Westernized upper and Russian lower classes, between Westernized cities, especially Petersburg, and Russian towns and villages. Among the educated the Orthodox religion and many native traditions remained lively forces (especially because of childhood experiences); but at the same time they often seemed quite incompatible with the secular and drastically rationalistic presuppositions that underlay much of Westernism, Russia's borrowed modernity. Let it be noted also, that the whole problem was not simply one of just any old cultural conflict. The Westernism that came to Russia was laden with all those ahuman, functionalistic cultural and institutional patterns, typical of modern times, which have long been the basis of cultural maladjustment and soul-searching in the West itself.[19] Often viewed as foreign in the very areas of its origin, modernity was doubly problematical in Russia.

Under these circumstances there flourished in Russia prominent intellectual schools (like the Westerners and the Slavophils whose conflict in the forties shaped much of Russian intellectual history in the past century) feverishly concerned with the spiritual, cultural, and intellectual problems that Westernization, both official and unofficial, was raising.[20] Alert and sensitive people felt a great need for a sense of meaning and continuity in their lives, particularly in an age that was still in many ways romantic. How meaning and continuity were defined, however, depended on personal characteristics and backgrounds, on varying sets of ideas and values, native or borrowed. Some wanted more Westernization, others, less, still others weird combinations of more and less, more for the sake of less, less for the sake of more. As Western influences grew in quantity and as, over time, the West went through periods of change itself, it became increasingly difficult even to define the problem of Russia's Westernization. Varying and changing solutions and contradictory intellectual imports served to compound the situation of cultural anxiety that any particular intellectual scheme was designed to solve. Though the phenomenon is more striking in the sixties than in the forties, even in the earlier age, especially in Danilevsky's rather precocious milieu, there was a tendency for cultural dualism to change, though only from our point of view, into relativism and pluralism. To appreciate this the historian might, on the basis of his knowledge of traditional Russian culture patterns, try to determine whether Westernism or Slavophilism was more in line with these. It would not be difficult to make a case that Slavophilism[21] was more Western European than Westernism. It was more individualistic, subjective, particularistic, more potentially innovative than Westernism. Slavophilism was an individual-oriented school of thought in a mainly community-oriented culture. It was their individualism which made the Slavophils both anti-Western and critical of modern "progress." Had things not been changing in Russia, they might have been progressive-minded and more than only potentially innovative. It is also probably significant that the Westernist view of the problem of Russia's Westernization was more acceptable to the Russian reading public than Slavophilism ever was. The very nature of the traditional culture made peculiar additional difficulties in the quest for meaning.

Especially during the reign of Nicholas I (1825–1855), that is, during Danilevsky's formative years, there was also an official solution,[22] in line with which, subjects like the "Law of God," conservatively selected history and literature, and some appropriate pedagogical orientations became compulsory in the schools. With an eye both on political stability in a revolutionary age and on national, spiritual, and cultural identity, Nicholas I advocated, indeed practically ordered, a "correct" intellectual orientation combining only technical Westernism with unreconstructed legitimism and established religion. The covering slogan was "Orthodoxy, Autocracy, Nationality." However, while many of the newly enlightened did turn out to be conservative or mildly progressive monarchists, others, like Danilevsky and his early intellectual associates, found it impossible to relate their new scientific and technical backgrounds to the concepts of God and Holy Russia, at least in the unimaginative forms in which these were presented in the official cultural program. In such cases that

program often had the effect of keeping alive the idea that a
literal continuity with the past was of overriding importance,
while at the same time rendering its own solution quite absurd.
In short, the tsarist cultural policy, like the Westernist and
Slavophil doctrines, often served simply to make the whole
situation more difficult, confusing, indeterminate. All approaches
were becoming mixtures, parts of a culture by nature paradoxical
and ambiguous.

Although Danilevsky's existential ambiguities and bizarre intellectual positions had roots also in his rather special personality
and life history, in his sometimes mistaken, sometimes keen intellectual perspectives, and in some moral successes and failures,
they were also part and parcel of the pluralistic cultural situation
of his age. His life history may be taken as a study of a sensitive
man looking for a mode of cultural and spiritual adjustment, a
satisfying sense of meaning in a society undergoing a process of
development under foreign influence, rapid and fragmented development from rural to urban, religious to secular, traditionalist
to modern. The fact that in this search for identity and for a
mode of discourse he became what we now call a totalitarian intellectual makes his story an especially noteworthy one, for it
highlights both the kinds of interests, mainly nonpractical, and
some of the motivations that go into the making of that kind of
intellectuality. It also suggests the cultural conditions that make
totalitarianism possible.

Because of the paucity of data it is necessary to fill in and interpret Danilevsky's story using general social and intellectual history of Russia. Even the most interesting possibility, that of de-
termining how he became a fanatic, is blocked at one important
point by an unusual shortage of information concerning his middle years; here one has to be satisfied with little more than a
stimulus to theorizing. But there are some compensations even
beyond that of describing a rather badly misunderstood historical
figure whose importance has been exaggerated. Used intensively,
the data are sufficient to give Danilevsky a sort of identity of his

own. With the addition of relevant historical, anthropological, philosophical, and social-scientific knowledge, it is uniquely possible in this case (for his life situation and his interests related to an especially significant combination of cultural and social phenomena) to elucidate the human meaning of a large segment of the intellectual history of modern Russia. Danilevsky's being in many ways typical and the data about him being just sufficiently plentiful to identify him, he is an unusually good subject, not for biography, but for biographical history. It is not that Danilevsky illustrates key developments in modern Russian intellectual history. Nor is it a matter of seeing that history through him. We can rather see the history *in* him and thus come to appreciate better the very important fact that that history was made not by impersonal forces but by men, ordinary and fallible, and often not very significant.

Part One

An Intellectual Biography

2

YOUTH

Danilevsky was born on November 27, 1822 (Old Style),[1] into a gentry family of Central Russia in the village of Oberets in the Liven district of the province of Orlov.[2] At the time of Nicholas Iakovlevich's birth and throughout his early years his father, Iakov Ivanovich, was a regular army officer, the commander of a hussar regiment. Iakov Ivanovich was a man of wide experience. In his youth he had studied medicine at the University of Moscow. His education had been interrupted by Napoleon's invasion of Russia in 1812; he had marched with the victorious Russian army all the way to Paris. Thereafter he had made a profession of the army. Iakov Ivanovich was a cultured person, an amateur of science and literature. Danilevsky's father, at least by example, probably influenced his son toward a public service career. Indeed, both Nicholas and an elder brother were to become state servants. The brother, whose full name is not known, followed the military vocation. Unfortunately there is no direct information available about Danilevsky's mother.

There are only scattered hints in the sources regarding Danilevsky's childhood, that important period in anybody's life.[3] He was sickly, thin, and had a twitch in his face, which, Peter Semenov says in his memoirs, was "like St. Vitus dance." Semenov also says he was a "religious and conservative boy." Given the fact of Danilevsky's lifelong regressive behavior pattern, there is a possibility that he was over-mothered in his early years because of illness. If such was the case, his mother could have been the transmitter of an unusually large dose of Orthodox, traditionalist, and even folkish cultural influence. Her influence might also have rendered him particularly susceptible to gentry class attitudes not well exemplified by his father — especially contempt of work as an unpleasant and plebeian affair, an attitude that would have helped enhance Danilevsky's continual sense of a need for meaning in his busy life.

At any rate it is reasonably certain that in his earliest years Danilevsky was exposed to two different cultural worlds: the one, Westernized, progressive, secular, and innovative; the other, Russian, traditional, rural, passive in some ways. At first the latter seems to have marked him more. Then the former's influence was enhanced and expanded by the Russian educational system. His formal education began in 1833 with attendance at a series (the family apparently at times followed the regiment from station to station) of private boarding schools (*pensions*), one in Lifland, two in Moscow. These exclusive establishments prepared him for the Lyceum at Tsarskoe Selo, which was one of the training grounds for the elite, both conservative and innovative, of the imperial bureaucracy. In the nineteenth century the Lyceum was the alma mater of the ministers of foreign affairs Gorchakov, Giers, and Lobanov-Rostovsky; of the ministers of education Golovnin, D. A. Tolstoi, and Saburov; of Reutern, minister of finance under Alexander II; and of many other prominent officials. Personal data regarding Danilevsky's years at the Lyceum and at the University of St. Petersburg later are sparse, but it is possible to expand upon them considerably by the use of sources concerning the educational programs of these institutions. There can be no doubt that Danilevsky's formal education constituted for him an intensive exposure to officially sponsored Westernism. The effect on his future development, professional and intellectual, was enormous. Like his Russia, Danilevsky was rapidly Westernized and modernized chiefly because of the policies of the tsarist government. His educational "sponsor," however, was at the same time ideologically legitimist. Here was another probable source of confusion and ambiguity.

The curriculum[4] of the Lyceum, which Danilevsky worked through in outstanding fashion between 1837 and 1842,[5] was appropriate for the training of bureaucrats who were to be at once professionally skilled in a modern way and loyal, Orthodox, "Russian." On the more practical side of the mostly fixed curriculum there were a number of obviously vocational subjects: the "juridical sciences" ("legislation in general," the history of Roman and Russian law, jurisprudence, civil and criminal law); statistics, geography, and political economy, all really aspects of *Staatskunde;* diplomacy. Intensive study of languages — Russian, Latin, French, German, and English — seems also to have had a partly vocational rationale. The same was true of science. The six years of study included physics, chemistry, and mathematics from arithmetic through solid geometry and trigonometry. But the humanities were also studied and the boys were given some selected materials with which to work out a view of the world. A six-year study of the "Law of God" was evidently regarded as basic. This included Bible study, Church history, and catechism. There were philosophical subjects like ethics, logic, psychology. Courses in history and literature were given too, and that not simply as propaganda for God, Holy Church, and Tsar. History, however, was presented with some caution; the general course, for instance, stopped with Louis XVI's accession and omitted the French Revolution. There was a marked tendency, in the teaching of literature, to emphasize the merits of ancient and French classicism and to neglect or even denigrate "modern" authors like Schiller, Goethe, Pushkin.

Limitations on the studies of the humanities were reinforced by the administration of the school. Both in St. Petersburg and at Tsarskoe Selo, it was in the hands of the military. The director of the Lyceum when Danilevsky entered was a Major General Goltgoer, who used the rod on recalcitrants. His chief assistant, Obolensky, also the teacher of moral philosophy and psychology, helped keep order by encouraging the students to spy and tell tales on one another. There were also minor harassments. The Lyceum had been founded in 1811 by Alexander I as a progressive school along modified Rousseauist lines. This was, of course, known to the students and they contrasted the intention with the reality, especially the use of corporal punishment. The library was stocked with good books, but students could not take them out without a specific order from a professor. They were no longer allowed at all into the once very popular periodical room. This control did not crush or necessarily alienate the students, however.[6] There were important compensations. The teachers were generally of the highest caliber. There were organized sports (an unusual feature in Russian educational institutions), dancing, fencing, singing, and drawing. It was possible to let off steam by reading romantic literature or by writing poetry. There was a regular cult of Pushkin, who had graduated in 1817. Pranks were not unknown. And there were the good social connections and the sense of being an elite. Graduates usually took great pride in their school. They were one of the few bodies of alumni in Russia to hold annual reunions.

There are a few interesting bits of evidence regarding Danilevsky's reactions to all of this. He told the investigators of the Petrashevsky affair that he had preferred the scientific to the other parts of the curriculum, some of which seemed stuffy and unimaginative, and that he had therefore decided not to go into government service but rather to try to develop himself into a sort of free-lance scientist. This testimony is quite credible, for he went from the Lyceum to the University of St. Petersburg where he studied mathematics and biology. This was entirely voluntary, though as a Lyceum graduate he was entitled to tuition-free education at the university.[7] His status there was that of "free auditor" but he received a degree like any paying student. Danilevsky deprived himself to obtain this education, for a civil service position was open to him upon graduation from the Lyceum, whereas in Petersburg he had to do hack periodical

writing to help support himself. It seems quite certain that on
the whole he found the generally high caliber of the Lyceum
curriculum, especially the science, stimulating and worthy of
commitment. Fittingly he graduated with a record well above the
average.[8]

On the other hand, he also associated at the Lyceum with
some incipiently radical students, some of whom were, in the
forties, to make up the nucleus of the utopian socialist circle of
Petrashevsky.[9] These included M. V. Butashevich-Petrashevsky
himself. At that time this future Fourierist was only a vague
freethinker. He was a great perpetrator of practical jokes at the
faculty's expense, a factor that helped put him at the bottom of
his class at graduation. Other such friends were the Kaidanov
brothers, A. V. Khanykov, A. P. Beklemishev, all future Petrashevskians; Michael Evgrafovich Saltykov, later the radical satirist
"Saltykov-Shchedrin"; and the already mysterious N. A. Speshnev, said to have been one of Dostoevsky's models for Stavrogin
in *The Possessed*. Among these students there was talk of Belinsky, who was just then turning to the left, of the supposed political implications of Pushkin's tragic death in 1837, of Schiller,
and of the Western Europe left out of their Westernist education. Radical ideas and attitudes were as yet vague among these
people, however. It might have been difficult to draw an "intellectual" line between a romantic student poet like Danilevsky's
close, quite unradical friend Nicholas Semenov, and Petrashevsky,
his more casual associate.

Here there seems to have been another kind of reaction of
Danilevsky's to the Lyceum. It was partly just a matter of adolescent behavior. Also involved was annoyance at the official re-
strictions imposed on studies of the humanities and on student
life. If we may judge by the later history of the same group,
freethinking seems also to have been related, particularly in
Danilevsky's case, to difficulties of emotional and spiritual adjustment to new cultural patterns, especially scientific ideas and
rationalist values. Fashionable late romanticism encouraged rather

open expression of feelings too; and it provided a language for this that was different from that of Orthodoxy or Russian traditionalism. On a more rational and practical level, however, Danilevsky was not much of an adolescent rebel, for he planned a professional life, if not within the official then within the political and social circumstances of that time. He was probably but a slightly more disturbed version of his close conservative friend, the student poet and future senator Nicholas Semenov. Even Petrashevsky went on as a free auditor to study law at the University of St. Petersburg. Danilevsky's double reaction and ambivalent behavior pattern seem, however, to have been a youthful anticipation of a lifelong combination of work and discontent.

In accord with his apparently dominant idea of preparing himself for social service through science, he entered the University of St. Petersburg in the summer of 1843. There he studied in the Physico-Mathematical Faculty until the spring of 1849. His exposure to officially sponsored Westernism was now greatly intensified. The university was not as emphatically vocational as the Lyceum but a Petersburg in distinction to a Moscow education was regarded at the time with justification as a rather practical affair.[10] And then, Danilevsky with his preparation and aspirations concentrated on the more practical side. There having been no fixed curriculum as at the Lyceum, one cannot see so many aspects of his university education. But looking at the courses offered at the time in the Physico-Mathematical Faculty, considering the disciplines used by Danilevsky later, and utilizing some direct evidence in Peter Semenov's memoirs, it is possible to identify some of the more important aspects. He undoubtedly studied statistics, probably under Professor Victor Iakovlevich Buniakovsky, who was an important figure in the history of operational mathematics in Russia and was later one of the founders of actuarial statistics there.[11] There was also extensive study of biology: botany under Professor I. O. Shikhovsky; zoology, comparative anatomy, and paleontology with Professor S. S. Kutorga. The days of speculative and romantic science or *Natur-*

philosophie in Russia were all but gone. Danilevsky received experimental training. Shikhovsky founded the botanical garden at Petersburg and was a scientist with only marginal philosophical interests. He based his courses on the work of such (for the time) unspeculative scientists as Jussieu, Cuvier, Brogniart, De Candolle, and Schleiden. The fancies of Geoffroy Saint-Hilaire did interest him some, however. Kutorga was more consistently interested in philosophy. Nevertheless Blainville, Cuvier, Purkinje, and Baer were his scientific models; and he was basically an experimentalist. On the whole, one is struck by the up-to-dateness and apparent excellence of science teaching at Petersburg in this period.

Danilevsky's years at Petersburg marked a repetition, on a larger and more serious scale, of his behavior, conformist and otherwise, at the Lyceum. He persisted in the idea of becoming a free-lance scientist and serving society, as his selection of a program, his associates, and his efforts to find appropriate employment show. While at the university he was very friendly with Peter Petrovich Semenov, the brother of his Lyceum friend. They all roomed together on Vasilevsky Island. Peter Semenov, who was also a student of science, continuously made an emphatic point of his determination to avoid what he regarded as the useless drudgery of the bureaucracy in favor of a "socially useful," as he called it, scientific career. In his memoirs he tells how Danilevsky shared this view and how unfortunate they both regarded the lot of Nicholas Semenov, who worked in the Ministry of Justice. In their evening conversations at home they had considerable fun at Nicholas' expense. In line with his determination to pursue a scientific career, Peter, in the winter of 1848–49, joined the newly founded Russian Geographical Society and got a position there as librarian.[12] Danilevsky followed him into the society. Toward the end of his stay at Petersburg Danilevsky managed, in partnership with Semenov, to obtain a three-year monetary grant from the Free Economic Society[13] to map and analyze the soil and vegetation of the black soil region of European Russia.

It seems reasonable to conclude that he thought of this opportunity as the achievement of something he had consistently sought for ten years.

One important purpose of such education from the government's point of view was to train people to do practical work, inside or outside the bureaucracy, in order to improve material conditions in Russia. The Danilevsky of 1849 was in many ways a product of the system. He had learned scientific skills and picked up a strong sense of purpose about using them to help modernize and rationalize Russian conditions. His idea of avoiding the bureaucracy in favor of employment with private scientific institutions suggests some sort of critical view of his education's sponsor. But whatever its particular motive, it was not a subversive or rebellious view. As far as practicalities went, he was willing to work within the *status quo*, though at the same time, as his behavior suggests, he seems to have had an idea that some of it was not conducive to the full use of his talents. This was a sort of loyal oppositionist attitude.

Although he did become an active participant in the Fourierist Petrashevsky circle in the late forties, there is no good reason for believing that this resulted, to any significant degree, from the frustration of a desire to work constructively for the improvement of Russian conditions. His situation, besides confusing him, had probably overstimulated rather than stifled him. The officially sponsored educational system had provided him, partly free of charge, with some outstanding professional skills. He had had a reasonable opportunity to choose the kind of work he wanted to do. There was even some chance, which he made use of, to disapprove, in a way, of the government's rather narrowly defined purposes and to develop an original position in opposition, yet still loyal and "socially useful." Moreover, there is no evidence that Danilevsky's or Peter Semenov's determination to avoid the bureaucracy involved any big political or ideological issue. He remained on close terms with Nicholas Semenov. They were to be friends for life: in the eighties Danilevsky was to dedicate his

Darwinism to Nicholas, an amateur naturalist. Nicholas seems to have been something of a loyal oppositionist himself, for he went on to become one of the architects of the emancipation of 1861; evidently he was not particularly stifled even in the civil service. The teasing that Danilevsky, Peter, and the Semenovs' uncle (who lived with them and was later to become a provincial governor) undertook at his expense in the apartment on Vasilevsky Island was probably more temperamental and professional than political or ideological in origin. They twitted him about some of his jobs, such as having to spend hours hand sewing files together. They helped him, sometimes in quite unorthodox ways and with his full connivance, in catching up on mounds of paper work he found it necessary to bring home. Then too they were scientists and he a lawyer; differences in professional orientation were an important root of their friendly disagreements with him and also of their desire to avoid the bureaucracy. Their practical attitude, like his, one with little ideological content, may be described as liberal.

Nevertheless Danilevsky participated most actively at this time in the radical discussion circle of Petrashevsky. He was a leading figure in that circle in 1846 and 1848 and was regarded as an expert on Fourier's system.

2

In Europe at large this was the time of preparation of the great revolutions of 1848.[14] It will be remembered that these political events constituted one of the more spectacular aspects of a lengthy struggle between the forces of political legitimacy and absolutism, on one side, and of liberalism and nationalism, on the other. By the mid-1840's liberal-nationalist political activism was in the air all over Western Europe. The years prior to 1848 saw an upsurge of another kind of movement, utopian socialism and modern communism. This was the heyday of Saint-Simonism, Fourierism, and similar doctrines. It was the time when Marx wrote the work now titled *Economic and Philosophical Manu-scripts of 1844* and Engels, *The Condition of the Working Class in England*; when together they conceived *The Communist Mani-festo*. Now, this whole movement was quite different from and had an unusual relationship to the burgeoning liberal, nationalist, "bourgeois" political forces that were to spark the events of 1848. The radicals partly identified with the liberals but they also op-posed them. Liberalism was thought to be too narrow, timid, and class bound in its conception of goals. This kind of critical atti-tude did have some empirical and ethical basis. The masses, urban and rural, were living under very harsh conditions and the liberals were often insensitive to this, partly because they were human and could not do (or even think of) everything at once, partly because they had some selfish economic and social vested inter-ests that were undemocratic. But on the whole this earth-bound situation was not the main root of radicalism. The typical radical intellectual documents of the time indicate as much or more in-terest in a quite different and distinctly nonpractical, relatively unempirical direction. The radicals thought the liberals narrow because the latter wanted a mere reorganization of this world. The radicals wanted the whole modern, antidynastic movement to push forward, not simply to such a reorganization, however fair and equalitarian that might be, but rather to the construction of a heaven on earth. This particular desire, a basic one with the radicals, had spiritual, cultural, and sociological rather than prac-tical political bases.[15] These radicals were antimodern, antiurban, and, in appropriate places, anti-industrial, though they also recog-nized the inevitability of the changes taking place around them. They wanted to push forward to a future that would have had many qualities in common with the traditional past (now highly idealized, even itself partly modernized in their minds). In a sense they were legitimist and traditionalist rebels. It is not very useful to regard them as simply a left wing of the liberal movement, for they were political and social thinkers only in a wholly extraordi-nary sense.

This romantic radicalism, often politically revolutionary, sometimes not, flourished all over Europe in the era of 1848. As the
historian shifts his attention from Western Europe to Russia,
however, an interesting change of pattern becomes evident. In
Western Europe romantic radicalism flourished side by side with
a strong and ideologically self-conscious movement of political
liberalism. In the East there was almost no liberal movement, and
radicalism stood much more alone. In the historical picture, as
it can now be observed, radicalism was a central movement in
Russian thought, a marginal one in Western European. In the
East, radicalism, on the eve of 1848 and way beyond, became the
continuing intellectual concern of many of the best minds — of
Herzen, Belinsky, Bakunin, Chernyskevsky, Pisarev, Lavrov, Mikhailovsky. In short, Russian radicalism was a more serious intellectual movement, involving more people for a longer time,
than was Western European.[16]

This difference of emphasis between Western and Russian intellectual history has sometimes been attributed to the fact that
the political situation in Russia was a singularly difficult and oppressive one. Radicalism rather than liberalism, it has been held,
was an understandable practical response to this. Though internally logical and attractively simple, this interpretation does not
relate fully enough to the facts. Placing too exclusive emphasis
on irrelevant differences between the Russian and Western European situations, it fails to take sufficient account of the distinctly
chiliastic, millenarian temper of all romantic radicalism. The interpretation thus either bypasses the real problem of motivation or,
noting the chiliasm, explains it as a symptom of political frustration in an authoritarian system. One cannot in a study of one
man undertake satisfactorily to refute the view that Russian radicalism (unlike American or British, for example) was by and
large an ordinary political movement skewed by tsarist oppression.
But one can point out the poverty of the human and psychological assumptions (for example, that men are basically self-interested, that impractical dreaming is a symptom of inactivity)

underlying the view and, asking better questions, take more seriously the actual behavior of the Russian radicals and what they had to say. The differences between them and their Western counterparts are better understood as variations on a common theme.

Modernization in Russia had a mainly bureaucratic impulse; Russia lacked a middle class with autonomous social power. The process did not therefore give rise to a nonbureaucratic, oppositional, modernizing movement — to liberalism. But the general process of change in Russia — together with the cultural dilemmas it generated — was the same as that in the West, and it made possible similar "anti-modern" intellectual responses. There could even be, and was, straight intellectual borrowing by Russian radicals from Western. In analyzing the history of radicalism in Russia, it is important to bear in mind the fact that the autocracy was not merely reactionary; with all its obscurantism it was the most significant initiator and maintainer of the forces of change, in a way, a progressive institution (the splendid scientific education it made available to Danilevsky and others is a good illustration). Appropriately Russian chiliastic radicalism, from the 1840's to the 1870's, was as much an effort to cope with the spiritual, intellectual, and psychological difficulties of social and cultural transition to the modern age, as it was the result of ordinary rational and ethical reactions against tsarist obscurantism and Russian socio-economic decadence. In its important nonpractical or speculative dimension, radicalism in Russia was chiefly a response to the continually deteriorating state of spiritual and cultural confusion, the catalyst of this process having been the tsarist government itself.

The relative strength and longevity of radicalism in the Russian intellectual scene may also be attributed, to an important extent, to nonpolitical factors. The forces of modernity came to Russia relatively suddenly and in highly developed forms. The confrontation of traditionalism by modern technical rationalism was especially abrupt. This confrontation also involved the problem of national identity more seriously than in Western European countries, for Russia was more backward and its culture different. Modernity in Russia was foreign as well as new. There was the additional difficulty, mentioned earlier, that varying intellectual solutions, both the unofficial and the official one, compounded the cultural problems they were designed to solve. Persisting at least through the seventies these conditions tinged Russian political and social thought with romanticism long after Western Europe had become more realistic. While the fifties and sixties did mark some shift to realism in the arts and in thought, romanticism, superficially recast, lingered on in the East; and utopian radicalism continued to be its main expression. It is likely, too, as suggested earlier, that the particular religious background, the national character, and the educational system conduced to the popularity of communal, leftist, progressive, scientific, and existentially concrete (rather than individualistic, aestheticist, and more obviously fanciful) kinds of romanticism. That is, the general temper or spirit of Russian romanticism (now "classical," now "realistic" [17]) was such that it found easy and natural expression in social and political language of a progressive kind. Moreover, such a romanticism may have been unusually susceptible to adaptation and thus able to survive longer in an increasingly this-worldly European climate of opinion. On the other hand, the oppressive political situation, the really backward social and economic conditions, did contribute to the popularity and longevity of radicalism in Russia. The phenomenon cannot be understood without making allowance for ethical responses to real evils. The point is that these evils and men's ethical common sense were only influences in a movement whose main energy, as it were, came from other-worldly aspirations. Indeed, it was probably the case too that the rather desperate condition of the country, and the deceptively obvious ("but for the autocracy") practical possibilities of doing something about it, encouraged the idea that fantastically ambitious changes in the society not only of Russia, but of mankind at large, were entirely reasonable.

The Petrashevsky circle may be taken as a particular instance of the general phenomenon of romantic radicalism, Western European and Russian.[18] The core of the circle was made up of young minor bureaucrats, junior army officers, students attending the University of St. Petersburg, and a few literary people, of whom Dostoevsky, who had recently completed an engineering education, was to become the most famous. Many of them were in situations similar to that of Danilevsky. They were not all men of scientific training; they did not all, because of their skills or temperaments, try to avoid government work. A number, however, had had a not dissimilar practical training and were impatient with the pace at which Russia was being reformed. This helped focus their romanticism on society. But their radicalism and Fourierism owed much more to two other, related sources. First, Western progressive and scientific influences picked up, higgledy-piggledy, at school, in the press, and from reading (especially forbidden books stolen by Petrashevsky from foreign clients in connection with his legal practice) served to exaggerate their expectations about the possible nature of Russia's future. Second, they all had an intense desire for a comforting sense of identity and of continuity with their own now highly idealized traditional backgrounds. Judging from the temper of the intellectual documents that have come down to us, the second was probably the more decisive stimulus. Western ideas seem mainly to have provided a modern conceptual language in which could be expressed, on the one hand, a desire for progress, science, democracy and, on the other, a desire that progress would have a terminus (an odd notion in itself) resembling somewhat the Orthodox heaven and a fanciful version of Russian traditional community life. In other words, the Petrashevsky circle was made up of recently Westernized, educated Russians in search of their own and their society's cultural and spiritual identity.

In the history of Russian radicalism the circle is notable as the first important manifestation of romantic radicalism in realistic trappings. The Petrashevskians were forerunners of the nontotalitarian radicals of the later fifties, sixties, and seventies. There were more Diderot-like scientific naturalists than Hegelian idealists among them. They often talked about serfdom, economic problems, the law, social classes, national minorities, education, forms of government, and about revolution and how it might come about. Most of them did not share Fourier's apoliticism. Many thought that the overthrow of the Russian monarchy and the setting up of a federated republic like the United States would have to precede the full reform of society along Fourierist lines. Petrashevsky himself and a majority of the others believed and argued that a large education and propaganda effort would have to come before a political overthrow. A minority of more orthodox Fourierists argued against any political action as being unscientific: utopia would have to come through direct social action; if some phalanxes or socialist communities were set up, people would quickly remodel their lives on the example of this most naturally human institution. A happy few like Speshnev and Chernosvitov took a Jacobin position: revolution must come first; agitation among peasants and workers would get a large *jacquerie* going and this could be used to overthrow the tsar. Because of the interest of so many Petrashevskians in enlightenment and propaganda, there was also frequent adverse talk about censorship and there was discussion of a free press. These people were realistic also in another sense. They made some subversive gestures in accordance with their beliefs. Petrashevsky himself was a leader in such gestures. Curiously for a Russian progressive, he wore a beard as a sign of defiance against the shaving tradition begun by Peter the Great. He also bore sartorial witness, in this case to the whole European left, by wearing an "Almaviva cloak" symbolizing Beaumarchais' *Barbier de Seville*. He harangued people on the streets, especially merchants, in whose progressive potentialities he had great faith. To spread the ideas current in his own circle, he got associates to hold their own "evenings," develop their own subsidiary groups, and bring in more people. He tried from time to time, with only partial success, to get his

writings by the censors and into the legal press. He developed a
good library of forbidden books. Speshnev, acting on a suggestion
originally made by Petrashevsky but later abandoned, tried to
work out a project for a secret printing press. It is also said, although the story is not fully corroborated, that Petrashevsky
built a phalanstery, as the central building of a Fourierist community was called, on his estate near St. Petersburg. However, so the
story goes, his peasants burned it on the day of its completion.

This kind of talk and action within this small radical movement
indicates reaction against Russian political, social, and economic
conditions. There is here more obvious influence of the immediate situation than in the case of the radicalism of older Russian
contemporaries, Hegelians and post-Hegelians like Herzen,
Bakunin, or Belinsky. At least one student of the circle, Leonid
Raisky, a Soviet historian, has even detected a marked influence
of the socio-economic position and interests of the lesser gentry
— to which class most of these people belonged — upon the
thinking and program of the Petrashevskians. Raisky, a reasonable Bolshevik of Pokrovsky vintage, points out with considerable persuasiveness that many aspects of their utopian dream were
"petty bourgeois." As gentry, impoverished by changes in the
Russian economy, these Fourierists wanted a type of community
which would at once assure a luxurious standard of living for all
and include the institutions of private property and inheritance.
In this thesis, they were particularly attracted to the phalanx because it took account, in the distribution of profits, of the inequalities of men's talents and wealth as well as of their productive
contributions. It all makes considerable sense and Raisky, especially if we interpret him in an un-Marxist spirit, provides insight
into the nature of the circle. The Petrashevskians may be seen as
impoverished gentry, ethically concerned with the welfare of the
Russian people, trying to make Russia into a country of socialist
latifundia. These would have been technically modern, econom-
ically most productive, democratically organized; they would also
have guaranteed private property and inherited social status —

even utilized (and thus justified) them as indispensable economic, social, and psychological mechanisms of the system. Thus Petrashevskianism was both a *laissez-faire* socialism and a modern form of feudalism.

Yet these lines of observation obscure more important and decisive phenomena. Anyone concerned with the whole, human — not just the socio-economic — meaning of the circle can hardly ignore or play down the beliefs which the Petrashevskians themselves took most seriously, namely, those they had borrowed from thinkers like Saint Simon, Fourier, and Ludwig Feuerbach. The published collections of documents, memoirs by former members of the circle, and Semevsky's unfinished biography of Petrashevsky (still the best treatment of the whole subject) — let alone Danilevsky's own writings — indicate beyond doubt that overriding importance was attributed to these beliefs.[19] Chiliastic and millenarian ideas, though derived mainly from books, were no mere academic playthings. Petrashevsky seems to have been diverted from suicide by them. He described his circle's motives by saying that the core of the matter was organization, "the reaction of the human spirit against the influence of liberalism, an influence which is anarchic and destructive of social life." Though an unbeliever, he once called socialism "the dogma of Christian love seeking realization in practical life." [20] So serious was he that he even tried, after his arrest, to convert the investigating committee and to persuade them to recommend to the government that it finance the organization of a phalanstery near Paris. Analysis of such commitments in terms of reflexes of frustrated (itself a bizarre word for these Bohemian characters) practical aims or of subconscious economic interests makes neither human nor psychological sense. The factual evidence, taken seriously, indicates rather that the Petrashevskians, though by no means utterly fanatical, believed with passion and dedication in their ideas for the same kinds of positive reasons that were the basis of belief in quite similar ideas elsewhere in the Western world (Brook Farm is a splendid example). The ideas themselves were the main center

of interest in the circle and the more decisive basis for all of its
activities, theoretical and practical. In short, it is best to assume
that the Petrashevskians meant what they said.

In effect they said repeatedly that they wanted Russia transformed into a land of Fourierist communities or phalanxes. The
phalanx was to them much more than an economic and social device. Men living in these communities would naturally and
easily experience self-fulfillment. All their spiritual and psychological potentialities would here, and only here, be realized. Work
and play would be the same thing. The Petrashevskians did not
seek to change Russia according to some mere practical plan. They
sought to direct Russians, as human beings not just as citizens, to
a heaven on earth. With Feuerbach and others (even Marx and
Engels were in their library) they believed that the type of society existing at that time, whether Russian or Western European,
was the main, indeed the sole, cause of man's existential troubles,
his anxieties, confusions, despairs. Modern science, engineering,
jurisprudence, sociology were wonderful new tools that created
the possibility for the first time in history of correcting and
ameliorating the human condition.

The subversive activities of Petrashevsky and his associates were
less reactions against political and social conditions in Russia than
they were positive actions taken in the light of a (usually) atheist
humanist spirituality. They wanted a revolution and put in some
diffuse effort on behalf of one, because they wanted to work out
a scheme in which they believed. They did not by and large develop the scheme in the course of a rational and ethical rebellion
against tsarism and serfdom. They rebelled against the evils of
Russian society, and also ultimately against liberalism, nationalism, history itself, because of their eschatological beliefs. The
doctrines of Fourier and others appealed to them on account of
their promise, not because they strengthened or rationalized a
mere idea of eliminating political and social abuses, however dire.
The Petrashevskians talked and acted more realistically than their
older neo-Hegelian contemporaries. But this was mainly due to the

fact that their dream about the future was made out of more worldly materials. Lower gentry social origins, practical educational backgrounds, and the changing European climate of opinion were key factors in attracting them to a dream that had a "realistic" quality. However, a very similar sense of cultural confusion, of spiritual and psychological uprootedness in an age of rapid change had been in part the occasion, in part the cause, of a quest for some new kind of spirituality and for a large societal myth in the cases of Khomiakov, Herzen, and Petrashevsky alike.

Despite the precocious elements of "realism" in the circle, there were significant differences between the Petrashevskians and their more hard-boiled, sometimes totalitarian, successors in the sixties and seventies. Danilevsky's friends have frequently been maligned. They were not intolerant fanatics but authentic humanists. There are several indications of this. First, the speculative elements in the thought of the circle were more prominent than the activist or potentially activist elements. Most of Danilevsky's radical friends were as fascinated with the process of dreaming as they were with the problems of implementing their dreams. This means, on the one hand, that they were not absolutely sure of the dream, and on the other, that they felt a strong sense of responsibility for it (it was regarded as human in origin). There was thus considerable intellectual difference among them; some regular participants in the circle were not even Fourierists. Then too the enjoyment of the speculative process itself suggests that the ideological was not the only important basis of the circle's existence. It was as much an auxiliary means to a social end *hic et nunc* as it was a basis for revolution. In contrast to later radical groups, this was a gathering of friends — some of whom, as we know, had been together since school days — not just of believers.[21] People met, in part, simply because they liked one another's company. Fittingly newcomers brought in were welcomed quite casually and there were no rules of membership or initiation practices. Intellectual discussion was frequently interrupted or omitted entirely in favor of just plain conversation or literary readings or drinking. The Friday gatherings offered stimulating people, readings (Dostoevsky, for instance, read part of *Netochka Nezvanova* at one meeting just prior to its publication), occasional ceremonial dinners in honor of Fourier. No doubt a simple desire for comradeship was a significant element in the life of the circle. Practically all of the members seem to have had some motive of this kind. There were even an exceptional few for whom interesting associations were almost the only attraction. A certain Captain Kropotov, for instance, told the Commission of Investigation after his arrest, though no doubt with some exaggeration, that he was innocent of any subversion because he had gone to Petrashevsky's only for dinner, that he was deaf in one ear and had earlier read Thiers on the dangers of socialism. Semenov says in his memoirs, "We all went to Petrashevsky's because he had his own house and could arrange a nice evening; we often thought Petrashevsky eccentric if not crazy." [22]

The circle may be said to have had its sociological origin both in gentry class, school, and vocational groups *and* in ideological convictions. Thus the Fourierist dream was valued as much for itself as for its promise of a radical transformation of this world. Many of the most typical "realists" of the next generation had more exclusively ideological ties and were appropriately more fanatical, more prisoners than orchestrators of ideas, more possessed than possessors. They were to be more concerned with squaring means to ends than the Petrashevskians; and fittingly they made themselves means to ends, seldom hesitated to excommunicate unbelievers from their midst, or, like Ivan Karamazov, to love their "neighbors in the abstract, or even at a distance" but not "at close quarters." While the changed social and historical situation of these later radical intellectuals together with the different nature of the cultural problem and materials with which they worked helped make all this possible, it is difficult to believe that a Chernyshevsky, a Dobroliubov, a Pisarev, or a Tkachev could not have done better for themselves. Some radicals of the sixties and seventies, for example, Lavrov or Mikhailovsky, found it possible to be human as well as committed. It would seem that the Petrashevskians deserve some praise from the historian.

On balance it appears that the famous judgments[23] upon the circle of both Alexander Herzen ("tsarism turned upside down") and Dostoevsky in his later years ("Shigalevism") were unfair. Both thought the movement fanatical, dangerously out of touch with reality, maliciously hyperideological, and inhuman. It must be granted that in comparison to the circles of Granovsky, Herzen, or Khomiakov, at Petrashevsky's there was less playfulness, less skepticism and irony about favorite ideals, and more willingness to sacrifice the self and mankind to abstractions. The very ideas of the Petrashevskians were narrower, yet most of Danilevsky's friends were genuine humanists, "men of the forties." This small radical movement *was* seriously revolutionary, though only in its members' minds; it did propose to overturn the world in the name of its ideal, its answer to the problem of Russian and Western European spiritual and cultural change. But at the same time, like the other more aristocratic groups, it was a social institution in the real world, one which provided (within the Westernized city of St. Petersburg) a chance to develop affective ties that were continuous with those that had once been known in idealized memories, in the country with its secure traditionalism and its lazy gentry social life. Dreaming of the future that would be something like, though also better than the past thus helped make it seem as though there had been little change at all. The Petrashevskians, like the other "men of the forties," acted as though in some obscure but meaningful way they knew about this dimension of their activities and prized it. Their sense of folly blunted their tendencies to fanaticism.

3

It seems reasonable, in view of the nature of Russian radicalism in general and Petrashevskianism in particular, to assume that Danilevsky's active participation in the circle over a considerable

time indicates that he was upset, that he felt spiritually and culturally uprooted, intellectually disoriented by his Westernist,
scientific education and by the whole new world into which that
was leading him. At Petrashevsky's he found some sense of continuity, some comfort, some hope of meaning. He also found a
chance to work on the problem of direction and purpose for
himself and others. As of the later forties, therefore, there becomes evident the first full picture of the typical Danilevsky,
simultaneously the professional scientist and the philosophic
quester, ambiguous, dualistic, self-contradictory. Of course, there
were, as has been mentioned, people in the circle who were not
Fourierists and some who were just interested in a good time.
But Danilevsky was not one of these. His writings and the more
intellectual part of his testimony before the Commission of Investigation of 1849 attest beyond doubt that he was deeply committed to Fourierism and that he took it as a kind of *Nouveau
Christianisme*. The available biographical evidence regarding this
episode of his life, though meager, further confirms the whole
picture and in addition provides several interesting insights into
the specific nature of his state of mind.

The most plentiful source of biographical information is his
testimony before the Commission of Investigation.[24] Let us sum-
marize this and then inquire into its credibility and usefulness as
a historical source. As did others among the accused, Danilevsky
emphasized that he was apolitical — like Fourier himself. Fourierism to him was a scientific doctrine. It would succeed because
Fourier had discovered the true nature of man and invented the
perfect social mechanism for his fulfillment. Once the doctrine
became widely known, especially through the establishment of
exemplary phalanxes, it would be enthusiastically implemented
by private efforts on a large scale. It was not a subversive program but, on the contrary — since it would alleviate economic
and social discontent — a powerful antidote to such dangerous
ideas as egalitarianism or communism.

He stressed that his Fourierism had been different from that of

many of the others, whom he had known to be "freethinkers."
His interest in the doctrine had developed long before he had
begun to go to Petrashevsky's. He had first learned about it,
"quite by accident," entirely on his own. Shortly after leaving
the Lyceum, he had come upon a book about Fourier's system
by a certain Gabriel Gabet (evidently *Traité élémentaire de la
science de l'homme considéré sous tous les rapports, enrichi de
figures*, 2 volumes, Paris, 1842). Inspired by this he had read
original works by Saint-Simon, Fourier, and Robert Owen. He
had then, in the winter and spring of 1846, gone to Petrashevsky's,
not with an interest in disseminating the doctrine of Fourier but
only in discussing its scientific validity. "I . . . undertook to
meet someone with knowledge and a speculative turn of mind,
who would join me in a common effort to penetrate more deeply
into the doctrine in order to elucidate several aspects of it to our
own satisfaction." [25] His activities in the circle during this first
period of participation had been limited to discussion with
Valerian Maikov, the chief literary critic of the journal Annals
of the Fatherland. Maikov, a liberal and something of a left
Hegelian, had proved to be more of a critic than a collaborator.
His resistance had led Danilevsky to a deeper study of Fourier,
not to an effort to win over the unconvinced. This was a further
proof of the purely scientific nature of his thinking.

From January to May 1848 he had again, after a period of absence occasioned by work on his master's thesis, gone repeatedly
to Petrashevsky's and also, though less frequently, to gatherings
at Dostoevsky's, where the main concern had been literature, at
the poet A. N. Pleshcheev's, and at N. A. Speshnev's. His main
interests had been in reading the Fourierist magazine *La Phalange*
at Petrashevsky's. Its reports on the revolution of 1848 in Paris
had raised hopes that there was about to be a practical testing of
Fourier's project. Also he had sought another intellectual dialogue. Maikov having died, he talked with Speshnev, who had
recently been to France, about the latest developments among
Fourier's disciples. He thought it to his credit that he had tried

very hard, by lecturing on Fourier and through conversation, to win the freethinkers, especially Speshnev, over to an orthodox and apolitical Fourierism. In short, his activities had remained chiefly scientific. His only guilt in his own eyes, he said, lay in having associated with people he had known to be freethinkers, in having failed to win them over to his own more solid views, and, on one occasion, in having discussed with Speshnev a project for a publishing venture abroad. This last idea had been scientific too, however; a journal published abroad would have given him a chance to expand Fourier's views in great depth and detail. Anyway, "I thank God that the idea left me when I reflected that it was useless and illegal." [26] In the end, once it had become clear to him that a political situation was developing in France that was unlikely to be conducive to Fourierist experimentation, he had given up the doctrine, which he still thought scientific, however, as being impractical except in the remote future. Intensification of freethinking in the circle (especially after many drinks) and the fear that his activities might be considered illegal, though Fourier's doctrine was harmless and his works not banned, had led Danilevsky to give up his associations.

On the whole, this testimony is credible. He could well have discovered the doctrine prior to his entry into the circle. Fourier's writings, as he said, were not banned in Russia. He might even have heard Professor Victor S. Poroshin,[27] the "Granovsky of the University of St. Petersburg," lecture on Fourier at the university. The doctrine was evidently more widely known among the educated in Russia than it was in Western Europe.[28] Coming upon it in this legal fashion may have helped give him the idea that it was purely scientific. Moreover, in the circle itself there was constant insistence that Fourier was "the Newton of the social sciences." Danilevsky could have found there much agreement with the general attitude he described as his own.

There is only one really suspicious element in the testimony: the degree of stress on political loyalty to the tsarist regime. Danilevsky seems too consistent and innocent; he protests too much. Had he really been so apolitical on principle, we might expect him to have mentioned a close association with N. S. Kashkin, the leader of the orthodox Fourierists, of the "right wing" of the Petrashevskians, rather than with Petrashevsky himself or especially with Speshnev, the leading Jacobin of the circle, a blatant rebel, atheist, and communist. Moreover, Speshnev seems to have admired Danilevsky and possibly thought of inviting him to join a secret society he was planning to form.[29] Then too in 1848, Petrashevsky, who was beginning to become disgusted with the informality and ineffectiveness of his circle, seems to have regarded Danilevsky and Speshnev together as allies in his effort to give the movement more direction and form.[30] It is unlikely that, in the circle itself, Danilevsky insisted on his apoliticism as firmly and consistently as he did before the commission. This aspect of his defense is further rendered suspect when it is remembered that many a one among the accused also chose to emphasize the "true" nature of his Fourierism.

But, in general, Danilevsky was undoubtedly mainly attracted by what he regarded as the scientific quality of Fourierism. His writings and the more intellectual part of his testimony indicate beyond doubt that he thought the doctrine's relationship to nature, to history, and to empirical science to be such that the realization of its promise was highly likely if not inevitable. Though he may at times have spoken with Petrashevsky, Speshnev, or others about the desirability of propaganda and even of giving nature, history, and science a little revolutionary push, he seems to have believed, in the main, that the doctrine's scientific validity was the chief guarantee of its being practical and realizable. It is also possible that he now and then objected to the adventurous politicism of some of his friends because he feared too much human tinkering would interfere with the workings of benevolent larger processes. In his testimony he seems to have chosen, quite understandably, to present his activities in a light somewhat more favorable than the facts warranted; but still there was only exaggeration, not outright falsification.

His reputation among the others and the role he played at Petrashevsky's meetings corroborate the idea that his interest in Fourierism was more purely ideological ("scientific") than that of practically any of the others. Several primary sources describe him as the expert in the circle on Fourierism.[31] Speshnev said that along with himself and his friend K. I. Timkovsky Danilevsky knew more about socialism than anyone else in Russia. The best historians of the Petrashevsky movement agree on this point. Fittingly, Danilevsky became an important leader in the circle in 1848, just when there arose a definite trend toward greater intellectual rigor. At that time his lectures on Fourierism became a regular feature of the Friday meetings. He seems to have been, as he suggested in his testimony, a sort of Olympian figure in this little radical movement. N. N. Strakhov, in his biographical sketch, describes his first meeting with Danilevsky at the University of St. Petersburg as an appropriately "public" affair. He says that one day he heard some students crying "Danilevsky! Danilevsky!"; and our hero gathered them around and "spoke to them concerning the existence of God." Danilevsky was an atheist at that time.[32]

In view of the fact that Danilevsky was later, in the 1860's, to become an intellectual fanatic, it is worth inquiring whether or not we can see any anticipation of this in the forties. Was he markedly more dogmatic, less humanistic than the majority of the others? A case of sorts might be made for some such interpretation. The evidence we have pictures him as more serious than most of them. We see him now participating, now sitting in a corner reading. His emphasis on the science in Fourier sounds hard-boiled as well as apolitical. Yet it does not seem that such an interpretation of the young Danilevsky is at all warranted. The fact that his behavior in the circle was distinctive can better be attributed to differences of personality (a certain shyness and diffidence in personal relationships) and of education (after all, he had had a most rigorous scientific training and was an advanced graduate student in biology by 1848) and probably of general intellectual sophistication. There is no evidence that he was "possessed" by Fourierism. No doubt he was fascinated with the doctrine. But, as he suggested repeatedly in his testimony, he thought of it as an idea not as a kind of revelation of nature's or history's will. In a series of review articles on Humboldt's *Cosmos* of this same period, he vehemently protested against Hegelianism and all such deterministic thinking about the development of ideas in history. True, he thought of the doctrine in connection with scientific as well as historical developments in modern times. But again, as we shall see in discussing his articles on Dutrochet, he did not hold to a narrowly positivistic view of science. To him science was a humanistic activity operating on certain definite methodological criteria, not the voice of nature. Thus he was prepared — indeed, it was one of his main interests — to discuss Fourierism, to explore it, but he was not prepared to believe in its practicability until it had been submitted to a test. When he despaired of the possibility of such a test, he gave it up. The attitude and behavior of an intellectual fanatic were not significant aspects of the make-up of the young Danilevsky. His real hesitancy about and objections to overly adventurous political actions and propaganda on behalf of the promotion of Fourier's ends apparently sprang partly from genuine doubts and reservations about the doctrine. He is quite believable in his testimony when he says he felt really guilty for having entertained an idea of starting a publication abroad. For this had been an illegal action, in the name of an idea. It had implications of hostility to his countrymen and was contrary to his deepest moral convictions. "I am very conscious of my guilt because I do not hold to the sophism that the end justifies the means." "I oppose political changes because, whatever their apparent advantages, they cause suffering and bloodshed." [33]

Danilevsky was intellectually more systematic than most of his associates. But systematism is not *prima facie* evidence of dogmatism; if that were the case, pessimists and skeptics like Turgenev would become the sole heroes of nineteenth century Russian cultural history. It is more accurate and fair to recognize that he was in tune with the humanism as well as with the Fourierism of the circle. As to his particular role within the circle as a group of friends, our evidence may not be well rounded. After all, he *had* known Petrashevsky, Speshnev, and others at the Lyceum. His relations with them could have been more than ideological. It does not seem to have troubled him that his friend Peter Semenov, who was most skeptical about the whole business, sometimes went to Petrashevsky's with him, chiefly for a good time. Evidently too, as Semenov says in his memoirs, all-night "bull" sessions about Fourier, Saint-Simon, the French Revolution, and related topics were a regular part of life in the apartment on Vasilevsky Island. It is entirely possible that there was considerable continuity between Danilevsky's everyday humanity and his rather formal intellectual activity.

Although there seem to be no good reasons for believing that Danilevsky's intellectual fanaticism of the sixties was anticipated in the forties, there was perhaps one aspect of his experience with the Petrashevsky circle that is of importance for his later unfortunate intellectual development. This has to do with the possible effect that his arrest (in June 1849), imprisonment in the Peter and Paul fortress (to November 1849), and exile to Vologda had upon his willingness, henceforth, for over three decades, to work directly, explicitly, and humanistically with a strong sense of uprootedness, meaninglessness, and disorientation that continued to arise in him as Russia's modernization and Westernization, especially in his milieu, intensified. As will later become all too clear to the reader, *Russia and Europe* was the work of a man with strong feelings of cultural alienation and intense spiritual longings, feelings and longings which he would not fully admit to himself and which at the same time, however, he tried to alleviate and to satisfy in curiously oblique ways. More intense and, for him, new modernistic cultural and social influences played a considerable role in this; they were such as at once to frustrate and enhance his feelings and aspirations. But there was another factor: his own state of mind. It is very likely that something — or more probably some things — that happened in Danilevsky's personal life helped make possible a profound change in him between the 1840's and the 1860's. One of these things may have been the dreadful experience of 1849.

Fully to appreciate this possibility, it should be remembered that there was much more to Danilevsky's life in the later forties than his activity in the Petrashevsky circle. He was working hard at his studies. He received his candidate's degree in mathematics in 1846 and worked on his master's degree[34] in biology down to the spring of 1849 when he was arrested. That same year, with a view to his future career, he entered the Geographical Society and, with Peter Semenov, began a survey of the black soil region for the Free Economic Society. It had been work, probably on the flora of Riazan and Tula provinces, for his master's thesis, that had taken him away from Petrashevsky's and Petersburg in 1846. He had left the circle "forever" nearly a year before he and Semenov, in April 1849, began the survey which again necessitated prolonged absence from Petersburg. The "main front," as it were, of Danilevsky's life was scientific, "socially useful" work, not radicalism.

It should be mentioned also that he fell in love in 1846 or 1847. The lady was one Vera Nikolaevna Beklemisheva, the childless widow of a major general. She lived at Russkii Brod in the Liven district near his birthplace and was apparently a friend of his family's. He courted her while engaged in field work for his master's dissertation. Semenov, who was with him, tells us that Danilevsky was painfully shy and could not at this time bring himself to make a proposal of marriage. That came, at Semenov's firm insistence, only in May 1849, when the two scientists, after some weeks of study of the soil and flora of Riazan and Tula, went to Russkii Brod to write their first report for the Free Economic Society. Vera Beklemisheva accepted and, as Semenov says, Danilevsky was "in seventh heaven."

Looking at the whole situation, it seems very possible that

Danilevsky left the Petrashevsky circle because, in addition to loss of hope for an early Fourierist experiment and to fear of compromise with the law in the jittery atmosphere of 1848, he was by that time achieving a higher degree of maturity and better sense of adjustment in his professional and private life. He suggested something like this to the Commission of Investigation.

There comes a period in the lives of many people, especially those who do not belong to rich families, when they pass from work and privation to an attainment of their ends. This could be called "the critical period." The present year is my "critical period" . . . This year my scientific studies were a success. I passed my master's examination and received a commission from the Imperial Free Economic Society to make a study of the black soil area of European Russia, its agronomy and natural history. I hoped that the successful completion of this mission . . . would put me on the road to life and give me means to continue my studies so that I could be of use to my fatherland and to myself. To these hopes are joined others [his engagement] which it would be no easier to give up than life itself. This mission also gave me the chance to visit my mother, whom I have not seen for seven years, and to comfort her in the absence of my father and brother who are in the war [putting down the Hungarian revolution], and to give her a chance to rejoice at my success in my chosen profession.[35]

By 1849 radicalism may have seemed to him more and more merely a stage of development, although he was not yet entirely through this phase. He told the commission that he still thought Fourierism scientific and, in the intellectual part of his testimony, which constituted a sample lecture on Fourierism, he could still apparently be quite persuasive; at least, Ia. I. Rostovtsev, the head of the Judicial Commission, which reviewed the record of the investigation, jokingly remarked that, upon reading the lecture, the judges all became more or less Fourierists.[36] Moreover, Danilevsky still thought enough of the circle to agree to go to its annual ceremonial banquet in honor of Fourier on April 7, 1849, though he failed to attend because of fear of the police.[37] But, on the whole, the available data suggest that, had he been left alone at this point, he would have completed a development that was very typical in his time and his Russia: from youthful radical to liberal or conservative-liberal professional man or civil servant, perhaps, in his case, with continuing philosophical interests, though of another, nonradical kind.

The axe fell at just this delicate point. The Petrashevsky circle had never been a desperately subversive group. Hardly anyone, least of all Danilevsky, was prepared for his ordeal by a prior sense of really willful major transgression of the law. Even the final official announcement of the sentences found only the *possibility* of a *future* "dangerous turn." Yet of the 252 people involved in the investigation, seventy-two received punishment of some sort. Of the seventy-two, twenty-one were sentenced to death for "intent to subvert the existing laws of the fatherland and the state order." After a deliberately cruel mock execution ceremony ordered by Nicholas I — a scene immortalized by Dostoevsky — the twenty-one were shipped to Siberia for long sentences at hard labor. Another twenty-three, including Danilevsky, went before the special court-martial or Judicial Commission and were given lesser punishments. Though the remainder were barely touched, it was quite a harvest. "During the reign of Nicholas there had not been a political case of comparable magnitude since the Decembrists," remarks Sidney Monas, the historian of the Third Section or secret police.[38]

Being among the twenty-three turned over to the court-martial, Danilevsky did not personally suffer the very worst of it. It is not likely, however, that he suffered only as an individual. As was intended the terror generated by the worst sentences probably affected all to a considerable degree. The terrible sufferings of old friends could hardly have been viewed without pain, Danilevsky underwent something of an ordeal himself. It began with a sudden arrest in Tula province, where Danilevsky had been on his survey, by one Colonel Nazimov, a typically polite agent of the Third Section. Then came the months of incarceration in the Peter and Paul fortress, interrupted briefly for the investigation and the "trial." Though the Judicial Commission found Danilevsky innocent and recommended he be set free, Nicholas I sentenced him to administrative exile in Vologda. It was a mild sentence compared to what happened to the others. It simply meant that he had to go and live in that province, work in the chancery of the provincial governor, and remain under the governor's supervision. But the sentence was no joke either. It meant a considerable interruption of carefully laid plans. According to Semenov, Danilevsky even thought for awhile, although he turned out to be wrong, that his engagement would have to be canceled. Moreover, Vologda was a provincial backwater, and even kindly supervision by a governor cannot have been a desirable situation.

How did Danilevsky react? Perhaps he wished intensely that he had somehow matured more quickly and abandoned Fourierism and the circle much sooner. After all, had he not been almost about to do so anyway at the time of his arrest? It would not have been much of a step from such a wish to a further one: that he had never been attracted to utopian ideas and Bohemian friendships in the first place. What had been the matter with him? What a fool he had been! And then, almost inevitably came the thought that he would never let anything like this happen again. He would be tough-minded, practical, loyal, "clean" from here on. He would stick to his work and "be of use to my fatherland and myself." We might say that he would henceforth avoid and repress the feelings and longings that had led him into this situation.

Unfortunately there is no good direct evidence regarding what he thought to himself at this point. Semenov, who met Danilevsky right after he came out of prison, has a few things to report. He says that Danilevsky had become physically more robust, that the twitch in his face had disappeared, that he had returned to the "religious and conservative" outlook of his earlier days, but that he was also still a lover of mankind and interested in serving it. He had spent his time in prison reading the Bible and a French translation of *Don Quixote*. It is difficult to make much of this, one way or another. *Russia and Europe*, though written in the sixties, is a bit more suggestive. There is the author's obsession with the thinkers (especially Westerners) of the forties, the heaping of scorn upon their type of poetic, metaphysical, speculative thinking. And there is the fact that, despite this, Danilevsky in the 1860's still had utopian socialism (now blended with Slavophilism) in his intellectual "craw." The impression of the close reader of his major work is that its author is trying to say something he is ashamed or afraid of saying. The state of mind that helped make this possible could well have had one important origin in Danilevsky's reaction to the experience of 1849. But there is no definite evidence. We can only theorize.

Nevertheless, the problem is worth thinking about. If Danilevsky did react in a negative, self-resentful, repressive way to what he regarded as the consequences of his own feelings and spiritual aspirations, then such a reaction could easily have become a habit. Other developments, personal and environmental, in the fifties and sixties could have confirmed and intensified this habit. As a result although his feelings and longings would not have disappeared, their growth and development may have been stultified to a certain extent, and as time went on, they would have become more not less of a problem to him. Moreover, his expression of them would have become oblique, indirect, contradictory, both tough and sentimental. On the basis of this theory, Danilevsky seems not to have outgrown his early romantic radicalism. To do this, he would have had to deal with its spiritual and psychological bases much more squarely, explicitly, indeed, charitably. Like its repressed bases, his stultified romantic radicalism kept coming out in monstrous form. Danilevsky's hatred of mankind seems to have begun in a hatred of himself. We cannot be sure that this began in 1849. But the circumstantial evidence is rather persuasive, so much so, indeed, that, at the risk of diverging at this point from the conclusion that the reader may wish to draw, I shall take 1849 to have marked the beginning of an important change in Danilevsky's existential psychology.

One thing does seem certain. Danilevsky, the totalitarian philosopher, was made, not born, not simply produced by his environment or by some fixed personality trait. The young pre-1849 Danilevsky, unlike his successor, was an individual of considerable moral and spiritual stature. His contradictory attitudes are, from the historian's viewpoint, much in his favor. He was caught in some difficult personal and societal contradictions. Yet he cherished his freedom too much, he was too honest and open-minded to attempt some elaborate, final, hasty rationalization and stabilization of his outlook and situation.

Some recent historians of the Russian radical intelligentsia have severely criticized these intellectuals for their relative lack of realistic and practical attention to the serious problems of government, economy, and society.[39] These historians seem to regard as perverse, wasteful, and harmful the typical radical intellectual's preference for speculation about God, truth, beauty, the condition of man, the meaning of history. This is narrow criticism. The story of Danilevsky's youth suggests that there were plenty of good reasons for romantic soul-searching and that it was not harmful or wasteful. Besides being a tribute to his humanity, it helped make his professional and "useful" side possible. More generally, Danilevsky's radicalism contributed, in a small way, to Russian cultural development, for the radicalism of circles like Petrashevsky's, however fanciful, helped significantly over time to raise the moral tone of public life. Moreover, the Russian political parties, constructive as well as totalitarian, that emerged at the end of the nineteenth century owed institutional as well as ideological debts to such circles. The story of Danilevsky's middle years strongly suggests that the intelligentsia and Russia might have been better off without the advice of puritanical utilitarians.

3

EARLY IDEAS:

SCIENCE AND UTOPIA

THERE ARE three sources[1] for the study of Danilevsky's outlook in the forties. There is a series of two articles, published in
1848 in the Annals of the Fatherland, reviewing a work by the
French biologist René Joachim Dutrochet (1776–1847) on some
aspects of the chemistry and physics of digestion. The work reviewed, *Agent immédiat du mouvement vital dévoilé dans sa
nature et dans son mode d'action chez les végétaux et les animaux*,
1828, is devoted to a discussion of the phenomenon of osmosis,
whose importance in the study of physiology Dutrochet had
been one of the first to appreciate. Second, there is a series of
three articles, also published in the Annals in 1848, on the Russian
translation of the second volume of the once very popular book
Cosmos, A Sketch of a Physical Description of the Universe, by
the German naturalist and explorer Alexander von Humboldt
(1769–1859). This volume of *Cosmos* dealt with the development
of the idea of the unity of nature in broad historical perspective.
I have only two of the articles in this series. Finally, there is the
lecture on Fourierism, now called *The Doctrine of Fourier
(Uchenie Fourier)*, which Danilevsky delivered before the Commission of Investigation on the Petrashevsky affair. These "works"
are of mainly biographical and historical interest, neither intellectually original nor very sophisticated. The ones on Dutrochet and

Humboldt, while containing some interesting passages in which Danilevsky set forth his own ideas on science, knowledge, history, and other subjects, are mainly résumés with commentary of the books under review. They were probably products of hack work for the publishers of the Annals. The lecture is a summary of and commentary on Fourier's social doctrine.

For Danilevsky's biography and for the intellectual history of the Petrashevsky circle, however, the writings are not without value. They specify many of the ideas Danilevsky held in the forties and the relationship, in his mind, of these ideas to one another. They attest that he took these ideas both seriously and without fanaticism. They underline the fact that he was more concerned with cultural change and with spiritual, human, and emotional problems than with the real evils of Russian society and state. Given the scarcity of primary materials about him, they are an indispensable source. Besides this, careful study of them throws some new light on the history of Russian Fourierism, which Danilevsky had a considerable role in defining.

I

The writings provide insight regarding both Danilevsky the professional and Danilevsky the utopian dreamer. As to the first, they attest to the rigor and modernity of his scientific training and to his considerable ability and emphatic willingness to use that training creatively. They also indicate his attitude toward science, scientific method, and nature.

Danilevsky the student of science was a tough-minded experimentalist. "In all of its studies," he said, "there have been two paths before the mind of man: the *a priori* and the *a posteriori* path. According to the first, some idea, considered as axiomatic, is taken as a starting point and from it a whole scientific system is deduced as a consequence. Up to now this method has been successfully applied only to mathematics, for the basic concepts of mathematics are essentially indisputable axioms and the methods utilized by it in its deductions do not admit of error. But, as applied to other branches of human knowledge, the *a priori* method has yielded false results; it has also shown itself inapplicable to the social sciences." [2] The proposition was no abstraction. He was speaking on the basis of personal experience and from a deep sense of commitment. This is indicated especially strikingly in the Dutrochet articles. Danilevsky had a warm sympathy and great admiration for Dutrochet, a severely empirical biologist, [3] and easily grasped, explained, and even waxed enthusiastic about such matters as the breathing and movements of plants, the permeability of organic membranes, cell theory, the mechanics of digestion, the nature of the role of atmospheric pressures in experiments on endosmotic flow, the relationship of organic irritability to oxidation.

Consistent with this emphatically physical attitude toward scientific method and the quality of true science was Danilevsky's mechanism. Just as he disliked deductive reasoning in scientific work, so he made vigorous objection to the projection upon nature of anthropomorphic thought patterns. Much of his admiration for Dutrochet's work on digestion was connected with the fact that that work promised to render obsolete many a naïve presupposition about how the organism took in its nourishment. There is a good statement of this mechanism in the second of the Dutrochet articles.

We can divide all phenomena into the constant and general and into the exceptional and particular. The first depend on causes such as gravity and chemical affinity, to which everything without exception is subject. The second depend on more particular forces. As soon as these particular forces stop operating, the substances governed by them are subject to the activity of the general forces. Putting several of the general forces of nature in artificial juxtaposition, we can produce phenomena such as do not exist in nature . . . If we mix potash with iron in a vessel and subject it to powerful heat, then the potash is dissolved and a metal is produced which exists nowhere in pure form in nature. To produce this phenomenon, we used only the general forces of nature, combining them in a way that is not encountered in nature. As soon as our artificial action stops, the potassium, being subject to the external forces of nature, is oxidized . . . To this kind of unusual phenomenon should be attributed the vital phenomena in plants and animals. We know that the very diverse plant and animal substances are made up of a few entities which are the same as those that make up the inorganic part of nature. Utilizing this fact, we can by analogy rationally conclude that the forces common to all nature *are also always linked with matter* — and that, uniting in various ways and changing their organization according to the situation in which they arise, they consist of complex forces which we call by the general name of *vital force*. Just as in the example of the artificial dissolution of potash, so in this case there occurs *by itself*, as a result of the action of this force (which is not self-sufficient but derivative), the renewal of those conditions on which depend the unique phenomenon of the existence of organic bodies. The supposition that such derivative complex forces exist, regardless of its probability, would be completely arbitrary if it were not at least partly corroborated by experiment. But we have seen the brilliant corroboration of this view in the exposition of the application of endosmosis to the way in which plant sap rises and to the movement of plants. Indeed, what is endosmosis if not a complex derivative force having its origin in the combination and mutual limitation of many general, more physical forces? This hypothesis, which does not belong to Dutrochet, but to which he gives brilliant support by his discovery and application of endosmosis, thus receives a degree of probability more than which physiological theory cannot at the present time demand. Moreover, this corresponds with the basic principle of every scientific explanation: *to accept only in an extreme case the existence of radical elementary forces.* Precisely in the same way in chemistry, only in an extreme case do we acknowledge some kind of body [*telo*] as a cause. Similarly, in logic, only in an extreme case do we acknowledge some truth as axiomatic. Only by such a theory can we avoid mysticism in science, and demolish such explanations as: the organs select the food necessary for them, the leaves call the plant sap to them, and similar psychomorphisms.[4]

The modern reader of Danilevsky's mechanistic and empiricist statements, mindful of the narrowly positivistic and materialistic currents that developed in nineteenth century European scientific thought, will wonder about the more specific nature of his views. It is an important consideration, central to the problem of Danilevsky's humanism, for if his view of science excluded an irreducible element of mystery from nature, and a sense of creativity, responsibility, and inevitable incompleteness from scientific thinking, then there would be grounds, assuming a high degree of consistency on his part, for describing him as distinctly unhumanistic. It will be recalled that he thought of Fourierism as a scientific doctrine. Does his attitude toward science and nature suggest that we interpret this as a sign of dogmatism?

It has been said of Marxism, for instance, that it became an evil and vicious doctrine from the moment that Marx began to claim that his social poetry was social science (that is, economics). Now neopositivist critics of Marx see in this a lesson about the importance of not mixing science and philosophical history, "fact and value." But this is only one way of viewing the issue and that a rather limited one. It is historically more useful to notice that the trouble arose because Marx's view of science was relatively positivistic (though his *ultimate* rationale was ever left Hegelian); to him science was less a dialectic — human in origin — of reason and fact, man and nature, than it was a revelation of nature's or society's own immanent reason. Marx was a kind of Comtean, though for historicist reasons.[5] Historically, however, science — precisely the respectable, experimental, tough-minded sort — has not excluded a sense of human limitation, of Erasmian folly, a respect for the mystery, for the irreducible brute objectivity of nature. But historically too, especially in the nineteenth century, some scientific thinkers, abdicating a sense of human responsibility, attempted such an exclusion. Such thinkers were not humanists. And those of this persuasion who claimed their social and anthropological doctrines to be scientific tended at best toward dogmatism, at worst toward being enemies of human freedom, beginning with their own. Where did young Danilevsky stand in all this?

One very interesting aspect of the story of his intellectual development concerns his changing attitude toward science. In the forties it was to him a human activity, not the voice of nature or history evoked by certain rituals in the laboratory or library. To say that some piece of knowledge was scientific meant to him that it had a certain rigorously factual quality and that it had been arrived at by certain recognized methods; scientific knowledge came to be when the efforts of rational imagination and empirical conscience coincided. Nor was the empirical approach the only one that Danilevsky was prepared to use. By the sixties science had become to him a struggle, consecrated by Nature and History, to work out final truths about nature and about history and man as well; all modes of knowing other than the empirical were mystical, fantastic, unreliable.[6] The eighties, however, saw a reversion to the scientific humanism of the forties and an explicit defense (fittingly against some pontifical Darwinists) of the importance of metaphysical and general philosophical awareness in science itself. This whole intellectual development is interesting, especially because it coincides with Danilevsky's change from humanistic socialist to totalitarian and then away from the totalitarianism. His totalitarianism was ultimately the product not of his own narrow positivism but of moral and human failure. But the changing climate of opinion, affecting science as well as affected by it, helped make it possible. Similarly, his less original and interesting yet morally superior social thought of the forties seems to have been strengthened by a certain attitude toward science, a more responsible one.

Thus we find that Danilevsky in the forties admired Dutrochet's work but was over and again sarcastically critical of his aggressive materialism and positivism. "In saying this," he noted about some of his remarks on Dutrochet,

I do not wish to belittle the factual or so-called empirical study of nature. On the contrary, I am completely convinced that this is the only road to truth, not only in the natural sciences but in the whole circle of human knowledge. If I call observations fruitless which do not begin from some general idea, theory, or analogical induction, I find the justification for this in the intellectual structure of man himself, according to which attention cannot be equally apportioned completely without distinction to all phenomena and to all the modifications of any phenomenon. However huge the point of view of the man observing, he always sees only that which has some kind of link with his individual nature. In a word, only that, or almost only that, which we seek do we see in any phenomenon. I use the word "almost" because accident plays a role to a certain degree here also. The importance of the facts discovered will always be proportional to the importance, depth, and generality of the thought that inspires the observation — a thought which the facts themselves establish, corroborate, or overthrow. An observer advocating accident entirely in doing his research, that is, the pure empiricist (in the strict sense of the word) by the very essence of his method cannot but be refuted by the laws of chance, that is, by the laws of probability; and as the number of facts is increased with the degree of their particularity [and as] their importance is inversely proportional to this particularity, so his discoveries will necessarily consist more or less in paltry things [*nichtozhnost*], depending on the degree of his zeal for work. Therefore, the gathering of any facts without any idea of guiding their collection leads only to meaningless results, for these facts remain without any grouping, without any generalization, without assignment to some hierarchy, and that is just why the most important facts remain unobserved.[7]

It would seem that in attitude and, to some degree (for his philosophical self-consciousness was evidently limited), in idea young Danilevsky was a scientific rationalist. Mainly through his training at the Lyceum and the university, he had come to be a participant in a scientific tradition, often called the Cartesian, running back to the Renaissance. It was both a speculative and an empirical tradition, a deductive and an inductive one. To its proponents and participants, in the words of one historian, "it appeared natural to believe that the world possesses a rational structure . . . that reality possesses an organization coincident with the organization of the human intellect, taking this, of course, in the form of mathematical reason." [8] Danilevsky's separation of the *a priori* and *a posteriori* methods should not be taken as contradicting this. The whole picture suggests that this was but one aspect of a larger viewpoint. He seems to have thought of his mechanism as a mathematically biased product of deduction (the very way he sets it forth in the quotation above suggests this) and to have seen the scientist as a human being involved in a permanent dialectic of reason and fact. In the tradition to which he belonged at this time, the goal of science was to build up a mirror of nature and thus diminish the gap between human and some conceivable ultimate wisdom. Man was a rational being. Science was a method by which man put a big question to nature: did human rationality correspond to the nature of things? Asking and finding answers, and sometimes, in technology, acting practically on the answers, was a uniquely appropriate way of being human and becoming more human, not of struggling with, possessing, or mastering nature. As we shall see, Danilevsky's enthusiastic review of Alexander von Humboldt's volume on the successful development and empirical corroboration, through the whole history of mankind, of the idea of the unity of nature was consistent with his scientific rationalism. So, indeed, was his espousal of Fourierism, a fittingly mechanistic doctrine — and also his refusal to commit himself to it until it had been tested.

But while Danilevsky's views of the development of science set forth in the articles on Humboldt and his Fourierism were not *logically* at variance with his professional scientific outlook, they reflect more the other, the dreaming Danilevsky. After all, his scientific training ran in a practical, "socially useful," not in a pure let alone a specifically philosophical, direction; even the articles on Dutrochet were probably not fully typical of the Danilevsky of practical science. It is doubtful that he thought of his romantic speculations as part of one consistent intellectual effort, beginning at the laboratory level and ending up in the empyrean. His scientific attitude was probably more of a cultural matter than one of rigorous intellectual decision. The spirit of the Dutrochet articles was rather different from that of the other writings. In his other work rational imagination soared far above the world of organic membranes, fluid levels, and digestive absorption. Other forces were at work in Danilevsky, neither deductive nor inductive but existential. Scientific rationalist habits of mind both colored the intellectual response to those forces and perhaps, even in some fashion, encouraged Danilevsky to take his feelings seriously and honestly at this time. But these habits were not the more important source of his utopianism. That source was his response to what seemed to him a vast cultural change, at once exciting and disturbing.

2

Science was a sober, experimental activity to Danilevsky the professional. To the young man rather recently up, as it were, from the village of Oberets in the Liven district, it seems to have been a distinctly heady affair. With the help of some ideas, myths, and shibboleths floating around in the air of the European scientific milieu, he convinced himself all too easily that a great and lengthy human effort was just about to reach a marvelous conclusion. Scientific knowledge was now progressing at such a rate that the whole human situation could soon be straightened out. Man and his social world could be rationalized, for man was on the verge of a knowledge of nature so complete that he would be able to adjust himself fully to nature's benevolent laws and thereby achieve prosperity, happiness, and even emotional and spiritual fulfillment.

Danilevsky's more euphoric scientific rationalism, or better his scientistic romanticism, apparently owed something to his close experience with the dramatic achievements of modern science and to the related influence of the widespread enthusiasm about science that marked his age. Though distinctly unprofessional, his romanticism had a link with his more sober self. He was especially struck by the fact that the ancient and hitherto mostly intuitive idea of the "unity and coherence" of nature was now for the first time being verified empirically and experimentally. "The history of the physical contemplation of the universe is now joined to the history of the separate scientific disciplines, for through deeper and more detailed research they begin to arrive at a consciousness of the coherence of nature — and this by *empirical* methods." Experimental science was already establishing that "light and heat, electricity, magnetism, and galvanism represent manifestations of something unified and all pervasive, probably of that ether whose existence is proved by the slowing down observed in the movement of Halley's comet." In many scientific fields empirical triumphs and strong hints of the existence of some great unity had for some time been coming together. "The introduction of a rational system in botany by the work of the immortal Adanson and Jussieu, Goethe's and De Candolle's idea of the metamorphosis of organs, and the zoological and anatomical works of Geoffroy Saint-Hilaire . . . introduced into the study of the organic world, by empirical, experimental methods, the deep concept of the unity of the type both in plant and in animal beings. Physics is inseparably united with chemistry, chemistry with physiology. Plant and animal morphology are becoming, instead of mere mnemonic devices, a kind of actual expression of the plan, according to which nature acted in the formulation of organic beings — justifying, in some degree, the title 'natural system' given to descriptive zoological and botanical works." Moreover, recent work in the geography of plants and animals, in physical geography, crystallography, and astronomy had resulted in a final unification of the phenomena of the terrestrial and celestial realms. The work of Cuvier and Brongniart had been particularly important in this latter triumph. Danilevsky registered his own and, as he saw it, everybody else's happy agreement with the great Liebig, who "in his *Letters about Chemistry* expresses his thought on the relation of astronomy and chemistry. 'The universe represents a huge body, the atoms of which are . . . indivisible and unchangeable.' " [9]

Modernity, in the form of science, was not, to the young Danilevsky, simply a cold, functional affair. It was not just a this-worldly one either, for his scientistic romanticism was not only euphoric, it was also distinctly spiritual. His hearty approval of and elaboration upon the nature philosophy in Humboldt's *Cosmos* attest to more than overexcitement about a rapid series of empirical successes. Science was a mode of communion with a great sacred power and its history a sort of religious pilgrimage.

The task of reviewing the second volume of *Cosmos* brought the spiritual interest of Danilevsky (the self-styled atheist) strongly to the fore, probably because of that famous work's peculiar blend of metaphysics and science.[10] Humboldt's outlook differed in temper from that of Schelling, Oken, and other specifically idealistic *Naturphilosophen* of an earlier age. He had much more regard for fact and experiment; he had a better physical sense. Danilevsky admired him particularly for this. Nevertheless, Humboldt had modified Schelling's ideas rather than discarded them. To him "Nature" was Being in the fullest sense. "She" was the equivalent of God, a sort of pagan Mother Earth. "Nature [he quoted Schelling himself on the point] is not an inert mass; and to him who can comprehend her vast sublimity, she reveals herself as the creative force of the universe — before all time, eternal, ever active, she calls to life all things, whether perishable or imperishable." [11] The ultimate human happiness, then, was "communion" with nature through "contemplation."

Danilevsky shared this idea. He was especially struck apparently by the fact that, nature being ontological reality, the individual and (this was his own addition) social lives of men were and should be a process of quest for a proper relationship with nature, one involving actualization of ultimate potentialities. This meant that history was and should be the story of the progress of scientific knowledge and of its application. Intellectual knowledge, more particularly science, was in itself a basis of communion with the beloved; but it was also a guide to happy, ultimate existence, to the good society and the good individual life, to man's discovery of and adjustment to his real place in the universe. Science was thus regarded as a sort of ritual technique. Though many people had a more hard-boiled view of it, science was not, in fact, a struggle with or search for conquest over nature. Danilevsky emphasized that this idea of a struggle with nature was erroneous and he cited "German philosophical dialectic" on the point.

In nature itself, the struggle of elemental forces is only apparent, and every set of contradictions is resolved into a harmony of a higher sort, just as a set of apparently dissonant musical notes, when arranged by the hand of a person knowing the laws of musical harmony, become very pleasing to the ear. So too the melodious elliptical courses of the planets appear to be the result of two contradictory forces: the centripetal and the centrifugal. The disturbing influences of one planetary mass on another produce regular oscillations in the orbit, never disarranging it but, so to speak, only varying the mathematical straightness of its form . . . Is this struggle? The result of a struggle is the destruction of one competitor and the enfeebling of the other; the result of the contradictions found in nature is their unification into a harmonious third phenomenon. Such a struggle, if we are not mistaken, is called cooperation or love . . . Man does not . . . struggle with nature, but adjusts himself to her; he does not free himself from her power but, learning her laws more and more deeply, finds them identical with the laws of his own nature. These laws express his own natural aspirations and, in submitting himself to the laws of nature, he acts only in accordance with his own aspirations.[12]

Optimism about science's promise for man's spiritual, psychological, and group life was carried by young Danilevsky to lengths that may be described as chiliastic, for his scientistic romanticism had a continuously historical and societal reference. He was prepossessed with the idea that science was going to rationalize the world. He tried to convince his readers that science could soon sponsor a happy end to the traditional vale of tears. To appreciate these convictions of his, it is only necessary to study his opinions on history, opinions he adduced in illustration of his idea that man did not struggle with nature but adjusted himself to her and thereby, at the highest possible level, fulfilled his own "natural aspirations."

Hitherto, historians had concentrated mainly on politics. This had been due, however, only to their incompetence in other fields. In fact, the most important thing in history was science. "The activity of man has been scientific, artistic, or productive, that is, he has been engaged in satisfying his intellectual, his aesthetic, or his material needs. Every activity (in history) is valid only insofar as it contributes to these satisfactions. Every historical event must be judged by us accordingly. Of these three realms of activity we must give predominance to the scientific and industrial. Only in Athens were the fine arts a real factor in social life. But in all periods and among all peoples, industrial activity determined the present of a nation and scientific activity its future. Since industry rests on scientific progress, the history of science is the most important of all." [13]

This was not, to Danilevsky, just an academic observation on history. He believed that men in their various ways had long consciously known scientific knowledge to be central and had acted accordingly. "Even [the history of] the most primitive societies, past and present, engaged in the (*erroneously called*) struggle with nature, show the predominance of science." The earliest societies of hunters or nomads or primitive agriculturalists (Danilevsky saw these as successive social stages in history) had differed in social organization because of the differing states of men's knowledge of nature, not because men had ever directed their main attention to or patterned their lives according to anything but science. On this distinctly Saint-Simonian view of things, men who had known only the most elementary laws of nature had become hunters and fishers. Those who had learned more, for instance, the dietary uses of selected herbivorous animals and the ability of the dog to herd them, had become nomads. The scientific discoveries of the plow and of the possibility of nourishment from a wide variety of plants had led to peasant societies. The "greatest age," that of "civilization," had begun about 1800. It had been made possible by "empirical successes in mechanics and chemistry" in the seventeenth and eighteenth centuries. The growth of workshops and factories, based on these successes, had led to the rise of life in great cities. Whole nations

(England and Belgium) were being transformed into great factories. For the future, Danilevsky found it difficult to imagine the huge technological and social changes that would take place as a result of the latest scientific advances, especially the changes that would arise from the spread of the use of the telegraph and of electromagnetism as a driving force. He felt reasonably sure, however, that electrical machines would one day be used to drive balloons, steam engines being too heavy for the purpose. No doubt the Russian in Danilevsky was speaking when he said he thought this particular technical advance, by making it no longer necessary to worry about the conditions of the roads, would be the basis of a tremendous revolution in communications. He may have been especially excited by another prospect because he was a poor student. "From the time that Humphry Davy analyzed alkali and Pélouze analyzed uranium, we have no longer been sure that our metals are simple bodies. Consequently, it is possible that precious metals, which are the measure of value and the means of exchange, can be analyzed and synthesized." In general, regarding the future, "the immeasurable changes in social life that will arise from these as yet unmade but still very possible and probable discoveries are clear to anyone who will penetrate into the essence of human relations." [14]

History, then, was the story of man's discovery of the laws of nature, his adjustment to them, and, through this, the fulfillment of "his own natural aspirations." It is as though Danilevsky thought all human history a unified and purposive quest for a state of living communion with what he, following Humboldt, called nature, a deity very like the old Russian pagan Mother Earth. Fittingly, there was a kind of necessity in Danilevsky's "history"; it was the unfolding of a large, immanent, teleological pattern.

He was much concerned with pointing out to his readers just what kind of necessity it was. It was not the Hegelian kind. Many people, in his view, had the erroneous idea that *everything* in history was determined. "It has been clear that history is not just a mass of unconnected facts, but that there is some link between them, some logical sequence. In recent times this has been turned into a strange theory of historical necessity. According to this theory, 'all that is must be'." To this was sometimes added the "still stronger idea about some sort of self-generating time which by itself completes everything and prepares everything." The whole notion of uncontrolled and unselective determinism was, in Danilevsky's opinion, "pure psychomorphism" and "very harmful." *All* history was not a necessary development. Only the history of science and its application was inevitable, logical, sequential. Other aspects of history, particularly political history, were accidental and capricious. "Several historical events, namely those which can be called the practical realization of scientific activity, represent a completely logical sequence in their development. All external, political events are by their very essence accidental and it takes a great deal of talk to make one believe otherwise." [15]

Historical necessity was actually much more benign and readily understandable than Hegel had thought. The real was not rational. On the contrary, only the rational — and comfortable — were real. To illustrate this Danilevsky undertook to show that the drama of man had been precisely one in which science had been gradually triumphing over politics, and mathematical reason over political caprice, as the dominant forces in human affairs. His discussion of the point has some methodological interest too. It is clear that he was toying with a new way of studying society, for his little "philosophy" about the imminent ending of history includes an effort, precocious at the time in both Russia and Western Europe, to apply graphical-statistical methods to the analysis of social phenomena. Here there may have been an influence of Victor Iakovlevich Buniakovsky, the great statistical scientist under whom Danilevsky probably learned statistics at the university. The latter evidently believed not only that science was about to end history but also that scientific method was about to supersede the historical.

Indeed, he began by asking his reader to think of world his-

torical development graphically and statistically. Let us "picture
to ourselves the course of the historical development of mankind
. . . graphically, as a kind of line, the waves of which express the
degree of swiftness with which, in various periods, mankind has
moved in its progress toward perfection (just as physicists represent the course of the temperature of a day or year) . . . Since
we have distinguished the separate elements that make up the
history of mankind (the course of scientific development and its
practical actualization from the course of accidental, external
events), then the line of actual historical development imagined
by us must be the mean between the line of scientific movement
and the line of movement which we call accidental-political;
just as . . . the isothermal line is a mean line between the rather
straight isotheres and the more crooked isocheims." [16] While the
straight line (the scientific) was expressible algebraically, the
other (the political) oscillated crazily back and forth without
regard to whether or not these oscillations helped or hindered the
straight-line development of mankind.

Taking the scientific line as an accelerative movement and the
political line as an oscillating movement, the reader was asked to
imagine the horizontal, straight, scientific line as divided into a
number of equal parts. With each of these points representing
the beginning of a century, an imaginary perpendicular was
erected at each point. The mean line of historical development
was then arrived at by marking off, on each perpendicular, the
highest point of scientific development of man in each given
century and connecting all these points. At the beginning of
history, this mean line would be observed to go almost parallel
to the horizontal, but then it dipped downward sharply, almost
approaching the vertical. From this low point the mean line then
gradually climbed back to its previous level and again approached
the horizontal. The first stretch of horizontal movement represented Greek and Ptolemaic science. But by the third century
after Christ the line began to dip sharply downward and con-

tinued on this course until some time in the later Middle Ages. Then, with varying degrees of speed (the fourteenth century being especially slow and the seventeenth especially rapid), it again reached the level of Alexandrine science by the early nineteenth century.

The reasons for the deviation in the mean line were accidental political events. Graphically they appeared as a capriciously oscillating line which had a completely irrational and inconsistent effect on the mean. But by the nineteenth century their influence was waning rapidly. As the result of the increasing influence of science on all aspects of life, the mean line was becoming straighter and straighter. Danilevsky predicted that, in the end, this mean line would become absolutely parallel to the straight line representing the movement of science. In other words, science would eventually, necessarily, be applied to all activities and relationships. Then, in Danilevsky's view, "a theory of historical necessity would be just." [17]

In the two of three articles on Humbolt's *Cosmos* that are available for study, Danilevsky does not mention Fourier or socialism. Yet we know that he was an ardent utopian socialist at this time and something of a political radical. Both the Saint-Simonian and the anti-Hegelian aspect of his historical ideas were undoubtedly influenced by discussions in the Petrashevsky circle. So also was his selection of the capricious and obstructive politician as the villain of history. It seems likely that his historical thought and his socialism were closely connected. Evidently Fourier's scheme, in Danilevsky's mind, was to be the terminator of history. As a mechanistic doctrine, it fitted his ideas about the nature of science. As a purportedly scientific social doctrine, it fitted his conviction that history was about the progress of science and its application to human living arrangements, for Fourierism was a science and a technology in one. As a utopian doctrine, it fitted his scientistic spirituality. Danilevsky wanted everything rationalized and harmonized and that in a way which would allow for a permanent living communion between man and nature. Fourier promised just that—harmony between reason and the passions, society and nature.

In fact, it looks very much as though young Danilevsky saw the Fourierist utopia as a kind of pagan heaven. As a whole, his thinking has a strikingly Joachite quality. That is to say, he seems to have believed in the coming of a new dispensation, a kind of end of the world and beginning of a new heavenly life within this world itself. That he had such a belief is strongly suggested by the apparent juxtaposition in his mind of the idea of a necessary, benevolent, and imminent end of history with the idea of the transformation of society into a series of small utopian communities. His sympathy with Humboldt's Schellingian ideas suggests the possibility of this belief also. Moreover, Fourier himself and also Saint-Simon, Proudhon, Cabet, and other utopian socialists, many of whose works were in the Petrashevsky library, were of this same persuasion. Latent Joachism had been a feature of millenary sectarianism all over Europe (including Russia's schismatics) for a long time. Utopian socialism was one nineteenth century, humanistic, partly secularized expression of a large tradition. It was both a social and a religious movement.[18]

Danilevsky rejected Fourier's wild cosmology and philosophy of history. But a less fanciful nature philosophy, something like Humboldt's together with a kind of Saint-Simonian philosophy of history took their place. He was a disciple of a *Nouveau Christianisme*. The whole spectrum of such a religion was present in his thinking: nature as God, science as religion, history as pilgrimage of reason, the new worldly dispensation, the utopian community. Here was the center of gravity of his outlook. An examination of the lecture on Fourier corroborates much of this picture. Even his rather restrained explanation, before the Commission of Investigation, of Fourier's utopian socialist doctrine does not obscure the spiritual and humanistic nature of his interest in it. It was clearly not an interest based on a desire merely to reform Russia but rather one based on an attraction to Fourierism's spiritual and psychological promise, a promise set forth, however, with "scientific" rigor.

In Danilevsky's interpretation of history, it will be recalled, human nature was definite and constant. And it had one possible, objective, discoverable, happy, fulfilling relationship to nature. History was therefore the story of man's increasingly successful quest for his ultimate relationship to nature. It was this assumption, rather than one of some transcendent force using men as its tool, that made Danilevsky's history patterned and deterministic. His theory thus differed from the Hegelian in two ways: in regard to what should be included in real history, and in viewing men, conscious and responsible, as the motive force of development. In interpreting history, Danilevsky, under the influence of some Western ideas, projected onto the ages his own self-image as a progressive and practical scientist. It was therefore appropriate that he was so deeply interested precisely in an individual thinker and in one with a broad "social scientific" proposal; men had to find the answer to the puzzle of the human condition by analyzing it rationally and mathematically and then testing for empirical correspondence. Danilevsky saw in Fourier a thinker after his own heart. To him (not inaccurately) Fourier's "basic idea is that every being is endowed with certain forces which are proportional to its end or destiny (*les attractions sont proportionelles aux destinées*). The result of this is that the being . . . [can find] . . . a state of harmony or equilibrium. Every being strives toward harmonious equilibrium. Before it arrives, it is subject to various vacillations and the more complex the being, the greater the vacillations. The equilibrium must be attained consciously — otherwise it is easy to lose it again . . . [Fourier] saw rightly that societies come and go, but human nature remains constant, has a constant set of needs and demands." [19] On the basis of what we know of Danilevsky's view of history and its mechanics, it seems reasonable to conclude that he viewed Fourier as a scientist, perhaps the last ("the Newton of the social sciences") of a long parade of great scientists, who had made a direct assault on

the big problem itself: the harmonization or equilibration of man
with himself, with his fellows, and with nature. If a test proved
successful, Fourier had solved the ultimate problem of fulfillment.
The solution would not just happen in some mystical, secret,
interior fashion as Humboldt seemed to suggest. It would be
demonstrated in a fittingly scientific way.

In Danilevsky's (again accurate) understanding of Fourier,
there were three divisions to be bridged: between nature and
society, between man and man, between society and the human
"passions." Fourier had simplified the three problems into one by
concentrating on the relationship between work and play. If these
could be somehow harmonized, then the passions, which were fully
engaged in play but not in the usual work situations, would be at
once free and socially integrated. Happy and unfrustrated men
would be on good terms with one another as they were in play
(though not, of course, without friendly rivalries). And man
would be in harmony with nature: nature in the form of the passions inside him and nature beyond society, for Fourier thought
the new playful kind of work the key to economic plenty for
all. The whole question of world history, of man and nature, of
man's quest for fulfillment had, therefore, in Danilevsky's view,
now taken one final, nodal form. "Is it possible to make work
attractive? Leave a man for several consecutive days with nothing to do and he will be ready to exchange this situation for
any kind of suitable work. But if you give him complete freedom
and means, he will not seek work but amusements and diversions.
However, the great majority of so-called amusements such as
riding, fishing, and hunting are essentially work. Why is work
of one type considered attractive and the other burdensome?" [20]

Danilevsky explained to his inquisitors that Fourier had shown
the answer to this problem of work and play to be really quite
easy. Men disliked inactivity and liked play because of the nature
and configuration of their emotions as "passions." They disliked
work, not because it required an output of energy, but because,
as presently organized, work warped and frustrated the passions.

This circumstance, by making possible the monstrous development of some passions at the expense of others, had in turn provided a basis for the widespread erroneous belief that the passions were evil and dangerous. And thus men, in their superstitious fear of their own emotional lives, found it all but impossible even to think out the problem rationally. What was needed first was a scientific enumeration, description, classification, and "natural system" of the passions.

Danilevsky communicated to the Commission of Investigation Fourier's great discovery that to be exact — and Fourier was always exact — there were thirteen passions in all. First, there were five "material passions" which corresponded to the five physical senses and strove naturally for a variety of appropriate objects: not only for food, drink, and the like (Fourier was no vulgar materialist), but also for scientific knowledge, travel, and commercial, industrial, and artistic activity. Then there were four "social passions" which had to be satisfied: ambition, love, "familisme," and the passion for friendship. The next three, the "distributive passions" consisted of (1) the *composite* or *exultante*, (2) the *cabaliste* or *rivaliste*, and (3) the *papillonne* or *engrenante*. The *composite* passion could be seen satisfying itself in situations where men enjoyed several pleasures simultaneously, such as eating a sumptuous Fourierist meal while engaging in pleasant conversation and listening to music. The *cabaliste* was to be seen in men's great love for competition and intrigue. The *papillonne*, the "butterfly passion," was the basis of men's endless practice of flitting from one occupation to another. The thirteenth and most refined passion was a sort of super *composite*. It was satisfied by the happy union of the other twelve, expressing itself satisfactorily in various forms, as patriotism, as love of mankind, as religious feeling. Fourier called it *unitéism*.

Now anyone looking at the "facts" could see that the problem of work was not one of activity. The passions were wholly of an active nature. The problem was rather to create a society that would satisfy all the drives. Fourier had shown this really to be quite simple also. While it was possible, in Danilevsky's view, that the simplicity and rigor of Fourier's system were deceiving and that perhaps a practical test would show that he had achieved them by omitting some important factors, nevertheless he thought the proposals most intriguing. Communities (or phalanxes) of a thousand people each should be set up. Within these, people with the same type of personality (for people varied, though again in mathematically predictable fashion) and with a liking for the same kinds of work would gravitate into "natural groups." Danilevsky estimated that a thousand people would break themselves down into fifty or sixty such groups. The passions for friendship, love, and "familisme" would be fully engaged within these and community and group spirit would thus be deeply rooted. Then these natural social groupings would also satisfy and be further consolidated by the passion for competition and intrigue while at the same time providing an excellent frame for the operation of the *papillonne*. Ambition could have its day as the groups vied with one another; it would also structure and limit flitting. On the whole, an infectious spirit of fun would soon arise and engage even the most stubborn quanta of passionate energy. Productivity would zoom. The resulting combination of material luxury (*roshkosh*, a favorite word of Danilevsky's at this time), love, rivalry, and vocational inconstancy would, of course, appeal further to the *passion composite* and lead at the highest level to a wonderful sense of *unitéism*, a feeling of complete harmony and utter fulfillment, evidently to young Danilevsky the same feeling he had spoken of as "communion" and "love" in his articles on Humboldt's *Cosmos*. One wonders too whether a knowledge of Feuerbach, whose ideas were much discussed in the Petrashevsky circle, may not have also been in the intellectual background here.

While some of the exact linkages between the various aspects of Danilevsky's early thought must remain in the realm of probability, there is little doubt that the most immediate occasion for his thinking was his desire for meaning and hope and not a wish practically to confront the evils of the Russian state and society. The very nature of his ideas indicates that Danilevsky the romantic intellectual was simply not by and large facing in the direction of political and social practicalities. He was acting not reacting, or if he was reacting in part, then it was to cultural rather than practical problems. Certainly conditions in Russia and his dissatisfaction with them had some effect on him. Most striking evidence of this perhaps is his insistent transposition of Humboldt's nature philosophy into historical and societal terms. There is also his selection of the politician as the reactionary villain of history. And it is possible that Russian socio-economic problems, especially those of the poverty of the peasantry and lesser gentry, influenced his advocacy of Fourierism. He brought up the problem of social justice himself at one point when he stressed another dimension of Fourier's theory: "The whole social problem will, consequently, consist in how to arrange relationships between men in such a manner that the passions of one group of people will not collide with the passions of another . . . in other words, to exchange the struggle between private interests and the common interest for the eternal cooperation of those interests." [21] But, on the whole, it would require some painfully esoteric reading of his main statements if one wished to make much of this really minor aspect of his thinking. His commanding interests were obviously spiritual and humanistic. Indeed, even the heavy societal emphasis of his thought may have had a mainly cultural origin. A man of his education and milieu was likely to develop a historical and social rather than a more purely contemplative theory. His Russian Orthodox spiritual background was probably also a factor in his historicist transposition of Humboldt. Russian Orthodox intellectuals had been thinking out mythlike history since the Middle Ages[22] and Danilevsky would hardly have worked out a surrogate religion in terms that were at variance with the spirit of Orthodoxy. The very lack, relatively, of an ethical component to his thinking and his concern with the meaning of great, "objective" historical forces, bad and good, seem very Russian. The sacramental (rather than the ethical) style of his thought is also suggested by the fact that he had more interest in thinkers like Hegel, Humboldt (or Schelling), and Fourier than he did in Bentham or Tocqueville, who were represented in the Petrashevsky library and discussed in that circle. The distinctly spiritual nature of young Danilevsky's doctrines and the mixed scientistic-Orthodox style of his thinking strongly suggest an intimate connection with the spiritual and cultural change taking place in Russia in his rather advanced milieu. The close connection between his thought and his own biography and the more general cultural and intellectual history of his time also confirms this picture quite strongly.

The pattern, quality, and detail of Danilevsky's early thought (set again in the context of his biography and his time) indicate something else also: although he was most concerned with problems generated by spiritual-cultural change, he was also attentive to some of those raised by social-cultural change. That is, besides his concern with Orthodoxy and science, he worried about the living and working arrangements of the developing new cultural world, the one centered in St. Petersburg but extending widely over the social surface of European Russia. It is neither difficult nor inaccurate to read some of his thought as an effort at understanding a contradiction between, on the one hand, a peasant-gentry society of face-to-face relationships, relative local self-sufficiency, slow tempo, production for consumption, cooperative working arrangements and, on the other, a bureaucratic and national specialized society, production for exchange, large and abstract social groupings. From this point of view, Fourier's phalanx meant something to Danilevsky other than an institution in a spiritual land of milk and honey. It was attractive to him as a way of organizing everyday life, a way that was at once continuous with traditional Russian society and yet capable of integrating and using modern scientific techniques. The phalanx that he wanted was modern in form but traditional in content. Like a traditional institution, it was small, local, a little world of face-to-face relationships. Production and exchange were subordinated to consumption. Inherited inequalities, prescribed statuses, would, in some form, have continued there. The phalanx was not a compulsive, vulgar, bourgeois, *meshchanskii* workshop but a place where a gentleman could lead a leisurely life. However, the phalanx would have been better than the gentry estate, for it would have been scientifically (*á la* Fourier) organized and much scientific knowledge would have been used in its operations.

In the lecture on Fourierism, Danilevsky criticized both gentry-peasant, and more modern, social arrangements. But the general economy, as it were, of his criticisms and the nature of his positive recommendations show his thinking to have been more directed to the past than to the future — or, perhaps better, to a future that was to be like the past. On the one hand, he said he thought "family production," that is, the economic and social organization of the Russian village, inefficient. Mainly there was too much duplication of effort, what with every family having its own living quarters, cooking arrangements, barn, cellar, and pantry. Fourier's principle of "association" should be applied to this situation; within phalanxes, these activities should be consolidated. This would save time and money; and it would allow for specialization and, through this, for the utilization of modern scientific and technological discoveries. Besides furthering productivity, the new arrangement would also (and this was most important) remove several of the causes of dissatisfaction with work, dissatisfaction hitherto considered endemic to work but now subject to alleviation. First, work would no longer be so "complex." The number of operations in which a worker had simultaneously to engage to get anything at all done would be greatly reduced. This, said Danilevsky, who thought even wood-cutting too "complex" for some kinds of personalities, would make for more satisfying work. Second, the heightened efficiency of less "complex" work would favorably affect productivity and thus remove dissatisfaction arising from poor results. Third, a degree of specialization would provide a basis for competition, which would increase productivity, but, more important, satisfy men's passionate love of intrigue.

All this may be regarded as criticism by a "modern" of traditional society. However, Danilevsky had some other and more extensive things to say about work and its organization. These criticisms were directed against the kind of work arrangements for which Danilevsky's education was preparing him and in which it was, to some extent, already involving him. It is clear that he was prepared to advocate specialization only in a limited way. "What is peculiar about work (and not about amusements)," he asked in this connection, "that makes it burdensome?" [23] Work was too "continuous." It lasted too long. It was too much of one thing. Moreover, it put the worker in a "solitary" situation, whereas people needed and wanted company. Then too, work was too compulsory; one had to do it whether one felt like it or not. The phalanx with its variety of activities, its togetherness, and its provision for flitting would solve all these problems. It appears that Danilevsky wanted what he called (after Fourier) "serialization" of — that is, maximization of the groups in — the Russian village, more because he wished an alternative to modernity for unhappy modern men of traditional background, than because he wanted a really fundamental change in the Russian way of life. One gets a similar impression from his enumeration of the kinds of people, "now unproductive," who, once the phalanx took over, would "go into productive work." As we might expect, these included the neither modern nor traditional, lazy ones and the "contrabandists, criminals, and vagabonds," people avoiding work because it was universally badly organized and thus unpleasant. But Danilevsky lumped with them some others, usually associated with a nationally organized, relatively specialized society.[24] Thus all "traders" or "commercial capitalists" would disappear under the new dispensation, for they "would not be needed in a situation of direct product-to-consumer relations." Along with them would disappear "the army, customs guards, collectors of excise taxes and imposts." The phalanx, to Danilevsky, as it had been to Fourier, was an anti-modern modern and a modernized traditional, not a really modern institution.

Danilevsky's one detailed example[25] of the social change that he wanted illustrates specifically both that he desired a continuation of basic features of Russian societal life, and that intellectually he was prepared to enter the wider world of nations only in sociological terms that were rural and localistic. In a section of his lecture that sounds curiously like an anticipation of the nostalgic, Slavophil account of hay mowing in Tolstoi's *Anna Karenina*, Danilevsky explained to the Commission of Investigation that many native agricultural activities (plowing, sowing, harvesting, but especially hay mowing) were *already* good examples of the kind of things Fourier had had in mind. He emphasized that the sociological principles immanent in such activities could be studied with profit, for, with but a little improvement and extension, they added up to Fourier's own principles. Russian rural living and working arrangements constituted a naturalistic, though still somewhat primitive model for the way in which, with a small assist from Fourier and science, *all* work should be organized.

Only a few improvements were needed to turn a Russian hay mowing for instance, into a Fourierist game, an unimaginably productive one. Some official should set the harvest time in advance so that everybody could plan on it. Good weather should be chosen by studying scientific meteorological data, while the work rate should be set at three hours a day for four days rather than twelve for one. Most important, one should follow nature's way further by encouraging and arranging for more "serialization" (more groups). Hay mowing was already pretty well serialized and thus competitive, playful, so that men's passions for competing and intriguing were satisfied by it. Men (the cutters) vied with women (the tossers), the skilled groups with the unskilled. Boredom was almost out of the question where the opportunities for flitting were so great. Under these happy natural circumstances, it would only take a little effort to turn hay mowing into something like the athletic games in ancient Greece.

Once the job was done, the whole idea would spread like wild-fire. But the movement would not tear the world asunder. Just as group rivalries within the phalanx were settled in the interest of rivalries between phalanxes, so national rivalries would check the disruptive possibilities of those between phalanxes. Indeed, the further the whole movement went the better. The atmosphere of Olympic games in the Russian village would become the spirit of the whole happy world. In a burst of enthusiasm, Danilevsky pictured to the Commission of Investigation huge international haying games on the "pampas of South America." The best mowers of each nation would be sent there. So would the best poets and artists in the world, making it a great holiday. "What a mowing!" he exclaimed.

Here was a kind of Russian messianism, for Danilevsky saw the native communal life as containing the germ of a socialist organization that could, by exemplifying the phalanx to the world, transform all society and all kinds of work, and save men not just from poverty, but from boredom, drudgery, and lone-liness. Franco Venturi, the historian of populism, has rightly seen Danilevsky as one of the earliest formulators of that very Russian idea.[26] One wonders too, in this connection, if Danilevsky was not subject to the influence of a famous book in the Petrashevsky library: *Studien über die inneren Zustände, das Volksleben, und insbesondere die ländlichen Einrichtungen Russlands* (the first two volumes appeared in 1847) by Baron von Haxthausen. *The Russian Empire,* as it has come to be called, was at that time the source of many a romantic and "socialist" conception of the Russian village.

Danilevsky did not want the phalanx so much as a way of Westernizing and modernizing Russia as he did as an up-to-date way of Russianizing and traditionalizing the West, St. Petersburg, and the new cultural and institutional life which was emerging in Russia. The fact that Fourier was a Frenchman seems but to have served to suggest and confirm the idea that everyone felt estranged and uprooted just as he did. A little like the tsar who had sponsored his education, he wanted to borrow techniques without significant spiritual, cultural, or intellectual implications. Like the tsar also, he failed. Remembering the fact that he did not involve many of his best energies in the effort anyway, it may be said that, on the "main front," he had given up before he started. His dreams were mostly a device to help him through a difficult spiritual and psychological time, one that had ensued from that understandable and perhaps inevitable surrender. They were not centrally related to tsarist despotism, Russian backwardness, or practical socio-economic problems. Neither, for that matter, were his dreams twenty years later. In the forties, however, he could admit and engage in his follies honestly. Later he was too filled with resentment against himself (and, largely because of it, against mankind), too ashamed of one part of himself and too proud of another, not to insist that he was a thorough modern, unidealistic, unromantic, tough, empirical, positivistic, skeptical, utilitarian. It is now our task to examine the nature and making of Danilevsky, the totalitarian philosopher.

4

THE MAKING OF A

TOTALITARIAN PHILOSOPHER

D<small>ANILEVSKY</small>'S exile to the provinces for his participation in the Petrashevsky circle lasted from late 1849 to June 1853.[1] Most of this period was spent in Vologda province; in November 1852 he was transferred to Samara. In both places he had to work in the chancery of the provincial governor. There is almost no evidence on the kind or quality of his work. But it must have been at least satisfactory, for the transfer to Samara was a move to a better and more regular bureaucratic position. There are a few things known about his unofficial work. He found time to pursue his own scientific investigations, which may have been related to his work for the governor of Vologda. The results were published, between 1851 and 1853, in a number of articles: six on the distribution and movement of the population of Russia in the year 1846; four which constituted a partial statistical description of Vologda province; several others on the climate of that area.[2] The articles on population earned him the sum of three hundred rubles from the Ministry of the Interior (the ministry was interested in this kind of work because the unscientific "revisions" of the population census, made periodically by the Ministry of Finance, were not too useful for administrative purposes). The articles on climate won him half the Geographical Society's annual Zhukov prize (two hundred fifty rubles) in 1853. Skimpy as these few facts are, they do suggest that Danilevsky tried to make the best of things and to rebuild his career.

In addition to official and professional activity, he also entered into the provincial social life. He became especially friendly with one Alexander Pavlovich Mezhankov, the son of the marshal of the local nobility; the Mezhankov village, Nikolskoe Selo, was the object of frequent visits. There was an added attraction in young Mezhankov's sister, Olga Alexandrova; she was later to become Danilevsky's second wife. There could hardly have been a serious attachment at this time, however, for Danilevsky was known to be in ardent correspondence with the widow Vera Nikolaevna Beklemisheva, of Orlov and Russkii Brod. In September 1852 his fiancée came to Vologda, and they were married.

If any general impression of Danilevsky is warranted on the basis of the information about the years after 1849, it is one of hopefulness, satisfaction in work, improving fortunes, good social relationships. Danilevsky was not crushed by his exile, it seems.

But then, after the transfer to Samara, trouble struck him again. Strakhov records in one bald sentence what was undoubtedly a great tragedy: on June 10, 1853, Vera died of cholera in Samara. Strakhov adds that Danilevsky was deeply depressed for a full year thereafter.

However, he did not suffer this lingering depression as an exile or in the provincial backwater of Samara. Only eight days after Vera's death a whole new world, challenging and different, opened up for him. On June 18 he was reprieved (friends in the Geographical Society apparently exerted influence on his behalf) and ordered by the Ministry of State Domains to participate in official capacity as the statistician in an extensive expedition devoted to studying the lower Volga and Caspian fisheries. This was government work, of course, and Danilevsky, as we know, had tried to avoid this kind of career earlier. But it was government work with a difference. It seems reasonable to assume that in his mind it fitted in with his earlier plans for a career and that he was not averse to it. Indeed, as we shall see presently in more detail, this particular work was much more like that of a really professional scientist (even of the free lance sort that Danilevsky had wanted to be) than it was of a drudge in a bureaucratic routine. The Geographical Society had played an important role in the initiation and planning of the expedition. Its object was not only the investigation of the declining catch in the fisheries, which was the basis of the government's interest; there was also to be a broad technical, statistical, and "natural historical" survey of the fisheries. Moreover, the expedition was being headed by Karl Ernst von Baer; this was a clear sign of the enterprise's professional scope. Baer, a Baltic German and a Russian subject, was one of the leading scientists in Europe, the discoverer of the mammalian ovum, a founder of the Russian Geographical Society, a man of great renown.[3]

The period of Danilevsky's exile at Vologda and Samara may be viewed as a kind of interlude. The data available for the years 1853 to 1869, the year in which *Russia and Europe* was published, and a little beyond suggest that these years may have marked a new period. Since the data do not allow for a really sequential account, let us look at his life during the fifties, sixties, and early seventies, first as a chronological whole and then as a set of circumstances which impinged on him and, on one level, apparently engaged him in certain commitments.

The Caspian expedition, headed by Baer, lasted from June 1853 to the early spring of 1857. Thereafter Danilevsky himself headed a whole series of expeditions and related enterprises. He was ordered to lead his first expedition in 1858, after spending a year in St. Petersburg working on the statistical data from Baer's survey. The new expedition took him to the far north to study the fisheries of the White Sea and the Arctic Ocean. It lasted till March 1861; New Year's Eve of 1860 and Easter of 1861 were spent in Trondheim in Norway. Immediately, in the spring of 1861, he returned to the Caspian to participate in a commission studying the fish and seal businesses there. This commission sat until June 1862. In November 1862 Danilevsky was sent to investigate violations of fishing regulations on lakes Pskov and Chud.

During the years 1863–1867 he headed his largest expedition. Like Baer's Caspian enterprise, it was really a joint Geographical Society–government affair. The government wanted a fisheries survey of the Black Sea and its tributaries; the society wanted a physical geographical one of the same area. Baer and Peter Semenov, Danilevsky's friend of student days, planned the society's part of the investigation, while Danilevsky set up the government side. From the latter part of 1863 until late in 1867 he made a series of six surveys: around the Sea of Azov, to the Dnieper, to the Manych, around the Black Sea, to the Kuban, and to the Danube. For an outstanding performance in providing geological and geographical data, he won the coveted Constantine Medal, the highest award of the Geographical Society. It was during the quiet winter months of these years that he wrote *Russia and Europe*.

His life was literally one journey after another up to the mid-seventies with only occasional short stays in St. Petersburg. In 1868 there was a survey of fishing and agricultural conditions in the Archangel province as well as another trip to Astrakhan to sit as president of another government commission on the Caspian fish and seal businesses. The year 1869 brought him again to Astrakhan, 1870–1871 to the northwest lakes. In 1872 and 1875 there were two more Crimean expeditions. The northwest lakes trip marked the completion of the Ministry of State Domain's planned survey of the major fisheries of European Russia. On the basis of the nine huge volumes of Studies of the State of the Fishery in Russia (*Izsledovaniia o sostoianii rybolovstva v Rossii*) and on the basis of his own experience, Danilevsky wrote in the seventies the basic part of that fisheries legislation which was to remain in force throughout the rest of the prerevolutionary period of Russian history and somewhat beyond. He was almost personally responsible for one of the lesser of the reforms of Alexander II.[4]

Professionally, Danilevsky's role in these years was much more that of a "socially useful" scientist than of an official. Though in the employ of the government and though on many occasions engaged in strictly government work (like making up statistical reports, drafting regulations, sitting on the official commissions in 1861–1862 and 1868), his work required much professional practice of the sciences of statistics and biology. In this he was working as much with, if not for, the Geographical Society as with the Department of Agriculture of the Ministry of State Domains. We do not have to assume that this was only because Danilevsky, continuing his earlier reservations about the bureaucracy, emphasized the more professional side of his work. The ministry had appointed him to participate in and to head the expeditions chiefly because of his scientific training. The ministry was working closely with the Geographical Society on the whole project of surveying the fisheries and had probably got his name from his old friend Peter Semenov. The society, on its side, particularly wanted Danilevsky in the expeditions. Indeed, the Black Sea survey of 1863–1867 was postponed because he was still involved in the investigation of the violation of regulations on lakes Pskov and Chud and because Baer and Peter Semenov of the society wanted only him to head that survey. Both the government and the society were interested especially in Danilevsky's competence as a statistician. On the society's side, there was more than simply an interest in seeing that a big government job was done professionally. Let us look at this matter a little.

In the nineteenth century the science of statistics was developing rapidly all over Europe.[5] This development was concerned with revising and making more rigorous the ancient sciences of *Staatskunde* and political arithmetic, the study of the military and economic potentials of nations. New techniques of sampling, collection, and evaluation of data and, particularly important, mathematical theory of probability were being applied to the older forms of statistical science. And there was increasing application of this whole reinvigorated science to a rapidly growing range of subjects. Adolphe Quetelet (1796–1874) of the Royal Academy of Brussels was the leader of the statistical movement in Europe.[6] His influence was strongly felt in Russia. Professor Buniakovsky of the University of St. Petersburg, under whom Danilevsky had probably studied the science, was a Russian Quetelet. For example, in a sort of statistical manifesto, published in 1848, Buniakovsky had advocated an extensive introduction of probability theory into the field of statistics and the application of that science to the study of population, culture, linguistics, even morals.[7] A sign of the great vigor of the statistical movement was the inclination of Quetelet, Buniakovsky, and others to let their enthusiasms run away with them. A mystique of statistics arose out of fascination with the possibility of predicting the course of human events. The comparative study of the lengths and stages of human lives and of civilizations was one particularly noteworthy aspect of this, as we shall see in a study of Danilevsky's *Russia and Europe.*[8]

The most important institutional center of the statistical movement in mid-nineteenth century Russia was the Statistical Section of the Geographical Society. The historical picture is one of a regular campaign on the part of this section, particularly in the forties and fifties, to interest the Russian government in statistical reform.[9] The government, which, according to one story, had once been extremely wary, even to the point of confusing sociology with socialism and demography with democracy, was beginning to surrender in the mid-fifties, for it founded the Central Statistical Office and agreed to abandon the old census revisions after 1858 (no scientific census took place until 1897, however). The leading figure in this campaign, continuing through the fifties and sixties, was Danilevsky's friend Peter Semenov (now called Semenov-Tian-Shansky, a title honoring him for an exploration of the Tien Shan mountains).

Danilevsky had already been involved in the efforts of the Statistical Section to convince the government of the value of scientific statistics during his exile at Vologda. This activity had eventuated in his articles on population, climate, on the province itself and in his winning half the society's Zhukov prize. From 1853 onward the society evidently saw Danilevsky as a campaigner in an important statistical cause. The government had at first wanted the Caspian expedition only for some *ad hoc* reasons (for instance, to stop complaints in the capital about the high prices of tastier Caspian fish products like caviar). The society had seized upon the government's interest, expanded the purpose and scope of the Caspian expedition, got approval for its plans and for a whole series of other surveys, and recommended that Danilevsky become Baer's statistician (Baer, as mentioned before, had been one of the founders of the Geographical Society). The temper of the society's interest and its dim view of previous efforts by the government alone are reflected in Baer's introduction to the volume of statistics that Danilevsky helped compile on the Caspian expedition. "The cause of these inconveniences [that is, problems with the Caspian fisheries] and of the frequent changes in legislation was, without doubt, the lack of scholarly studies of fish life in the Caspian Sea and the streams running into it, and of conditions making for their multiplication or diminution and the relationship of these conditions to the methods of fishing now in existence and to the regulations published in regard to them." [10]

After the first Caspian expedition, the government (now, under Alexander II, embarking on a general policy of reform anyway) decided to continue this type of work and to maintain the unofficial partnership with the society at least as far as major efforts were concerned. In view of Danilevsky's proven competence and the society's enthusiastic sponsorship of his effort as part of its own cause, he was kept in charge of the whole enterprise for two decades. Thus his vocational role in the entire period of his life presently under study was emphatically that of a professional scientist. Many of his fisheries expeditions were all but indistinguishable from purely scientific enterprises.

It will be remembered that in the forties Danilevsky had wanted and had started to become a free lance "socially useful" scientist. On the professional level, his attitude toward the government had been rather negative. He had evidently developed little faith in bureaucratic efforts at reform; and he had therefore intended to work with private scientific societies, the Free Economic and the Geographical. Objectively and on the pragmatic level he might have been classed as a loyal oppositionist. His situation in the fifties, sixties, and seventies could well have seemed to him like a perfect fulfillment of his earlier plans. Politically, though only on one level, Danilevsky in his middle years still looks, on the basis of the available data, like an operative, unideological liberal. His more professional writings of this period, which are quite untouched by any fanaticism, further confirm the picture. He did not, it seems, become a totalitarian philosopher — any more than he had earlier become a Fourierist — because he was rationally estranged from the political *status quo* in Russia.

Other pieces of data confirm the idea that he was largely occupied with science in his middle years and that, whatever his overall state of mind, he found some satisfaction in that. He did not restrict his scientific and scholarly interests to fish and commercial fishing practices, but continually sought to satisfy his own scientific and general intellectual curiosity. Evidently there was plenty of time to read and he took advantage of this, as the great amount of knowledge behind his philosophy of history and his other nonofficial writings of this period attests. Moreover, he could and did explore the geographical, ethnographical, and historical points of interest on his journeys: the rivers, lakes, and inland seas of European Russia; the Caucasus mountains; the great salt lakes of Elton and Baskunchak; the ancient Echmiadzin monastery, the seat of the Armenian primate; Mount Ararat; the northern Persian plateau near Resht; the ruins of the old Volga Bolgar kingdom. He also visited the wild Mordvinians; Prince Tiumen of the Kalmyks near Astrakhan; the Arctic peoples of the north; the Volga German colony and the Ural Cossacks. Danilevsky was with Baer on a strictly unofficial excursion on the lower Volga when Baer made a study that resulted in the formulation of "Baer's law" regarding the bank formation of rivers.[11] With Baer, too, according to one story, he studied the problem of the edibility of the Volga-Caspian herring, a fish thought "mad" by the local inhabitants and hence used only for oil. They succeeded in bringing this fish into the Russian diet.[12] The extent of Danilevsky's extra-official activities again suggests that he operated more like a scientist who had been retained by the government than like an employee, and that he was satisfied with this situation.

Looking at his situation from a little different angle, another quality of it may be identified. In the nineteenth century when ill-equipped expeditions into a still pretty wild nature were the order of the day in many fields of science, the scientist had to be an adventurer and outdoorsman. Alexander von Humboldt was a famous example of this kind of person. This sort of life often brought the scientist an exhilarating sense of freedom, moral cleanliness, and self-sufficiency. Kropotkin, the anarchist prince, who was a good Russian example of the type, described in his memoirs the life of "outdoor science" and some of the good feelings that expeditions made possible. "From the age of nineteen to twenty-five I had to work out important schemes of reform, to deal with hundreds of men on the Amur, to prepare and to make risky expeditions with ridiculously small means . . . and if all these things ended more or less successfully, I account for it only by the fact that I soon understood that in serious work commanding and discipline are of little avail. Men of initiative are required everywhere, but once the impulse has been given, the enterprise must be conducted, especially in Russia, not in military fashion, but in a sort of communal way, by means of common understanding." [13] Experience of this sort influenced Kropotkin's whole view of nature and was an important basis of his criticisms of Darwinism and its vision of an unremitting and quite uncommunal struggle for survival among organic beings of the same species.[14]

I mention Kropotkin in particular because he was particularly articulate and helps us appreciate attitudes expressed less clearly and explicitly in some of Danilevsky's writings. There are statements on the natural communal self-sufficiency of men in the wilds in an article on the Ural fisheries, for example. They sound like the statement quoted from Kropotkin.[15] In a rare moment of reminiscence in *Darwinism,* a work published in the eighties, Danilevsky made a point against the Darwinian theory that sounds much like Kropotkin's view; and he cited as evidence this same kind of personal observation made while on the great Caspian expedition of the fifties.[16] The pages of Baer's fascinating autobiography that deal with the Caspian expedition give a similar impression of an adventurous, dangerous, and morally satisfying life.

Good direct evidence is not available to indicate that Danilevsky not only lived this sort of life, off and on, for many years but also, in some fashion, took to it, became a happy scientific adventurer, so to speak. There are nevertheless two pieces of evidence which strongly suggest that it was so. D. A. Miliutin, the Minister of War, was a friend and neighbor of Danilevsky's in the seventies. He pictures Danilevsky's manner as that of a hoary, absent-minded, eccentric outdoorsman. He draws a curious comparison between Danilevsky and Don Pedro II, the emperor of Brazil, a symbol of pristine nature to Miliutin as to many Europeans of the time. "Today Livadian society had some amusement; it was busy, to the exclusion of all else, with the Brazilian guests, who, by their originality, simplicity, and ease, provided a rare contrast to the formal, strained tone of our court manners. The Brazilian emperor travels so modestly and casually that, upon his arrival at Yalta, he did not have any hat with him and, upon leaving, took somebody else's in the hotel. Don Pedro II has the look of an old man (though he's not more than fifty) with a large grey beard, tall, and rather stout. He reminded me of our Crimean neighbor and friend N. Ia. Danilevsky, not only in outward appearance, but also in manner." [17] Another bit of evidence is provided by N. N. Strakhov, the neo-Slavophil publicist, also a friend of Danilevsky's in the last period of his life. Strakhov relates an incident in connection with some government work that Danilevsky was doing in the eighties, combating phylloxera (plant lice which destroy grapevines) in the south. Strakhov was visiting Danilevsky in the Crimea and he told him that friends in St. Petersburg thought he should be up there "legislating" rather than running around the countryside. Danilevsky answered disdainfully, "this legislation is a word, but the fight with phylloxera is action." [18] He seems always to have preferred field work, to have enjoyed the wide open spaces and the pursuit of scientific and other knowledge, useful and not. Sometimes it seems all but impossible that this man could have been the author of *Russia and Europe*.

Danilevsky's social and personal circumstances also suggest that there were many at least potential sources of personal satisfaction in his life at this time and that he took some advantage of them. His personal situation steadily improved. In October 1861 he remarried. His bride was Olga Alexandrovna Mezhankova, whom, it may be remembered, he had known at Vologda. Eventually they had five children. In the sixties he took his family along on the Black Sea expedition, settling them in a rented house at Miskhor on the south shore of the Crimea between Yalta and Sevastopol. In 1867 he bought from Count Kushelev-Bezborodko, a wealthy Moscow nobleman, a small estate, called Mshatka, in the same vicinity. Incidentally, Kushelev-Bezborodko played host that same year to the Slavic guests at the "Panslav Congress" in Moscow. The estate was run-down, for the French had burned the manor house during the Crimean War; but it had a large garden, a vineyard, and a small overseer's house in livable condition.

The purchase of Mshatka is also indicative of an improvement in his financial situation. This must have come from earnings rather than inheritance. Danilevsky's parents had not been rich and, like many a gentry family, their fortune seems to have declined. They had had the money (2500 rubles a year for tuition, a great sum in those days) to send him to the Lyceum. But he had had to make much of his own way at the university, "free auditing" to avoid tuition charges and doing hack work for Petersburg publishers. He mentioned his straightened circumstances to the Commission of Investigation in 1849. When his father died (in 1855, of cholera, while raising a *levée* in Orlov to fight in the Crimea), Danilevsky had probably inherited very little. His improved financial situation was thus another possible basis of satisfaction with his career and his life.

Then, too, there were social advantages. In October 1857, right after the Caspian expedition, he was given a regular appointment as an official in the Department of Agriculture of the Ministry of State Domains. In March 1858 he received a title, "junior engineer." The details of his subsequent promotions are not known. But they must have been steady: having begun with the tenth rank in the civil service table, he finally reached the fourth, that of Actual State Councillor. Professionally he was a respected member of the Geographical Society, a winner of its highest awards. His acquaintances included people like Karl Ernst von Baer of the Academy of Sciences; Peter Semenov-Tian-Shansky of the Geographical Society; Dmitri Miliutin, the Minister of War. Nicholas Semenov was closer to him than these; he had an important role in the framing of the emancipation of 1861 and became a senator in 1868. Danilevsky also probably had good social connections outside official and scientific circles — with businessmen[19] in fish and seal enterprises and with socially prominent people interested in Panslavism like Kushelev-Bezborodko.

On the whole, the available data again and again indicate that to a high degree Danilevsky had succeeded in the fifties, sixties, and seventies, in his intention, as a student, of getting ahead and becoming a professional man among practically minded professional men. Now, as we know, there had been in the forties another side to Danilevsky. He had been zealously interested in the problem of the meaning of Westernism and modernity. His inter-

est had led him into a discussion circle, a sort of intellectual-
spiritual institution of the time, and also to some late romantic
doctrines about man, history, society, and nature. At that time
there had been discontinuity and contradiction between the professional and the human Danilevsky; he had found satisfaction in
his scientific work but was not generally satisfied with the world
of science and technology.

There are data which suggest that by the later fifties or early
sixties he had become much better able to integrate his aspirations,
his spiritual life, his world view, and his values with his professional life. Indeed, the impression one gets at this time is of a
much more consistent, rather bourgeois Danilevsky. Look again
at his friends and acquaintances, for instance: Baer, Miliutin, the
Semenovs, and undoubtedly many businessmen, liberal bureaucrats, members of the Geographical Society (including even several other former Petrashevskians now evidently quite tame: A. P.
Balasoglo, D. A. Kropotov, E. I. Lamansky, Vladimir Miliutin,
N. A. Mordvinov). The cultural atmosphere, at its best, in this
social milieu may be inferred from the tone of works like Miliutin's diary or Semenov's memoir and his history of the Geographical Society. While none of these is a properly theoretical work,
each attests to values and a world view that were liberal, pluralistic, rather secular, though at the same time pretty conservative
and not hostile to sacramental religion. Parts of *Russia and Europe*,
as we shall see, seem to fit Danilevsky right into this picture and
to suggest that there was considerable liberal ideology as well as
attitude in this social environment of his: there is, for instance,
his warm praise of the reforms of Alexander II, especially the
liberation and the jury system; complaint about censorship; emphasis on the importance of the free play of varying ideas and
points of view in the progress of science and civilization in general.[20] Undoubtedly, too, his militant, anti-metaphysical, philosophical realism and utilitarianism — other features of *Russia and
Europe* — had their origin in the culture of this social milieu. All
this suggests that Danilevsky had now managed to work out a

more consistent life. Institutions like the scientific society and the more professional side of the imperial bureaucracy had become the focus alike of his aspirations and of his professional life. His renewed adherence to Orthodoxy in 1849 also continued; Christian (whether genuinely or only sociologically so) conservative-liberal professional men were not by any means uncommon in nineteenth century Russia. Everything seems to indicate that Danilevsky had become a loyal oppositionist, an enlightened Russian bureaucrat, in his heart as well as his mind. If, however, one is inclined, looking at this picture of change in Danilevsky, to think it perhaps a little too abrupt to make human sense, then one finds even further evidence to the point. He finds that Danilevsky also became, probably in the fifties sometime, a Panslavist and that his Panslavism can be taken as a sign of *some* feeling of cultural maladjustment to modernity, though fittingly not a sign of such serious maladjustment as his radicalism in the forties had been.

Bearing in mind that this whole picture of Danilevsky's ideological *embourgeoisement* is belied by the import of his *Russia and Europe*, let us nevertheless look at the development of his interest in Panslavism and attempt, on the basis of general knowledge of that movement, to work out what this interest could have meant, that is, what the whole picture, except for *Russia and Europe*, seems to have been. Let me say that I am not filling out what can later be shown to be a false story simply to bemuse the reader. There is a historiographical problem here. It cannot be straightened out nor a better portrait of Danilevsky be drawn without an appreciation of its specific nature.

Danilevsky joined the Petersburg Slavic Welfare Society on March 30, 1868.[21] However, this could not have been the beginning of his interest in Panslavism, for in 1868 he had already finished *Russia and Europe*, which contains an elaborate Panslav program; when he joined the Slavic Welfare Society, he was in St. Petersburg looking for a publisher. He had spent years working on his philosophy of history; his interest in Panslavism must

have considerably predated 1868 (the year of the founding of
the Petersburg branch of the society), perhaps by a decade. While
evidence is again scanty, it does seem rather definitely to indicate
that he first became interested in Panslavism through the Geographical Society. Some people and currents of thought within
the Ethnographical Section of that society[22] were probably the
sources of his initial contacts both with the Panslav movement in
general and, within it, with the important philosophical strand of
Slavophilism.

The ethnographers of the society were naturally greatly interested in all sorts of questions about folklore, linguistics, popular
customs, cultural differences between people. Particular attention
in the fifties and sixties was given to the Slavs. A leader in this
was Nicholas Ivanovich Nadezhdin, the man who had suffered
with Chaadaev in the famous *Telescope* affair of 1836. Nadezhdin
was the chairman of the Ethnographical Section from 1848 to his
death in 1856. An official nationalist with some Slavophil ideas,
he had a lively interest in the study of the Kashubs, the Bulgarians,
the Macedonians, the "Ugro-Russians," and other Slavic peoples.
Other active and influential scholarly members of the section interested in the Slavs were A. F. Hilferding (1831–1872) and
V. I. Lamansky (1833–1914). While a student at the University
of Moscow, Hilferding had come directly under the influence of
the Slavophil circle of Khomiakov. His ethnographical activities
in the Geographical Society in the fifties and sixties included the
collection of *byliny* (epic songs), an extensive study of the
Kashubs (whose Germanization and Polonization he decried),
and a visit to Herzegovina, Bosnia, and Old Serbia. He wrote a
lengthy account of this expedition, which was published in the
Zapiski of the Geographical Society. Vladmir Ivanovich Lamansky was also a scholar of Slavophil persuasion. An accomplished
Slavicist, for his master's dissertation at the university he wrote,
in 1859, an emphatically Panslavist and Slavophil work. He translated Ljudevit Shtur's important Panslavist work *Slavdom and
the World of the Future*. His own book *On the Historical Sig-*

nificance of the Graeco-Slavic World in Europe, published in
1871, was to become a minor Slavophil classic. Especially interesting in the present context is the fact that Lamansky was one
of the most important founders of the Petersburg Slavic Welfare
Society.[23]

Besides specifically Panslavist and Slavophil currents in the
Ethnographical Section, there was a widely shared atmosphere
of nativism and patriotism. This had first manifested itself in the
late forties when the Russian members of the section had ousted
Baer as chairman in favor of Nadezhdin. The ousting had been
an episode in a "fight against the German group" in the whole
Geographical Society. The patriotic enthusiasm continued strong
through the fifties, being reinforced by a belief that the Russians
were progressive and the Baltic Germans too conservative.[24]

Danilevsky himself was more active in the Statistical than in the
Ethnographical Section. But the Geographical Society was not
enormous and interests within it were never rigidly separated.
He had friends and acquaintances all over the society. Moreover,
he seems to have followed its publications closely. This included
ethnographical writings; we find, for example, quotations from
such writings by Baer and Nadezhdin in an article of his on the
Ural Cossacks.[25] This article was the outgrowth of a paper read
by him before a general meeting of the society on February 19,
1858. Its subject was both economic and ethnographic. There are
some distinctly Slavophil elements in it: the moral advantages of
organic customs over written laws were extolled, while the "Russian" communal life of the Cossacks was depicted rather idyl-
lically. It appears likely that Danilevsky first came upon Panslavism and Slavophilism within the circle of his professional life in
the fifties. His writing of a philosophy of history focused on
Panslavism in the mid-sixties and his joining of the Slavic Welfare
Society in 1868 were parts of a development that had begun as
much as a decade earlier.

Taking Danilevsky's developing interest in Panslavism at its
face value, what does this tell us about him? On the one hand,

it suggests again that he was adopting a personal outlook more consistent with his modernistic professional life. The institutional contiguity of the Slavic Welfare Society and the Geographical Society attests to this. So does the nature of Panslavism[26] in the fifties, for that doctrine was in some important ways a distinctly modern one.

It advocated the strengthening of supposedly potentially strong ties of cultural unity between the Slavs. As of the fifties and sixties, the idea of political unification was also becoming popular, though it was not as yet frequent or well developed among either Russian or non-Russian Panslavists; the main emphasis was still on the development of a specifically Slavic culture in Central and Eastern Europe. It was believed that this would protect the national identities of the individual Slavic nationalities and of Slavdom as a whole against (as Panslavists saw the situation) the cultural imperialism of Magyars and especially Germans and against the potentially denationalizing influence of Western European (that is, modern) culture. Cultural unity and development would also, it was believed, make possible a distinctly Slavic, quite spiritual contribution to modern materialistic civilization. But the Panslav idea was not, for the most part, an anti-modern one. Many Panslavists of this time were professional men, scholars, businessmen, bureaucrats. They sought a way of preserving their sense of identity *within* modern Europe as it was developing in the nineteenth century. By and large, they did not, as had the Petrashevskians, for instance, refuse to accommodate to any type of modernity that was not structured and defined in some traditionalistic, folkish, decentralized way. In this sense, the Panslav movement, outgrowing its romantic intellectual forerunners in the fifties, was basically a nationalist movement, though a somewhat amorphous and confused one. The deepest motive behind it was a quest for community *within* modernity. In Ferdinand Tönnies' famous terminology, the Panslavists' *Gesellschaft* (their "society," collectively the functional groupings in which they lived) was not greatly at variance with their sense of community

(*Gemeinschaft* — the emotional and spiritual group).[27] Panslavism such as that in the Petersburg Slavic Welfare Society was a less humanistically attractive movement, but it was sociologically a more mature one than utopian socialism or populism. In both the latter, the sense of community was at much greater variance with the facts of life, of "society"; internationalism and millenarian localism, peasant or proletarian, were out of tune with the irreversible developments of national economies, national regimes, and the nationalist sense of community and meaning that was sweeping away traditionalism all over Europe.

On the other hand, it must be noted, in considering the question of Danilevsky's adjustment to the modern age, that Panslavism was still a rather peculiar sort of nationalism. Indeed, the movement may also be taken as a sign of some inability or unwillingness, in the part of budding Russian or other particular Slavic nationalists, to find a fully satisfying sense of community and meaning in the nation-state and nationalism per se. Panslavism made little concrete historical or sociological sense, for "Slavdom" was really an abstraction. Appropriately the Panslav movement was heavily intellectual, scholarly, and distinctly without popular roots. Fittingly too, each national Panslavic group had its own nationally colored brand of Panslavism. Russian Panslavism was often indistinguishable from a kind of Panrussianism. Non-Russian Panslavists, on their side, hardly ever faced the fact that, indeed, the majority of Slavs *were* Russians and that if Slavdom *was* a reality, its leadership, political and cultural alike, was bound to come mostly from Russia. Each national group saw Slavdom in a markedly particularist way. According to this line of thought, the Panslav movement may be said to have had roots also in feelings of doubt about nationalism — among Westernized professionals and intellectuals, people in social milieux in their own lands only rather recently starting to undergo an all too rapid process of modernization. Basically these people were nationalists, loyal to Russia or other Slavic areas of more real historical and sociological vitality than Slavdom. But their properly nationalist sense of community was still in process of formation. There was still a sense of strain and some groping. The Panslav idea, the idea of the nation as a sort of locality in a supernation, fed on their lingering doubts. Some of the most progressive people in Russia had still, in the fifties, sixties, and seventies, not worked out a fully comfortable modern sense of community, a nationalism particularistic in regard to the external world, antiparticularistic in regard to internal localities. The Panslav movement of that time was both a sign of these men's cultural maturity and a symptom that they were only just reaching it. The temper of their ideas was realistic enough; the project they envisioned was only ambiguously so.

On balance, it seems proper to place the emphasis on the modernity of the Panslav movement rather than on the signs of discontent with that same modernity. The history of the movement's institutional development in Russia illustrates this in another way, for that development owed nearly everything to the influx of progressive people into a formerly quite romantic, poetic, and wholly intellectual movement. Intellectual proponents of the Panslav idea are to be found at least as far back as the eighteenth century. By the time of Nicholas I, thinkers like Pogodin, Shevyrev, Khomiakov were making the idea the subject of more continous discussion. But as an organized, institutional affair, the movement really dates from the era of the reforms of Alexander II, a time of intense modernization and of development of Russian professional life. What had been a strictly intellectual strand in Russian thought was put on an institutional basis with the founding of the Moscow Slavic Welfare Society in 1867 and its Petersburg branch in 1868, and it was done not only by intellectuals but also by professionals, scholars, bureaucrats, scientists, businessmen. Another sign of the new practicality in Panslavism was the arrangement in 1867, in connection with a scientific and ethnographical exposition in Moscow, of a Slavic "Congress" (consisting really of a series of conferences on cultural unity between leading Russian Panslavists and invited guests from other

Slavic lands). Moreover, the influx of professional and other practical men into the movement during the later fifties and sixties, together with the new realistic European climate of opinion, seems also to have inspired a more political turn in what had hitherto been an almost strictly philosophical and cultural affair. Of this period in the history of the movement, one contemporary wrote, "Never before was the Russian language and literature so studied in Slavic lands. The number of Slavic pilgrims, especially Czechs, in Russia grew significantly from that time and the number of Russian pilgrims and tourists in Slavic lands increased. Private and public links of friendship were more strongly knitted between Russian and South and Northwest Slavs. In Russian literature, with unprecedented frankness, sincerity, and knowledge, there began to appear judgments and talk about the Slavic and 'Eastern question.' To show this it is enough to point to the work of Shtur, *Slavianstvo i mir budushchago*, the book of N. Ia. Danilevsky, *Rossiia i Evropa*, and the brochure of Fadeev, *Vostochnyi vopros.*" [28]

In general, Danilevsky's interest and participation in the Panslav movement would seem to have been wholly consistent both with the impression that he had undergone a really fundamental change and with the idea that, given his previous difficulties of adjustment, the change was not being undergone without some continuing sense of strain. The impression the properly biographical data give is one of a dedicated, public-minded, professional scientist adhering to an incipient utilitarian liberal ideology and developing a really modern (though still uneasy) sense of community. Danilevsky's should have been what Goncharov called the "common story" of a romantic young radical maturing into a conservative-liberal professional man. Only the philosophy of history in *Russia and Europe* really contradicts this. Though that philosophy in part shows heavy (though rather formalistic) influence of liberal and liberal-nationalist-Panslavist ideas and can even be used, along with the other biographical data, as evidence of some kind of adherence, on the author's part, to such ideas,

these liberal and nationalist ideological strands are flatly and
aggressively contradicted elsewhere in the book. Danilevsky did
not really adhere fully to these doctrines. His book rather indicates that he was at once greatly involved and greatly discontented with them. It is scarcely an exaggeration to say that the
book was written by a man who felt himself entrapped in this
kind of thinking. It is as though Danilevsky hated utilitarianism,
liberalism, liberal nationalism, and even, in a way, Panslavism, but
felt himself somehow compelled to think in ways which resembled
theirs, a case reminiscent of Marx's attitude toward "capitalism."

The old romantic, culturally regressive Danilevsky was still
very much alive in the 1860's. He had not been matured by his
experience since 1849. He rather seems to have been confused and
upset by it. The journeys around Russia, the professional associations, and the changing climate of opinion fragmented his older
sense of place, time, and meaning, but did not replace it. There
is an interesting moment of reminiscence in *Darwinism* which
probably suggests his state of mind at this time better than all the
biographical data we have seen. In the winter of 1860–61, he
tells us, he was far from home, in Norway. He was reading the
Revue des Deux Mondes. Here he came upon an account of the
Darwinian theory of evolution. He recalled his confusion as similar to that into which he had once been led by a mathematical
puzzle.

I remember how some one once showed me how there could be two
right angles in a triangle and this without recourse to the fourth
dimension — it was all done in terms of ordinary Euclidean geometry.
At first I did not see what the trick was. What could I do in such a
position? Prove the theorem by the usual method that was taught in
every textbook? To this my opponent would have had the right to
answer: "Very well, I have no quarrel whatsoever with you; it is
very possible that your proof is true, but mine remains true also until
you are able to disprove it; and if both are true, then I have proved
much more than I proposed in the beginning. I set out to convince you
of the inconsistency of one of your axioms, but now it turns out that
I have disproved the validity of the logical process in general. What is

left of logic after you are forced to admit that two mutually exclusive truths can exist side by side?"[29]

It seems that this may be taken as more than a commentary on a scientific conundrum. Danilevsky in the sixties felt himself to be living in two contradictory worlds, two or three kinds of time. He was deeply disturbed, and probably felt more like the classical Russian figure of the superfluous man than like a reasonably well-adjusted modern.[30]

2

A big work of historical philosophy is hardly a readily usable biographical source. Danilevsky did not write *Russia and Europe* in order to reveal himself (quite the contrary, it appears), but rather in order to establish the meaning of Russia's Westernization and the modern age in Russia and in the world. He did this for the same general reasons, spiritual, intellectual, cultural, psychological, that had earlier led him into the Petrashevsky circle. *Russia and Europe* is in the form of a treatise; unlike Herzen's writings, for instance, it lacks almost all personal overtone and belongs rather strictly in the history of Russian formal thought. It will therefore be necessary to seek biographical information from it more indirectly, by observing Danilevsky's behavior, as it were, in philosophy and then, on this basis, trying to reconstruct his state of mind and to reinterpret his story. Let us begin with a brief look at the philosophy itself.

Russia and Europe is a bizarre work, in length over five hundred pages of finely printed Russian in its original serialized publication of 1869. It is a mixture of angry, dated, political Panslavist journalism; primitive, at times brilliant social science; *Realpolitik;* sentimental romanticism and populist-utopian socialism; fanciful theology and philosophy of history; and mad prophecy.

In the early stages and, at one level, throughout the whole book the author seems to be a political realist or hyperrealist, a tough-

minded Panslavic and Russian nationalist. In this vein he ex-
coriates all those "thinking men of Russia," Westerners, humanitarians, and political moralists who would apply idealistic standards to Russian foreign policy. Though he praises the Slavophils
for their insistence on Russia's distinctness from the West, he
also roundly criticized their "humanitarianism." Russian idealistic
foreign policy, in Danilevsky's view, was an epiphenomenon of
a national upper-class habit of self-devaluation in the presence
of Western European civilization. Unrealistically soft and dis-
gracefully hesitant foreign policy, based on this habit and rationalized on grounds of morality and truth, was making Russia
appear the fool and suffer the lot of the puppet in international
power politics. Stressing the Darwinian quality of international
political life and evoking Bentham's principle of utility as the key
to all proper foreign policy, Danilevsky calls upon Russians to
assert themselves, to lead the Slavs to unite and to construct their
own native civilization.

He thought this program necessitated elaborate demonstration
that Western European civilization was not the same thing as
civilization itself. Without such demonstrations, the moralists, the
Russian Westerners, the "thinking men of Russia," could not be
cured of their deeply rooted habit of self-devaluation, the most
important basis, in Danilevsky's view, of the current unfortunate
Russian and Slavic international political situations. His famous
theory of cultural-historical types or civilizations, which has
seemed to many scholars like an anticipation of Spengler's philosophy of history, was designed to prove his point. A theory of
limited cultural relativism, it removed world history from the
linear-progressive, ancient-medieval-modern scheme and placed
it in one of a number of civilizations, each with its own version
of these three supposedly archetypal periods. On the basis of this,
Danilevsky attempted to establish the fact of the presence in
world history of a nascent Slavic civilization, separate from the
"European," one that was as morally justified as any other in
fighting for its own existence. This former Petrashevskian tried

other ways too of changing the intellectual political habits of his educated contemporaries. He debunked tender-minded, romantic, metaphysical, myth-historical ways of thinking in general as well as in regard to politics. Though there is little formal general philosophical argument in *Russia and Europe*, it is for realism against romanticism, for positivism against metaphysics, for secularized transcendentalism against immanentism and sacramentalism. Finally, to the same didactic ends, he even set forth some explanations of the mechanics of internal development of civilization, explanations which suggested that romanticism in general and humanitarian views of foreign policy in particular were really expressions of the tensions of a civilization's growth at a certain, still fairly primitive stage, one out of which Danilevsky was attempting to lead his fellows.

If he had left the argument at that, he could not now be classified as a totalitarian thinker, for in this part of his doctrine there is no sign of an impulse to reach spiritual and metaphysical ends by contradictory instrumental and violent means. Also Danilevsky's goals are here spelled out and clear as well as limited; they are stated as his own not history's, vaguely revealed. He said that the world was a hard one and dangerous to anyone who did not recognize this. Using appropriately scientific ways of thinking, often brilliantly, he sought to establish the truth about the international political world and to persuade his contemporaries to act accordingly. He confused fact and value and he was quite Machiavellian. But in this aspect of his theory he was not totalitarian.

Biographically speaking, if he had left the argument here, we should be strongly inclined to see *Russia and Europe* as the conclusive evidence that a definite *embourgeoisement* had taken place in Danilevsky's thinking. It all sounds as though he had become something of a conservative liberal, utilitarian in philosophical persuasion. As mentioned before, *Russia and Europe* expresses real enthusiasm for the reforms of Alexander II, praising the emancipation and the jury system, urging a democratic society and a more even distribution of national wealth, complaining of the continuation of censorship, and yet also stressing that the emerging new system was authentically Russian and relatively complete. Danilevsky's vision of a future world balance of power and of cultural influence between the United States, Western Europe, and Slavdom, a balance ensuring cultural variety and political freedom for all peoples, was also liberal in spirit. The influence of Tocqueville upon this vision seems quite possible. The proposed constitutional arrangements for the future Panslav Union included a free capital (like Washington, D.C.) at Constantinople so that the little Slavic brothers would not be dominated by Russia. This too was liberal; so was Danilevsky's insistence on the importance of national pluralism in the Union and his advocacy, just after the revolt of 1863, of a reconstitution of the Polish nation, even though he regarded it as a cultural traitor to the Slavic cause. It all seems to corroborate the idea that since the forties Danilevsky had succeeded in adjusting to the spiritual, cultural, and intellectual life of the modern age into which his professional life had taken him.

His too hard, Bismarckian tone and even his ominous tendency to insist that the further rational and ethical reform of Russia had to be preceded by the achievement of a very strong, politically guaranteed sense of national community, do not, it should be emphasized, contradict the general impression that Danilevsky had worked out an intellectual and spiritual accommodation to modernity by becoming a utilitarian conservative liberal. Though the degree of such insistence, together with his wish to see the nation state as a sort of locality within a supernation (Slavdom or "Europe"), suggests some continuing uneasiness or at least feeling of unfamiliarity with this same accommodation, by and large the aspect of *Russia and Europe* here described in no way suggests that Danilevsky was still obsessed by his (or, as he saw it, Russia's) past or that he was trying to think out his own or Russia's problems in ways like those he had learned in the Petrashevsky circle. The initial impression one gets, leaving academic distinctions aside, is that his nationalism-Panslavism is appropriate in spirit to his militantly utilitarian liberalism. He seems to have wanted to see the Slavs build a politically independent community of their own in order that they might, from the very experience of building it, become more worldly, more secular, less eschatologically expectant and thus more psychologically, as well as politically and culturally, able to rebuild their own societies in practical, modern ways. On one level of *Russia and Europe*, Danilevsky simply gave philosophical expression (his book was a "codex and catechism" of Panslavism) to the socially useful but also stuffy, shallow, philistine, spiritually pessimistic, neurotic, bumptiously realistic social psychology current, from the fifties and sixties, in the Westernized layers of Russian society—among progressive bureaucrats, professional men, budding entrepreneurs, and members of institutions like the Russian Geographical Society or the Petersburg Slavic Welfare Society.

However, as one reads through to the end of *Russia and Europe* and then examines it more closely, it turns out that the utilitarian liberal Panslavism and its rationale were by no means all that Danilevsky had in mind. Indeed, these make up only part, and, though they take up most of the space, an intellectually subordinate part of a much larger theory, one rather briefly and vaguely stated. In what appears at first to be a blatant contradiction of the letter and spirit of the more prominent, but actually subordinate, theory, we are told that the whole course of world history had been generally laid out in advance by God, and that beyond this, He had been continuing to work out His predetermined pattern in more detail by means of occasional interventions. Danilevsky claimed that only God Himself could really know such things; mere human beings could, however, especially as history drew toward the end, get occasional glimpses of them. According to Danilevsky, God had arranged and was continuing to arrange the course of world history so that it would all end in one final "panhuman" and Russian socialist civilization. That wholly utopian civilization would realize a perfect political,

economic, social, artistic, technological, scientific, and, most important, spiritual balance. Nothing in it would be undeveloped;
no development would be out of harmony with any other; and
there would be no progress possible beyond all this. World history was a quasi-Hegelian process in which first one people and
then another had worked up and were continuing to work up
various aspects of this socialist, panhuman, highest possible, and
final civilization. Each people but the last (the Slavs, "the chosen
people of God") was a means to the one end. "Europe" was now
making claims to its finality and universality. But the Russian
Westerners were both wrong and idolatrous to believe these
claims. Indeed, this belief was blocking God's purpose and the
completion of the whole drama of world history. In fact, Europe,
though great, was only penultimate. Russia or Slavdom was to
be the ultimate. Whether in the final analysis mankind as a whole
(or at least the West) was to be saved through Russia's and
Slavdom's beatification, seems not to have been entirely clear
to Danilevsky. Mainly he held that a really "universal" civilization was impossible. Slavdom's future would not be universal but
panhuman, that is, the ultimate historical synthesis would be
realized in Russia and Slavdom alone. However, in a lyrical passage at the very end of *Russia and Europe*, Danilevsky did hint
that Slavdom's fulfillment would lead to everybody's salvation.
His neo-Slavophilism, his emphasis on the important role of Christianity in the whole providential course of world history, his
scientism, and his socialism suggest that his hint was not entirely
contrary to the spirit of his theory. But mostly he spoke of the
beatification of Slavdom alone.

But whatever he meant by his messianic reference, there can be
no doubt that he wanted, or was happy to know that God wanted,
a kind of heaven on earth. The future civilization he predicted,
with its finality, its harmony, its many-sided development, its extreme yet orderly democracy (social and economic not "merely"
political), its successful integration of science and religion, tradition and reason, modernity and community, the things of the

body and the things of the soul — all this was way out of tune (except geographically) with the Panslav Union he spoke of in his *realpolitisch* theory. There he decried all such dreams and even damned the habit of dreaming itself because, in his view, it kept men in Russia and elsewhere from achieving what happiness and progress were possible in this — as he insisted over and over — quite secular, Machiavellian, functionalistic, Benthamite-Darwinian world. His providential theory of world history, in temper, in intention, in the end it envisaged was more in line with his utopianism of the forties and with the theological and metaphysical side of Slavophilism, which he also said he rejected, than it was with the increasingly positivistic culture of the Russian fifties and sixties, the culture that so definitely marked the properly realistic Panslavist aspect of his book. He did say he wanted a Panslav Union that would have been merely another worldly civilization, a protected base on which the Slavs could develop their own version of modernity, a guarantee of a world balance of power, a preserver of variety and true (quite secular) progress. But there can be no doubt that he really wanted much more, something (though now with Slavophil overtones) like the old utopian dream of the forties, not a compromise between, but a full synthesis of traditionalism and modernity.

The relationship between his two theoretical standpoints is a little difficult to work out because he never explicitly told his readers what he had in mind. He rather acted out the relationship himself, rhetorically, especially by making his subordinate theory more prominent. Given the meaning of his doctrine as a whole, this was an entirely logical thing to do. Though the practice makes understanding of that doctrine rather a struggle, his meaning is not really obscure. It seems that God did not expect mere men, especially in their present transitional, incomplete state of spiritual and intellectual development, to be able to think out the bases of their lives or actions on the highest level. The objective form, as it were, of their still alienated consciousness was for the most part now modern, scientistic, realistic, Machiavellian. God had therefore arranged that the chosen people in Eastern Europe would at the right historical moment be thinking (and that, providentially enough, greatly under the influence of the positivist values and ideas of the Western or European penultimate civilization) about a Panslav Union in narrowly utilitarian and realistic political ways. The thing for them to do was to go on, *à l'outrance*, with what they were doing and with their ways of thinking about it. God had also arranged that the continuing practice by Russia of *Realpolitik*, oriented to the realization of a Panslav Union with its capital at Constantinople, would eventually trigger off a great war between Slavdom and "Europe." God knew that the Slavs, especially the Russians, who were their military and political leaders, would be preparing for this and that it would not be unexpected, though the reasons for their preparations and some of the content of their expectations would be false. In line with their expectations the war would unite the Slavs militarily and then politically, raise their national spirit, and make their victory over the materially superior West possible. Beyond their expectations the long process of war would be a liturgical event: it would raise their spirit to a level of unity and vitality at which it would be possible to realize their great potential for the final synthesis of civilization. This would be the end of history; there would be a new dispensation, a Russian socialist heaven on earth.

It seems clear that Danilevsky preached a dialectically contradictory utilitarian, realistic, positivist Panslavism and *Realpolitik*, not because he meant it fully but because he believed this to be an "objectively" determined, providentially arranged action. His utilitarian, modernistic Panslavist theory was thought by him to be part of a cosmic pattern, one whose next step of development was to be a war that, like a liturgy, would ontologize the Slavic soul. He believed that only God could really see the whole picture, act and think directly in relation to it. All that men (including Danilevsky) could see was (a) Panslavism, realistic politics, war preparations, (b) occasional flashes of something else, just enough to keep high their zeal for the more proximate tasks before them, just enough to give them a feeling that their cause was not just practical but categorically moral, loaded with appropriately absurd but at the same time believable promise. Thus Danilevsky not only concentrated his own and his readers' attention on utilitarian Panslavism, he even stated rather fully some comparatively limited, this-worldly ends for his program. This was in order that he and others might not poach upon God's domain and in order that they might do the work laid down by God, without hesitancy or reservations, in and for itself. Without this, indeed, the world historical pattern could not be worked out.

Thus Danilevsky never really stated but rather acted out rhetorically (especially by twisting the focus of and emphases within his book) his overall meaning because he was following out the logic of his odd dialectical theory. For the most part he really did concentrate on the tasks at hand. He tried to teach men by example rather than by word because, in his view, any but the vaguest and briefest explanation would have implied that he could put himself on God's level, or even that *he* and not God wanted a war in order to synthesize traditionalism and modernity in the Russian soul. Thus his was mainly a philosophy of the deed, a typically totalitarian doctrine. All the big questions, including moral responsibility, were matters of cosmic forces arranged by Providence. These would take care of the relationship between Machiavellianism and beatification. Indeed, these forces had themselves set up the seeming contradiction between them. Thinking and acting dialectically were thus not only permissible; they were both morally necessary and the sole ways in which, under present alienated circumstances, men could share in the life of God. Now like Adam Smith, now like Bakunin, Danilevsky believed that evil was the motive force of good. In a sense he thought it evil to do anything but evil, for good and responsible action implied a questioning of the transcendent ordering of the universe. He preached and meant to preach only one thing: realistic Panslavist policy for Russia and that at the risk of war with "Europe." But his ultimate reasons for so preaching were different from the

ones he stated. He limited his ostensible rationale for unlimited
reasons. He was realistic, modern, and hard for romantic, traditionalist, and soft reasons.

There are many things about this theory which remind one of
Marx. There is the connection of religious and spiritual-psy-
chological considerations with quite secular social and political
conditions and with mundane though violent action. There is the
imposition of quasi-theological patterns on factual historical situations and the odd blending of metaphysical with social scientific
language. Both thinkers' interests were primarily spiritual and
humanistic, yet neither felt himself capable of enough detachment
from his social and existential situation to state these interests, or
even to concern himself with them, except obliquely and dialectically. Each felt himself and his contemporaries to have suffered
an inner split in a time of transition from the traditional to the
modern. Each thought pregnant with all but inarticulable meaning both their sense of inner alienation and the societal incon-
gruities supposedly related to it. Both preached actions and values
oriented to violence as though these were ends in themselves.
Each hinted at an age of beatitude to come and at a violent historical liturgy that would ontologize human souls, fitting them
for beatitude. Both were socialists. Both wanted not a return to
the past, but a growth and fulfillment of the traditional through
complete synthesis with the modern (in this sense the Danilevsky
of the sixties was still as much a Petrashevskian as a Slavophil).
Each in his own way was a rationalistic, scientistic, progressive,
action-oriented, "Russian" totalitarian philosopher. Overall, the
similarities in spirit between Danilevsky and Marx are so striking
that the really vast differences in detail between their theories
seem not decisively to distinguish them, except as two representatives of one intellectual historical type.

Turning again to the biographical problem in the light of these
facts about *Russia and Europe*, it is evident without any deep
analysis that intellectually and spiritually Danilevsky had settled
down very little since the forties. There can be no question of

any but a superficial *embourgeoisement*. His book was basically about Holy Russia's Westernization and about the meaning of the modern age. His approach to these questions shows that he was as deeply concerned as he had been in the forties about problems of ultimate purpose and identity in the cultural confusion around him. By the sixties he was more involved with the modern than he had been in the forties. Indeed, he seems to have become so involved that he was having difficulty thinking about it in other than its own categories. But he was still profoundly discontented and bent on achieving some sense of meaning that would have done justice to all sides of the cultural situation he suffered. It is also clear that he had lost his humanistic sense of folly somewhere along the line. He was a fanatical, totalitarian Panslavist, one without any reservations or sense of responsibility. It would be difficult to excuse him of not in some sense wanting the great war, the liturgy of destruction, that he insisted would be God's doing, in order to achieve a utopian "Russian socialist" idea not so unlike the one to which he had adhered some twenty years earlier. Undoubtedly he was to a marked extent a prisoner of his own fantasies about God and world history. But only a rancorous, aggressive man could have worked out such a fantasy in the first place. He had more than abandoned the idea he had spoken of so proudly to the Commission of Investigation, the idea that ends never justify means. He now markedly tended to dwell on forceful and violent actions for their own sake. From one point of view, his philosophy of the deed was a sign of an irrational fascination with force and aggression, in and for themselves. Similarly, it would seem that his dialectical rhetoric was the result not only of his interpretation of cultural conflict as theologically meaningful but also of deep seated hypocrisy, for Danilevsky was extremely good at not saying what he meant. Sheer hatred and hypocrisy were key ingredients in his new philosophy. Clearly then his story since 1849 had not been — though the properly biographical data and even much of *Russia and Europe* indicate otherwise — Goncharov's "common" one.

What had really happened? The data will not allow any satisfactorily empirical explanation. But it is possible to advance a
theory of his development since 1849 that is not contrary to the
data at hand.

In order to work out an idea of what had happened to Danilevsky since the forties, we must specify more fully the feelings and
attitudes, and their interrelationships, symbolized in *Russia and
Europe*. But before getting into this, let me emphasize again that
I do not see any reason for believing that the philosophy was
simply a projection of the state of mind of its author. Many ingredients outside of Danilevsky's control went into the making
of *Russia and Europe*. Most obviously there were formal systems
of ideas: romantic Slavophilism (blended with and recast, in turn,
by the influence of Fourierism and scientific naturalism) and the
doctrines of thinkers like Adam Smith, Bentham, and Darwin,
whom Danilevsky regarded as modern, if not chronologically in
the case of the first two, then in spirit. The philosophy no doubt
also owed a crucial debt to the situation of rapid cultural change
in Russia. The fifties and sixties, the age of the great reforms, saw
a marked acceleration of the growth of modernism and Westernism in Russia; it was the time of the great debate among the intelligentsia between the romantic "fathers" and the realistic "children," the Hegelian Kirsanovs and the utilitarian Bazarovs.[31]
The very rapidity of the change from tradition-oriented romanticism to modern-oriented realism made it uniquely possible for
Danilevsky to apply utilitarian and realistic canons to Slavophilism
and Petrashevskianism, to come up with his secularized Slavophilism or main Panslavist theory, and then, contrarily, to ask a
quite romantic, Russian, sacramentalist, and immanentist question
about the meaning of the disturbingly this-worldly meaning he
had worked out. His intellectual habit of working with ideas and
groups of ideas as though they were, in some mystical way, epi-
phenomenally representative or somehow equivalent to large
social and historical movements; his related belief that a successful synthesizing of ideas was tantamount to a catching of the

historical world's changing "idea" or consciousness and to proof of a prophetic mission for himself — these owed debts, less, I think, to Hegel than to immanentist culture patterns set up by Orthodoxy and by folkish gentry-peasant society.

But *Russia and Europe* was also a product of its author's free creativity and, most important in the present context, his state of mind. After all, the same (or similar) general factors mentioned above made other kinds of romantic-realist, traditionalist-modern, Russian-Western philosophies possible at about this same time. One has but to think of the later Herzen, of Lavrov, Fedorov, Soloviev, or Dostoevsky (a most interesting case of a humanistic thinker who occasionally lapsed into a totalitarianism not dissimilar in many ways from Danilevsky's). Moreover, the cultural circumstances under which Danilevsky had worked in the forties had not been *so* different, while, under conditions which were really not different at all, he was able after about 1880 to work himself toward a new and quite humanistic outlook. Without reductiveness, *Russia and Europe* may indeed be used as an index of a certain state of mind and thus become a basis for reinterpreting the more properly biographical data and working out a more satisfactory picture of Danilevsky.

3

It is possible and useful to work at the problem of Danilevsky's personal development from 1849 to about 1869 in the light of some concepts drawn from the philosophical social psychology of Max Scheler.[32] I have in mind especially aspects of Scheler's work on the psychology of *ressentiment* (Scheler owed Nietzsche a debt here) or existential hatred. Seen from this perspective, the Danilevsky of the fifties and sixties was a man possessed by impotent hatred and by repressed feelings of vengefulness. He felt unable, however, openly to act on his aggressive impulses, so that the hatred spread, taking on a life of its own relatively without an object. His inability to express his feelings stemmed from fear

and from shame. He was afraid of spoiling his life by further
radical commitments and arrests. He was ashamed of his radical
past, ashamed of his continuous tender responses to the world in
general and to modernity in particular. Given the large, human,
spiritual, and emotional meaning that utopian radicalism had for
him, it may be said that he was ashamed of his own identity. He
wanted revenge against a world ("Europe"), which, as he saw
it, had required his self-denial and self-effacement. But ultimately,
it seems, he hated his own falsified selfhood.

Scheler tells us that *ressentiment* develops by stages.

> First of all, there is the repression of the original object of an emo-
> tion. I hate a certain person or want to take vengeance on him, and
> I am fully conscious of my reasons — of the act by which he harmed
> me, of the moral and physical trait which makes him distasteful to
> me. If I overcome my impulse by active moral energy, it does not
> disappear from consciousness, only its *expression* is checked by a clear
> moral judgment. But if, on the contrary, the impulse is "repressed,"
> it becomes more and more detached from any particular individual.
> First, it may come to bear on any of my enemy's qualities, activities,
> or judgments and on any person, relation, object, or situation which
> is connected with him in any way at all. The impulse "radiates" in
> all directions. At last it may detach itself from the man who has in-
> jured or oppressed me. Then it turns into a negative attitude toward
> certain apparent traits and qualities, no matter where or in whom
> they are found. Here lies the origin of the well-known modern phe-
> nomena of class hatred. Any appearance, gesture, dress or way of
> speaking which is symptomatic of a "class" suffices to stir up revenge
> and hatred . . . When the repression is complete, the result is a gen-
> eral negativism — a sudden, violent, seemingly unsystematic and un-
> founded rejection of things, situations, or natural objects whose loose
> connection with the original cause of the hatred can only be discov-
> ered by a complicated analysis.[33]

If the "original object" of Danilevsky's hatred is taken to be cultural rather than personal or social, that is, intellectual and institutional modernism and Westernism as he saw these in his professional milieu, then it makes considerable sense to assume that
Scheler's is a good general description of Danilevsky's develop-

ment from the 1840's, when he curbed the expression of his "hatred" (actually it seems a rather strong term for his earlier attitude) by a clear moral judgment, to the 1860's, when repression had become all but complete and *ressentiment* was at full tide in his soul. *Russia and Europe* attests to the presence of *ressentiment*. Interpreted from the point of view of existential psychology, Danilevsky's book shows a fascination with violence, aggression, and destruction largely for their own sake. The thin intellectual rationale given for these attests mostly to the author's desire to abdicate responsibility and to some of the origins of what can accurately be called his nihilism. "A secret *ressentiment* underlies every way of thinking which attributes creative power to mere negation . . . Let us . . . mention the principle of the 'dialectical method,' which wants to produce not only non-A, but even B through the negation of A." [34]

I emphasize that none of this can be established to any satisfactorily empirical degree. After all, the data are so slim that it must be wondered if we even have mention of all the really important elements. Scheler's framework merely provides a useful basis for explaining the puzzle presented by the contradictory biographical data available and for elaborating a thesis about Danilevsky's middle years.

The philosophical sin committed by Danilevsky in the sixties was that of justifying, rationalizing, even glorifying and sacramentalizing violence and hatred. His philosophy would not have been possible unless he could have drawn on a rich fund of hatred and (recalling the twisted focus of *Russia and Europe*) of deceptiveness or hypocrisy. The "fund" was not brought into existence simply for the occasion of writing *Russia and Europe*. Danilevsky was no academic philosopher. His philosophy was deeply felt, existentially most serious, "committed," in this sense quite Russian. It is not much of an assumption to say that the moral qualities of *Russia and Europe* should be taken as indices of similar and continuing qualities in the man who wrote it, as indices of the presence of *ressentiment* and of its twin, hypocrisy. These qualities evidently went back to some ordinary moral and human failures. Let us try to sketch out the story.

It began with Danilevsky's arrest and trial in 1849. Just at the time when he was outgrowing his youthful romanticism, accommodating healthily to a modern professional life, and establishing himself, he was punished, indeed, unjustly and harshly, for an intellectual and social commitment he had made, primarily on account of his own feelings of estrangement, confusion, and despair. These feelings had had some mutually reinforcing general sources. For instance, there was an individual, psychological source, for Danilevsky seems always to have been more maladjusted to the world in general than we might normally expect. There was also a cultural source, consisting of the conflict between a world view learned in a Russian childhood and the unsystematized but numerous modern Western ideas and values encountered in the world of Russian science. Romantic radicalism, utopian socialism, frequent visits to and active participation in "circles," had greatly helped to provide him with a sense of large purpose, of continuity, of meaning, of identity, and, on the individual psychological level, of distance from the world in general (it is notable, in this connection, that he was no convivial fellow even inside the Petrashevsky circle). Anger at the commitments that had led to his arrest, imprisonment, trial, and exile would not have been, in this case, mere anger at a foolish intellectual and social mistake. It would have been anger at Danilevsky's own selfhood as he understood it. In my biographical thesis, then, Danilevsky began a long period of self-rejection, self-repression, self-alienation, and false psycho-cultural adjustment in 1849. In the catalog of his writings from 1848 to 1869 there is a notable lack of titles that suggest, considering the time and place, any but the most emotionally and spiritually arid mind — a startling contrast to the Danilevsky of the forties.

But at first Danilevsky (so my thesis continues) was not the fake, "modern" tough guy of *Russia and Europe*. He had only taken some initial steps at self-repression and false accommodation. At Vologda he probably had the look of a young man chastened by suffering and being cautious and restrictive about his ideas and associates. The death of his first wife in 1853 was the next important event. In the context of the decisions Danilevsky had been making about himself since 1849, Vera's death and the terrible year of depression he suffered over it confirmed his idea that his own tender feelings (here more of a personal than a cultural phenomenon) were a source of great discomfort and trouble to him. He began to develop a "sour grapes" attitude toward his more spontaneous expectations of life. It may be notable that he courted his second wife by mail, in letters written from one of his fisheries expeditions in the far north. Strakhov tells us these letters (now lost) constitute one of the best sources available for the study of the expedition. At any rate, the new sour grapes outlook and the post-1849 attitude of intellectual and spiritual caution fitted together very well. Self-alienation moved on apace in 1853–54.

Then also in 1853 came his big chance for professional success. The data we have examined indicate that he seized upon the chance. Success as a socially useful scientist had been a central purpose of his life since his days at the Lyceum. He had stumbled once off the road. But now he was going to be the master of himself. Strakhov says that Danilevsky buried himself in his work to forget about Vera's death. It should, it seems, be added that he undertook simply to bury himself in his work. In the context of his existential development since 1849, the work was more an escape from the self of which he was ashamed and afraid than a mere diversion from external trouble. In *Russia and Europe* Danilevsky told his readers again and again that only realistic, hard, political action could burn metaphysics, romanticism, and poetry out of the Russian soul. Work had earlier become his own *rite de passage*.

Now culturally and intellectually times were changing in Russia and in Western Europe by the mid-fifties. Romanticism was coming under heavy attack. Realism, positivism, pragmatism, encouraged in Russia by the preparations for the great reforms, were very much in the air. Being modern was coming to mean something new, for modernity was now — or so it seemed to many men — beginning not only to challenge traditionalism, but also to dictate, as it were, the ways in which that challenge should be understood. In the new climate of opinion, spiritual and intellectual not just vocational commitment was demanded. I believe that Danilevsky interpreted the cultural change of the 1850's in this fashion and that he viewed the demand of the times for a deeper commitment to modernity as one to which he was eager to respond. A commitment to the utilitarian, the sectarian, thin, mechanistic liberalism and to the nationalism and Panslavism now rampant in his immediate and larger environments offered several advantages. Such a commitment would provide a firm social reinforcement to his own difficult effort at self-repression. More important, however, a commitment to a much more modern way of thinking would ostensibly provide him with a socially and culturally acceptable way of seeking meaning and identity. He could thus relieve tension, for ostensibly escape and self-repression would no longer be so necessary — if one could find a sense of meaning in the modern age. This idea was rendered even more attractive by the anti-West but pro-modern nationalist and Panslavist element in the new climate of opinion. This element suggested that the very practice he had in mind — to reject himself as a way of being himself — was an authentically human one. The new cultural and intellectual atmosphere seemed to provide a call to conversion rather than to further repression. From my point of view, it provided him with a chance to falsify the fact of his own hypocrisy. Strong commitment to the new cultural strands became the linchpin of his existential edifice. The liberalism, nationalism, and Panslavism in *Russia and Europe* are both overzealous and false. This is because they were developed in the light of a personal world view which was a subtly false surrogate for something (the old attitudes and ideas of the forties) that Danilevsky, on some level, still believed that he believed; for he had never really taken the effort to check his former thinking; he had only run away from it. His liberalism and nationalism were to him crucial aspects of an effort at ultimate self-deception.

The "liberalism" and "Panslavism" which he tried to implant in himself fell upon peculiarly rich soil, for by now his insulted and injured self was reacting strongly out of impulses of revolt, anger, and hatred. These feelings blended well with modern ideologies, so negativistic almost by definition at that time especially. And Danilevsky, now rancorous and aggressive, found it possible to a degree to express himself by championing a somewhat too utilitarian and bitter realism and by attacking romanticism, altruism, immanentism, humanitarianism. The conversion to realism, utilitarianism, and to nonmetaphysical and militant nationalism served him well. It allowed him to deceive himself about his own refusal to seek a sense of meaning and identity. It provided him with a socially acceptable language for sublimated expression of his anger at himself. It also deflected his anger at himself for his repression of his true longings. It allowed him to view his problems as external and general to his country and his time rather than as internal and specific to himself. It promised, in short, a way of aligning his uncomfortably conflicting angers: the anger at his more genuine identity (as he saw it) and the anger against his self-effacement. He was now able to a degree to transvaluate his values. What had once been challenge (modernity) to him became response; what had once been problem became solution; what had once been other, self. He who had been an honest and attractively human radical intellectual had made himself into a negativistic hypocrite.

The flowering in Danilevsky of that human and moral disease which Scheler called *ressentiment* was, of course, made possible by circumstances as well as by our subject's own existential decisions. I picture him, from the early or mid-fifties, committing himself repeatedly and increasingly subconsciously to a fake but potentially dangerous toughness, to a forced accommodation with a world and with ideas that really upset him. As he began to achieve some success in working out this way of life, however, some forces, external and internal, began to work with him. There was the temper of the time — as Herzen noted so perceptively,[35] sour, "bilious," militantly "realistic," utilitarian, antipoetic. Even the scientific culture of Europe was changing and the newly dominant popular positivism that replaced the older rationalism was, appropriately for the time, narrow, dogmatic, and apodictic. *Russia and Europe*, as we shall see, shows definite influence of the new scientific culture. It must have seemed to him sensible, even human, to have repressed and then transvalued his own longings. Was not everybody doing it? The new cultural materials which Danilevsky found at hand provided excellent grist for his mill. As Scheler has noted rather persuasively, the culture of modernity is laden with rancor, especially, it might be added, for one who is susceptible to this aspect. The more spacious ideas and the more humanistic values of the previous decades might have made Danilevsky's project more difficult. On the other hand, the culture and thought of those same earlier decades, lingering into the fifties and sixties (especially in Danilevsky's mind, for he had never taken the trouble to re-evaluate his earlier commitments squarely and honestly) may themselves also have contributed to his moral and spiritual decadence. One who saw quest for meaning and human identity in terms of the fantasies of Fourier, for example, may be said to have been confronted, as the climate of opinion shifted radically, with a dilemma as well as a choice. Danilevsky may have been encouraged to dishonesty by the language in which he was inclined, by his previous cultural and intellectual experience, to understand intellectual and spiritual honesty. If the culture of modernity was so sourly realistic that it could provide him with a language in which to express the rancor in himself, then the romantic version of traditionalism that he knew was so sickly sweet that it may have seemed to impugn itself. The rapidity and the specific quality of the cultural and intellectual change of the fifties was most conducive to Danilevsky's existential project. Then, too, as time went on, there may well have developed a sense of financial, status, and interpersonal vested interests in maintaining an established image, an image dependent on a false life style. To have "gone back" might have cost money, position, genuine friendships — or so it may have seemed to the increasingly successful Danilevsky.

There should be noted too the very real possibility of the operation of other psychological forces inside Danilevsky. In working with Scheler's insights we need not and should not omit the possibility of contributions to Danilevsky's existential hatred from psychic forces such as those described by Freud and his successors.[36] Without allowing for the operation of these, I find it difficult to understand the mechanics of the psychological phenomena described by Scheler; indeed, he himself allowed for such factors. In ordinary language, there are lurking bestial qualities in all men. Thus under some circumstances love is difficult, creative, and provokes anxiety, not just because the external world is complicated and challenging, but also because of contrary drives within us. Hating is easy and the appetite comes with the eating. More specifically, it is not difficult to appreciate that Danilevsky's ethical and rational decisions about himself allowed his unconscious negative feelings to be brought to the surface. For instance, *Russia and Europe* may be interpreted, from one point of view, as an expression of a rampant oedipus complex. Europe, aggressive, intrusive, imperialistic, a distinctly male, paternal symbol was the object (insofar as he had one) of Danilevsky's hatred. Russia, an obvious mother figure, permissive, cooperative, easygoing, needed to be rescued. That would take a war, perhaps because Danilevsky's father had been an army officer, for Danilevsky had had no other close contact with the military in his life. Success in the war would allow Danilevsky to have "Russia" to himself. And then there was even associated with this the dream of an end of time, a return to the beginning. Copulation with the mother in a Freudian oedipal drama has the purpose of a return to the maternal womb. Danilevsky's probably extraordi-

narily deep attachment to his mother ("Russia") in the first place
may have originated in another problem; his idea that violent behavior would eventuate in a satisfying union is reminiscent of a
weaning tantrum. Or we may put the business in different way,
in terms of Freud's later metapsychology. The more a person
surrenders to the utilitarian reality principle (and this was precisely Danilevsky's story in the fifties) and chances of implementing the pleasure principle became increasingly remote and
scarce, the more that person is inclined both to despair and to
aggressive feelings against himself. Projection of these aggressive
feelings outward, in socially acceptable form, is necessary to keep
him from suicide, or from facing himself. The world-encom-
passing, nihilistically destructive nature of *Russia and Europe*
suggests that Danilevsky could well have "benefited" from some
such cycle of forces, a cycle rendered unusually volatile by his
own repeated and willful self-repressions. But, let it be emphasized, even allowing, as it seems we should, for many extenuating
contributory factors, external and internal, in the development of
Danilevsky's angry soul, it does not appear at all possible to assign
to anything but his own decisions the ultimate responsibility for
his unfortunate development. These factors were not causes; they
were *conditiones sine qua non*.

On this general line of observation the puzzling contradiction
between the properly biographical data and the import of *Russia
and Europe* may be explained. If we posit that Danilevsky was,
on the whole, only falsely and superficially accommodating to
his professional life in the fifties but nevertheless making a serious
and partly successful effort at this false adjustment, then we might
expect to find just such a contradiction, one between data suggesting a pretty thorough *embourgeoisement*, on the one hand,
and data (*Russia and Europe*) suggesting that this was not genuine, on the other. The puzzle in the sources appears itself to be
one key to the problem of Danilevsky's personal development.

Prior to his decision about 1860 to return to romantic philosophizing, then, Danilevsky's personal story seems to have been

one of lengthy self-repression and self-effacement. These actions were undertaken because he feared the consequences (political or just plain accidental as in the case of Vera's death) of honest spiritual and intellectual commitments and of too optimistic expectations of life. And they were undertaken also because of shame, in the presence of successful, modern, and quite honestly adjusted friends and associates, about his past and about being "Russian" in a now socially unacceptable sense. That is, he was ashamed of being backward, sentimental, romantic, unscientific, unprogressive, impractical. Kept up persistently over years, self-repressive practices became relatively habitual. Developing material vested interests and socially flattering connections helped to consolidate and to justify the new spiritual, intellectual, cultural, and emotional habits. But psychological factors, existential and behavioral alike, led to an unintended (though still accepted) consequence: the development of explosive, only partly controllable and increasingly objectless feelings of hatred and revengefulness.

Thus the "fund" of hatred and the facility of doubletalking that were key prerequisites for *Russia and Europe* had been developed in Danilevsky by Danilevsky over a long period. Appropriately his big philosophical work contains a most prominent but false doctrine of utilitarian liberalism and nationalism. Biographically speaking, this may be taken as a symbol of his hatred of tradition and of his romanticized self. Equally appropriately, on the other hand, *Russia and Europe* also suggests the presence of a still deeper hostility, a hatred, as it were, of his own hatred of the traditional. Danilevsky was angry at himself for his own self-repression. He was thus only partly successful in his project. He was unable to consolidate fully, even with the help of society, ideology, and culture his modernistic existential strategy. And that was apparently an important reason for his writing *Russia and Europe* in the first place.

Now in this last connection, it should be noted that *Russia and Europe* itself (that is, the acts of working it out and publishing it, acts to which its existence attests) must be taken as evidence not only of self-repression, but also as evidence of some moving away from this practice on Danilevsky's part. There must have been another stage of development beyond that just described, a step back, some sort of return to honesty. After all, the book does come out publicly, however obliquely and vaguely, in favor of the traditional. While modernity is not interpreted as a historical deviation — quite the contrary — Danilevsky did "say" that he was uncomfortable with it, that it was alienating and uprooting and that there was need to find its meaning. Moreover, he published the work in a new magazine, *Zariia*, whose editorial policy was frankly and proudly one of defending higher values, "Russia," and the like against the onslaught of materialism, secularism, and Westernism. Danilevsky accepted help in finding a publisher from N. N. Strakhov, a basically romantic neo-Slavophil and a renewed acquaintance of the forties. Through Strakhov he may have had other similar contacts. Perhaps it is notable here that he met Dostoevsky again in 1871.[37] Both the content of *Russia and Europe* and the circumstances surrounding its publication attest that, sometime in the later fifties or early sixties, Danilevsky decided to turn again to the old business of philosophic searching, for himself and for his country. His life historical pattern as a whole in the sixties thus resembles the dualistic pattern of the forties. The main difference (leaving aside the presence of new ideas like Slavophilism in the later period) is that the man of the sixties was a fanatic. And this raises again our basic question, by no means as yet fully explored: how had he come to be this way?

Of course, we cannot really know. But let us place his philosophizing of the sixties in the context of his existential development since the forties. At least, we can close our theoretical traverse. Danilevsky's intellectual fanaticism had several roots. He had been away from philosophy for a long time and that for the reasons I have described. But he had not been entirely successful in his personal project. A spiritual and intellectual crisis had set in. His inner tensions had become unbearable and he had decided to go back to his older more honest ways. In the context of his life experience and culture, this meant searching for the spiritual meaning of history, particularly in regard to Russia's modernization and Westernization. It also meant becoming a utopian socialist again; and perhaps too, as his renewed contacts with Strakhov may suggest, it meant seeking out members of the intelligentsia proper, for Danilevsky seems ever to have associated the institutional foci of his life with his varying senses of the desirable qualities of meaning. But the prodigal son found that life had gone on in his absence. The intelligentsia and its particular kind of intellectuality were changing. Without losing basic commitment to tradition, much of Russian philosophic life was being heavily influenced by the new realism, utilitarianism, and positivism. Danilevsky would have seen this in Strakhov himself.[38] Russian intellectuality was now more of a mixture of realism and romanticism. Thus Danilevsky's apparent intention of returning to the intellectual "fathers" of the forties had to be worked out intellectually in new ways. One had now to be an up-to-date romantic. And there was involved in such a task of redefinition the possibility, actually more real than the intellectual situation of the forties had provided, of what is now called totalitarianism, for that sort of doctrine is characteristically a dialectical mixture of romanticism and realism. Now let us add two other elements to this whole situation. The Danilevsky who confronted the mixed intellectual situation of the sixties was not a morally, spiritually or emotionally healthy person. He could not quickly turn off his aggressive and rancorous feeling. A mere return to philosophic searching could not, in the short run anyway, help him. He was not now the sort of human being likely to be tolerant and constructive. Then add the fact that the ambiguous intellectual situation offered him a chance to relieve his tensions directly and quickly, without the necessity of really facing himself, his failures, his dishonesty; the intellectual and cultural situation of the sixties offered the possibility (which, as we know, Danilev-

sky seized upon) of an expression of his conflicting angers in
social and cultural language. Taking advantage of this, he thus
achieved, not an advance toward truth but a further degree of
human and moral decadence: his philosophy is all too easily taken
as a destructive nihilism with some elaborate rationalizing and
self-exonerating intellectual paraphernalia. As an intellectual document *Russia and Europe* is a fanatical book about the spiritual
meaning of modern times. As a biographical document, it tells us
of an evil man, one using good for evil purposes, "honesty" to
maintain some lies about himself. Danilevsky was partly like
Dostoevsky's man from underground. He was openly resentful
and aggressive because he had made himself that way; he had
to begin to be himself by accepting the self he had degraded
and by acting on its induced feelings and taking the responsibility
for them. Yet *Russia and Europe* does not in fact indicate that
its author was consciously resentful and hostile, and, in a way,
proud of it. That author rather claims that forces, "history,"
"Providence," are responsible for his predicament. Thus Danilevsky was probably more like Stavrogin in *The Possessed*, the character who used a false repentance as a defense against a true one.
The character Shatov in the same novel also comes to mind.[39]
Danilevsky continued to blame his *ressentiment* on the world.
He thus refused to forgive and to accept himself. He preferred
to justify and even sacralize his sins against himself.

While it is useful to compare Danilevsky to literary characters
like Stavrogin or Shatov, the limitations of such parallels must,
of course, be recognized. Men in history are much more complex
than characters in novels and the historian can scarcely ever pattern his material completely. Thus to say that Danilevsky of the
sixties was a hypocrite, a fanatic, and a hate-monger is only to
describe one facet, however striking and important, of his makeup. No doubt he was much more complicated than that. After
all, his constructive professional work on the fisheries was carried
on at the same time as his philosophical work. Danilevsky was
only a part time Stavrogin.

Much has been written by modern scholars about the origins of totalitarianism as an intellectual, spiritual, and moral phenomenon. There seems to be fairly general agreement that it is occasioned by a sense of loneliness and uprootedness and superfluousness, a sense of "alienation," developed under at once stimulating and frustrating modern cultural conditions. Totalitarianism can arise (it is a "disease of transition") when modern secular, scientistic culture and more tradition-oriented, sacramental culture confront one another; when a lonely man attempts to maintain the temper of the latter in the language of the former; when there is advocated the use of modern means to traditionalist ends; when such practice is regarded as providential or "necessary." Danilevsky's story seems to fit the pattern closely. But let it be emphasized that the "freedom," the loneliness, the *Meinungschaos* from which he sought to escape were not just the products of modernity. Danilevsky alienated himself; modern culture was but an appropriate vehicle for this. While his story may illustrate the dynamics of several similar theories of the origins of totalitarianism, it seems also to testify that he used his freedom in his effort to escape from it. Maybe there was a necessity in that.

5

LATER YEARS

D ANILEVSKY's thinking continued into the eighties to follow the lines of *Russia and Europe*. But toward the very end of his life he was beginning to work himself away from his totalitarian intellectual position. At the time of his death this change was apparently still in process. A brief discussion of his later years (about 1875 to 1885) will serve several purposes. Besides "completing" his biography, it will record the morally important fact of some change for the better in his thinking. And such change attests again to his intellectual and moral freedom.

The available biographical facts[1] are few and quickly told. The years 1875 to 1880 marked a lengthy respite from the usual official duties and field work. Danilevsky spent much of his time at home at Mshatka in the Crimea[2] doing research in biology, especially regarding Darwin's theory of evolution. Toward the end of this period he became interested in the imperial botanical garden in the Yalta district, the Nikitsky Sad;[3] from September to December 1879 and from May to November 1880 he was acting director of this center of research and education on grapes and wine. This last activity became the beginning of a return to his former role as full-time government scientist. On October 2, 1880, he discovered vinicultural lice or phylloxera in the arbor of a Crimean neighbor. He petitioned Alexander II to forbid the importation of foreign grapevines (the lice really were a "Western" influence in Russia). The tsar acted accordingly and also appointed Danilevsky chairman of a Crimean Phylloxera Commission charged with supervising the destruction of infected and suspect vines in Thessaly (outside the Russian border) and in the Crimea. Danilevsky took a two-month trip, starting in December 1880, to Switzerland and southern France to learn more about methods of dealing with grape lice. The affair became so important in the eyes of the Petersburg authorities that it was decided to put someone with more prestige at the head of it. One Baron Andrei Nikolaevich Korf became Danilevsky's superior until 1883. When Korf retired in that year, however, Danilevsky, who had continued all along in the field work, resumed the directorship. As late as the year of his death he was still fighting this "battle," [4] as he called it, for he attended a phylloxera congress in Tiflis in April 1885. But it is perhaps appropriate that he died while on a last fisheries expedition, an arduous one over the Caucasus mountains to study the causes of a decline in the catch on Lake Gokcha. A leg injury and a mild heart attack during his April visit to Tiflis had impaired his vigor. He completed the fish survey but, back in Tiflis writing his report, he died of a heart attack, on November 7, 1885. His body was brought back to Mshatka for burial.

As to the overall pattern of this decade, the dualism of practical and intellectual activity continued. Danilevsky published a number of angry Panslavist articles during and right after the Russo-Turkish war of 1877–78 and then, in the eighties, some others dealing with currently controversial cultural subjects. He also made some notes for a revision of *Russia and Europe*. Most of the intellectual effort of his later years, however, went into biology and philosophy of science. The biggest of his later works was in this field, the monumental *Darwinism*, in two huge volumes. It was still unfinished at the time of his death. In connection with these intellectual interests, all through this last period he continued his close friendship with the neo-Slavophil N. N. Strakhov. Strakhov, who was also on good terms with Dostoevsky and Tolstoi, was a frequent visitor at Mshatka. He regarded himself as Danilevsky's disciple and he was later to set forth his own version of his master's ideas, both historical and biological, in numerous articles, lauding Danilevsky as a man of great "Russian" wisdom.

The diverse intellectual writings from this period do not present a clear picture. Neither the chronology nor the precise nature of the change in Danilevsky's thinking can be satisfactorily traced. His articles on the Russo-Turkish war and those on liberal constitutionalism, the origins of nihilism, and Vladimir Soloviev's ecumenicalism were conceived almost entirely in the spirit of *Russia and Europe*. He cited it frequently in the discussion of the war. But turning to *Darwinism* we are confronted with several new phenomena. There is the fact that Danilevsky now presents himself, honestly and lengthily as an anti-Darwinian. His criticism of Darwinism is no longer, as in *Russia and Europe*, merely one of the details of the theory (mainly that the struggle for existence took place between groups rather than between individuals). The fundamentals of the doctrine are criticized. This means that Danilevsky was now rejecting a point of view which, though used ambiguously, had been an essential ingredient of *Russia and Europe*. The doctrine set forth there is inconceivable without some kind of adherence to utilitarianism, Benthamism, and Darwinism. In *Darwinism* Danilevsky explicitly and fully rejected all these facets of what he called "the English outlook." Moreover, the theory of evolution to which he now adhered, a theory borrowed chiefly from Karl Ernst von Baer, was a neo-Aristotelian teleological one. This was also quite inconsistent with *Russia and Europe*. Though that work does contain a teleological philosophy of history, it is an aspect that is kept latent (it is "God's" point of view) and entirely separate from the tough action program, whose conception is based on Bentham's and Darwin's theories. Apparently, at least in regard to biology, Danilevsky was now being more consistent, straightforward, and honest about his ultimate convictions. Finally, he explicitly recognized that his teleological theory of evolution had to be developed on philosophical grounds. He even defended the practice of philosophical speculation. *Darwinism* therefore seems to attest to a drastic change of outlook. The impression one gets from the whole body of his later writings is rather confusing — especially when one remembers also that Danilevsky, as Strakhov tells us and as Danilevsky's own fragmentary notes show,[5] was preparing a revision of *Russia and Europe*.

If we remember, however, that Danilevsky worked mainly on biology and the philosophy of science during this decade and further that *Darwinism* was written later than most of his other work (it was unfinished when he died), it is possible to see some order in all of this. On this line of observation, he may be said to have been undergoing a process of intellectual change all through his later years, a process that apparently accelerated and strengthened as time went on. But by the year of his death this change was still largely restricted to the area of biology and related philosophy, and had not yet extended into history, political theory, and cultural analysis. There was a lag on these matters, though there are appropriately some vague signs of change even here.

Had Danilevsky lived on and extended his biological ideas into the philosophy of history, it seems quite probable that he would have developed an outlook similar to that of Herzen or, with a Christian bent, of Dostoevsky, whom he occasionally cited in these years. That is, he would have posited (in a mythopoetic but responsible, nontotalitarian fashion) an immanent, divinely instituted or at least objectively existent teleological principle in world history; and, on this basis, he would have viewed the developments, sequential or contemporaneous, of nations and civilizations as orderly steps in a progress toward an all-human, Christian (or utopian) socialist civilization and an end of history, a sort of Joachite new dispensation. Russia would have been assigned a messianic role in the last stage of history. As his commentaries on Humboldt and Fourier suggest, Danilevsky had been groping for something like this since the forties. Behind the utilitarian, Darwinian facade, there is in *Russia and Europe* such a view of history. The evolutionary theory in *Darwinism*, though relating only to organic nature, is even similar in spirit to some of the less prominent historical theory in *Russia and Europe*. There was a marked consistency of sorts in Danilevsky's most fundamental philosophical convictions throughout his life.

Such appears to be the picture of Danilevsky's last intellectual period. Only the most general outline is discernible. It does appear reasonably certain, however, that by the eighties he was changing intellectually for the better, becoming both more rational and more responsible. What I have called his totalitarianism was breaking up. Dealing first with his articles and then with *Darwinism*, let us view the situation as it is reflected concretely in his writings.

2

The Russo-Turkish war of 1877–78[6] was one of a series of nineteenth century events growing out of the Eastern question, that large international political conundrum posed by the simultaneous decrepitude of the Ottoman empire, the rise of Balkan nationalisms, and the jockeying of the European powers, now in the interest of aggrandizement, now simply in that of preserving the balance of power. For a time, both politically and militarily, the Russians did well in the war of 1877–78. At the beginning much of European opinion (Disraeli stood out as one notable and fateful exception) was pro-Russian, for the war had been precipitated by rebellions of obviously much oppressed Balkan peoples against a villainous Turkish regime. The massacre of rebels and innocents by Turks, together with Gladstone's public protest, *The Bulgarian Horrors*, further enhanced Western European sympathies for Russia's military actions. In a politically friendly atmosphere the Russians were able to push vigorously against the Turks. After a difficult campaign in the Balkan mountains, they drove easily to Adrianople. With Constantinople threatened, the

Turks sued for peace. By the treaty of San Stefano, Turkey ceded Russia Batum and Kars, granted independence to Serbia and Rumania, promised reforms in Bosnia, and granted autonomy to a large new Bulgarian state, which would clearly become a Russian satellite. The Western powers, however, now found themselves unable to tolerate such an accretion of Russian power. Disraeli and Bismarck undertook, at the Congress of Berlin, to force a revision of San Stefano. Under the new treaty of Berlin the Russians kept Batum and Kars while the Serbs and Rumanians were still granted independence. But the tsarist diplomats had to agree to a smaller, less easily dominated Bulgaria and — in return for even this reduced gain in influence — to compensation of Austria-Hungary with the right to "occupy and administer" Bosnia, and compensation of the British with Cyprus. Both Russian official circles and public opinion were bitterly disappointed.

As far as Russian public opinion was concerned, the war had been an unusually heady affair. The years of the "breakfast war" (so-called in England because of interest all over Europe in daily morning newspaper dispatches) marked the high point of Russian political Panslavism. Under the circumstances it seemed realistic to many people to believe that Russia was now after centuries actually saving little Slavic or at least Orthodox brothers from the terrors of Islam and the barbarian Turks. European sympathies for Russia's cause helped encourage the complementary notion that the war was in the interest of the highest ideals of civilization. The press was full of Panslavic editorials and articles, at once euphoric and belligerent. Charitable contributions and volunteers streamed to the south. Because of all this furor and jingoism the Berlin congress proved unusually disappointing to the public.

Danilevsky's two nearly book-length sets of Panslavist articles, "The War for Bulgaria" and "Woe to the Victors!" [7] were occasioned by the war, the public uproar, and the Berlin congress. Connected as closely as it was with international politics where continual and rapid change was the rule, Danilevsky's totalitarian philosophy required at least occasional commentary on the shifting political scene. He had felt called on before, in 1871, to discuss the significance of a major event, the Franco-Prussian war; his article on this subject was published as an appendix to the 1871 edition of *Russia and Europe*.[8] The articles of the later seventies were another effort of the same kind. Those collected under the title "The War for Bulgaria" were written during the war; "Woe to the Victors!" concerns the Congress of Berlin.

Both sets contain detailed political discussion of the changing situation. During the war itself Danilevsky was concerned with the elaboration of immediate war aims. He advised an effort to achieve a personal union between Russia and Rumania together with Russian diplomatic hegemony over Turkey and specific gains by various Balkan peoples. He desired all this mainly in order that there be created a basis for the eventual breakdown of the "moral barriers between northeastern and southern Slavs." This would be, in his view, an important step on the road to later Panslavic political achievements and the furthest point which, practically speaking, could at present be attained. Though he thought it might not be impossible to acquire Constantinople, he advised against it: out of deference to friendly Europe (the Western powers and public were still pro-Russian at this point) and its fears for the balance of power, "Tsargrad" should be left for now in Turkish hands. During the preparation for the Berlin congress and the meeting itself, he undertook an analysis of Russia's diplomatic and military mistakes (Erzurum, Gallipoli, and the Bosporus should have been seized as a basis for a firmer bargaining position), gave an explanation straight out of *Russia and Europe* of the history and causes of Russian softness in international politics, and thoroughly vilified the Western powers, especially England. While the adjective "moderate" is scarcely descriptive of Danilevsky's tone, the reader unfamiliar with his philosophy could easily mistake this discussion for mere nationalist political "realism." But, in fact, on closer examination, the consistency of these writings with *Russia and Europe* is most apparent. To appreciate this it is important to find out why Danilevsky insisted on keeping his own and his readers' attention focused so tightly on the immediate political realities.

In the first set of articles he advised his readers, whom he regarded as unduly excited, not to expect a *solution* of the Eastern question from the current war. That question was actually much larger than they seemed to think. Its ultimate solution would require a whole "period of struggle" and not just against the Turks. The present war was only "the first step." This was its true significance and it would have this even if Russia lost the war. "Some years ago I devoted a large book to the Eastern question, both in its cultural and in its political aspect. Now I will talk only about politics not just because people are interested in this at the present moment but also because it is my firm conviction that the political is the base on which a cultural edifice can be built and not the reverse as many people think." [9] Here he was expressing his old idea (in itself extreme but nontotalitarian) that the national psyche needed to mature and that that could be achieved only in the practice of *Realpolitik* or, as he sometimes put it, *Gelegenheitspolitik*. "The Serbian revolt did more for the development of Slavic consciousness than reams of literary works." [10] "Every organism, whether individual (like man) or complex (like the state) or collective (like a system of states) becomes conscious of itself only when the ego is faced with the non-ego," he put the point more generally in "Woe to the Victors!" [11] On this level Danilevsky was not concentrating on the events at hand because he was being moderate or realistic. The process of struggle was a cure for national psychological immaturity, a cure far superior to any mere intellectual discussion. In his view, it was important to make maximum use of the belligerent opportunities at hand. Hence his insistence on the significance of the war ("the first step") for the Panslav cause even if Russia lost.

A little later on in the first set of articles he suggested another reason for concentrating upon the tasks at hand. "The logic of events, the logic of history is often opposed to individual logic. Whoever recognizes that history is run by some higher (unknowable) reason will prefer the logic of events to individual logic." [12] Here was the totalitarianism again. Men were toys of a mysterious but orderly History. "The hand of God is clearly visible in this whole affair, beginning with the revolt of Herzegovina." [13] The deeds of the moment were determined. *Realpolitik*, narrowly conceived, was a series of sacred actions, ways at once of being with and becoming closer to a developing, immanent sacred force struggling for integration. Thus too, as he was soon to explain in "Woe to the Victors!" what appeared as evil was really, dialectically, but the objective form of goodness. "In order for the policy of Russia to be successful . . . it should adhere to its constantly guiding principle, to *Russo-Slavic egoism* [his italics] . . . But 'what about the selfless interest of mankind generally?' cry naïve political idealists . . . In the first place, strictly speaking, no one knows, in fact, what the selfless interest of mankind generally consists in . . . in the second place, at the present period of history, Russo-Slavic egoism corresponds with the selfless interest of mankind generally." [14] In these war articles of the later seventies Danilevsky concentrated attention upon concrete and limited political goals, not because he was a mere realist but because such concentration was a way of realizing a presumed providential historical role. This intellectual behavior was entirely consistent with his most important presuppositions.

Given his evident belief that intense and irresponsible concentration on the deeds at hand was an imperative laid down by a mysterious Providence, these articles must be taken as elaborations of the philosophy he had worked out a decade earlier. He was still a crank about the Eastern question, "the knot that is the straits." Providentially, man's (or Russian man's) currently modern, realistic state of mind, properly accepted and acted on, was the objective form of God-in-History's present state of consciousness. Human actions were providential actions. A lengthy existential state of *Realpolitik* and war related to the Eastern question was in the offing. Gradually the Panslav Union with its capital at Constantinople would be achieved. At every step there would be worse trouble between Russia and "Europe," but at every step too Russia, at once more mature psychologically and more united politically and morally with the Slavs, would be more able to fight and to succeed. Eventually, at about the time the Union was realized or nearly so, there would ensue a final total war between East and West, a war that would burn out all human imperfections and end with the dawn of a "pan-human," final civilization, a utopian socialist heaven on earth.

The attentive reader of these war articles will readily detect the mystique behind the superficially sober political realism. Danilevsky was not concerned only with an international political situation. Larger things, he kept insisting, were involved. Thus Russia was not really fighting with the Turks but with Europe, as Danilevsky had long ago predicted.

In my book *Russia and Europe* I said of Russia's relations to Turkey and Europe after the Crimean War, "the Mohammedan-Turkish episode in the development of the Eastern question is finished. The fog has dispersed and the opponents stand face to face, awaiting awesome events; in fear both sides hold back as long as possible to avoid the inevitable war as long as God permits. Henceforth a war between Russia and Turkey has become impossible and useless, a struggle between Slavdom and Europe, possible and inevitable — a struggle which will be decided finally not in one year, not in one campaign, but which will take up a whole historical epoch." Were my words justified? Did this prediction come true . . . ? Evidently only in part; but if we penetrate into the essence of the matter, things turned out completely as predicted . . . Though the external facts indicating the contrary are indisputable, we assert that all this is only appearance, only a mirage, an illusion . . . in reality, under the guise of a war with Turkey, we fought a war with Europe.[15]

Nor was Europe to Danilevsky just a political entity; it was rather the historical incarnation of evil. In general the Europeans were "wolves" trying to maraud the Christian innocents of the East. More specifically (and here Danilevsky's peculiar radicalism manifested itself), they were the philistine, commercial, materialistic English with their allies on the continent, "the banking, stock-exchange, speculating Europe, generally recognized under the name bourgeoisie, with their organs, the *Revue des Deux Mondes* and the *Journal des Débats*." [16] If, as some people proposed, "Tsargrad" or Constantinople were to be made a free city, these reactionary, jesuitical schemers would destroy all moral and human decency there. With their "stock-exchange materialism" they would debauch the city morally and make it into a breeding ground for nihilistic radicals and papal subversives alike. England, now in Danilevsky's view the dominant force in Europe, was a "plunderer," a "thief," and an "incendiary." [17] In this paranoid historical world, not Russia and Turkey, not even Slavdom and "Europe," but Good and Evil were at war in 1877–78.

From this last period of Danilevsky's life we have also three articles on cultural topics: "Some Words about the Constitutional Agitation in Our 'Liberal Press' " (1882); "The Origins of Our Nihilism" (1884); "Mr. Vladimir Soloviev on Orthodoxy and Catholicism" (1885).[18] In the first he addressed himself to some proposals in the "liberal press" for a written constitution and a Russian parliament. He said the proposals were ridiculous, for the existent political institutions of Russia were organic to its unique historical development and to the character of the people. The autocracy was unlimited because this was the will of history and of the people (*narodnaia volia*). Any but a merely opinion-sampling national representative body (he vaguely echoed the Slavophil idea of restoring the *Zemsky Sobor*) would be meaningless, for, despite the paper limitations imposed by a constitution, "the people would continue to regard the tsar as unlimited." If a Russian parliament were to be instituted and along with it a Left, a Right, a Center, "white gloves," journalists, ladies in the gallery, oratorical fulminations, the word "foolishness" would ring out "from all corners of the Russian land."

The article on the origins of nihilism was similarly self-assured and dogmatic. It was directed against two articles in the journal

Rus, by a certain Constantine Tolstoi, a physician of intellectual bent, on the subject of the origins of nihilism. Tolstoi, an amusing hedonist of the worst imaginable variety, had held that nihilism ("I am the number one") had been a new morality; it had arisen in response to the decay of Christianity and as a replacement of Christian ethics. "Yudushkas and Tartuffes" had ruined it, however, by mixing it up with altruistic morality and leftism; and this made it now easy to misunderstand its true origins and significance. Danilevsky, of course, utterly disagreed. Orthodox Christianity had never decayed nor had modern culture made it irrelevant. Nihilism had never had any basis, situational, cultural, or spiritual, in Russia. Indeed, it had originated in the West as an appropriate expression of European "violent" national character. European history (Danilevsky repeated some theory from *Russia and Europe*) had been the story of the gradual uncovering and ever purer realization of the "violence," the authoritarian negativism of that character. Catholicism, Protestantism, deism, secularism, revolution, exploitative capitalism, anarchism (which Danilevsky thought a perverted, "European" version of socialism), and nihilism — these had been the key stages of development. Feuerbach, Strauss, Stirner, Vogt, Moleschott, Büchner, Haeckel, Lassalle, and Marx — these expressed the ultimate essence of European character. Being a doctrine of Western origin, nihilism was without any historical or cultural basis in Russia and Tolstoi was entirely wrong. The only native condition that had bred nihilists had been the insidious Russian tradition of "imitativeness," which had begun with the Westernism of the forties.

Soloviev was criticized harshly. Danilevsky found only nonsense in the theory that Orthodoxy and Roman Catholicism were but Eastern and Western divisions of one ecumenical Christian Church.

Mr. Soloviev is without doubt a man of philosophical turn of mind. This is a rather rare and very valuable quality, but, like every intellectual and indeed moral quality, it also has its weaknesses, which compel it to fall into the defects of its own virtues. Experience shows that the chief deficiency or defect of philosophical minds, that is, metaphysically philosophical, is the tendency toward symmetrical conclusions. In their construction of the world according to the logical laws of the mind, there appears a schematism; and within schemes, everything is beautifully reduced to symmetrical headings, which are, in turn, subdivided symmetrically. Then they (the philosophical minds) find justification for their schematism in that which is supposedly clearly manifested in the objective phenomena of the world . . . When the crude, stubborn facts have not surrendered to this symmetry, they have nudged and pushed them, they have given them, in the apt French expression, a *coup de plume*.[19]

Danilevsky found it appropriate to refute Soloviev by contrasting his vision of the ecclesiastical world with a mass of "crude, stubborn facts" organized to reinforce some stock Orthodox theory about the history of Catholicism and Orthodoxy. He concluded that Soloviev's foolish ideas were mostly the result of his fascination with the number three.

It is a little difficult to characterize these articles. On the one hand, they show affinities to *Russia and Europe*. There are affinities of detail: the dogmatic neo-Slavophilism according to which Europe was providentially damned and Russia saved; the crude idealization of the Russian people, Russian history, the Russian form of government (the "real" one, that is, the democratic Rousseauist monarchy, not the perverted one he criticized in 1877–78, the one in the hands of the "stock exchange materialists"); the hints of socialism, native to Russia, warped and impossible of realization in the West; the iron determinism. Danilevsky's intellectual style is also reminiscent of his big work. I mean his positivist-scientific approach to large, basically philosophical questions. In regard to cultural and political matters alike, Danilevsky was still not prepared to admit, most of the time, that values, beliefs, and goals were matters of human, of rational and ethical responsibility. Using scientistic language he was still bent on assigning responsibility for his own versions of these ultimates to forces that were as objective and knowable, to his way of thinking, as those discoverable in nature by scientific methods. His description of Soloviev's "metaphysically philosophical" mind could accurately have been applied to his own. But he was not so applying it. On the other hand, there is no sign in these articles from the eighties of the further, related, specifically totalitarian conviction that the theories Danilevsky articulated were History's or God's or that he was the spokesman of Providence. Though the articles utterly muddle fact and value and though they are most dogmatic, they seem to lack the final old Danilevskian touch. It is difficult to say whether or not this fact about these fragmentary, occasional pieces is significant.

There are, however, a couple of hints, in his articles of the seventies and eighties, of the advent of a more responsible attitude, the dawning of a sense of moral and intellectual responsibility. There is a passage in the "War for Bulgaria" series, for instance, in which he seems, quite inconsistently with the rest of what he has to say, to be advocating a tough stand in the war for frankly moral rather than "providential," deterministic reasons. The remarks occur in the course of a discussion of the "Russian view of political affairs," a view whose tender, unrealistic, selfless moralism he had long been decrying as both politically harmful and out of touch with "higher" real morality ("Russo-Slavic egoism"). Now he seems to say that the Russians should protect themselves and the Slavs against Europe simply because this was the right thing — in an ordinary ethical sense — to do. "The Russian view of political affairs is characterized . . . by astonishing humanity and the finest delicacy. We do not wish to take others as our example when their actions do not correspond to the strictest justice, with the highest demand of civilization, with the most self-satisfying disinterestedness; we do not wish to act like wolves because we live with wolves . . . God forbid judging such qualities of the Russian political outlook. But we only regret that these political virtues are overdone by us, overdone in the sense that, in pursuit of selflessness, we sacrifice interests only because they are our interests. We sacrifice them on behalf of others only because these are foreign." Contrary to his usual practice Danilevsky urged a deeper appreciation of moral values rather than their abrogation in favor of a providentially correct belligerency. He urged a look "at the inner qualities" of Russia's interests, "at the fact that our interests are lawful, just, holy, human, while the foreign interests are selfish, egoistic, even barbaric. We forget that magnanimity is not always magnanimous." [20] Here for once Danilevsky preached Machiavellianism as a means to an ethical end rather than as a ritualistic near end in itself.

There is a similar suggestion of an incipient sense of responsibility in his article on the origins of nihilism. But in this case his awareness is intellectual rather than moral. The passage occurs as an aside.

With phenomena of such complexity as all social phenomena and especially trends of thought and public opinion, the direct method of proof by itself has rarely been sufficient and fully convincing. Here we must look at all sides and be most careful that our conclusion is not altered by various collateral circumstances that do not enter into the realm of those bases on which we have built our conclusion and that nevertheless should influence it essentially. And we must be careful that we have not come to erroneous conclusions through this one-sidedness, however logical and unbiased we think we have been. This rectilinearity of thought, as it seems Dostoevsky has called it, is simply what is called radicalism, which is nothing but extreme rationalism. But this extreme rationalism or radicalism, even in the realm of thought, is appropriate only in one branch of knowledge — mathematics.[21]

It does seem that here Danilevsky is at least worried about being dogmatic and that he has some sense that, in the study of "all social phenomena and especially trends of thought and public opinion," one can never be quite sure of one's conclusions. While there are a few scattered remarks in *Russia and Europe* about being tentative and cautious, there is little in the spirit of that work as a whole to lead us to take them seriously. There is just as little in the political and cultural articles of the later years.

But when we turn to *Darwinism*, we find evidence of some really startling changes in Danilevsky's thinking. They are such as to indicate that a sense of responsibility is really beginning to dawn on him.

3

In his *Russia and Europe* Danilevsky described the conflict of civilizations, one with another, as the central phenomenon of world history — something like the way in which Marx described world history in terms of the class struggle. The struggle for survival of a civilization or cultural-historical type was not only necessary to its continuing existence, but also the way in which its mature cultural individuality developed. Its individuality was in turn an indispensable basis for contributions to "the common treasury of mankind," in science, the arts, technology, and other high cultural areas. This conception owed much to the Darwinian theory of evolution according to which species became differentiated through the struggle for existence: the fit organisms which survived also worked out their individualities in that struggle. This part of Danilevsky's doctrine alone, though extreme, was not totalitarian, for it did not set up any but this-worldly ends, survival and cultural maturation. These ends were not inappropriate to their means, tough, realistic diplomacy and instrumental war. However, as we know, Danilevsky also expected that somehow, providentially, Slavdom's struggle for existence would bring an end to all need to struggle and, ontologizing Slavdom ritualistically (through total or existential war), inaugurate an age of blessedness. In other words, his ultimate idea was that the metaphysical problem of man's alienation from God, nature, his fellows, and himself could be (and had to be) solved through forceful political measures. This idea was distinctly totalitarian.

Intellectually speaking, Danilevsky's totalitarianism had arisen in the fifties and sixties out of an effort to think in two contradictory ways at the same time: positivistically and metaphysically, at once like a utilitarian (a "modern") and like a myth-maker. Biographically speaking, according to my theory of his development, this intellectual practice had been made possible by Danilevsky's unwillingness to appear romantic in a world (as he saw it) of hard-boiled realists. Had he been more honest about his romanticism, utopian socialism, and immanentist spiritual aspirations, his philosophy might have been quite different. For one thing, under his own particular intellectual circumstances, more honesty might well have manifested itself in the form of some sort of criticism of Darwinism and of what to him were largely the same, the ideas of Bentham, Adam Smith, and the classical political economists, altogether in his view the most typical, essential voices of modernity. Now his *Darwinism*[22] is a work of great significance in his intellectual biography because it expresses honestly Danilevsky's true convictions. Indeed, in again viewing science as a humanistic activity, in openly championing higher things against scientism and materialism, and in proudly defending metaphysical thinking against Comteanism and Kantianism alike, the Danilevsky who wrote *Darwinism* recalls the author of the reviews of the work of Dutrochet and Humboldt, the young humanist of the Petrashevsky circle.

The intention of the work was frankly philosophical; its lengthy "positive-scientific" aspect was subordinate. The chief targets of criticism were, not Darwin himself, whom Danilevsky regarded as a great scientist and a basically sensible man, but pontifical Darwinists, in particular Ernst Haeckel and Kliment Arkadevich Timiriazev,[23] men who had uncritically extended Darwin's theory into a world view. It was the mystique of Darwinism ("the first scientific theory ever to become an 'ism' ") in Western Europe and Russia that troubled Danilevsky.[24] In his view, thinkers like Haeckel and Timiriazev, had been materialists even before Darwin's theory had come on the scene. They had adopted it less for scientific reasons than because it seemed to validate preconceived metaphysical systems. In particular, they thought it disproved scientifically the idea of a created, inherently rational universe; everything was a matter of pure chance not design. "Though the principle of accident played a role in several philosophies of antiquity such as those of Empedocles and Epicurus . . . Darwin was the first to apply it systematically . . . to a sphere of the most complex phenomena." [25] Seizing uncritically upon Darwin's theory, modern materialist philosophers now proclaimed it scientifically established that probabilist repetition of pattern, interaction of old and new patterns, and habitual human feelings about order (themselves, in fact, but parts of the "system" of nature) were sufficient explanation of the apparent orderliness of things. Danilevsky set out to defend Christianity, metaphysics, and the idea of design in the universe against this fashionable materialism and naturalism. Under the circumstances of the time, as he saw the situation, this required a "positive-scientific" critique of Darwin as well as a philosophical argument about materialism. His work thus involved both science and philosophy, not, however, because he was going to try to *prove* a philosophy but rather because his chosen opponents were trying to do so. In the light of Danilevsky's previous intellectual behavior, this marked a significant change in his intellectual style.

He was still capable himself, here and there, of a deterministic approach. Thus he expatiated at length on the idea that the broad acceptance of the new Epicureanism, as he called the outlook of Haeckel and Timiriazev, was an epiphenomenon of a godless, success-hungry age.[26] Citing *Russia and Europe*, he also assigned the English national character a large role in the development of Darwin's own thinking.

With Darwin . . . there are particular causes of blindness. His theory is a purely English theory, comprising not only all the peculiarities of the direction of English thought, but also all the qualities of the English spirit. Practical usefulness and competitive struggle, these two traits, in significant degree, give the tone not only to English life but also to English science. The ethic of Bentham and, in essence, also that of Spencer was based on utility; the political theory of Hobbes was based on the war of all against all — now called the struggle for existence; the economic theory of Adam Smith (and indeed the whole predominantly English science of political economy) was based on struggle and competition. Malthus applied this principle to the problem of population. Even the philosophy of Bacon is purely utilitarian, as was explained very well in Macaulay's study of Bacon. Darwin extended both the particular theory of Malthus and the general theory of political economy into the organic world.[27]

At such points, of course, Danilevsky was coming perilously close to his former practice of attempting to subvert those he regarded as his enemies with their own weapons. But such lapses were only occasional. More typically he took the position that the materialists and Darwinists were pretentious about their doctrines' *positive scientific* validity, that no world view could have such validity, that he disagreed because of his own beliefs in God and a created order, and finally that the materialist-Darwinian world was cold, unattractive, depressing, vulgar. It could not satisfy man's deeply felt need for a sense of meaning. "In the splendid poem *The Veil of Isis*, Schiller had the youth who dared to raise the veil hiding the image of truth fall dead at its feet. If the image of truth had had the features of a philosophy of chance, if the unfortunate youth had read on it the fateful words *natural selection*, then he would not have fallen in awe of its dreadful magnitude, but would have died of nausea and loathing . . . at the sight of the odious and abominable features of its miserable visage. This would also have been the fate of mankind if this theory were true." [28]

Danilevsky's procedure in criticizing materialism-Darwinism was first to establish the possibility, quite distinctly, that Darwin might have been in error scientifically at some crucial points and then, having made this opening, to discuss philosophically the problems of order and creation. In connection with the first point, he did not claim scientific originality or pretend to put himself on a level with "a great scientist like Darwin." He only undertook to point up the fact of disagreement, at the scientific level, between Darwin and equally distinguished men like Cuvier, Baer, Agassiz, Quatrefages, Wigand.[29] While his enthusiasm sometimes ran away with him, he was often as interested in showing that science was a process of humanistic discussion as he was in arguing for an alternative theory of evolution. In his more strictly philosophical discussion, he made particular use of Baer's philosophy of science, a source that apparently led him also to Aristotle.

The criticism of Darwin's natural selection theory was, in the light of present-day scientific knowledge, quite sophisticated. It was drawn from some first-class scientific works, newly available to Danilevsky, especially Albert Wigand, *Der Darwinismus und die Naturforschung Newtons und Cuviers*.[30] Following Wigand and others he concentrated much attention on one quite weak and at the same time crucial link in the Darwinian theory: the doctrine of the inheritance of acquired characteristics.

Darwin's theory of the origin of species stated that chance variations sometimes provided their possessors, in a given litter, for instance, with advantages in the continual, fierce struggle for existence with the environment in its many forms. This enhanced, relative to their parents, the probability of the survival of such mutants. Eventually after many such episodes, a new species would arise. Danilevsky rightly asked how it was that the more favorable variations, in this world of chance and struggle, could maintain sufficient identity over generations so as eventually to achieve the numerical strength necessary to achieve status as a species on the taxonomic table. What prevented their being absorbed back, through interbreeding, into the overwhelmingly numerous group from which they had sprung? Danilevsky's statistical background may have made him particularly appreciative of such arguments.

One might, for instance, look directly at the problem of heredity. This offered "an extremely difficult dilemma for the Darwinian theory," for it involved the assumption of a process whereby remoteness strengthened heredity, an assumption which, in fact, worked more against Darwin than for him.

To admit that continued inheritance does not strengthen acquired characters and does not make them fixed, is to strip the doctrine of an important prop. How then would continued selection attain its goal and fix the changes that had taken place? In fact, even if the unfit forms are destroyed . . . the fit can never multiply unless remoteness strengthens heredity. To admit, on the other hand, that fixity of acquired characters is strengthened with the increase of the number of generations . . . is tantamount to arming the basic species with a very powerful weapon in the struggle with the variations that have sprung from them. The elder species will continually transmit its own characters to its progeny, while those of the individual variations that have sprung up will be transmitted very weakly, even sometimes disappearing.[31]

Thus it would appear that, in the great struggle for existence, the new variations were only superficially fit.

To solve this problem, Darwin would have to show that somehow natural selection "consists in the more or less complete elimination of crossbreedings unsuitable to the conscious or unconscious end of the variation of the organism." Danilevsky evoked this as what he called his "first premise in favor of the refutation of this theory." His "second premise" was that "the struggle for existence in no way and in no degree eliminates crossbreeding, and Darwin never indicated that it should, nor how crossbreeding in nature should be eliminated." Since natural selection did not and could not do what, practically, it would have to do — eliminate crossbreedings — "*there is no such thing as natural selection in nature* — and I evoke again the two above premises in refutation of it. And from this it follows that so-called natural selection is not a real factor in nature, is nothing more than a fantasy, an illusion, *ein Hirngespinst* (as the Germans so expressively put it) of Darwin and his followers." [32]

It was not difficult, Danilevsky thought, to see how Darwin had come to put such unwarranted faith in the operation of natural selection. He had unwittingly treated it as though it had a life of its own and were an "intelligent critical agent." For he had drawn a false analogy between artificial and natural selection. An intelligence was at work in the former, that of the breeder, who kept the more desirable variations from breeding with any but their own kind. Artificial selection was a much more consistent and orderly process than natural. Darwin had treated the two as equivalent, thereby coming greatly to exaggerate the evolutionary effect of the latter.[33]

Another line of criticism, less solid in our eyes than that directed at the problem of heredity, but still, under the scientific circumstances of the time, respectable, involved the unrealistic quality of the Darwinian vision of nature.[34] In Darwin's view, nature was unverifiably efficient, ruthless, structurally systematic. The many well-known examples of inefficient animals and of useless organs in some animals indicated that nature was not so cruel nor so rigorous. What good was the rattle of the rattlesnake? It was really detrimental to him, for it frightened away his prey. The long branchy antlers of the reindeer were not useful in the struggle for existence. One look at an elephant or a peacock was sufficient to indicate through what a peculiarly distorted "English" glass Darwin viewed nature. Moreover, the struggle for existence in nature itself never looked quite as Darwin pictured it. It was not so intense nor cruel, nor did it operate over long periods in such consistent ways. At times it was suspended, at times great natural catastrophes overcame both the fit and the unfit. Sometimes the struggle changed its quality so that the "fit" became the "unfit." Yet, despite all this, many natural forms, some very inefficient, had survived over centuries.[35]

Internally, organisms often harbored organs which neither utility nor history could explain. "The swim bladder cannot have been produced by selection since, in the large majority of cases, it is useless. Nor can it have been called into being as a concomitant of growth, for no other special organ or special group of organs is related to it; nor can it have been the result of heredity, for it is present in various groups which belong in unrelated classifications — which, according to Darwin, is *the* mark of their genealogical relationship."

Such phenomena were thought by Danilevsky to be peculiarly compelling evidence in favor of the possibility that, in organic life, design was prior to and more important than any environmental influence. "Does not this example . . . show with the greatest clarity that, in the struggle of organisms, the morphological aspect is primary and essential, that it provides us with a guiding thread in the understanding of organic structure, and that the adaptive aspect is secondary, something that appears sometimes as a result, but in no case as a conditioning principle?" [36] Indeed, he was deeply interested, beyond the "positive scientific" level, in elaborating such possible implications.

In order to appreciate what the shortcomings he saw in the Darwinian theory meant to Danilevsky, we should remember that neither he nor practically anybody else at the time had any knowledge of Mendelian genetics; later elaborations of Darwin's vision of nature together with the twentieth century developments in biochemistry and their application to the problem of heredity, of course, belong to a different scientific world from his. Under the scientific circumstances of the time,[37] "the mistakes of Darwin" were quite readily interpreted by Danilevsky, as also by Wigand and the others, as evidence that the idea of some sort of created order in nature was still viable, though not necessarily proved. If the variation-selection doctrine was unsound, then there might be ready recourse to the continual influence of the Creator in nature.

At the point where the really scientific arguments ran out, Danilevsky found himself confronted with some intellectual alternatives. His choice among them is even more indicative of a fundamentally changing outlook, on his part, than is his direct and honest attack on Darwin's science.

He thought he could have stopped with the scientific criticism. Following the great biologist Rudolf Kölliker, he could have insisted, he said, that the scientist went against his nature when he did more than record verifiable regularities. If it could be shown statistically that 106 boys were born for every 100 girls, then that was a law and nothing more could be said of it. Danilevsky rejected this alternative, thereby registering another important change of attitude. Where he had once been so taken with positivism that he had been prepared to deal now obliquely, now directly, even with metaphysical questions as though they were physical ones, he insisted this time that it was the task of the scientist to explain, to seek meaning as well as to describe. His discussion of the point sounds like a triumphant confession of a new or newly recovered faith from a man with intimate knowledge of the pitfalls he described.[38]

He said that Auguste Comte's idea that the limits of positive knowledge were the rightful limits of human thought no longer awakened his sympathy. Positivism had no claim to the name of philosophy at all. He compared Comte to King Canute ordering the sea to stop at his feet. He also rejected Comte's idea that metaphysics and positive science were phases of development of the human mind. They were rather (and this was why the scientist had also to be a philosopher) two different ways of looking at nature. The only really valid position on scientific method was a middle one between "Scylla and Charybdis (apriorism and positivism)."[39] "At the limits of positive science begins the realm of metaphysics in the sense that Aristotle used this term (that is, the realm that lies beyond the limits of physics) or the realm of philosophy in the broadest sense of the word. The human mind cannot even wish not to go beyond these limits . . . It trusts no proof of the impossibility of this, though it be developed with Kantian strictness . . . just at the moment when it is convinced of the existence of any such limits, it begins to seek ways of getting around them."[40]

The facts of heredity and the overall look of organic nature provided the possibility of at least two extra-positivist interpretations. One was that of Cuvier: species were the result of separate creations; there was no such thing as evolution. The other was

that of Danilevsky's old friend Karl Ernst von Baer: there had
been evolution; its mechanics were teleological. Danilevsky es-
poused Baer's theory. His Bolshevik critics have been too hard
on him. He was always an evolutionist, never, strictly speaking,
an "idealist." He never hid from the problems of his time. In
Darwinism he was trying to confront them in his own way.

The influence of Baer (and through him of Aristotle)[41] upon
the later Danilevsky is unmistakable. *Darwinism* is larded with
references to his works. Danilevsky thought Baer the leading
scientific mind of the time. "Many of these mistakes [of Darwin]
have been noticed by various scholars and among them [his
italics] *the most significant minds . . .* of our time. The first
among these I name the great naturalist-philosopher Baer." [42]
Baer, a Baltic German, was, indeed, one of the big figures in the
history of modern science. Famed for the discovery of the mammalian ovum and for the elaboration, in place of some really
bizarre theories, of the fundamentals of modern embryology,[43]
he had long been interested in evolution. It was a natural correlative of his main study. In the early nineteenth century, for
instance, he had devastated the romantic, mystical, evolutionary
theory of J. F. Meckel and Lorenz Oken. One of the corner-
stones of their transformist theory had been their idea that the
ontogenetic development of higher organisms recapitulated, in its
various stages, the whole development of organic nature. This
had been like an invitation to criticism from Baer, the embry-
ologist. At that time a Cuvierian, he had easily refuted them.[44]
A lively and curious man, however, Baer had by the seventies
become himself a transformist, though of a different kind. With
the help of some of his writings, we can reconstruct the main
outlines of the rather casual theory of evolution which Danilevsky drew from him.[45]

Following Baer, Danilevsky held that the scientist should start
his philosophizing about evolution with ontogenetic development.
He should fix the picture of the evolving individual in his mind
before he looked at the question of the evolution of species. He

should see phylogenetic development or evolution after considering the facts of ontogenetic development — not the reverse, as Darwin had done. This would ensure that he did not distort empirical phenomena like the morphological roundedness of organisms.

Now ontogenetic development appeared to Danilevsky, as it appears to some scientists even today,[46] to be a peculiarly teleological process. It was as though the embryo unfolded according to a plan, for the pattern of growth was almost unimaginably complex, while, at the same time, it proceeded by stages, at once orderly and discrete. It seemed to go by jumps through a series of intricately coordinated steps. The scientist saw before him the actualizing of a structured potentiality, a physical analogy to the Aristotelian metaphysical order. He saw a teleological process.

If we wish to evoke a picture of epigenetic development, we can do no better than to turn to the example of a sculptor molding a statue. At first he gives the lump of clay a crude and general outline of the human figure . . . by which it is impossible to distinguish whether it will be a man or a woman, naked or clothed, in ancient or in modern dress. (Exactly as in the case of the development of a living thing, it is possible at first to distinguish only its type, then its class, its order, and so forth.) Nature, just like the sculptor, does not make all the particular parts at once (the final forms, for example, appear only at a comparatively late stage), but goes from the general to the particular. The particular parts (for example, the head) the sculptor gives only a general form and then molds the nose, scoops out the eye sockets, sketches the eyebrows, then makes the crook in the nose, the area of the nostrils, the nostrils themselves, and so forth. Let us add two presuppositions to this work of the sculptor: let him possess a Fortunatus cap and let all these moldings, scoopings, outlinings, and scrapings take place not as a result of the actions of any external instruments or methods, but by some internal process of swellings and contractions of the clay in the proper places and in a definite successive order — and we have something similar to the epigenetic process of development. It would seem that the gradual particularization of the form of the statue is the reflection of some ideal form. With the presupposition of our invisible sculptor we would not have been mistaken; the statue would have been the reflection of some internal form or ideal living within it and realizing itself by means of the process of swelling and shrinking which are at the disposal of its will.[47]

Danilevsky, like Baer, was at pains not to have his point sound naïvely vitalistic, anthropocentric. "We can understand epigenesis, from its morphological side, only as an ideal process (though realizing itself, as Baer expressed it, not by magic but through the medium of the forces of nature)." [48] However, without claiming any but philosophical verifiability for the idea, Danilevsky believed that phylogenetic development — or macrocosmic evolution — could be understood on the analogy of the microcosmic picture. In this view, life forms or species had once been much less fixed, more plastic, more subject to transformation than later. Once they had constituted, in Baer's words, a *"generatio originaria* or *primitiva."* Despite its indefiniteness and plasticity, organic life as a whole at that time had not been simply an open, unpredetermined affair. Like the embryo, it had had a definite structure, a definite potency. Its "end," when actualized, could be understood by reference to the structure of organic nature as now set forth in the Cuvierian taxonomic table. Evolution was not and had not been a matter, as Darwin conceived it, of gradually cumulating changes. When new forms appeared, they were full blown. This was called a "jump" theory of evolution (Baer had said it went *sprungweise*).

As Danilevsky put it

in our theory . . . there remains for us only to have recourse to jumps (*skachki*) from form to form . . . If phylogenesis is similar to ontogenesis . . . then the phylogenetic process will be a process of development. But development is epigenesis and we can understand epigenesis, from its morphological side, only as an ideal process. But an ideal process . . . is nothing but an intellectual process. And so, if we leave the ground of positive science but, in going beyond its limits, base ourselves on it by drawing out the probabilities involved, we will have recourse to a theory of descendence in explaining the multiplicity and variety of the forms of the organic world; however, in the final analysis, we cannot understand the descendence of the forms of the organic world except as an aspect of an ideal, or more precisely, an intellectual process . . . There cannot be a closer analogy to phylogenesis than ontogenesis, by which is meant, both in the case of processes that take place in the postnatal life of organisms (the metamorphosis of insects, the phenomenon of intermittency of generations, and so forth) and in the case of those that take place inside the egg or in the womb, only definite forms passing over into equally definite forms and being integrated and connected in a definite way. This process is known as development.[49]

This theory of evolution allowed for support from facts which, on the scientific level, contradicted the Darwinian theory. Here a new form was in no danger of being swamped by interbreeding with the still numerous stock from which it had arisen; it was different in kind. Here the struggle for existence could be seen for what it was: intermittent, capricious, a minor factor. Here swim bladders, peacocks' tails, and elephants' trunks could be included; they were signs of the essentially morphological rather than functionalistic norms of nature.

Such were Danilevsky's last ideas. His *Darwinism* was a great step away from the hypocrisy-laden dialectics and rancor of *Russia and Europe*. Philosophic and humanistic in spirit practically throughout, his work on modern biological theory attests to something like a return to attitudes he had had in the forties. Now he once again openly stated his disquiet with what he regarded as the most typical ideas and values of modernity and that in an appropriate language; and he proudly defended the idea of a created, objective order in the world. Regarding the content of his later scientific thought, his fascination with Baer (whose work he had known as a student at the University of St. Petersburg and with whom he had been closely acquainted on the Caspian expedition in the fifties) is especially interesting. Baer's fundamental and neo-Aristotelian idea of a basic unity between matter and spirit, a unity behind and responsible for the processes of evolution was a very Russian idea (though Baer was a Baltic German). The father of modern embryology was a thorough immanentist, and he viewed natural and human history together,[50] as though the whole thing was a process of incarnation. His most basic presuppositions were very similar in spirit to those of Herzen, of Dostoevsky, of Soloviev. Danilevsky's great interest in Baer again suggests his affinity to these typically Russian philosophers. It also brings up again the fact of the similarity of his thought to Marxism, for in Marx's and Engels' descriptions of matter's qualities there are expressed, sometimes right on the surface, a conviction very like Baer's and Danilevsky's. "The first and most important of the inherent qualities of *matter* is *motion*, not merely *mechanical* and *mathematical* movement, but still more *impulse, vital spirit, tension*, or, to use Jacob Boehme's expression, the *throes* of matter. The primary forms of matter are the living, individualizing *forces of being* inherent in it, which produce the distinctions between the species." [51] Danilevsky had been obsessed intellectually all his life with this kind of spiritualist materialism. The fact that he worked out the same at once most Russian and most Marxist idea, now in a humanist, now in a totalitarian, then again in a humanist way, besides attesting to his freedom and his not inconsiderable spiritual stature, makes the life history of this rather peculiar, quite undistinguished intellectual reverberate with historical implications.

Part Two

Russia and Europe

6

PANSLAVISM AND THEORY
OF CIVILIZATIONS

A DETAILED EXAMINATION of Danilevsky's *Russia and Europe*[1] is now in order. But there is one subject which must be discussed before starting the analysis. Slavophilism was one of the most important intellectual sources of his philosophy of history.[2] It will be necessary to refer repeatedly to it in this and the next chapters. While the doctrine has been the subject of a number of useful studies,[3] none that I have seen (except perhaps Berdaiev's) manages to communicate its meaning as a whole, that is, to describe satisfactorily what the Slavophils were worried about, what they wanted, how they hoped to obtain it. A brief discussion of their ideas with emphasis on such matters, together with a few preliminary remarks about Danilevsky's complex and subtle intellectual relationship to Slavophilism will facilitate understanding of what follows.

Slavophilism was in some ways a typical Russian intellectual "system" of the late thirties and forties: basically oriented toward the cultural problems that were arising out of Russia's modernization and Westernization, its temper was eschatological and "world historical." The doctrine was largely the invention of two thoughtful country gentlemen, Alexei Khomiakov (1804–1860) and Ivan Kireevsky (1806–1856). They responded to the problem of change in Russia by taking the stance of Christian philosophers criticizing their contemporaries, Western European and often Russian, for overinvolvement in the things of this world. They singled out as particularly symptomatic of evil, certain social and cultural phenomena in both "the West" and Russia: slavish imitativeness by Russia of foreign models; statism and bureaucracy; serfdom; too sharp social divisions; economic activities unsubordinated to humanistic purposes; religious, radical, and revolutionary movements which were only worse examples of the problems they were designed to solve. But the Slavophils were by no means entirely naïve and unrealistic. They understood that many of the things they criticized had deep historical roots. Godlessness and self-seeking were believed to be the ultimate origins of the social phenomena they disliked. But these phenomena were not thought to be merely the results of offhand perverseness. This kind of consideration led Khomiakov, in particular, to some elaborate theorizing about world history.

He saw the historical problem of his time as being rooted in a point of view he called Kushitism. World history was a dialectic process involving the interaction of two races of people, the Kushites and the Iranians. The Kushities were (or so it seems proper to interpret Khomiakov) the all but damned by predestination and the Iranians the all but saved. The Kushites by nature lacked sufficient fortitude to accept the rigors of the simple, bare, natural life as God had created it. They tried to figure things out and invented great systems of thought, economies, states, and even false churches in order to give themselves a sense of security. The Iranians had great fortitude. This kept them simple and good, but, at the same time, it also made them the easy victims of Kushite influence or even domination. Once this happened the Iranians, at given historical periods, became almost entirely Kushitized.

In the nineteenth century the Western Europeans were the Kushites and the Slavs (especially the Russians) were the Iranians. The historical situation of both was in an advanced state of deterioration. Western European civilization was characteristically out of focus, so much so that efforts at reform simply made things worse. This had, in fact, been going on for a long time. For example, protest against the Kushite rationalizing authoritarianism of the Catholic Church had led to the Kushite egoistic anarchy of Protestantism. Protests against this were leading to the empty secularism of liberalism and radicalism. By the nineteenth century, European Kushitism had for some time been infecting Russia with swollen bureaucracy, social divisions, serfdom, and godlessness. In general it had been conducive to the suppression of the volitional-emotional quality in men, an important basis of true perspective, in favor of the intellectual and rationalistic.

A simple general call to all men to return to the life of the spirit and to a search for salvation and for integrity of soul would have been irrelevant to this complex situation. Kushite Western Europe, and Russia too, in part, encased, spiritually, psychologically, institutionally, in their incarnated sins, were impervious to any simple, sentimental, spiritual appeal. Kushites lacked perspective to such a degree that they often could not appreciate the truth when confronted with it. Or when they did appreciate it, their actions on its behalf simply made the whole situation worse. The problems both of Western Europe and of Russia had to be attacked in some other way, in some way that gave adequate consideration to deep vested interests in institutionalized evil.

The Slavophils' often incisive analysis of the spiritual and human situation in their time might have led them into the kind of totalitarian errors Danilevsky was later to make. Their great emphasis on man's imprisonment in the social and cultural instruments he had invented in his own service might have led them, as it did Danilevsky, to advocate drastic reform, revolution, or war as, under the circumstances, the only possible roads to human wholeness. But they went another way.

In the view of Khomiakov, the current Russia-Europe situation was really different from all previous Iranian-Kushite ones. The Russians had the one true Church, the Orthodox, to strengthen their natural fortitude beyond any point previously known in history. In other words, the chosen people could be kept from damnation or near damnation in the nineteenth century because God was choosing them, as it were, a second time. A Biblical paradigm was at the base of Khomiakov's philosophy of history: the chosen people had a new dispensation; the Church, the mystical body of Christ, was with them. Through the Church and the sacraments, the Russians could regain perspective, a new level of knowledge and insight, in the midst of Kushitism. They could divest themselves of the tempting and comforting things of this world, for their fortitude and their keenness of insight were potentially unique. A new degree of interiorization, achieved through more active, dedicated, corporate life in the Church, would destroy the sinful institutions that had been grafted upon Russia. But even more, the shining example of the resultant ideal Christian society in Russia, free, simple, classless, communal, patriarchal, natural, yet not without the best (a small amount) of poetry, philosophy, and science, would save the West from itself, would support that potentiality for persistent goodness that God had planted in the Kushites themselves. Just as the Church would save the Russians, the Russians would save the West. Interiorization and exemplification, not revolution or war, were the keys to the new life — to the proper subordination of means to ends, in Russia, in Europe, in the world.

Slavophilism was an exciting doctrine in nineteenth century Russia. It had a large influence on modern Russian thought — on Herzen, Bakunin, Tolstoi, Dostoevsky, Leontiev, Lavrov, Mikhailovsky, Soloviev, to name only a few prominent thinkers. In a sense its great influence was peculiar, for despite its nationalist message and its stress on communal values in Church and society, it was in many ways not a typical Russian doctrine. Untypical was the degree of emphasis placed upon the volitional-emotional side of man, on individualism (national and personal), on particularism, especially of the ethnic kind. Slavophilism was shot through with elements of transcendentalist idealism and romantic primitivism. Khomiakov and Kireevsky (like Tolstoi later) envisaged the transformation of the world through purification and simplification; other more characteristic thinkers thought they foresaw something like the world's transfiguration. The Slavophils emphasized to an unusual degree *plebs* over *populus, narodnost* over *natsionalnost*.[4] In the history of Russian spirituality their doctrine was unusually Augustinian, quasi-Protestant in temper. They belonged more to the minor tradition of St. Abraham of Smolensk than to that of St. Theodosius.[5]

Some of the great influence of the doctrine was direct. That is, there were orthodox Slavophils in Russia right down into the early twentieth century. But its widest impact took place in a more complex way. In some hands Slavophilism became secularized and turned into nationalism and Panslavism. Other thinkers synthesized it with theories of their own. Herzen, for example, worked out a revolutionary Slavophilism, replacing Khomiakov's Christianity with his own humanism, assigning Russia a messianic role in a distinctly eighteenth century rationalist and utopian socialist, intellectual universe. Bakunin, Lavrov, and Mikhailovsky did something similar. Where Khomiakov had valued the agricultural commune pretty much as it was (or had been), a patriarchal, familial, neomedieval, mysteriously and peculiarly Slavic institution, the leftist Slavophils prized it for its supposed potentiality for realizing the European ideals of socialism and democracy. A number of important religious thinkers (Dostoevsky, Fedorov, Soloviev) were also deeply influenced by Slavophilism. But the very cores of their doctrine were no more Slavophil than those of the revolutionaries. Their attitudes toward civilization and progress were much more positive. They had a fittingly better rounded, less idealist, primitivist, and subjectivist view of man. And they envisaged Russia's mission as being accomplished less through withdrawal from and more through kenotic entry into the modern world. Russia, in their views, was destined to bring out the universal and integrating potentialities in the world and thus make possible its transfiguration.

In considering Danilevsky's relationship and intellectual debt to

Slavophilism, it is important to be mindful of the variegated nature of that doctrine's influence, for his thought presents another example of it. He was no orthodox Slavophil gone astray. He never wholly believed in the doctrine. One finds in his thought evidence only that he used it to help him articulate a world view whose center lay both in eighteenth century scientific naturalism and, though more remotely, in the major, immanentist tradition of Russian spirituality. Perhaps the most recognizably Slavophil part of *Russia and Europe* is that which sets forth a properly Panslavist program. But only the outline of Slavophilism is visible, for here Danilevsky, like many of his nationalist contemporaries, thoroughly secularized the teachings of Khomiakov and his circle. Elsewhere, in developing his ultimate ideas, he transformed those teachings in a way most reminiscent of Herzen and the Populist tradition, occasionally of Dostoevsky and Soloviev. Like the "Russian socialists," he associated Russia, not with will, inwardness, and the past, but with reason, the heavenly city of the eighteenth century philosophies and with the ideals of utopian socialism. His adulation of science and the too naturalistic flavor of his "Christianity" were also not Slavophil. His muting of the idea of Russia's and Slavdom's mission to the world in favor of emphasis on the idea that the East could realize a heaven on earth all by itself, by completing and synthesizing a cultural "treasury of mankind" laid up by others (especially Western Europeans), was another striking deviation. It suggests the presence of a residue of Danilevsky's former Westernist outlook, now informed by a contradictory desire to assert the East's superiority over the West. In a general sense it may be said that Danilevsky's totalitarian philosophy arose when he wedded Slavophilism with utilitarianism and proposed solving by war what Khomiakov had proposed solving through the Church, namely, the problem of man's alienation from God, nature, other men, and himself. But a closer look reveals that Danilevsky's "Slavophilism" was to a significant degree a synthesis of the original doctrine of Khomiakov and Kireevsky with ideas like those he had held in

the Petrashevsky circle. It could as well be said that he proposed
solving by war what Fourier and the Petrashevskians had proposed solving by the *example* of the phalanx. Like modern Russian
intellectual culture in general, Danilevsky's thought owed a
great debt to Slavophilism. In the final analysis, however, the
center of his intellectual commitment originated in those Friday
evening discussions in St. Petersburg in the forties and, though
more remotely, in the culture of his gentry-peasant Russian social background and in the main tradition of Russian Orthodoxy.

2

Danilevsky said he wanted a Panslav Union. It would have
consisted of a series of Slavic and culturally related or geopoliti-
cally neighboring autonomous kingdoms in personal union with
the Romanov dynasty of Russia. The Russian Empire, a Czech-
Moravian-Slovak Kingdom, a Serb-Croatian-Slovenian Kingdom,
a Bulgarian Kingdom, a Rumanian Kingdom, a Hellenic Kingdom,
a Magyar Kingdom, and a Polish Kingdom were the proposed
elements of the Union. There would also have been a Tsargrad
(or Constantinople) District, a kind of Slavic Washington, D.C.
This, the capital of the Union, would have belonged to no one
state; it would have been above all the states and possessed
equally by all. The Russian capital was to be in Moscow.[6]

The constitutional features of the Union would have included,
besides the union of kingdoms, one central directing power, a
central judiciary, and local administrative autonomy. It would
not, however, have been, at least in Danilevsky's intention, a
Russo-Slavic parallel to Prussia-dominated Germany. Danilevsky
decried what he thought of as Prussia's unjust suppression of
autonomy within Germany after 1866. He warned Russia
against this practice within the future Panslav Union. "From our
point of view . . . this would not be at all advantageous, but,
on the contrary, very harmful because, in the interest of the greatness and cultural significance of the whole Slavic family of peo-

ples, it is necessary that the Slavic world shall not take the form of a fusion of the Slavic streams into the Russian sea, as Pushkin put it, but the form of a broad ocean with independent, though united and mutually subordinate parts . . . not the fusion of the Slavs into Russia, but the unification of all Slavic peoples in the common idea of all-Slavdom both in political and cultural respects." [7] The future civilization of Slavdom would suffer from Russian domination. "The civilization proper to any cultural-historical type achieves its fullness, variety, and richness only when the varied ethnographic elements constituting it are not swallowed up in one political whole, but enjoy independence and form parts of a federation or political system of states." [8]

Indeed, the Union was not entirely conceived on the analogy of the emergent nation states of Italy or Bismarckian Germany. It was rather comparable to what Danilevsky called Europe, that is, all of Western Europe, including Germany. "Europe" was not a nation, strictly speaking, but a kind of supernation, constitutionally, a "political system." That Europe as a supernation lacked the detailed more centralized constitutional arrangements which Danilevsky proposed for the Slavic Union did not mean that Europe was not a comparable entity. The supernational, practically institutionless, constitutional form, "political system," or, as he also called it, "politically centralized state," was partly the expression, in an appropriate style, of a particular kind, a highly individualistic kind, of civilization, partly the result of a response to a certain degree of external danger. "The forms of the politically centralized state [for example, ancient Greece, Europe], of the united state [the tightest form, for example, the Roman Empire], and the union of states [proposed for Slavdom, partly in view of the example of the United States] . . . are conditioned, on the one hand, by the nature of the national personalities serving as their basis and by the degree of affinity between them; on the other hand, by the degree of danger threatening the national honor and freedom, for which the state must serve as protection and defense." [9] Danilevsky wanted the Slavs

to realize themselves as a supernation or civilization not merely
as a nation. The exact constitutional form this would take had to
depend on the Slavs' relatively unindividualistic culture and on the
very present danger of the hostile and powerful European neighbor.

The institution of the Panslav Union would serve two major
purposes in the world. The first of these was political and cultural; the second was more philosophical.

"Europe" was in process of dominating much of the world
politically. Its cultural and psychological domination was already
more advanced than its political and was, in fact, facilitating
European imperialism. Non-European peoples, most relevantly
the Russians, the natural leaders of the Slavs, were hesitant about
defending and asserting themselves politically because they considered forceful, self-interested international politics directed
against Europe, immoral, narrowly nationalistic, and unhuman-
itarian. These beliefs derived from their acceptance of Europe's
claims that its civilization was the culmination of all human
progress and, as such, universal, final. To counter Europe force-
fully was to act in a hostile manner toward the good and the
true, to act like a barbarian. Europe's claim to historical finality
and universality was both the basis of its own imperialistic ex-
pansionism and of its potential victims' docility. The institution
of a Panslav Union would directly block European expansion to
the East. But, more important, the union would make possible a
flowering of already promising native Slavic civilization and thus
put Europe's subtle claim to a monopoly on truth and universality in perspective. Other peoples would then find it much
easier to go their own ways. Europe itself would gain a much
needed and, in the long run, salutary sense of humility. A balance of world power and the development of separate cultures in
Slavdom, Europe, and another nascent civilization, the United
States, would replace the present monopoly Europe seemed to
have on civilization.[10] Danilevsky thought nationalistic individualism, free enterprise, *laissez-faire*, among the highest values. Above

all, true progress would be saved. "The danger consists . . . in the supremacy of one cultural-historical type [that is, civilization] . . . the present danger consists in that order of things which is the ideal of our Westerners: in the accession not of an apparent but of a real universal human civilization . . . That would be tantamount to cutting off the very possibility of any further success or progress in history, which consists in the introduction of new world views, new aims, new strivings, which always have their origin in the particular psychic structures of new elements arriving in the field." Real universal civilization was "multilocal and multitemporal" (*raznomestnyi i raznovremennyi*).[11]

Throughout the more strictly utilitarian part of Danilevsky's philosophy one comes repeatedly upon an operational, secular version of the original Slavophilism. *Russia and Europe* reflects a major intellectual attempt on its author's part to meld that traditionalist and metaphysical doctrine with what Danilevsky regarded as the intellectual spirit of the modern age. The ideas just described smack strongly of an effort at once to follow and to denature important doctrines of Khomiakov and Kireevsky.[12] These Slavophils had dreamed of a Christian society in Russia, one which would simultaneously give outer testimony of the Russians' own inner state of grace, save the larger community of Slavic souls from the Kushite, system-building, power-hungry West, and strengthen that West against its own innate Kushitism. In Danilevsky's theory, the Panslav Union would block European imperialism physically. This idea was only vaguely Slavophil. Much more in the spirit of his predecessors of the forties was his idea that it was an important Slavic mission to exemplify cultural variety. The similarity was not exact, however, for the mission of Danilevsky's Russia and Slavdom, like the way in which he conceived of these, was much more this-worldly, scientific, unpoetic. It was strictly cultural not religious. This squaring of ends and means kept this part of his theory nontotalitarian.

The same this-worldly emphasis appears in Danilevsky's conception of still another notable consequence of the institution of the Panslav Union. The Slavic political and cultural example and the consequent new free market of civilizations would also serve an important philosophical-psychological didactic purpose. The false Western dominance Danilevsky saw in being had its deepest roots, he thought, not just in an accidental conglomeration of historical factors, but also in a state of mind, an outlook, widely shared especially among Russians and Slavs. Its basic premise was that men could see God's purposes at work in history; they could see before them the progressive triumph of truth, beauty, universality in the history of human civilization. They could, as it were, see God gradually incarnating His ways in the world of politics, society, economics, culture. The Panslav Union and its hoped-for political and cultural consequences (illogical variety) in the world would be a fundamental challenge to this erroneous belief, this immanentism, and to corollaries of it like the idea of natural law or the relevance of metaphysical or theological considerations in historical thinking. Then, with men no longer attempting the impossible, historical life might lose some of its tensions and conflicts. If men could separate states, nations, history from their religious beliefs and metaphysical ideas, then, within limits, they might be able to relax a little, to concentrate their energies on smaller, more possible things, like the sciences, the arts, social welfare. The separation of politics from the ethics of salvation and fulfillment would prevent recurrences of the present unfortunate international situation. The world would, as it were, indulge less and less in politics. Even Europe might one day be happy to relax and enjoy a highly cultured period.

It is interesting, in this connection, to recall that Danilevsky wanted the capital of his union, presumably the most important political center of Slavdom, in Constantinople, outside Russia, and away from those aspects of national life that he thought, at least at times, really mattered. Dostoevsky, a staunch religious immanentist of the Orthodox variety, was later, in *The Diary of a Writer,* to excoriate him for this proposal.[13]

Danilevsky's second, more philosophical purpose again recalls the original Slavophilism. Khomiakov and Kireevsky had attacked men's overinvolvement with the things of this world. They had singled out as especially tragic men's sacrifice of their souls to politics, bureaucracy, class divisions. They had emphasized that, besides practical reforms, and ultimately more fundamental than these, men needed to think of ends and means in a very different way. The Slavophils had thus undertaken spiritual renewal as the greatest cause. Its furtherance in the world at large was to be particularly hoped for by the didactic example of a Christian society in Russia. Danilevsky did not call for spiritual renewal. He called for another, at once more Protestant and more scientific kind of separation of fact and ultimate value, a redefinition of ends as well as a subordination of means to ends. The more physical, factual nature of his conception of Russia and Slavdom and of his idea of "what was to be done" differed accordingly. Yet he was vitally interested in a kind of renewal of men's minds and he regarded Russian and Slavic exemplification as an excellent way of teaching the needed philosophical lesson. Up to a point, he was successful, after his own fashion, in modernizing Slavophilism without a bizarre confusion of Christian charity and gunfire.

Analyzing the concrete international political, cultural, and psychological situation of Europe, Russia, and Slavdom in the eighteen sixties, Danilevsky found the prospects for his Panslavic program most unpromising. There was the strength with which Europe was thrusting eastward. The Germans shared with the Turks political control of practically all the Slavic peoples except the Russians. Moreover, Europe supported and dominated the Turks, thereby also exercising indirect hegemony over the Ottoman Slavs. And European political imperialism was about to become much worse.[14]

From a detailed study of European history, Danilevsky thought he had discovered that imperialism had been more marked in some periods than in others. It was during periods of equilibrium, when the European balance of power system was in full force, that Europe was most dangerous. Disturbers of the balance of power —like Louis XIV or Napoleon—interrupted imperialistic periods, forcing the Western powers to concentrate their efforts on restoring the balance. But, by the eighteen sixties such disturbances were no longer likely. The meteoric successes of figures like Louis XIV or Napoleon had been based on the possibility of using the helpless and disunited areas of the continent, especially formerly disunited Italy, as makeweights. With the unification of Italy, the balance of power was likely to be permanent. Europe would now engage full time in imperialism, especially in the old eastward thrust, the *Drang nach Osten*.[15]

Culturally the situation was just as bad. Thoroughly Westernized were the intellectual classes of the awakening non-Russian Slavs. Polish culture, under the foreign influence of Roman Catholicism, had long ago been practically diseased forever by Westernism. The strength of European cultural influence in Russia was deplorable. Danilevsky (again reminding us of the Slavophils) traced the beginnings of "Europeanism . . . the sickness of Russian life" to Peter the Great. Beginning with a laudable program of technical borrowing in the interest of national security, Peter had soon gone on to "fall in love" with Europe. The rot had slowly spread downward from court circles. In Danilevsky's time it was evident in the ludicrously unnatural and unnational quality of the Russian way of life (*byt*): clothing, furniture, the arts, social customs, and upper-class popular culture generally.[16] An advocate of a free press, he even blamed Alexander II's new press law with its system of three warnings on slavish imitativeness of the West. But the worst of the consequences of the disease in Russia was the odd psychological habit of "looking at everything through European eyeglasses," for by it Russians were robbing themselves of their own resources for resistance, self-determination, leadership of the Slavs. Its chief manifestations were in the realms of foreign policy, of public opinion about foreign policy, and of Russian philosophy concerning the relationship of Russia to European civilization.

Psychological eccentricity being most appreciable in the light of reality, as Danilevsky thought he saw it, this subject is best approached through a discussion of his "law" of foreign policy. In foreign affairs, he held, idealism and humanitarianism had no place. The principles of altruistic morality were all very well as guides for the activity of the individual. But the individual was immortal and could expect rewards in Heaven. "But the state and the nation are essentially transient phenomena and consequently the laws of their activity can be based only on the demands of their temporal existence, that is, on politics. We are not advocating Machiavellianism but only asserting that each class of beings and phenomena has its own law. An eye for an eye, a tooth for a tooth, strict legality, the Benthamite principle of utility, that is, enlightened self-interest — this is the law of foreign policy, of the relations of state to state." [17]

This "law of foreign policy" was applied in different ways in different situations. In the case of relations between nations within a supernation like "Europe," it was applied not only by the individual nations to their own policies, it was also given the status of a more universal value. Under this latter circumstance, one nation, within the supernation, would judge another's actions justified if those actions were undertaken in accordance with national self-interest. There had been a clear case of this in the year 1864.[18] Prussia and Austria had attacked Denmark in order to further German unification by a favorable solution of the Schleswig-Holstein problem. This violation of the integrity of tiny, nonaggressive (as Danilevsky saw it), enlightened, liberal Denmark had been a violation of morality in the ideal sense, but not in the utilitarian sense. The powers, therefore, though they (including Austria and Prussia) had earlier guaranteed Denmark's integrity in the Treaty of London, had not protested. Here a "law of nationality" had been applied as a higher law. The powers had assumed that "every nationality [in this case, German] has a right to independent existence to the degree that it is conscious of having one and strives to have one." [19]

On the other hand, as between supernations, the ethic of self-interest was only selfishly and narrowly applied. No allowance was made for the pursuit of self-interest by others. The events of the year 1854, a striking contrast to those of 1864, illustrated this. Russia, unlike Prussia and Austria, had not even been seeking to add to its territory. It had merely urged Turkey, a barbaric despotism — in utter contrast to Denmark in 1864 — to respect the rights of its Christian subjects, a right guaranteed in the treaty of Kuchuk-Kainarji. Yet England, France, Sardinia, and Austria had fought Russia in the Crimean War. They had not allowed for Russian self-interest at all, but solely for their own. For Russia belonged to an entirely different world. Europe simply hated Russia in an irrational and irremediable way.

However long we search for the reasons for this hatred of Europe toward Russia, we cannot find them in this or that action of Russia, or in other rationally comprehensible facts. There is nothing conscious in this hatred for which Europe can account rationally. The real cause lies deeper. It lies in those unfathomed depths of tribal sympathies and antipathies which are a sort of historical instinct among peoples and lead them (regardless of, though not contrary to, their will and consciousness) toward a goal unknown to them. For, on the whole, historical process does not proceed according to arbitrary human plans, which determine only its secondary patterns, but according to unconscious historical instincts. This unconscious tendency, this historical instinct, is responsible for Europe's hatred toward Russia.[20]

The only reasonable basis for the foreign policy of a supernation, whether one in being like Europe or a potential one like Slavdom, was the less enlightened type of self-interest. The Americans had the right idea. "America considers its greatest man, not the man who freed her from the foreign yoke (Washington), not the men who helped her define her civil and political freedom (Franklin, Adams, Jefferson), not the man who freed the Negroes (Lincoln), but the man who proclaimed from the very height of the presidential chair that America belongs to the Americans, that any foreign intervention in American affairs is an affront to the United States. This simple and spontaneous doctrine bears the glorious name of the Monroe Doctrine and constitutes the supreme principle of the foreign policy of the United States. This doctrine should also become the Slavic slogan." [21]

Against this background the foreign policy of Russia, mainly since the reign of Paul I, looked strange indeed. It had been conceived in the light of altruistic morality. This had cast Russia in the role of a ridiculous Don Quixote. In 1799, for instance, Paul had fought a chivalrous war, first, on behalf of the Knights of Malta, then, of Europe. The years 1805, 1812, and 1813 had seen Russian wars on Europe's behalf. Russia had saved Europe from Napoleon, who had, in fact, if one considered the treaty of Tilsit, been Russia's friend. Nicholas I had continued the mistakes of his predecessors. In the Russo-Turkish war of 1829 he had withdrawn from the very gates of Constantinople when the European powers had insisted. In 1848 revolution had swept Europe. Nicholas could have taken advantage of this opportunity (as Catherine II would have done) and thrown down the gauntlet to the Turks. But he had desisted and even spent his efforts in saving the Austrian monarchy from destruction.[22] Russian policy since the Crimean War showed that no lesson had been learned. Alexander II's diplomats should have been manipulating the Franco-German and Austro-German situations for all they were worth. But the Slavic cause was still forgotten in favor of a fantastic mystique of humanitarianism.

Involved here, in reality, however, was not genuine humanitarianism but manipulation of Russia by European interests. Conscious humanitarianism was simply a comfortable and soothing rationalization for a relatively unconscious self-devaluating state of mind. Russian leaders had internalized Europe's image of itself and of its Eastern neighbor. In this view, Europe was civilization,

Russia barbarism. The Russian diplomats were thinking of Russia as a conquering, obscurantist power — in flagrant disregard (according to Danilevsky) of Russia's relatively clean historical record of conquests and of the Great Reforms of Alexander II. They were forever trying, therefore, to square their own national guilt feelings.

One major mode of behavior, expressive of this state of mind, was the formulation of Russian foreign policy in the interest of Europe or "civilization," a practice rationalized as humanitarianism. Another was acquiescence in European conquests or in continuing European dominance in Slavic areas that had come under European influence through lengthy historical developments. An informative example of this second mode of behavior was the partition of Poland. Though Danilevsky admired Catherine II, he detected the first signs of diplomatic decadence during her reign. On one important occasion, at least, abstract notions of human rights had deflected her from the old forceful Russian policy of gathering the lands which had obtained in previous centuries. This, in turn, had led, paradoxically, to real violation of human rights, to the partition of Poland. Some of Poland, the part Catherine had finally acquired for Russia, was simply former Russian territory to which Catherine had had a perfect right. But, in the light of abstract humanitarian standards, its acquisition was a conquest. Catherine, infected by these standards, had therefore felt hesitant and guilty about her designs on Russian lands under Polish rule. Austria and Prussia had then taken advantage of Catherine's state of mind, not in order to defend Poland, but to insist on a share of the conquest for themselves. Poland was destroyed. In similar fashion there had as yet been no effort by Russia to liberate and unite the Slavs. False humanitarianism of this sort also blocked the forceful Russification of the subject nationalities in the Russian Empire.

The government, in its habit of looking at everything through European eyeglasses, was reinforced by a vociferous public in the same state of mind. Two important strands of public opinion could be delineated.[23] First, there was the strand of the "thinking men of Russia." The position had its ultimate intellectual roots in the ideas of Peter Chaadaev, a Russian philosopher of the 1830's. Following Chaadaev, these Westerners (Danilevsky specified no names of contemporaries here) thought of Russia as a "historical pleonasm." Europe was the equivalent of civilization and progress; Russia, of barbarism and stagnation. Russia was therefore a hindrance to the spread of civilization and should make herself a *tabula rasa* in order to become fully civilized, that is, Europeanized. Russia's influence in its own borderlands should be weakened, the Russian element subordinated to the non-Russian. All aspirations for Russian national self-determination should be sacrificed at the altar of humanitarianism. Danilevsky compared this view to the ideal of one of Schiller's famous characters, the Marquis de Posa (in *Don Carlos*). This fictional Spaniard had gone around Europe seeking enemies against his native Spain because he considered it an obstacle to human freedom and welfare.

Another important strand in Russian public opinion was that of "external political patriotism." [24] The advocates of this view wanted Russia to be a "hollow nut with a strong shell." They were markedly less logical than the "thinking men of Russia." Like the thinking men, they presumed that Russia was a historical pleonasm, without a past and with a problematical future. But, illogically, they wanted to strengthen the external, military-political shell of Russia. Why not let Europe flow in and eradicate barbarism, Asiaticism, Orientalism? One could easily see the cause of this inconsistency. The external political patriots felt a degree of discontent with their lowly national self-image and were trying somehow to express this. Danilevsky was particularly annoyed with this strand of public opinion.

Reinforcing Westernist public opinion was the dominant outlook in Russian philosophy. The philosophers had, of course, been much more subtle. They had devalued Russia in the face of Europe by an elaborate theory of the relationship of the national to the universal, a theory, in turn, walled up in an almost impregnable fortress of immanentism. In this theory

the relations of the national to the universal are usually represented as an opposition between the accidental and the essential, the narrow and limited and the spacious and free — the national is represented as a wall, as swaddling clothes, as a cocoon, which must be broken through in order to get out into the light of God . . . A universal genius is a man who, by the power of his spirit, succeeds in getting out of the road of nationality and bringing himself and his contemporaries (in one category or another of activity) into the realm of universality. The civilizing process of peoples is defined as the gradual renunciation of the particularity and limitation of nationality and the entry into the area of the essential and the general — of the universal human. The service of Peter the Great consisted in his bringing us out of the captivity of national limitation and introducing us to the freedom of the children of mankind . . . Such a doctrine was developed among us in the thirties and forties, before the literary pogrom of 1848. Its chief authors and defenders were Belinsky and Granovsky; their followers were the so-called Westerners, to whose ranks belonged almost all the thinking and even the simply educated people of that time. Its organs were *Otechestvennye Zapiski* and *Sovremennik*. Its sources were German philosophy and French socialism . . . the fantasies of Leroux (*De l'humanité*) or Perty (*Die Mystischen Ersheinungen der Menschlichen Natur*).[25]

That it was the immanentism as well as the Westernism of this outlook that bothered Danilevsky becomes evident in his lumping the original Slavophils together with Belinsky, Granovsky, and company. While he praised the Slavophils for standing up bravely, despite the paucity of their numbers, to the strong current of Westernism, and while he sympathized with their defense of nationality, he upbraided them for adhering to "humanitarianism," a fact which he attributed to the influence of German philosophy. Slavophilism in its original form was too much like an inverted form of Westernism; for, while the Slavophils had wanted the Slavs to live their own life, they had also taught, according to Danilevsky, that a new civilization would succeed the European and perfect it into a universal civilization.

What all these philosophers were really doing, behind all the fancy verbiage, was devaluating Russia in the face of Europe or looking at everything through European eyeglasses. It was another symptom of a national psychic breakdown. The symptoms took different forms in diplomacy, journalism, and philosophy. But, they were all unmistakably rooted in a single disease — *zapadnichestvo*, Westernism. Russians' tender-minded immanentist ways of looking at the world only made them more susceptible.

Danilevsky had a problem. He wanted a Panslav Union, an original Slavic civilization, and a relaxation of the unreasonable tensions of life. But, like Khomiakov again, he found the world not only externally in bad shape but also internally, psychologically structured by the same bad shape. The evils of the world kept feeding back on themselves, consolidating themselves. People could not see the truth because they had to use a distorting lens to look at it. What was to be done? Khomiakov had called for spiritual renewal. Danilevsky, an Orthodox, was not against religion and spiritual renewal. But he regarded confusion of spiritual renewal with political, cultural, and even psychological reform as but another likely way of reinforcing the evils he wanted to get rid of. In his view, Westernism fed on religious and secular immanentism.

The first solution he found — within the context of his utilitarianism at any rate — was that of enlightenment.[26] If people could not see the way things were in their present state of mind, then he would do something about that state of mind. He would try to specify the nature of the historical world by bringing in science and applying it to history. He would show, once and for all, that Europe and universal civilization were two different things. He would show that Europe was by no means the only civilization in history; it was only one of many, past, present, and future. Then he would discuss how civilizations developed. By this he would suggest what was wrong with the diplomats, the journalists, and the philosophers that made them do and say the things they did and he would attempt to rectify matters. He would explain why it was that, at a certain stage, a civilization put forth false claims to universality and why men in another civilization were susceptible to belief in these claims. Applying this explanation to the current Russia-Europe situation, he would cure Russia of Westernism.

Once he had put Russian thought, opinion, and philosophy on the right path, advances would come more easily. The Panslav Union could be realized by some concerted effort on Russia's part. Once established, the example of the Union would advance and spread the very perspectives that had created it. Backsliding would be prevented by physical rearrangements of the geopolitical and cultural conditions that had helped so much to make the original problems of Europe, Slavdom, and the world possible. Finally, the agonizing feelings which arose from the belief that historical action was a form of cocreation with God would disappear. The greatest happiness to the greatest number would be assured.

3

In approaching the most famous part of Danilevsky's historical thought, it should be emphasized that his theory of civilizations has often been too closely equated with Spengler's.[27] Especially important is the fact that he was not the extreme relativist that Spengler was to be. He did not, in his effort to teach the Westerners, reject so completely the ideas of universality and objectivity. This meant too that he was partly sympathetic to the aspirations of his supposedly muddled audience. He made this clear, for instance, in his plea for another look at Slavophilism. "Where are we to seek the reconciliation between Russian national feeling and the demands, acknowledged by reason, for human prosperity and progress? Are we to seek it in the Slavophil dream, in the so-called doctrine of a particular Russian or All-Slavic civilization, a dream at which everyone has scoffed so long and at which many people (though not all) continue to scoff? Perhaps Europe has not worked out the final form of human culture and perhaps there remains more to do than simply to spread this culture over the face of the earth in order to make all races and peoples happy?" [28] He wanted to "move" his reader from Westernist thinking to Slavophil thinking, while at the same time taking the metaphysics out of Slavophilism. It hardly occurred to him to base his case on an idea that there was no such thing as truth, objectivity, universal value.

Similarly, from certain contemporary points of view, it might be said that he based an important part of his case on an attempt to revise the thought models in use in the study of world history; but it must be remembered that he conceived of this in the manner of nineteenth not of twentieth century positivism. That is, he thought, as it were, of substituting a true or natural intellectual model for a false or artificial one, not of substituting a merely clearer, more intelligible for an obscure one. The current erroneous historical thought model he found to be linearly progressive. In detail, it envisioned world history as a series of three worldwide stages, each better than, though based upon, its predecessor. These stages were called "ancient," "medieval," and "modern." In this scheme, modern Europe was the culmination of history, progress, and civilization. It was close to being, in Danilevsky's view, the specific root of Westernism and of all the evils he sought to remedy.

The trouble was that it was based on an outdated conception of classification or, better, of taxonomy, for Danilevsky regarded historical thinking and biological thinking as fundamentally similar. The classification of world historical phenomena into three hierarchically related stages was like an outdated, classical or neoclassical, taxonomic scheme. Based on consideration of only a few characteristics of organisms, such schemes had been phenomenologically and morphologically weak. Their at least implicit apriorism was patent, for such cavalier definition of the data had grown out of an impulse to systematize rather than to explain; it was reductive. The classical scheme of biological classification according to a few arbitrarily chosen characters had long ago been superseded by better work, particularly that in zoology of the great French biologist Georges Cuvier. Danilevsky especially liked Cuvierian taxonomy's phenomenalist and morphological methods of procedure.[29] It began with both the details of organisms and their organic arrangement. Classifying things as they were, it was a natural taxonomy. Even its constructs were relatively empirical, for they were elaborated from the comparative study of the ground plans of organisms (homology). Danilevsky liked this classificatory system's implicit permissiveness, its "democracy," its possible nationalist implications. As he pointed out, in pre-Cuvierian biology little plants like the cryptogams and many "lower" animals had once been considered merely unimportant appendices to the rest of organic nature. But now these poor relatives had come into their own. Each had come to be viewed, not as a mere subscript in some classical hierarchy, but rather as in itself an important type of organic life making peculiarly precious contributions to the variety of nature.

Such importance, for his larger purposes, did Danilevsky attribute to the problem of classification that he undertook to give his readers a thorough lesson on it. He concentrated first on the problem of the difference and historical relationship between an "artificial system" and a "natural system" of classification.

The degree of progress of any science, in his view, was not to be measured by the number of facts the science could muster, but by the degree of

preciseness that is reflected in what is called the system of the science. By system I do not at all mean a system of exposition, which is nothing more than a mnemonic device for better imprinting the facts of the science on the memory or for presenting them more clearly to the understanding. Systematism, understood in this sense, is very justly without much of a reputation in our time because it has often been

used for evil and, with its endless hairsplittings, has only made the
task more difficult — being, for the most part, a remnant of scholastic
pedantism. This kind of systematism is no more than a scaffolding
of scientific knowledge. It cannot be dispensed with but it should be
restricted as much as possible so that it will not blur the lines of
knowledge itself. I mean rather the internal system of a science, that
is, the arrangement, the grouping of subjects and phenomena belonging to the sphere of some science according to their real affinity and
their real relationships one to another.[30]

The discovery of such a natural system had been a decisive step
in the development of every science. Take astronomy, for instance. Like all sciences, it had begun with the collection of facts.
Then had come the first synthesis: the geocentric theory. This
had been an artificial system, perpetuated beyond its time by the
theory of epicycles. Copernicus' heliocentric system had inaugurated the next stage of the science, that of the natural system.
In fact, astronomy had become a real science only at this point.

The same thing appears to be true of every science. Only from the
moment when a science begins to realize the true or, as is more often
said, natural system in the sphere of its subjects and phenomena can
it be considered worthy of the name of science — though, properly
speaking, this is not fundamental, for it is impossible to define science
independently from the stage of development at which it finds itself.
A science is the whole science — just as a man is the whole man,
whether he is a child or an adult — provided only that it has as its
subject a sphere of phenomena which really exist and are not some
more or less arbitrary abstractions. I want to say that the organism
of man or the organism of society, for instance, can be subjects of
actual independent sciences regardless of the degree of perfection with
which the organism of man or the organism of society is studied, but
that the organs and process of digestion, for instance, cannot be the
subjects of an independent science, for there are physiological scientific truths and there are social scientific truths, but there cannot be
independent gastronomic or economic truths.[31]

It was impossible for a science, then, to discover the detailed
workings of its subject matter without the discovery of an appropriate natural system. A natural system made the facts more

meaningful, made it possible to deal with fewer facts and thereby gain more precise insights. Thus only after Copernicus' work had it become possible for Kepler to formulate his laws of planetary motion. Only the natural system of botany developed by Jussieu and that of zoology by Cuvier had made analogously detailed and fruitful results possible in these sciences. In history, valid judgments about progress and stagnation could not, in like manner, be made until that science had passed from the stage of the artificial to that of the natural system.

Danilevsky undertook to move the "science" of history to that stage. He thought that this would refute the Westerners' erroneous ideas about stagnation and progress and about East and West in two ways. On the one hand, a natural classification of historical phenomena would be a basis for a countertheory regarding the form of world history and the nature of progress. On the other, a countertheory based on a natural system would carry scientific and empirical, not merely philosophical, weight. It would thereby enlighten men in a more compelling way than usual; this was practically a necessity in the current Russian cultural situation as Danilevsky saw it. Therefore, though he went into some merely argumentative detail about Chinese history in an effort to discredit the Westerners' presumptions about Western progress and Eastern stagnation, he based his main attack on his ideas about historical classification. He would be both the Copernicus and the Kepler (and also, in a way, as we shall see, the Newton) of the science of history.

His first direct attack on the problem involved an enunciation of the requirements of a natural system and an examination of the linearly progressive theory in the light of these. There were three basic requirements for a natural system of classification: "(1) the principle of classification should include the whole sphere of that which is to be classified, penetrating into its most essential characteristics; (2) the objects or phenomena of any single group should have a greater degree of similarity or affinity among themselves than they have with the objects or phenomena of any other group; (3) the groups should be homogeneous, that is, the degree of affinity that unites their members should be the same in all groups." [32]

Danilevsky found that the going, artificial, linear system of history satisfied none of these demands. In the first place, the classificatory system of ancient, medieval, and modern did not include the entire field of study. The fall of Rome in 476, for instance, was supposed to divide ancient and medieval. But what did the fall of Rome have to do with Chinese history? Or with the earlier "falls" of Egypt or Greece? What significance did it have for Arabian history? Had not the fall of the Parthian empire or the rise of the Sassanid been more meaningful for the Euphrates area than the fall of Rome? Nor, he found, were the units within the groups, ancient, medieval, and modern, more similar to each other than to any outside units. Did not Rome and Greece have more affinity with modern Europe than with Egypt, India, or China? Finally, he could not see an equal degree of affinity uniting the members of the three groups. If Egypt, India, China, Babylonia, Assyria, Iran, Greece, and Rome belonged to "ancient," Germano-Roman (Western European or "European") history belonged to both "medieval" and "modern." Just as the Ptolemaic system had been geocentric in perspective, this artificial system of history was "presenticentric." The historian was blinded by the stage of history closest to him. He saw it as the final stage, with all other history as a kind of blurred background to it. Thus, he made the Germano-Roman phase of history equivalent to the fate of mankind and viewed Germano-Roman civilization as universal human civilization. This was an important source of the illusions of Russian Westerners and the related difficulties of Russian foreign relations.

It is interesting to notice in passing that Danilevsky did, however, recognize some empirical justification for the illusion of continuity in Western but not in Eastern history. Every people must eventually grow old, just like a plant or an animal. Geology and paleontology taught that whole species and kinds of life had died out. Each had a birth, growth, flowering, and decay. How or why this happened, no one knew — any more than they knew why individuals went through this cycle. (Here spoke Danilevsky the statistician.) In the case of "political organisms" there was sometimes an extremely prolonged old age or period of decay. This was the present state of China. Egypt and Byzantium had also had very long periods of senescence. But in Western history there had been much passing to and fro of new peoples and forces. They had killed off aging organisms and had been fertilized by their remains. Thus the lives of Western peoples seemed to follow one after another. This was an empirical prop for the illusion of linear progress. The presence of Christianity (which Danilevsky regarded as the one true religion in the very stringent sense that he thought all others "lies") and its transmission from people to people also added to the illusion. Elsewhere in *Russia and Europe* he found some similar ideas about affiliated civilizations pregnant with eschatological meaning.

But at this point he was mainly interested in emphasizing his conviction that there was no such thing as a universal human civilization, that Europe had no monopoly on civilization and progress. The artificial quality of the scientific basis of the linear system was further heightened by the elaboration of Danilevsky's "natural system" of history. He advocated the abandonment of the old linear scheme, based on the concept of "steps of development," for a morphological scheme based on "types of development." Evoking the morphological taxonomy of Cuvier as a model, he pleaded for variety and tolerance. There were many civilizations, not just one civilization. There were many human possibilities. None could rightfully be called better or worse than another because they were ultimately incommensurable. Each civilization had its own basic structural plan. Each was a type of development, just as architectural styles of various ages and peoples were "types of beauty," not steps toward beauty.

The forms of the historical life of mankind, just like the forms of the plant and animal world, like the forms of human art (styles of architecture, schools of painting), like the forms of language . . . like, finally, the manifestations of the spirit itself striving to realize types of goodness, truth, and beauty (completely independent and not developments of one another) not only change and perfect themselves with age, they also vary according to cultural-historical types. Therefore, properly speaking, only inside one and the same type or, as it is called, civilization can the forms of historical movement really be distinguished by the terms ancient, medieval, and modern history. This division is only a subordinate one. The chief one, however, must be the distinction of cultural-historical types, that is, independent, original plans of religious, social, moral, industrial, political, scientific, artistic, in a word, historical development . . . The natural system of history must therefore distinguish cultural-historical types of development . . . from steps of development.[33]

But what of the system of civilization as a whole? Should we not be able to say something of it in order to make history meaningful? No, at least not in any metaphysical sense. In this case the historian found himself in the same situation as the astronomer. The astronomer could plot the courses of the planets which lay under his investigation, some with exactness, others only approximately; but he could say nothing about the movement of the whole solar system. Such things could only be known to God.

The Russian Populist Mikhailovsky once suggested that Danilevsky was the kind of thinker who built up his readers' credibility in one connection and then, when in difficulty in some other connection, borrowed on this credibility in order to move over the difficulty. There was some truth in this. For, after all his pretentious methodological preparations, it is a little surprising to find Danilevsky telling us that the enumeration of "these [cultural-historical] types presents no difficulty, for they are well-known. These, in substance, are the cultural-historical types or independent civilizations arranged in chronological order: (1) the Egyptian; (2) the Chinese; (3) the Assyrian–Babylonian–Phoenician, Chaldean, or Old Semitic; (4) the Indian; (5) the Iranian; (6) the Hebraic; (7) the Greek; (8) the Roman; (9)

the New Semitic or Arabian; (10) the Germano-Roman or European. To these it is perhaps possible to add two American
types: the Mexican and the Peruvian, which suffered death by
violence and did not succeed in completing their development."
We are to learn later that a central question of the nineteenth
century was whether the American (mainly the United States)
civilization, which was according to Danilevsky already emergent, and the Slavic civilization would add themselves to this list
in the form of fully grown types or only in the truncated form
of the Mexican and Peruvian types, in the form of "ethnographic
material." [34]

Where Danilevsky got this "quick list" of civilizations remains
a puzzle. It probably came from some standard world history,
possibly Heinrich Rückert's, as Vladimir Soloviev thought, but
more probably from Gervinus or Rotteck or Weber, for these
nineteenth century historians, unlike Rückert, are mentioned in
Russia and Europe.[35] So is Hegel. The list may be Danilevsky's
own composite from such sources.

Besides these civilizations or cultural historical types, Danilevsky found other historical phenomena. On the analogy of Cuvier's
"promotion" of the cryptogams, the former stepchildren of the
taxonomist, Danilevsky found a place for some stepchildren in his
system too.

These positive cultural-historical types — successive and solitary —
do not, however, exhaust all the agencies of history. In a solar system,
side by side with the planets, there appear from time to time comets
which come and then disappear for many centuries into the darkness
of space. Falling meteors, stars, and zodiacal light are other forms of
the manifestation of cosmic matter. Similarly, besides the above positive cultural types of civilizations, there are in the human universe
intermittent temporary agencies like the Huns, the Mongols, and the
Turks who, having performed their destructive mission, having helped
dying civilizations to die and then scattered their remains, return to
their previous nothingness and disappear. We can call them the *negative agencies* of history. Sometimes, however, constructive as well as
destructive missions are performed by the same tribe, as for instance,

by the Germans and the Arabs. Finally, there are tribes or peoples whose creative élan is, for some reason, *arrested* at an early stage and who are therefore destined to be neither constructive nor destructive, neither positive nor negative agencies of history. They represent only ethnographic material, a sort of inorganic matter entering the historical organisms, the cultural-historical types. Undoubtedly these tribes increase the variety and richness of the historical types, but in themselves they do not achieve any historical individuality. The Finns and, to a greater degree, most of the tribes of mankind, are examples of this.

Sometimes dead and decayed civilizations disintegrate to the level of this ethnographic material until a new formative (creative) principle unites their elements with a mixture of other elements into a new historical organism, until this principle calls them to an independent historical life in the form of a new cultural-historical type. The peoples that made up the Western Roman Empire serve as an example of this. They became ethnographic material after the disintegration of the Empire and re-emerged in a new form, known as the Romanic peoples, after experiencing the influence of the Germanic formative principle.

To sum up: the historical role of a tribe or people is threefold: it is the positive role of a cultural historical type (civilization), or the destructive role — the so-called whips of God that render the *coup de grace* to senile, agonizing civilizations, or the role of serving the purposes of others as ethnographic material.[36]

While Danilevsky did not rely on his system of classification alone to settle the Westerners, it was obviously designed to move that cause a long way forward. From such a point of view, the idea of Europe as the universal and final civilization was not only clearly unscientific, it was also parochial, narrow, and inflated. So far did Danilevsky push his point about cultural pluralism that his readers at the time may well have wondered, as many have since, if he did not mean utterly to demolish the idea of progress in history.

But, on this point, it would be wrong to confuse his sometimes angry overemphasis with what he really had to say. An affirmation of order and progress fitted Danilevsky's purpose of redefining Slavophilism and enlightening the Russian public. It was besides a product of his own training and the climate of opinion of the fifties and sixties. Most important, it was central to his specific effort to convince the Russian Westerners that barbarism and chaos were not the only alternatives to their foolish imitativeness of the West.

He envisaged two types of interaction between civilizations, one falsely, the other truly progressive. One of his "Keplerian" laws stated that the ultimate "sources of the civilization of one cultural-historical type" could not really be transmitted "to the people of another type." They were necessarily of internal origin. "Each type works these out for itself." But this could and often had been done "more or less under the influences of previous or contemporary" civilizations.[37] To this latter type of effect, sometimes nutritional, sometimes actualizing, he gave the name *vozdeistvie* or "influence."

Influence was sharply distinguished from *peredacha* or "transmission" of ultimate sources of civilizational energy.[38] Alexander the Great's effort to Hellenize Asia was an example of attempted transmission. But after seventy years of superficial Hellenism, with the establishment of the Parthian and Sassanid Empires, the eastern part of his empire had reverted to its Iranian basis. In Syria and Asia Minor, Hellenism had apparently had more success. But, in fact, it had been very superficial, restricted to the ruling classes who lived in the great cities, and who had been Greek to begin with.

Genuine influence was also not to be equated with inoculation. Inoculation could be compared to the process of grafting in fruit trees. The process did not change the nature of the host, but the graft drew its nourishment from it and, as such, was a parasite. Though not to be confused with progress, this had not always been a bad thing, as the examples of Hellenism in Egyptian Alexandria or Roman civilization in Celtic areas indicated. In these cases the hosts had been useless for any other purpose. But in other cases the result had been monstrous, like the inoculation of a people with a disease. Such had been the case with much of the influence of Greek civilization on Rome. The Romans never produced any science or plastic arts that were worthwhile. Yet the Etruscans (the "old Italians" or the original Romans) had shown great potentialities in these areas. Cato and his party, the "Latinophils" had been right in their stringent nativism. If Rome had gone its way, it might have surpassed Greece in science and in plastic arts. This was a good lesson for Russia, which was already showing the unfortunate effects of inoculation in the form of "Europeanism, the sickness of Russian life."

Real influence, truly progressive and beneficial to the recipient civilization, took place in two ways. The first Danilevsky compared to the process of enriching and cultivating the soil in order to help plants flourish. Dead or dying civilizations or types left residue which had a nutrient effect upon new types fortunate enough to be located in the same general geographical area. We have already discussed his favorite example of the operation of this process in Western Europe; it was admittedly an empirical basis, though an unsatisfactory one, for the Westerners' illusion of the unique progressiveness of "Europe." The other type of "influence" is more significant and complex, and Danilevsky's explanation of it reveals many of his more fundamental assumptions.

There was, in his view, something in human experience that could legitimately be called universality or universal human civilization. It was not localized anywhere; that was the important point. It had the form of a "common treasury of mankind," a sort of world cultural bank into which the various civilizations deposited their ultimate achievements: artistic techniques; scientific laws; political, economic and social "rules" (*pravila*).[39] As time went on and the treasury developed, cultural-historical types could draw from it, improve the withdrawals by dealing with them from new points of view or in the light of often unique local natural or social data, then replace the improved products for the use of others.[40]

The chief example Danilevsky gave of the operation of this

process was the development of science. He divided the histories of the sciences into stages: data-gathering, artificial system, natural system, partial empirical laws, "general rational law." We have already seen a partial example of his view of the stages of science in his account of the historical relationship between artificial and natural systems. This is easily expanded, using again the example of astronomy. The primitive data-gathering stage had been superseded by Hipparchus' elaboration of the artificial, geocentric system. The names of Copernicus and Kepler were inseparable from the next two stages; Newton, with the law of gravity, had inaugurated the last, the final stage of astronomy.

Hipparchus was a Greek, Copernicus was a Slav, Kepler and Newton were "Europeans." Three cultural historical types had "cooperated" in the progress of astronomy. All the other sciences were viewed in the same general way, except that few of them were as yet complete. Though in many cases international cooperation in the development of a science had been mostly between nationals within "Europe" rather than between scientists belonging to different civilizations, Danilevsky repeated his point emphatically. Indeed, he worked out a rather elaborate scheme of the history of the sciences to indicate the very real possibility of future great Slavic achievements in science. He envisaged active future cooperation, as he defined this, in that area.

Science was his fullest example. But it was not the only one. He also thought the Slavic cultural-historical type would extend the political principle of liberty, discovered in Europe, into the socio-economic sphere, in the form of socialism based on the Russian peasant commune. This political principle of liberty was also being borrowed and worked upon by both the United States and Russia, Slavdom's present active member. Each would modify it differently. Danilevsky's exemplary Panslav Union would result in a new view of civilizational liberty in the world. In a sense, Danilevsky was still a Westerner himself.

The example of astronomy indicates that he thought it likely, at least in some fields, that elements in the treasury could be brought to a final stage of humanly possible perfection. "The simpler a field is, the less importance in the achievement of a true representation has the one-sidedness of the point of view from which we look at it . . . the degree of perfection which a science has attained has precisely the same effect. Thus, if the development of some branch of knowledge reached the point where a precise and positive method became available for studying it, then both the effects of personal and national views and the usual subjective admixtures would be, in significant degree, removed." [41] The whole process, indeed, was thought of in so orderly and progressive a manner that it reminds one of the development of reason in Hegel or of science in Auguste Comte. The idea of ultimately available "precise and positive" methods in the treasury of mankind, tried and true precipitates of long historical experience, even anticipates the rather dogmatic Soviet view of dialectic as a kind of Aristotelian logic.[42] Danilevsky was a long way from proto-Spenglerian relativism. The Westerners need have had no fear of turning from Europe to chaos.

Yet it would have been difficult for Danilevsky's readers, the Westerners, as he defined them, not to have seen their conception of universality seriously challenged by this. They were giving universality a metaphysical status and seeing it incarnate in "Europe." Insofar as Danilevsky was willing to grant the idea of universality more than nominalist stature, he insisted that it be viewed as something realizable only on a multitemporal and multilocal basis.[43] Universality and its actualizations in civilizations might be regarded, in his view, as analogous in relationship to that of the genus (a "treasury of similarities") to the species. The genus could never realize itself in any one concrete form but only in many. No particular vegetable could ever realize the "idea of vegetableness." Similarly, no individual could realize his "total self" at any one point in his life; he could not be child, adult, and old man all at any one time. None of his stages of growth was superior to any other. In like manner, a metaphysical universal (*obshchechelovecheskii*) civilization was an absurdity:

it would have had to be the equal of "Greece in art, Europe in science, India in fantasy, Rome in state structure, the Hebrews in their adherence to the Word of God."

Only God could know the story of progress and backwardness in this metaphysical realm or the relationship of it to the human kind of progress. Men had necessarily to concern themselves with a more human kind of universality, that of the common treasury. Here the historical picture was not one of European uniqueness either. Europe had been a great but only one of many contributors; this would continue to be true in the future. Indeed, the concept of a "panhuman" (*vsechelovecheskii*) civilization, one which brought the treasury to completion, was about as absurd as that of a metaphysically "universal" (*obshchechelovecheskii*) civilization. God alone was a real "pan-man." At least, Europe had obviously not been able to complete the treasury. There was plenty to be done by new civilizations like Slavdom or America.

Danilevsky's relegation of metaphysics and God's purposes to the level of the unknowable served not only his purpose of changing the Westerners' minds about the nature of Europe and the possibilities for Slavic civilization. It was also designed to make them more ready to support a more Machiavellian Russian foreign policy. For if men, in the nature of the circumstances, could not see the relevance of religion, idealism, and morality in public life but only in their own private lives, then a degree of forceful political irresponsibility, a giving way to "historical instinct," was justified. Equally important, if there was at the same time a God and He cared about men, as Danilevsky believed, then the consequences of relatively irresponsible self-assertiveness could be left to His invisible hand. Finally, it could be that assertiveness without consideration of its ultimate ends, which were unknowable, might even be the way of carrying out His mysterious purposes. In this spirit, the "Protestant ethical" spirit of Adam Smith and Bentham, Danilevsky praised the historical conduct of both Romans and Germans. "What is the interest of mankind? Who has this interest but God? Who knows its course? Without doubt, it was in the interest of mankind that Rome was destroyed and that in place of its civilization barbarism reigned temporarily. But no Roman or German knew or could know that the interest of mankind demanded this. Each understood or at least felt only what the interest of his own people demanded." [44] In similar vein, there is the famous brutal slogan: "For every Slav — Russian, Czech, Serb, Croat, Slovene, Slovak, Bulgar (I would like to add Pole also) — after God and His Holy Church, the idea of Slav-dom must be the highest idea, higher than freedom, higher than science, higher than education, higher than any earthly wel-fare." [45]

In the face of the entrenched Westerners, Danilevsky engaged himself in a series of cumulative and intricately related intellectual moves designed to set up a self-accelerating political process: na-tionalistic assertiveness, awakening on the basis of his ideas, would lead to changes in political and cultural circumstances which would, in turn, lead to more adherence to his ideas, and so on and on. Thus he began by bombarding the idea that Europe was progress and civilization, Russia, stagnation and barbarism. But at the same time he tried to limit the anticipated change of mind from Westernism to Slavophilism in such a manner that meta-physics would be left out. For this he found it useful to advocate a kind of controlled barbarism for Russia, thus partly compromis-ing his first move in the interest of his second. A more irresponsi-ble foreign policy, based on a giving way to "national instinct," would advance the Slavic cause. With this, perspective on Europe, Russia, history, God, and man would improve even more. The whole process would gradually build itself up to a successful con-clusion.

The key problem, given the current cultural and psychological situation, was how to start. Danilevsky was not satisfied that a new classification of historical phenomena and a new theory of progress were sufficient. He went on to discuss the natural his-tory of the human mind, a history that illustrated, in particular, why Europe made such claims to universality and why so many educated Russians believed these claims.

4

Westernism, *zapadnichestvo*, as Danilevsky defined it, envisioned history as a pilgrimage of mankind to a promised land on earth. It was a hopeful and optimistic outlook; it gave men a way of seeing meaning amid the contradictions of their lives. But it presupposed a number of things which Danilevsky did not like. There was the linearly progressive view of time. The mechanical inflation or deflation of individual peoples' worth, on the basis of their predefined historical "contributions," followed logically from this view of time, whether in Hegel's theory or in that of the English political economists. There was the moralistic view of historical action, values being hierarchically arranged on the arbitrary basis of progress toward the heavenly city. The localization of the end of history in a particular area was another natural corollary. These last two beliefs served to weaken in advance all of "Europe's" potential competitors.

A mere attack on the details of this view, such as Danilevsky made in his theories of historical classification and of true progress, was not sufficient in itself to raise meaningful doubts about it. For its most powerful prop was its ability to assure men of the possibility of human transcendence over the apparent contradictions of spatial and temporal particulars. It assured men not only that their lives were orderly and meaningful but that their minds were somehow above, outside of, the unpleasant, often absurd, earthbound facts of social existence. It gave them a sense of freedom and dignity, here and now, just as the Orthodox Christian doctrine of Heaven, of which *zapadnichestvo* was a secularization, gave men a feeling that they were growing metaphysical persons, not simply atomistic individuals. From this sense of freedom and dignity stemmed a certain sense of well-being, of joyfulness, of hope. Men would not abandon such precious things merely on the basis of a theory of historical classification and progress. Their vested interests in their own sense of dignity and hope would resist this to the end. Some such line of reasoning seems to have been at the root of Danilevsky's concerted effort to cultivate a degree of pessimism, doubt, despair, a sense of the animality of man in his readers.

The history of mortal, public man, he thought, was not like a pilgrimage to some city of reason. It was more like a series of funeral processions. "The course of development of cultural-historical types resembles most that of those perennial monocarpic plants whose period of growth is indefinitely long, but whose period of bloom or fertility is relatively short and exhausts their life force forever." [46] The inevitable civilization cycle of growth, flowering, decline, and death was not even rationally understandable; it was mysterious and fatalistic. "I said that the aging of individuals was somewhat more understandable. This is not so: in reality it is no more understandable than the aging of societies. The individual too is made up of ceaselessly self-renewing elements. Parts of his body burn up, decompose, and disintegrate, and are renewed by new parts. Why are these new parts inferior to and more poorly integrated than the old, so that the general effect of their activities is less beneficial for the whole? This is no less difficult to explain than why, with the continual renewal of the individual parts making up the social body, these parts lose their original qualities. Why, when once there were men born like Pericles and Epaminondas, Aeschylus and Sophocles, Phidias, Plato and Aristotle . . . among the Greeks, were they replaced by nonentities?" [47]

The process could not be understood. It could only be described statistically. "Let us take the course of daily temperature as the first example. It depends on the apparent movement of the sun in its heavenly arc. The sun reaches its highest point at midday, but, as a result of its [upward] movement, the temperature continues to climb for two or three hours after this, though the cause of it has already begun to decline." [48] Similarly, June was the seasonal peak of the year, but the real summer weather and the flowers came only during the first part of the period of seasonal decline. A man reached the height of his moral and physical powers at thirty, but few men had ever done great intellectual work until their forties. Languages always passed the peak of their development before great literary periods. So it was too with civilizations. Greece had reached its peak in the age of Pericles. But the greatest achievements in Greek art, thought, and science had come only afterward. Rome had reached its peak during the Punic Wars, but the great period of Roman civilization had been the Augustan age. Europe itself had reached its peak before the sixteenth and seventeenth centuries.[49] Names like Raphael, Michelangelo, Shakespeare, Kepler, Galileo, Bacon, and Descartes were the symbols of the flowering of Europe. After them there was nothing for Europe to do but to work along the same lines. It was well into its period of decline by the nineteenth century. The current brilliance of Western science should not deceive anyone. Science was a fruit of civilization. The blossom was the gift of early spring, the fruit of early autumn. The plant thus lived on after the time of blossoming to yield the fruit. The life of a civilization "continues even after the leaves, the chief organs of nourishment, have dried up. It sometimes continues even after the fruit have been plucked from the plant . . . It continues even on the shelves of the storeroom." [50] Even ghosts of dead civilizations continued to haunt the living long after death, necessitating some practice analogous to the old Slavic one of driving an aspen stake into the funeral mound to keep the ghost down.[51]

No one should let himself be misled by such lingerings. Every civilization "ends with that time when the creative activity of the peoples of a given type is exhausted: they either rest on what they have achieved, considering the testament of the past the eternal ideal of the future, and grow decrepit in an *apathy of self-satisfaction* (like China, for instance); or they fall into insoluble, from their point of view, antinomies, contradictions —

proving that their ideal (like everything human) was incomplete, one-sided, mistaken, or that harmful external circumstances deflected the ideal from the straight road. In this case there arises disenchantment and peoples fall into an *apathy of despair.*" [52]

The autumnal quality of Danilevsky's view of history was not only a device for discrediting the idea of Europe's finality and universality. It was also one for encouraging the Westerners in Russia to die a little, as it were, to die in order to live, to accept their harsh Panslavist political fate in order to achieve their high cultural destiny.

Danilevsky seems to have meant to sound scientistically sour and hard-boiled. But, in fact, he was not as far from the original Slavophils as he may have thought. To them, also, the genuine life had been sparse, exposed, without adornment. They had probably derived this idea not from science, but from Christian tradition. Life was a cross, an imitation of the way of the Lord, a witness of His presence.

If Danilevsky could not, under the circumstances, explain these mysterious cycles, he did attempt to show, at some length, that the condition of knowable, mortal, historical man was not at all inappropriate to them. Moreover, he tried to show that, given the nature of mind and its growth, the hardening and tempering of mind involved in political Panslavist activity would not spoil potentialities for high culture. On the contrary, it would make them possible.

As far as could be verified positivistically, the mind was earthbound. Men's minds were not transcendent over circumstances, nor separable from their mortal aspects, particular environments, practical activities.

First of all, men did not think alike. Different civilizations, even different nations within them, showed marked mental differentiations. In the history of scientific progress, for instance, the Germans had been frequent contributors of artificial systems. The German mind was one at once disturbed by quantities of disordered facts and strongly given to wild speculation, to the search for *ein durchgreifendes Prinzip*. The French mind, however, was practical and unspeculative. French scientists had worked more patiently, cautiously, and experimentally; they had contributed more natural systems to science than any other nationality. Both in science and elsewhere, Englishmen worked repetitiously in terms of ideas of struggle and free competition; Hobbes, Adam Smith, Darwin were typical. The structure of the American mind, at its present stage of development, expressed itself most naturally in technology; the structure of the Russian mind, at its present stage, had markedly bureaucratic, "state service," qualities. The European mind, as a general phenomenon, was a violent one. It had a strong feeling for the individual personality; this was expressed in authoritarianism, in anarchism, in economic exploitation, in the practice of free trade. The Slavic mind, in contrast, was tolerant, cooperative, selfless.[53]

Peoples, especially at the typal level of differentiation, had different "psychic structures." The characteristics of these reflected the particular, differing activities of peoples over long periods. Thus, the English were free traders; hence they thought about the world generally in terms of competition and struggle. At the present juncture of history, the United States had achieved more than Russia in the field of technology, Russia much more than the United States, just emerging from the Civil War, in that of political organization. In each case circumstances had dictated activities and activities had structured minds. The people of the United States had had no important foreign enemies, but had been confronted with a great struggle with nature. Hence American psychology was technological. On the other hand, Russia's enemies had been many and a high level of political organization had become a necessity. Political activity had stamped the Russian psyche by several means. State service had become an influential social norm, so much so that people looked with disapproval on anyone outside it. Many people had found privileges and advantages in state service; this had raised its cultural value too. Ultimately both family and school had become oriented toward the service. So strong, in fact, had the obsession with politics become that it had brought out special mental, even physiological characteristics, which, by the process of the inheritance of acquired characters, had become integral parts of the Russian physical and mental makeup.[54] Danilevsky gave Darwin credit for helping him develop his ideas on American and Russian character. Indeed, much of his theory of mind has marked social Darwinian overtones.[55]

In addition to such general observations on the contingent aspects of basic national or larger psychic structures, Danilevsky also made some remarks about the historical development of group minds during civilizational cycles. This further emphasized the naturalistic quality of mind. Cultural-historical types went through several more or less distinct periods of development: the ethnographic, the interim state, the state, the civilizational. The differentiating characteristics of the typal psyche were set in the first period. The last three were stages of maturation of this mental structure. Both the structure itself and its stages were, however, made possible mainly by prolonged group activities, practical and earthbound.

It was true that no people could live, except as a "historical pleonasm," without some integrating principle. "Every living organic thing must contain in itself an internal essence, meaning, idea — that which we call its spirit — of which it itself is only the outward casing, the visible expression. It is this idea alone that links the parts of the body into an organic whole, that makes it possible for [the organism] to resist harmful external influences and to arrange these parts according to its own specific morphological type." But this was not metaphysical spirit. "The idea which vitalizes a state . . . or a less loosely knit union of peoples . . . is not some abstract mystical notion, but, on the contrary, something living in the consciousness of all or of a large majority of the citizens of the state." [56] A particular natural or typal consciousness was the product of group activities in the ethnographic period. Here people cooperated in a struggle for existence against national obstacles, forest, floods, mountains.[57] In the process common ways of thinking or, what was the same thing, a common and very particular psychic structure emerged. Inwardly the people experienced this as group consciousness. They objectivized this consciousness in their mythology, their epic traditions, their first economic and social arrangements, especially their language.[58]

The ensuing maturation of a group mind was also, in important part, the product of common activity in a struggle for existence. Now, however, the struggle was not with nature, but (as in Marx after the stage of "primitive communalism") with other human groups or their cultural products. "The transition both out of the ethnographic stage into the state stage and out of the state stage into the civilization or cultural stage is determined by a shock (*tolchok*) or series of shocks, originating in external circumstances, which awaken or increase the activity of the people in a given direction." [59] For the Greeks, the attack of the Heraclidae (the Dorians) had been the first shock, the Persian Wars and "the knowledge of Oriental wisdom," the second. The first for Rome had been the wars between the Italian states, wars which had ended in the supremacy of Rome over Italy externally and in the establishment of the rule of the aristocrats over the plebeians internally. The Punic Wars and the knowledge of Greek civilization had been the second. The Germans had had the stimuli of their own invasion of the Roman empire, of classical culture brought into Western Europe by Byzantine refugees, of the discoveries overseas.

As the psychic structure matured, national self-consciousness increased and its manifestations became more and more sophisticated. Its ensuing expressions, states and "civilizations," were specific in nature; they were appropriate to the shock or series of shocks that had led to a degree of mental growth. Even though the historical shocks a people felt were sometimes not very distinct, there was always a political shock at the end of the ethnographic period. This usually resulted in the suffering of a foreign yoke. In the subsequent interim state period, the common interest became one of preserving some sense of national integrity. This led to an intensification and growth of national self-consciouness. The new level of consciousness eventually expressed itself in a drive for liberation from the foreign yoke and in the institution of a native state. Somewhat similarly, foreign cultural domination helped lead to simultaneous, though at first secondary preposession with national cultural integrity and to the development of a native culture.

The degree of maturity achieved in the interim state period made the state period psychologically possible. The psychology of the state period was a prerequisite for, a necessary stage preceding, the civilizational period; without it the wrong kinds of foreign influences arose, as in Russia. "In order for the civilization proper to a cultural-historical type to be born and grow, it is necessary that the peoples belonging to it enjoy political independence." [60] "By civilization period I mean that time in the course of which the peoples constituting a type — having left the unconscious, purely ethnographic forms of life (which is their so-called ancient history), and having founded, strengthened, and delineated their own inner essence in independent political entities (this is the content of every medieval history) — display pre-eminently their own spiritual activity in all those directions for which there are bases in their spiritual nature [that is, psychic structure], display it not only in the sciences and the humanities but also in the practical realization of their own ideals of justice, liberty, social welfare and personal well-being." [61] The implications of all of this for Danilevsky's Panslav scheme are evident. So is the pointed suggestion that the Westerners' passivity was partly a function of their national immaturity.

Much of this theory of development resembles Danilevsky's theory of the stages of development of a science: data gathering (ethnographic), artificial system (interim state), natural system (state), partial empirical laws (civilization). After the first, each was dependent on the progress made in the previous stage. The artificial system "oppressed" the data like a foreign yoke. The natural system arose when the data expressed their true nature. A people with a sense of national identity strengthened in the political struggle with foreigners and expressing itself in a native state was ready to go on to civilization; the scientist in possession of a natural system had sufficient control to go on to partial empirical laws.

But, if expectations of psychological growth and of capacity for original civilization could be justifiably associated with *Realpolitik*, these expectations, in Danilevsky's view, should be sharply limited. Men could not expect the civilization stage of their histories to be like a heaven on earth or even a Slavophil Christian society. *Realpolitik* would not lead to any degree of ontological fulfillment. Indeed, had he not insisted on this it would be impossible to speak of a quasi-liberal, nontotalitarian dimension of *Russia and Europe*. But it is possible to do so because, in his view, the coming of a people to political maturity not only prepared them for civilization. It was a step achieved at great, though necessary, psychic cost. Moving from the ethnographic to the state phase involved a sort of positivist version of original sin. The human psyche was irreparably injured, inwardly divided by the process of its own growth. This was one of the bitterest pills he offered the Westerners.

This national or typal psychic injury resulted from the fact that a people necessarily matured in a somewhat alien environment, responding to a randomly selected foreign domination. Under "ideal conditions," every people would develop its state in the general form of a decentralized federation. Here sovereignty would be distributed between central and local governments with more sovereignty in local than in federal hands. "The cantonal bond would be stronger and tighter than the district, the district than the area, the area than the provincial, the provincial than the state." [62] But such a state was only theoretically possible.

All historical states had developed in response to an external challenge, to varied forms of political dependency. There were three of these: slavery, vassalage, feudalism.[63] They differed in their severity and, under varying circumstances, the degree to which they were alien to the national psychic structure. Slavery was, in itself, the harshest form of domination. Maturation under it had resulted in the destruction of Rome, Greece, and other types before their time. China alone had been able to enjoy longevity after suffering it. A slave upbringing usually led to a master-slave mentality, to slavish institutions, and to an early demise of the type. Feudalism was less severe. This type of dependency involved the conquerors' taking over the land but permitting the use of it in payment for services. Europe had experienced this and had internalized the structure of the experience. Exploitative capitalism was appropriate not only to the "violent" nature of the European psyche, but also to its historical education. The lightest form of yoke was vassalage. Here the conquering nation was so different in mental structure, mores, language and the like that it feared harmful intermixture. It therefore kept its distance and dependency took the form of paying tribute. The Russians had suffered vassalage under the Tartars, the Slavs under the Turks. The experience had taught discipline and stimulated growth, but with a minimum of deleterious effects. The Russia of Alexander II lacked exploitative capitalism and the common people had their own land because of this as well as because of the cooperative nature of the Russian psyche.

The various forms of political psychic maturity were conditioned, like the states in which they found expression, "on the one hand, by the nature of the national personalities serving as their basis and by the degree of affinity between them; on the other hand, by the degree of danger threatening the national honor and freedom." [64] Consequently the national mind, at the state level of growth, was inwardly divided. It was partly a native, partly a foreign product. It could not remedy this. There was even no easy way of getting an objective, integral view of the national self.

The quality of the state reflected the situation of the stage of mind it expressed. The state had a chilly English quality. Danilevsky accepted "the English conception that the state is that social form or that social structure which guarantees its members the protection of personality and of property, understanding personality as life, honor, and freedom. Such a definition seems to me completely satisfactory if life, honor, and freedom are understood communally, that is, not only individual life, honor, and freedom, but also national life, honor, and freedom, for these constitute the essential part of these blessings." [65] Danilevsky rejected all integralist theories of the origin of the state, theories based on the social contract idea or on the idea of the naturally social nature of man and he rejected "mystical definitions," such as were taught, he said, to Russian schoolboys, definitions which identified the state as the highest manifestation of law, right, and justice on earth.

The achievement of civilization did not involve a solution to the problem of inner dividedness. It did not involve it in metaphysical terms. Danilevsky did not, in this context, even discuss this spiritual question, having relegated it to the unknowable, to God's mysterious ways.[66] Nor would it solve the problem on the naturalistic level. There could be no full return, on a higher level, to the integrality of youth. Civilization was only a *pis aller*. "From the data available on the histories of the known cultural-historical types, it is possible to conclude that the general characteristic of the state period of their development is the loss of a greater or less part of that original tribal independence (tribal freedom in one form or another) and that the general characteristic of the civilization period is a striving for liberation from this dependency and for a substitution of real liberty for the lost freedom of antiquity — a substitution which has never been fully achieved." [67]

It was a harsh though unspectacular truth. Adult national life was a kind of entrapment. Men longed for the freedom of their childhood, but they had lost the capacity for regaining it. The course of national life was not free nor prone to tragedy; it was largely determined and essentially pathetic. Danilevsky's view of national psychic development was similar to the view of the condition of man in the literary works of his contemporary Turgenev or, later, of Chekhov.

Genuine truth, beauty, civilization were always bitter sweet; they were not genuine unless more than a little cruel, a little incomplete. Men did not want to recognize this. They fell into dream lives which defended them against it. They tried to believe that civilization was a complete return. The extravagant claims for the universality of European civilization, which were at the root of Westernism and of the whole outlook of the forties, grew out of both ignorance of the true nature of history and resistance to the pathetic insight it implied.

Hardly anyone now believes that German philosophy really brought the absolute into human consciousness or that French socialism found a transcendent formula that solved the social problem. Nevertheless, everybody still continues to confuse Europe with mankind, to assert that it has emerged from the sphere of the narrow and national to that of the universal human. I see in this only a confusion of the concept of the civilizational stage of the development of a culture type with the concept of the universal human. This confusion arose because a civilization always tries to demolish those special forms of dependence under which tribal freedom is brought in the course of the transition of the peoples of any cultural type from the ethnographic to the state form of living. Civilization always tries to substitute known forms of liberty for these forms of dependence. These forms of dependence are understood as national and the corresponding forms of liberty as universal (in accordance with the commonly held historical view that misconstrues a stage of development and understands, for example, the modern history of the civilization period of the Germano-Roman tribe as a direct step in the development of all mankind).

Examples were legion.

The religious despotism of Roman Catholicism is taken as a national appurtenance of the European peoples, but the anarchic liberty of Protestantism as the universal form of Christianity; or: religious intolerance and the interference of the Church in all state, social, and

family relations is considered a narrow, national phenomenon characteristic of the Middle Ages, that is, of the national period of the life
of the European peoples; but religious indifferentism and state atheism,
along with civil marriages, and so forth, are considered universal.
Monarchical feudalism is a national German phenomenon, but constitutionalism in the English tune is universal. In just such contradiction are: feudal law against unlimited personal economic freedom
(that is, the proletariat and collective slavery); workshops and guilds
against economic disorder, expressed by the formula, *laisser faire,
laisser aller;* mercantilism and the exploitation of colonies against free
trade.[68]

The claims were in vain. The absurd truth showed through the
subterfuge. "Both these forms of dependence and the forms of
liberty corresponding to them are equally national and condition
one another." [69] Nationality at the state level of development
conditioned the forms of liberty, while they, in turn, showed the
fundamental national inability ever to be quite free again. By unmistakable implication, the Westerners were not only foolish,
they were also robbing themselves of the only possibility for
true liberty. It was a perfect analogy to the problem of progress.
A false version of it kept men from being truly progressive. A
false version of "liberty" kept men from being as truly free as it
was possible to be. False expectations of fulfillment in civilization militated against the degree of fulfillment that could be
gained.

Danilevsky's theory of typal and national mental development
was incomplete and, in spots, contradictory. But it was sufficient
seriously to challenge the Westerners' sense of the quality of life
and of history and, besides, perhaps to make them feel foolish,
romantic, childish, quixotic. It provided both a didactic and an
emotional reinforcement to Danilevsky's theories of historical
classification and of true progress. Everything historical was much
more contingent, relative, physical, contrary, earthy, animal than
the Westernist humanitarians presupposed. Convinced to a degree
of this, the Westerners might be much more willing to act force-
fully, politically, egoistically. This would further the Panslav

cause — and that was the key to all Danilevsky's other aims, even, as we shall see, to those he admitted much less explicitly.

It was certainly, both despite and because of its utilitarian, liberal trappings, an extremist doctrine. Its implementation would have involved, at a minimum, the destruction of the Austro-Hungarian Empire and the Ottoman Empire in Europe. This might well have led to major war or a series of major wars. Intellectually, the theory was overindividualistic, almost to a Nietzschean degree. Separating the ideas of liberty and equality in discussing the "law of foreign policy" and the selfish and unselfish applications of the principle of utility in world politics, Danilevsky set a basis for exaggerating the assertive, belligerent, irrational, irresponsibly willful aspects of utilitarianism. English radical liberalism was appropriately susceptible to this type of exaggeration. Nevertheless, Danilevsky violated both its letter and its spirit. He also rendered it doctrinaire, abstract, absurd; and he applied it, so transformed, to a level of human experience and on a scale that was most unusual. Liberal in form, illiberal in content — this is the correct characterization. The paradoxical quality of the theory reflected its author's simultaneous attraction to and revulsion from Benthamism, on the one hand, and his manipulation of the theory for curious metaphysical purposes, on the other.

Yet, in the interest of full expository analysis of *Russia and Europe*, it should be stressed again that, in this part of his whole theory, Danilevsky's aims were not cosmic. They were explicitly limited and appropriate to the means he wanted to use. He did advocate the use of political power to achieve cultural, psychological, and philosophical ends, but only while at the same time defining these in a special way. It would be wrong to evaluate this advocacy of political means to such ends too negatively, as though it were *prima facie* an evidence of totalitarianism. Much, in this connection, must depend on the way Danilevsky defined his nonpolitical ends. For, if they were limited suitably to the means proposed for their achievement, these means would not have been, if the theory had been followed, overapplied. Machiavellian *Realpolitik* is not by nature totalitarian;[70] we would have a strange view of history and of life if this were the case. It is totalitarian when its aims are metaphysical or religious.

Danilevsky's famous theory of cultural historical types, in itself, was not of this kind. It was basically a distorted version of utilitarianism, an outlook "found" by Danilevsky in the treasury of mankind, closely related to the climate of opinion of Victorian England, familiar to him through his associates and through reading Adam Smith, Bentham, Darwin, Macaulay (one of his favorite authors). In this climate, assertive, egoistic, somewhat irresponsible action was believed to be the method of progress; and progress was defined as a maximization of rather shallow ego satisfactions. The invisible hand of a mysterious (so much so as to be nonexistent for some theorists) God sorted out the wheat from the chaff. Danilevsky applied this to civilizations: nationalistic assertiveness built the common treasury of mankind, a secular, operational, banklike institution. A kind of cultural capital was slowly being built up for its own sake. Men only knew that the process of contributing made them feel a little better, a little less out of Eden than they knew themselves inevitably to be, made them feel, at the same time, brave, modern, realistic, illusionless. The basic aim of the typal theory and its program was to kill off a false sense of metaphysical perspective, not to realize metaphysical ends by physical means. After the Panslav Union got going men's "world historical" urges would have been, not fulfilled but kept permanently in abeyance by the ceaseless necessities of maintaining the national ego in the struggle for existence and of making civilizational profits and paying off civilizational interest. "The habit of calculation is in itself antirevolutionary." [71]

The theory of cultural-historical types proper was not totalitarian. The theory in *Russia and Europe* as a whole was. Danilevsky did not really believe his typal theory. In a sense, it was a dishonest theory. His advocacy of utilitarian psychology, philosophy, and behavior for utilitarian ends was a way of agitating to involve Russia in a cause in which he did believe.

7

EUROPE, RUSSIA,
AND METAPHYSICS

THERE is a whole relatively consistent, finished Panslavist and utilitarian philosophy of history on the surface, as it were, of *Russia and Europe*. The completeness of this philosophy together with the presence in Danilevsky's work of much more, indeed of things which are utterly contradictory, raises questions about his goals: whether he really wanted a Panslav Union for the merely political and cultural reasons he stated; or whether he had in mind higher aims, like spiritual fulfillment, the harmonization of man with God, nature, his fellows, and himself; and, if such was the case, why he did not say so more openly. The middle chapters of his book raise such questions particularly cogently, for one has to do very little probing beneath the surface to see that Danilevsky had a deep commitment to spiritual ends, to a theological-metaphysical view of history, and to the Russian traditions he so heartily decried in his typal, Panslavist theory.

His Slavophilism is not his most interesting doctrine and it is by far his least original one. He was scarcely at his intellectual best in this area. Nevertheless, while telescoping the exposition as much as seems feasible, it is important to look rather carefully at these beliefs. Though mixed with and partly obscured by the language of his utilitarian, Panslavist theory, they constitute some of the best evidence regarding his actual goals and the historical context in which he conceived them. Study of this doctrine also provides insight into the nature of Danilevsky's deviation — leftist, quasi-Hegelian, rationalistic, utopian socialist — from authentic Slavophilism and into the still "Petrashevskian" quality of his thought.

The chapters in question are VIII through X. They deal with the question of Russia's distinctness, as a cultural-historical type, from "Europe." The titles are "The Distinctions of Psychic Structure" (VIII); "The Distinctions of Confession of Faith" (IX); "The Distinctions in the Course of Historical Education" (X). As the chapter titles suggest, we do not find ourselves here in completely strange territory. There is a continuity of vocabulary, of tone, and of many concepts from the previous section. A detailed study of the distinctness of Russia from "Europe" seems, moreover, quite logical and justified, even necessary. Yet in these chapters the typal theory of history is drastically violated. Europe and Russia are not distinguished, as we might expect, on the basis of distinct psychic structures, earthly, pragmatic in nature and origin, maturing under varying circumstances or on the basis of their different stages of growth. They are rather distinguished by their differing "characters." "Character" is a new concept. The character of a cultural-historical type transcends psychic structure and historical experience. Indeed, these are, for the most part, simply emanations of character, differing modes of its being. Each type has a character. Its collective personality, style of life, particular process of development result from character's inevitable unfolding. Spengler's "prime symbol" comes very much to mind in the study of Danilevsky's new, quite metaphysical entity.

In searching for those qualities which could really be considered traits of national character, it is necessary to take a road other than simple descriptive recording of partial observations. If we can succeed in finding traits of national character that have been expressed in the whole historical life and activity of the peoples to be compared, then the problem will be satisfactorily solved. For if some trait or other of national character appears in the whole history of a people, then it must be concluded, in the first place, that this is a trait common to the whole people and that only exceptionally can it belong to some other people; in the second place, that this trait is constant, independent of accidental or temporal circumstances, of any situation in which a people finds itself at one or another stage of the development through which it proceeds; finally, in the third place, that this trait, since it can stamp the whole character of a people's historical activity, is of essential importance [*eta cherta sushchestvenno vazhnaia*]. We have a right, therefore, to consider such a trait the moral ethnographic symbol of a people, the expression of the essential peculiarity of its whole psychic structure.[1]

Familiarity with this new entity, character, and its expressions is an indispensable prerequisite to appreciation of its important implications for Danilevsky's philosophy as a whole.

We are put on our guard at the very beginning of his discussion of the distinctions between Russia and Europe. Following a spirited introductory quotation from Khomiakov's poetry, we learn that

the distinctions in character of peoples making up original cultural-historical types, those distinctions on which is based the difference between their civilizations (which constitutes the essential content and fruit of the types' living activity), can be reduced to the following three: (1) an ethnographic distinction; this concerns those racial characteristics which are expressed in the peculiarities of the psychic structures of peoples; (2) a distinction in terms of ultimate values, on which alone can be based fruitful civilizational development, social and political, as well as scientific and artistic; (3) a distinction in terms of the course and conditions of the historical education of peoples. From these three points of view we will examine the peculiarities of Slavic and, in particular, Russian character — since the Russian people alone have achieved and preserved political independence, a condition without which, as history proves, civilization has never begun and never existed and therefore, probably, never can begin or exist. The goal of this study will be to discover whether distinctions are sufficient to warrant the elaboration by the Slavic peoples of their own original culture, in fear of loss of significance as a historical race (in the highest meaning of this term).[2]

Evidently psychic structure and historical education are no longer to be taken so seriously. Their interaction is not the really significant operative center of life of a cultural-historical type. Each is like a mode of being of the really essential character that underlies everything; also the peculiarities of each, in the cases of various historical types, are simply symbolic of the differing natures of characters. Illogically but appropriately, "Russia" now stands for Slavdom. Russia has achieved its statehood. Russia and Europe thus seem to be much more like contemporaries than before when we were led to believe that Slavdom as a whole was in its ethnographic, Europe in its civilizational phase. On this basis, too, stage of development seems to be no longer an important basis of distinction between these two types.

Finally, "a distinction in terms of ultimate values" has been brought in. This might be taken in one of two ways: on the one hand, as a distinction in terms of religious and ethical outlooks considered only as societal, cultural phenomena;[3] on the other, as one in terms of these outlooks as true or false. In the first case, a people's ultimate values would be under view, simply as particularly nodal phenomena in cultural life useful for making sharp, meaningful distinctions. Danilevsky had, on the whole, no such limited, heuristic device in mind. "The distinction between the spiritual basis of the Russian along with the majority of other Slavic peoples and that of the Germano-Roman peoples consists in the fact that the former profess Orthodoxy and the latter Catholicism and Protestantism. Is the distinction between these religions sufficient to differentiate the Slavic world and the Germano-Roman world as cultural-historical types? Is not this distinction unimportant in the face of a general concept of a Christian civilization? And, on the other hand, is not the distinction between Catholicism and Protestantism greater than that between Catholicism and Orthodoxy . . . ? This can be answered very briefly, for the distinction of truth from a lie is infinite and two lies are always less distinct from one another than either of them from truth." [4] Toward the very end of *Russia and Europe*, there

is the further information that, "on the objective, factual side
there fell to the Russian and to the majority of other Slavic peoples, together with the Greeks, the historical destiny of being
the leading trustees of the tradition of religious truth, Orthodoxy,
and thus of continuing with the great role that fell upon Israel
and Byzantium: to be peoples chosen by God. On the subjective
psychological side, the Russians and the other Slavs were filled
with the thirst for religious truth." [5]

We are confronted here with a theory of separately created
typal characters, characters which are, by their original nature,
good or bad, true or false. These characters not only determine
the historical lives of peoples, they also either assure or deny, by
strict predestination, their salvation or damnation. Danilevsky's
theory of Russia and of Europe proper is a modified and vulgar-
ized version of Slavophilism. It is not here modified as to metaphysics. The Russians are the children of light and the Europeans
of darkness. It is modified by near complete elimination of the
elements of human freedom and responsibility.

This theory is applied with marked consistency[6] in the analysis
of the two types, Europe and Russia. Danilevsky treated Europe
first. Moreover, he had frequent recourse to the nature of Europe
in his analysis of Russia; Russia was "not Europe." Let us follow
his own sequence.

The fundamental character trait,

common to all the peoples of the Romano-German type, [is] violence
(*Gewaltsamkeit*). Violence in itself is nothing more than an extraordinarily developed feeling of personality, of individuality, in accordance with which a man possessing it considers his own way of thinking, his own interest so highly that every other way of thinking and
every other interest must, willy-nilly, give way to him. Such obtru-
sion of his own way of thinking upon others, such subordination of
everything to his own interest does not seem unjust from the point
of view of highly developed individualism, of an extreme feeling of
private dignity. It seems only to involve the natural subordination of
lower to higher; in a sense, it seems to be even a blessing that is
inseparable from natural superiority. Such a habit of mind, of feeling,

and of will brings various features, depending on circumstances, into politics and social life — aristocracy and oppression of peoples *or* unlimited freedom and extreme political factionalism. In religion it brings both intolerance and rejection of all authority. It also has good aspects. It is the basis of persistence in activity, of firm protection of one's own rights, and so forth. Let us follow the events of European history to see if violence does not constitute one of the basic qualities of the Germano-Roman peoples.[7]

Danilevsky concentrated on two major facets of European history: the history of religion and that of oppression and liberation.

In the history of European religion Danilevsky found a singular lack of respect for the Church and for the objectivity of revelation. European religious behavior was consistently either political or philosophical — it was subjective, egoistic, and "violent" — rather than specifically religious.

The political side was to be seen in Catholicism. Originally Europe had been given Orthodoxy, the one true religion. Before the time of Charlemagne, all had been well. The Pope had had no pretensions. "The high priest of Rome" had been honored in Italy, Gaul, and Spain, but only because of his location in that renowned city. He had been Orthodox. He could have been similarly honored in the East, for people there were searching for some makeweight against the despotism of the Byzantine emperors. But Europeans could not accept the truth. Their violent character had found its first effective religious expression in the person of Charlemagne. For the sake of his own "violent" political ambitions he had transformed the papacy into a theocracy. After this European Christianity was not longer Orthodox but Catholic. The pseudo-Isidorean decretals and the insertion of the *filioque* clause into the Nicene Creed had been the first striking symptoms of the politicization of religion. The use of Christianity for political purposes or at least interference with it by political leaders had become a continuing practice. Behind a missionary mask, Charlemagne had conquered East Germans and Slavs. The Teutonic knights in the Baltic and Henry VIII had been political

Christians. While Danilevsky was at times sympathetic to the papacy, even in the nineteenth century Church-state conflict in Italy, he thought that, in general, the popes had internalized their false theocratic position quite early and had contributed to their own politicization. He cited the Inquisition, "Jesuitism," the doctrine of papal infallibility. Papal intolerance and persecution of heretics were, in his view, unusually good proofs that Roman Catholicism was political and not Christian, an expression of "violence," for Christianity was not by nature intolerant.

Protestantism, too, showed itself but a false religion, basically another kind of expression of violent, hyperindividualistic European typal character. In Danilevsky's theory more so than in that of the original Slavophils, Protestantism was a religious phenomenon parallel to, rather than reactive against, Catholicism. It had been made by European violence more than by an honest but unsuccessful search, in a distorted spiritual environment, for the truth.

Typical was the fact that European protests against Catholicism had been made, not in the name of the objective Church and objective revelation, but only in the name of individual reason or conscience or both. In this situation, every man became his own judge. Protestantism was thus tantamount to religious anarchism. Without objective ecclesiastical control it had become increasingly indistinguishable from philosophy. Referring to their own arbitrary desires, Protestants took from the Christian tradition only that with which they felt comfortable. Thomas Jefferson's idea that he could take Christian ethics without Christian mysteries was characteristic. Along this line, Protestantism had proceeded from *Ausschnitt zu Ausschnitt*, revision to revision, right out of religion itself. Now, consequently, there loomed the latest horrors in Western thought, "radical rationalism," deism, nihilism. Danilevsky saw a direct, inevitable line of development from Luther, Calvin, Zwingli, Henry VIII, and Schleiermacher to Büchner, the mechanistic materialist, the author of *Kraft und Stoff*.

In the typal theory proper, Danilevsky explained states of mind and outlooks largely as functions of tensions of national psychic growth in an often alien environment. His theory of Protestantism, if it had been consistent with this, would have referred to Europeans' search for lost freedoms of the ethnographic period in their civilizational. But now "character," meaning the soul not the mind, explained almost everything.

The account of the European history of oppression and liberation is much less intelligible and coherent than that of religion. Danilevsky threw out a number of scattered observations on European political and social life and history. For instance, in contradiction to his pet idea that politics and idealism, public and private morality, should be kept quite separated, he pointed to European atheistic statism as an important and most unfortunate symptom of violent character.[8] Cavour's formula, "the law is atheist," had simply been the culmination of a long, typical European development. Elsewhere Danilevsky gave the familiar nineteenth century nationalist lament about dynastic states (especially Austria) oppressing nationalities. In this vein he intoned against the "oppression of the abstract state in the living nationalities," "the old universal dynastic principle," "Louis XIV's *l'état c'est moi*," Machiavellian diplomacy by congress for the sake of balance of power. True, the period of the French Revolution and Napoleon had begun the demise of this old oppressive order. Though he regarded Napoleon III, that self-styled champion of nationalities, as something of a fake,[9] Danilevsky even sounds a little hopeful about the future of Europe in this connection. But it mattered little. The main thing was Europe's insoluble socio-economic problem not its nationality one. Indeed, fixation by European leaders on the latter was mostly a way of drawing attention from the former. It will seem highly significant to anyone familiar with Danilevsky's intellectual development that a kind of socialist analysis and critique of capitalism is the subject of the only sustained effort at discussion of the history of oppression and liberation in Europe. He drew a black picture. "Vio-

lence" had been and still was rampant; it was about to have its
reward. The "Cimbri and Teutons" were "at the gates"; another
"age of Marius" was at hand.

At the root of Europe's social problem was the fact that, while
the people had won and were winning important elements of
political and national freedom, they were making no progress
at all in the achievement of the socio-economic basis that was
absolutely indispensable for that freedom. In short, the common
people did not have land. This situation was a hangover from the
distant feudal past of Europe. Individualism, an especially significant epiphenomenon of violent character, had expressed itself, first, in the economic and social domination of the feudal
nobility, then, with their decline, in that of their direct successors, the bourgeoisie. Danilevsky, the old socialist, decried this
fundamental and subtle oppression, highlighting its evil by contrasting the situation of the European landless masses with that
of the Russian landed peasantry after 1861. He emphasized the
seriousness of the whole situation of European socio-economic
division by quoting Carlyle's *Sartor Resartus* at length (and the
editor of *Zariia* had the passage reproduced in Danilevsky's own
handwriting):

Or better, I might call them two boundless, and indeed unexampled
Electric Machines (turned by the "Machinery of Society"), with
batteries of opposite quality; Drudgism the Negative, Dandyism the
Positive: one attracts hourly towards it and appropriates all the
Positive Electricity of the nation (namely, the Money thereof); the
other is equally busy with the Negative (that is to say the Hunger),
which is equally potent. Hitherto you see only partial transient
sparkles and sputters: but wait a little, till the entire nation is in an
electric state; till your whole vital Electricity, no longer healthfully
Neutral, is cut into two isolated portions of Positive and Negative
(of Money and of Hunger); and stands there bottled-up in two
World-Batteries! The stirring of a child's finger brings the two
together; and then — What then? The Earth is but shivered into
impalpable smoke by that Doom's-thunderpeal; the Sun misses one of
his Planets in Space, and thenceforth there are no eclipses of the
Moon.[10]

Such was Danilevsky's "Europe." It was not, it would seem, just another type. Its contemporary state was not one of normal typal decline; it had never had any future to speak of. Europe was, had long been, without divine grace. Lacking this, it was doomed to self-inflicted sufferings and antinomies. That was its destiny, its character. Russia's was a different story.

Danilevsky's picture of Russia and its character suggests that he used two major criteria in elaborating it. First, Russian character was distinct because of the absence in it of "the European trait of violence, which the Romano-German peoples, in centuries of civilizing effort, succeeded only in transferring from one field of activity to another. Will not this inborn humanity [of Russians] be reflected as a peculiarly original quality in the nature of the civilization that they succeed in creating?" [11] Second, Danilevsky's Russia has the quality of a utopia and that of the scientific naturalist rather than of the Augustinian-Slavophil tradition. Where the Slavophils had emphasized the will and the emotional quality of Russia, Danilevsky praised Russian inherent prudence and reasonableness.

Anyway, we are told that the Russian people were tolerant.[12] They had never oppressed religious and national minorities. They were natural eighteenth century rationalists. They had not needed the enlightenment and the ideas of the encyclopedists in order to learn tolerance.[13] Nor had they needed "the wisdom of Beccaria" to learn humanitarianism in the treatment of criminals.[14] The death penalty had been abolished in Russia centuries before the eighteenth.

The outward appearance of the historical process in Russia, the land of "inborn humanity," prudence, reasonableness, was quite different from that of the process in Europe. Great historical decisions had been made in an atmosphere of calm and unanimity, not of strife and egoistic factions. Each event thus seemed to the historical observer to have taken place without preparation, for all the preparation and struggle had been inward, in the rational processes of men. At the crucial moment a great man arose who was simply the embodiment and executor of the consensus of the people. One example was the conversion of Russia to Christianity. Unlike the European, the Russian conversion had not involved conquests, martyrdoms, extensive missionary work. Vladimir, the embodiment of the rational consensus of the people, had thought through the problem of Russia's spiritual thirst, sent out ambassadors to look over neighboring religions, and then, it would seem, on the basis of the evidence, chosen Orthodoxy. All Russia had been converted immediately and without force. Another example was the liberation of the serfs in 1861. Alexander II had embodied the national consensus. The serfs had been freed and given land, all without any significant opposition and difficulty. "It would be quite incorrect to conclude from this general character, which works all the important revolutions in the life of the Russian people, that it is devoid of all energy and activity, that it is soft as wax and can be molded at will." [15] Reasonableness should not be confused with passivity.

Danilevsky's distinctly metaphysical presuppositions are particularly evident in his discussion of Orthodoxy and the Russian people.

Again he emphasized the objectivity of revelation. "Since the Christian Church and all Christian societies that call themselves Churches acknowledge Divine Revelation as their basis, they cannot call any doctrine that rejects Revelation Christian . . . this indispensability [of Revelation] is acknowledged because it alone can give a completely authentic, unshakable foundation to faith and morality." Ostensibly, man, in this view, was not predestined. "Revelation, that is, the communication to creation of the will of God, can be understood either as acting directly on the will, that is, as necessary, acting like an utterly irresistible instinct — or as having an indirect influence through understanding and consciousness. It is clear that, in the case of man, who is in essence free, only this latter kind of Revelation is possible."

But man was imperfect. He could not therefore, by himself, embrace revelation directly and fully. "Everything that is given to our human understanding can be taken in all its objective truth or in a form utterly different from it or in a form partly different from it. This last way of taking what comes to us is the only probable or practically possible way. Therefore, Revelation, in entering our consciousness necessarily loses its authentic meaning, and therefore loses its essence, the cause of its very existence; it is stripped of its force and significance; it becomes, as it were, unontological." Some mechanism was needed to counterbalance the imperfection of man and of his grasp of revelation. "Revelation is something completely useless, completely incapable of attaining its goal and thus not possible unless some means is given with it of guaranteeing its authenticity, its true meaning, and correct application to each given case. This is done by means of that which we call the Church, which by necessity is so infallible, as infallible as Revelation itself, that it is the only guarantee of the latter's infallibility, not in itself, but in our consciousness of it. The relationship of the Church to Revelation is exactly the same as the relationship of a court to the civil law, with the exception that inner veracity is not the same as external compulsion." [16]

This was in itself undoubtedly good Orthodox ecclesiastical doctrine. But in the context of Danilevsky's character theory of Europe and of Russia, it was a clumsy heresy. For Danilevsky was extending the whole idea another step. In his theory, men needed the Church to guarantee the authenticity of revelation; and they *also* needed a special kind of character to keep them from either distorting or abandoning the Church. The Europeans' violent character, not their sinfulness (as in the Slavophils' emphasis) had made it impossible for them to accept the Church. Therefore they had lost revelation and respect for it as well as for the Church's objectivity. In fact, it would appear that European character had first expressed itself in abandonment of the Church (the Catholic "heresy") and then of revelation and its objectivity (the Protestant "heresy"). On the other hand, the Russians, with their "inborn humanity" or reasonableness, had, quite naturally, stayed with the Church. What else could they have done? The reasonable could not be unreasonable. Actually they did not need the Church at all. It was superfluous. Its function was to stabilize and ontologize imperfect human reason or "our consciousness." There was as little that was imperfect about human reason in Danilevsky's Russia as there was about it in Fourier's phalanx. This whole theory is one of predestined peoples.

Danilevsky was not always consistently predeterministic, however. After all *Russia and Europe* was addressed to the problem of Westernism, the idolatrous *zapadnichestvo*, in Russia. At least the chosen people had been free enough to commit this sin. Yet even here Danilevsky's thought had a particular emphasis. He usually referred to Westernism as a disease never more than implying that it was a sin. Moreover, in his view, it had never touched the chosen people in their essence; it was a superficial (though very serious) thing, only a pseudomorphosis, to use an appropriate Spenglerian expression. Indeed, as we shall see, even *zapadnichestvo* was, in a way, given a providentialist rationale, for Danilevsky indicated he thought God was going to make use of Slavdom's effort to cleanse itself in order to usher in an ultimate, utopian civilization in Slavdom, maybe even in Europe also. There is inconsistency in Danilevsky's "theology," but the spirit of deterministic providentialism, distinctly immanentist and rather un-Slavophil, is clearly there. It attests, for one thing, to the rationalistic, scientistic, and naturalistic quality of his Orthodoxy.

The Russians, by and large, were predestined to be "free." Still even the saved, in Danilevsky's view (now state-oriented and quasi-Hegelian), had had to grow and mature. The Russians, unlike the damned Europeans with their crippling historical experience of feudalism, had matured under the influence of a series of what seem providentially beneficent authoritarianisms. Maturation under alien circumstances had not, as we might expect from Danilevsky's typal theory, injured the Russian soul at all. The

Russians had not merely been given an admirable character. They had also been blessed with a wonderful "historical education."

Oddly enough too, this Russian education recapitulated all three of the possible types of experience of dependency described in the typal theory proper: slavery, vassalage, and feudalism. The "first shock," which had started the Russians on the road to maturity, had been the coming of the Varangians at the invitation of the people themselves. This could have turned into a conquest. But (perhaps, we might guess, because the Russians had made such a reasonable choice) the Varangians had been a very small group and had been rapidly absorbed. This yoke had been very light. Russia needed another impulse; it was ready, presumably, after its first experience, for a stronger one. This had come from the Tartars. Under their yoke the Russian state, a symbol of national maturation, had developed markedly. Collecting tribute for the Tartars and protecting the people from direct contact with them, the princes of Moscow had developed into native and beloved rulers. Yet in the sixteenth and seventeenth centuries the Russian nation had still been too incohesive. Still another educational experience had been needed. The Russians were, at this point, evidently mature enough to take a hand in history themselves. For their own rulers now visited serfdom upon them. Boris Godunov had had the idea first; but Peter the Great had carried it out fully. Serfdom had been the Russian feudalism. It had been self-inflicted like European feudalism. But in Russia it had been a beneficient experience. Like the previous yokes, it had been light, as Danilevsky put it, a vaccination rather than smallpox. The lightness of the yoke he attributed to the facts that the masters and serfs had been of the same race and religion and that the Russian character was soft and humanitarian.

Under these circumstances, the Russian people were emerging from their "period of dependency" in the nineteenth century in wonderful shape. The land was in the hands of the people. The whole popular mass was in a state of "disciplined enthusiasm." [17] The Russians were ready for a higher state of liberty; [18] and the

Great Reforms, especially the serf law and the judicial reform, were a sign of their highly mature inner state.

The contradictions between Danilevsky's typal theory and his view of Europe and Russia are many. Most striking, perhaps, is the insistent this-worldliness of the one and the obvious immanentism of the other; from a position which stated that man could know almost nothing of God's purposes in the world, we pass to a statement of those purposes so complete as to leave hardly even an illusion of human freedom. One theory envisaged man living a difficult, alienated life in a hard, physical, power-hungry world; the other projected nearly all difficulties westward, leaving man in Russia in the benevolent, all too proximate hand of God. The world of cultural-historical types was complex. The view of it was fittingly external and statistical. The world of "Russia" and "Europe" was simple; it was viewed dogmatically.

These contradictions are highlighted by the differing views of time and of the general structure of historical experience in which each theory participated. The typal theory was a progressive theory. Time and history spiralled upward toward a treasury of knowledge and technique. The Russia-Europe theory was a cyclical theory; time was basically a series of repetitions of the same thing, superficially varying expressions of unchanging character. Here was Danilevsky's myth of the eternal return of the same. Had Danilevsky chosen to project this theory upon the canvas of the world history of civilizations, we would undoubtedly have had, except for the business of the truth of Orthodoxy, a theory much more like Spengler's than his typal theory ever was; the unfolding of mutually independent "prime symbols" explained everything.

Existentially the typal theory of time and historical experience suggests the hustle and bustle of nineteenth century England or of the progressive bureaucratic milieu in reforming Russia. The Russia-Europe discussion evokes the quiet, metabolic, changeless peasant and gentry life of rural Russia. One of Danilevsky's languages was secular, Promethean, innovative; the other, sacerdotal, receptive, traditional. In one, man made time and history; in the other, men were encased in a great medium, one which made their whole lives. For Russians, evil arose from failure to accept their fate, destiny, character. This was the disease of Westernism. It was fittingly archaic that Danilevsky saw ahead an orgiastic war that would purge the chosen people.[19]

It is important not only to see the fact of contradictory theories in *Russia and Europe*. Equally necessary is an understanding of the nature and quality of the contradiction. There is, for instance, the possibility that the contradiction is simply ridiculous, stupid, amateurish, unintended. It would be misleading not to recognize that the contradiction does have some such quality. Even regarded as a totalitarian work, *Russia and Europe* is not perfectly coherent and unified. Danilevsky seems to have had some compositional difficulties, as it were. He says too much at times and tends to damage his hard-soft, physical-metaphysical rhetoric. "Ideally" a totalitarian philosophy should be presented so that its metaphysical aspect is seen but only most dimly. On occasion Danilevsky was unable to maintain proper control and one gets the impression of just plain contradiction. It is as though, in writing the chapters presently under discussion, he had set out, having developed much of his typal theory earlier, to prove the distinctness of Slavdom from Europe by using "character" only as a convenient heuristic device, but had in this delicate intellectual situation fallen into a version of Slavophilism. In the light of the spirit of his whole work, however, this was certainly not the case. One should see Danilevsky's contradictions not in terms of category mistakes or stupidity but in terms of meaningful paradox.

The tone of his work, even from the very beginning though with varying emphases, seems to reflect a mind in a paradoxical existential and ideological state, one in which old and new, religious and secular, static and dynamic, utopian socialist and nationalist, and metaphysical Slavophil and realistic Panslavist currents are at war with one another. The Russia-Europe theory

just described is not really as purely metaphysical as I have had
to make it sound in order to explain it. The language, concepts,
and tone of the typal theory pervade the chapters on Europe
and Russia. On the whole, the effect of Danilevsky's tone is not
one of philosophical idiocy. The reader gets a sense more like
that of confronting an unstable personality, one in which the
ego masks the id but only incompletely and with great strain.
Russia and Europe is Quixotic in style and its author seems to
feel like Sancho. Russia, the self-sacrificing fool of European
politics, the insulted and injured, the "gigantic superfluity" was
really his hero as well as his butt.[20] As Dostoevsky says, Sancho
— "the personification of common sense, prudence, cunning, the
golden mean — chances to become a friend and fellow-traveller
of the insanest man on earth; precisely he and no other! He de-
ceives Don Quixote continually; he cheats him like a child, and
at the same time he fully believes in his great mind; he is tenderly
fascinated by the greatness of his heart; he also gives full credence
to the fantastic dreams of the valiant knight, and not once does he
doubt that the latter finally will conquer the island!" [21] Keeping
in mind that the two sides of Danilevsky's philosophy bear a
paradoxical more than a simple contradictory relationship to one
another, we may examine some of the implications of what we
see in the middle chapters of *Russia and Europe*.

The more explicitly stated occasion and purpose of the book
are supposed to be taken in some special way. Explicitly, the
author seems to have wanted a Panslav Union. Its purposes included guaranteeing the possibility of future variety in the world
and teaching men, by exemplary contradiction of their erroneous
immanentist assumptions, that metaphysics (or theology) and politics did not and should not mix. Learning this last lesson, men
would set themselves smaller, more possible goals and achieve
a modicum of happiness. The means to the ends of the Union
and its many hoped for consequences was to be a Machiavellian
and Bismarckian Russian foreign policy carried out even at the
risk of war. The means were, at least theoretically, appropriate

to the ends. Life, seen realistically, was an alienated, difficult, somewhat pathetic affair. *Realpolitik* was a plausible part of it. Danilevsky, on this more explicit level, seems to have had no expectations that would have led to the unlimited use of hard, realistic, political and military means. But, in the light of the theory of the saved and the damned in history, Danilevsky's purpose seems rather different. He wanted a Panslav Union. He thought that the union was a necessary prerequisite for the flowering of a native Slavic civilization; culture and psychology in Russia and Slavdom were so Westernized that an extraordinary new force was needed to produce a native version of them. Westernism, however, now took on a new meaning. It was not simply a cultural and psychological aberration. It was a spiritual disease, an infection by the devil of the national soul of the chosen people. Curing the disease also included, by implication, the expectation of a return of the national soul, enriched by suffering, to its natural, ontological state. As we shall see in the next chapter, Danilevsky thought the Slavic civilization of the future would be both "panhuman" and maybe even "universal"; its realization was to be not of mere historical but of metaphysical and theological significance. It was to be the ultimate expression of the spiritual psychology of the redeemed elect.

The means to such a metaphysical and theological end remained *Realpolitik* and the achievement of a Slavic Union. The theory now therefore looks objectively totalitarian, advocating violent physical means to metaphysical ends. *Realpolitik* was not a plausible part of Danilevsky's second historical world. His demands on it were unlimited. He expected it to produce a metaphysical result. It was, for him, in fact, a liturgical and purifying more than a political means. Indeed, it becomes clear, in the last chapters of his book, that he wanted the Panslav Union not so much as a protected political base for a cultural flowering, but more because its institution would bring on a war with Europe — a war that was providential in origin and liturgical in function. Slavic practice of *Realpolitik*, including war, was per se more important to Danilevsky than the Panslav Union; the union seems to have been proposed as a means of intensifying this practice even more than as its goal. Slavic acceptance and overacceptance of the judgment of God upon the sins or the spiritual "disease" of modern men and a subsequent achievement of a blessed innocence — this was what our old Joachite Fourierist now turned liberal, positivist, and modern ultimately wanted.

The continuity of Danilevsky's thought in *Russia and Europe* with his ideas of the forties should be stressed. That continuity is clear from the temper of his quasi-Slavophil metaphysical and historical theory. In chapters VIII–X of *Russia and Europe* he broke with the idea that Slavophilism was a good guide to secular nationalist thinking but harmful in itself because of its metaphysics (it too was diseased by *zapadnichestvo*, which he originally identified with metaphysical thinking). But though he reversed his position on metaphysics, he did not come up with an authentic Slavophilism. Like the Slavophils he did criticize Western European society and culture, especially by pointing up their fragmentation; but, in his view, that fragmentation was not due to "Europe's" rationalism but rather to its individualistic voluntarism, its highly developed feeling for personality, its "violence." Khomiakov and Kireevsky, emphasizing the importance of the will, the senses, the empirical, often remind one of the later Schelling's criticism of the Hegelian universe.[22] But Danilevsky was in spirit like a left Hegelian criticizing a Schellingian one. His "Europe" was fragmented because it was merely "real," too shortsighted, willful, pragmatically one-sided; the Slavophils' Europe had been fragmented because it was too unspontaneous, stiff, formalistic, impersonal, univocally "rational," both objectively and subjectively. The Slavophils' European man had been out of touch with a true volitional and emotional selfhood; Danilevsky's was out of touch with a prudent and reasonable one, one with which the Europeans had never in any case been endowed.

There are interesting differences of emphasis between the Slavophils and Danilevsky also in regard to social institutions and to Western European cultural achievements. Like Danilevsky the Slavophils had had a high regard for the Russian agricultural commune. But they had prized it as an organic primary group institution, historically and thus humanly developed, natural, primitivistic, unrepressive of the Tolstoi-like individual, a man of will and feeling. The Slavophils' commune had been hoary, patriarchal, bearded, gloriously all but incapable of further development. But Danilevsky saw the commune as an institution potentially mediative between the individual and larger secondary social groups, particularly the nation. He valued it for its unique promise of bringing natural man into civilized society without dehumanizing him. The story about the successive benevolent authoritarianisms of the Varangians, the Tartars, and Peter may readily be interpreted as one about the commune's role in Russia's social development. And "Europe's" nationalist movement was hopeless in his view because the nation by itself was too abstract and distant an institution to be able to accommodate the individual directly, while European society because of its violently feudal historical formation lacked the essential mediative institution, the commune. The commune was to Danilevsky the concrete institutional form of a benevolent historical education, an education of natural man for civilization, the realm of "disciplined enthusiasm" — a distinctly un-Slavophil theory. In a similar spirit was his evaluation of "Europe's" cultural achievements. The Slavophils had been critical of or at least much more ambivalent toward these, for they had connected them symptomatically with Europe's deviation from the natural, bare, Christian life. But Danilevsky criticized Europe rather for its inability (again partly because of the absence of the commune) to make proper social, human, and spiritual use of its cultural achievements. The Slavophils had been pretty consistently particularists, individualists, quasi-Schellingian transcendental idealists, relatively negative toward change, progress, and reason. Danilevsky did not share their most basic ideas and values.

Like a left Hegelian too, Danilevsky justified (and minimized) the sufferings of the Russian people in the course of their historical development, under state auspices, from the Varangians through Peter (the Slavophils' *bête noire*) and beyond.[23] His view of revelation and the Church was fittingly legalistic. Their main function was controlling subjectivist (not objectivist as in the Slavophils) deviation. Danilevsky's authoritarian and rationalistic idea of the Church is a startling contrast to the Slavophils' conception of the Church as an all but voluntary community, unrepressive like the commune, dominated by the principle of collegiality or *sobornost*. The association of the Russian and Slavic national style with eighteenth century rationalism; the naturalistic, scientistic, deterministic derivation of Russia's reasonableness from "character" more than from Christianity; the socialist critique of Western capitalism and nationalism; the celebration (developed more fully, even obsessively, later in *Russia and Europe*) of Russia's natural potentialities for socialism; the only slightly qualified admiration for Western cultural achievements — these combined with the Hegelian overtones of Danilevsky's metaphysical theory about the distinctions between Russia and Europe identify his thinking of the sixties as basically continuous with that of the forties, utopian socialist, left Hegelian, populist. He had been influenced since the forties by the Slavophils but mainly in such a way as to become a revolutionary or left Slavophil, something like Herzen or Bakunin. The doctrine of Khomiakov and Kireevsky seems to have helped Danilevsky elaborate the incipient populism of his Petrashevsky period rather than to have worked a fundamental change in his thinking.

It is informative to compare Danilevsky's attitude toward Bentham, Smith, and Darwin — on the secular Panslavist side of his theory — with his leftist Slavophilism. His anti-individualist emphases are striking. He did not, it may be remembered, completely accept the "English way of thinking." He accepted the English idea of the state as the protector of rights, for instance, but only where this meant group or national rights. He praised English political economic doctrines but demanded that Russia's communal social structure be the context in which they were to be applied. He borrowed much of Darwin's theory of evolution, applying it to society, but insisted that the struggle for existence took place between internally cooperating groups not individuals. Just as he filled Schellingian and metaphysically transcendentalist Slavophilism with a left Hegelian content (he had done much the same in the forties with Humboldt's Schellingianism), so he filled individualistic and secular transcendentalism with socialism and other community-oriented, quasi-traditionalist ideas. While making allowance for some more authentically particularist elements in his secular Panslavism (itself a sort of communalistic nationalism), that latter doctrine was, except for the matter of metaphysics, very similar to his left Slavophilism. The Panslavism was like an alienated or "frontist" version of the radical Slavophilism — as in Marx secular democratic socialism is an alienated version of metaphysical communism. Danilevsky's Panslavism was the objective form of his "Slavophilism"; it was Slavophilism expressing itself in a world linguistically and conceptually diseased by *zapadnichestvo*, which turns out in the final analysis to mean the intellectual universe of Bentham, Smith, Darwin, and company, that is, the ideas and values of modern man in Russia of the sixties. His Panslavism was an attempt to deal with this universe in its own hard-boiled, egoistic terms but only in order once and for all to banish all such terms — so that even realistic Panslavism, except perhaps for its geographical focus, was to Danilevsky mostly part and parcel of *zapadnichestvo*. This may be why at the very end of *Russia and Europe* he dropped for a moment his vaguely official nationalist and xenophobic idea that Russia and Slavdom alone would be beatified, and burst into poetry prophesying (as he had in the forties) an end of the division of Russia and Europe, and salvation for everybody through Russia's unparticularistic kenoticism.

The chapters under discussion leave us one other curious impression. Coming to them from the earlier chapters setting forth the typal, Panslavist theory, the reader sometimes gets the idea that Danilevsky was trying to manipulate his audience, to agitate them into taking actions the likely consequences of which he was trying to hide. It is as though he had approached his readers most directly in a utilitarian and political Panslavist spirit because, over-generalizing his own experience and reading, he believed these intellectual strands to be increasingly and unfortunately dominant in Russian thought and public opinion. His subtle distortions of the strands suggest both that he was trying to use them against themselves and that he was trying to involve their proponents in a situation that would destroy their views. Danilevsky seems here to indulge in doubletalk, to be adept at an intellectual front technique. He spoke of liberty but left out equality. He spoke of individualism but meant hyperindividualism. He spoke of Slavic self-determination but urged its forced realization and that in necessary connection with Constantinople, the powder keg of European politics. On realistic grounds he urged more pessimism, animality, forceful assertiveness; barbarism, he insisted, would be self-limiting. It is as though all this was only a device for starting men on the way to a liturgy of destruction. The experience of war would destroy Westernism which, for Danilevsky, included utilitarianism, *Realpolitik*, liberalism, Panslavism, and the world they represented to him. What are we to make of this impression?

It certainly appears justified. But it would be unwise to make too much of it. *Russia and Europe* is too complex to have been a product mainly of conscious manipulation. While Danilevsky must bear the responsibility for putting things together and focusing them — processes he evidently enjoyed in a sort of manic way — the traditional-modern and romantic-realist situation and the Russian intellectual practices of his time appear to have contributed greatly to his philosophy. He was a manipulator but he was also much the prisoner of his own fantasy.

8

TOTALITARIANISM

THE LAST SIX chapters (XII–XVII) of *Russia and Europe* lead
the reader to a careful scrutiny of his assumptions about Danilevsky's point of view. For it becomes particularly evident here that
Danilevsky did not want to identify himself as a detached, positivistic, Cartesian observer, a social scientist and engineer, gathering data, reasoning, concluding, proposing, enlightening, manipulating. Like Marx and other totalitarian thinkers, he played the
role of social poet not of social scientist. Though he made use
of the language and concepts of the social scientist, he wanted
it believed that he did so not with a view to furthering rational
knowledge or encouraging merely ethical action, but rather in
order to elaborate a vast, angry, socioreligious metaphor, one
that would express his own and his generation's sense of being
in the modern world. Danilevsky wanted to be thought a myth-
maker who was really articulating History's myth about itself,
a myth functionally necessary to History's teleological development. His scientistic and manipulative language was supposedly a
function of his symbiosis with History (or God-in-History) in
its struggle for integrality, with its consciousness in its current
state. In this specifically totalitarian fashion, Danilevsky's philosophy was not authentically rationalistic; it was visionary, shamanistic, magical. Supposedly the author was at once witness, prophet,
and tool of History. Thus there was only dialectically meaning-

ful contradiction between the positivism and the metaphysics, the voluntarism and the determinism in his doctrine. And he could not fully state his real ends because (allegedly) he could not more than glimpse them himself until History had arrived at a new stage, making a further development of incarnate cosmic consciousness possible.

This is a subtle subject.[1] It is wise to proceed cautiously in discussing it. Let us note the main topics in these chapters. There is more speculation about world history, its task, and God's relationship to history. There is an "analysis" of the historical and cosmic meaning of the Eastern question, of Constantinople (Tsargrad), and of the function of political action, grandiose and violent, in world history. In discussing these subjects, though he keeps insisting that he can only glimpse the large patterns, Danilevsky really says too much at times, again marring his "totalitarian composition." But the import of what he says leads him with utter consistency back to the language and scientific-ethical pose of his theory of cultural-historical types and its Panslavist action program. It leads him away from saying what he wanted and why, lest apparently, for one thing, he and not history would seem responsible for what in the final analysis *he* was doing: hating, preaching war. Let us look at his nihilism. Unifying his schizoid doctrine, it is something like the Eastern question, the key to everything.

I

Looking closely at the text we find what amounts to a new view of world history, which Danilevsky developed in the course of a discussion of Slavdom's (obviously metaphysical) potentialities for civilization and of the likelihood of their actualization through Slavic political unification and war. Fittingly, it turns out to be a doctrine of the providential determination of all human history. History was a closed drama with a beginning, middle, and end; time was linearly progressive, objective, and sacred.

Danilevsky emphasized, however, that this order was not by any means entirely knowable. Men had still mostly to concern them-selves with the brutal practicalities of international politics; ra-tional certainties were still thought by him to be confined to the scientistic order of mere cultural-historical types and *Realpolitik*. But a higher drama could be glimpsed, at least by the very sensi-tive.

According to this new theory, there were four main categories of possible cultural activity.

(1) *Religious activity*, embracing the relations of men to God; man's conception of his own fate as something moral, indivisible from the general fate of mankind and the universe; that is, expressing it in more general terms: a people's *Weltanschauung*, conceived not as theoretical, more or less hypothetical knowledge available only to a few, but as a firm faith that makes up the living basis of the whole moral activity of man.

(2) *Cultural activity in the narrow sense of this term*, embracing the relationship of man to the external world: in the first place, theoretical-scientific; in the second, aesthetic-artistic (for man him-self, as an object of study, thought, and artistic expression, belongs to the external world); in the third, technical-industrial, that is, the taking and fashioning of objects of the external world according to the needs of man and according to the understanding, by theoretical means, both of these needs and of the external world.

(3) *Political activity*, embracing the relations of people to one another, as members of one national whole, and the relations of this whole, as an entity of a higher sort, to other peoples. Finally —

(4) *Social-economic activity*, embracing the relations of people to one another, not direct relations, as those of moral and political persons, but indirect, in regard to the conditions of utilizing the objects of the external world — and consequently the taking and fashioning of these objects.[2]

This somewhat Saint-Simonian categorization of cultural activities (Saint-Simon had them as religion, science, polity, *beaux arts*) was used to study the kinds of such activity in which most of the cultural-historical types had participated and at the same time to work out a theory of linear progress that culminated in

Slavdom. Danilevsky sounds very, though not strictly, Hegelian.[3]

The "first cultures," the Egyptian, Chinese, Babylonian, and Iranian, had not taken up any single cultural activity. Because they had been the "preparers of culture," they had developed all the possible activities together. Not specializing, they had been unable to bring any activity to a very high level of performance. The Hebrews had been the first to specialize. They had been a religious people *par excellence*. Religion had been their whole cultural life; they had had no art, no worthwhile social or economic institutions, no science; and they had been weak, even absurd, politically. Religion, however, had been so highly developed by them that they had come to be called, quite justly, "the chosen people of God." They had put the stamp of their religion on the highest civilizations. The next great culture had been that of the Greeks. Their forte had been art. Greek social and economic institutions had been based on slavery and hence were despicable. Their ineptitude for politics had shown itself again and again in the city-states' suicidal particularism. Greek religion had lacked depth, content, metaphysics, and cosmology. They had had no idea of universal Providence. The only thing even close to it had been an idea of "blind, inexorable fate, the incarnation of the law of physical necessity."[4] The real religion of the Greeks had been the worship of beauty, which had been expressed in art. The Romans, on the other hand, had developed the political side of culture to the exclusion of all others. Their peculiar genius had expressed itself in the organization of empire and in the development of law.

These three early specialized civilizations had all been "one-sided." The further development of history had therefore depended not only on the possibility of the higher development of the fourth, the socio-economic activity, but also on the elaboration of cultures that were more than one-sided. As in Hegel, the cultural condition of mankind had gone from a relatively undifferentiated state of mere potency, in China and the other early cultures, to one-sided specialization and sophistication of the various cultural fields. Historical thesis had been countered by historical antithesis; the next step had therefore been a new synthesis. It had been achieved by "Europe." "Similar to the logical process of thought in the individual spiritual being, there are revealed also in the logical course of world history — by means of analysis — distinct aspects of cultural movement, out from a primeval, mixed (undifferentiated) state, whose representatives were the ancient states of Asia and Africa; and after that, it seems [the course of history] approached a moment [appropriate to] the process of synthetic fusion in the history of the Germano-Roman peoples." [5] Danilevsky's "Hegelianism" was really rather superficial, however. His immanentism was somewhat more relative than Hegel's had been. The divine was not only in history, in the form of marvelously potent and magically synchronized national "characters." God was also above it, like a Newtonian mechanic, adjusting it occasionally.[6] Thus, the first two-sided culture in history, the European, had not simply been a high point in a predetermined, immanent process. It had also been made possible by the coming of Christianity, a factor that had raised human cultural potentialities to a new level. "The circumstances of the time favored the realization of such a synthesis. Religious truth in the ultimate form of Christianity was discovered and assimilated, at once obediently and exultantly, by the new peoples, by their richly gifted spiritual natures." [7] It would seem too that the advancement of the socio-economic dimension of culture had been, in Danilevsky's view, particularly difficult. For the first rudimentary progress, beyond the earliest Afro-Asian phase of history, had come only with God's special revelation, the new Christian religion. Only thereafter had slavery disappeared. Both cultural syntheses and socio-economic progress were regarded as exceptionally difficult and significant steps throughout this historical theory.

That ordinary potentialities for civilization, ever more deeply actualized by the accumulating fruits of immanent cultural progress, were insufficient for a final synthesis was evident in Europe's cultural failures as well as in its successes. Europe had benefited initially from some "extra" divine intervention. But this seems to have been insufficient or too short-lived or both, for Europe had had and was having difficulties. Gifted in politics, science, industry, and to a lesser extent, art, Europe had failed religiously and socio-economically. The violence of Germano-Roman "character," heightened and focused on politics by the tradition of Roman civilization, had turned Orthodoxy into the despotism of Catholicism. Ecclesiastical despotism, together with feudal despotism (another expression of violent character) and "the despotism of scholasticism" (involving "the worship of ancient science"), had turned the history of Europe into a great struggle between oppressors and oppressed. It had ended in a three-sided anarchy: religious (Protestantism), philosophical (materialism), and socio-political (bad kinds of socialism and anarchism). This failure apparently indicated that Europe had been a means not an end. Europe's greatest achievements, science and the working out of a good political compromise between state power and the individual, would be materials for a higher and more complete synthesis.

It is by now little surprise to Danilevsky's reader to learn that he thought the future Slavic cultural-historical type would likely realize "a synthesis of all aspects of cultural activity — aspects which were elaborated, either in isolation or in incomplete union, by its precursors on the historical scene." [8] Nevertheless, though obviously rather firmly convinced of this happy probability, Danilevsky continued to be cautious. He only allowed himself, on the basis of current, factual evidence, projected forward statistically, as it were, to spell out some of the "historical desiderata." However problematical his caution may seem to us, it is essential that we keep it in mind. For his method, at just this juncture, is more than a quaint illustration of the influence of statistics on his thinking. The unity of his whole philosophy depends greatly upon it. In a sense he was being true to his conviction, voiced strongly in his typal theory proper, that only God could see the whole of the ultimate historical order. Human certainties were limited to the level of the theory of cultural-historical types, the "natural system" of history. Human actions could only be marginally, absurdly affected by anything else. This self-consciously provisional way of seeing is the first unmistakable hint of Danilevsky's totalitarianism. With statistical caution, then, Danilevsky identified in the Slavdom (mainly the Russia) of his time startling potentialities in all the now nearly perfected fields of human cultural activity *and also* in that still relatively unworked area, the socio-economic.

The story of the happy marriage of the Russian people and the one true religion is familiar to us. Unlike the Europeans, the Russians had persisted in Orthodoxy from the first.[9] This had been because of humble, reasonable, pliable "character." Christianity had come to Russia not through political force or propaganda, but through frank dissatisfaction, on the part of the whole people, with paganism. Russian capacity for religious achievement was comparable to that of the Jews. Superficial observers might deny Slavic and Russian political potentialities. But closer scrutiny showed the error of this. Except for the Russians, the Slavs were still in their ethnographic phase; political achievements were not yet to be expected of them. (Even so, they had had an active, successful political life in the Middle Ages.) As to the Russians, the evidence of their political capacities was abundant. First, they had behind them a great imperial achievement. Russian imperial ability was historically unique. The empire had been organized slowly, in an organic way. Russians had never set up "colonies," areas of settlement distant from the homeland, always susceptible to particularism. This was symptomatic of the fact that Russians themselves had lacked the bent for building showy overseas empires. Their expansiveness had been natural and spontaneous not artificial, overly self-conscious, chauvinistic. The natives of newly annexed areas had been thoroughly absorbed without force or violence, for they had had no reason for irritation with their tolerant, self-confident, integral, humble masters. Second, there was good evidence that the Russian people had an unusual capacity for the advancement and exercise of political liberty. On this point the contrast between Russia and France was instructive. It had taken France centuries to get rid of serfdom. The Russians had eliminated it in a very short time. The French liberation had come finally only out of revolutionary upheaval. The Russian had been absolutely peaceable. Moreover, the fear of conservatives that the Russian people would be disorderly after the liberation had proved utterly unfounded. Even though the censorship had been lifted just before the liberation, allowing Westernized radicals to fill the press with all kinds of vicious and inflammatory articles, there had been no trouble. The Russians could handle huge doses of freedom. They had great actual and potential political ability.

There seem to be Diderotian, Fourierist utopian overtones in Danilevsky's account of the Russians' religious and political achievements and potentialities. We have noted the same thing before in Danilevsky's account of Russian typal distinction from Europe. In his description of his own people's socio-economic potential, there is some almost frank socialism. Indeed, it would hardly be an exaggeration to say that our old Petrashevskian regarded a kind of socialism as the linchpin of world historical development. Specifically, Russia was the only powerful empire in history that had not been built upon some kind of social and economic oppression. In Russia there was therefore no great political and socio-economic contradictions such as those which had put Europe "between the Charybdis of Caesarism and the Scylla of social revolution." The bases of the social and economic health of Russia were "the peasant allotment" (*krestiansky nadel*) and communal landholding. Those who confused the commune with communism were wrong; the connection was merely etymological. "In this something very important is forgotten, namely that our commune, whether good or bad in its historical consequences, is a historical right." Socialism in Russia was therefore a conservative, not a radical, doctrine. "European socialism, on the other hand, is a revolutionary doctrine, not so much in itself, but because of the ground on which it must operate." [10]

Like Herzen and other Russian thinkers, like himself in the forties, Danilevsky regarded the agricultural commune as a natural, organic socialist institution. It would make possible, for the first time in history, a solution of the social and economic difficulties of human societal organization.

As to culture in the ordinary sense, there could be no doubt, in Danilevsky's view, that the Russians and the Slavs had thus far been weak in these fields by comparison with the Europeans and the Greeks. But this was because of their comparatively youthful stage of development, not because of lack of ability. Names like Copernicus, Rokitansky, Purkinje, Shafarik, Ostrogradsky, and Pirogov indicated great promise in the field of science. But science was always the last fruit of a civilization; hence the "seeds of the future" were more striking in the artistic than in the scientific field. There was Ivanov's painting, Pimenov's sculpture, Glinka's music, Mickiewicz's poetry. There was Gogol's *Dead Souls,* comparable to, even better than, Cervantes' *Don Quixote. The Old-Fashioned Landowners* and *The Overcoat* were also outstanding. *Boris Godunov* by Pushkin merited comparison with Shakespeare's history plays and was superior to Schiller's *Wallenstein* or *Wilhelm Tell.* These had all been Slavophil favorites. Danilevsky added only one. Let Europe point to a work as good as *War and Peace* by Leo Tolstoi. As an example of an epic interpretation of the past it was a masterpiece.[11]

Slavdom, then, seemed to hold unique promise for the fulfillment of the drama of world history. At the very time when that four-sided development had reached a state of cosmic pregnancy, it seemed undeniable that the offspring would be Danilevsky's favorite cultural-historical type. Yet there remained a problem. Previous history had shown the possibility of the immanent development of one-sided high cultures of the religious, artistic, and political kinds. But both cultural-historical synthesis and higher elaboration of the socio-economic activity had depended, in the single relevant case of Europe, upon the additional, occasional intervention, the magical midwifery, of a transcendent Providence.

Was Slavdom likely to be the object of such divine attention? We know already, from Danilevsky's discussion of Russia in the middle chapters of his book, that he thought the Slavs had already been again and again the darlings of Providence. Not only their wonderful "character" but also their remarkable, three-staged "historical education," attested this. He went on now, much more explicitly, to accumulate evidence that would strongly suggest that they had been under the attentive eye of God for centuries and centuries. A study of the history of the Eastern question seemed to indicate that He had long been nurturing and protecting them for some high purpose.

We shall be unable, however, to look at Danilevsky's lengthy and complicated study of the Eastern question solely within the present frame of reference. For that study not only illustrates that he thought the Slavs the ultimate darlings of Providence. It also shows the form he thought providential help in actualizing Slavic potentialities would take. God was about to involve the Europeans and the Slavs in a great war over the Eastern question, over the Panslav Union, and over Constantinople, the Gordian knot of the Eastern question. Participation in this war would actualize the Slavic civilization and ontologize the chosen people. It would be a kind of holy war, an "objective" war, a liturgy of destruction, something with a life and meaning of its own, beyond the petty diplomatic and Panslavist causes that would set it off.

Its ultimate effect might even surpass that of the completion of a final, purely Slavic, panhuman civilization. Europe and Russia might somehow become one in a universal civilization. If so, there would be an end of time and history, an achievement by mankind of spiritual integrity and innocence. In the final analysis it seemed possible to Danilevsky that "the main stream of world history originates from two sources on the banks of the ancient Nile. The one, celestial and divine, passing through Palestine and Tsargrad, attains its final purity in Kiev and Moscow. The other, earthly and human, splits into two important branches of culture and of politics, the one passing through

Athens, Alexandria, and Rome, the other into the European countries where it dried up temporarily and is now being enriched
by more plentiful waters. In Russia a new spring has broken
through which justly guarantees the popular masses socio-
economic security. All these streams must run together into one
broad basin in the wide plain of Slavdom. And I believe," he went
on in verse, "that the hour is approaching when the river will
overflow its bank. It faces the blue sky and the sky contains
everything. See how extensively the waters run over the green
valley as foreign peoples gather with spiritual thirst at the
shore." [12]

This final vision was apparently too vague to be discussed
fully, however. Danilevsky went into detail only about the relatively clearer possibilities of a Slavic panhuman civilization, of
God's way of bringing it into being, and of the role that would
be played in all this by blind, instinctual, human motives, expressing themselves in a Machiavellian Panslavism and rationalized
by the positivistic certainties of the theory of cultural-historical
types.

2

The Eastern question concerned the emergence in Eastern
Europe of some great state. Danilevsky vaguely echoed his typal
theory; this state would be the necessary historical prerequisite
for the realization of an ultimate panhuman civilization. This
civilization, in turn, depended also, as we know, on other things:
on the immanent historical development of religious, political,
and cultural human potentialities, on the transcendentally directed
development of the socio-economic potentiality and of the capacity for synthesis of civilization. But the early protagonists of the
historical drama had not known this. They had each attempted
(objectively speaking, for their subjective motives had been narrower) to build a great state. Danilevsky seems to have thought
that their futile efforts had served a purpose of setting an

archetypal habit of grandiose political behavior, a classic focus of political action in the East. In the fullness of time God would, in His synchronistic wisdom, tie this in with the other lines of human development. Thus the Eastern question had concerned more peoples than the Slavs. It had been involved in the struggles of the Hellenic and Iranian types, of the Roman and the Old Semitic, of the Roman and Hellenic, and of the Roman and the German peoples as well as the struggles of the Slavic and Romano-German or European types. It had gone through three major periods: from Philip of Macedon to the schism between Catholicism and Orthodoxy, from the schism to Catherine II of Russia in the later eighteenth century, from Catherine II to the present. A fourth period was about to begin.[13]

It was no mere question of *Realpolitik*. Danilevsky set the tone of his discussion with a lyrical quotation from the poetry of Khomiakov: "The voice of God: 'Peoples, gather to the court of justice, gather to the East!' And blindly following out the appointed task, the peoples stream over the earth, hasten over the stormy waters." Then he explained:

The Eastern question is not one of those questions subject to the decision of diplomacy. History leaves the little transient trash to the bureaucratic operation of diplomacy. But it announces decisions which become the law of life of peoples for whole centuries, its own decisions, with thunder and lightning, like Jehovah from the heights of Sinai, without any intermediaries. It is unnecessary to prove this. In the general consciousness the importance assigned to the Eastern question is such that no one thinks of putting it into the narrow confines of diplomacy; no one would think of a congress to decide it. Diplomacy itself, after many efforts, feels that it is inadequate to the task and only tries to put off the approach of a decision in order to give everyone time to enjoy the present in the face of a historical crisis that will for a long time attract all the attention, all the energies of peoples, pushing all other tasks and anxieties into the background. Acting in this way diplomacy only fulfills its obligation, which consists, according to its powers, in smoothing the paths of historical movement and, if not deflecting, then slowing down and weakening colliding forces. This relative impotence of diplomacy — this impossibility of deciding the most important international questions by means of peace treaties — seems to be a mark of the imperfection of the condition in which all human societies find themselves. The natural and lawful striving for peaceful historical development more and more attracts the sympathy of peoples to the stock-exchange view of politics. But if storms and thunder are necessary in the physical order of nature, no less necessary are direct collisions of peoples, who are tearing their fates out of the sphere of the narrow, merely rational views of political personalities . . . passing under the direct leadership of world historical Providence . . . In the fact that world decisions of the fates of men are always completely removed from the small and narrow political wisdom of the statesmen contemporary to any great historical revolution should be seen one of the most benevolent laws ruling historical movement.[14]

On the other hand, Danilevsky took care that his reader not take the question merely as a bit of historical mythology. He took pains to dissociate himself from S. M. Soloviev's metaphor for world history, one which described it as a great dialectic between West and East, Ormuz (the sea, the good) and Ahriman (the steppe, the bad). This was just fantasy. He had something much more scientific and factual in mind. He illustrated this by an account of the history of the question. It showed that God had long had curious purposes in the East, had been working for the Slavs, and that a final intervention was imminent.

The first of the four phases of the story had been that of "the preparation of the Eastern question." Here the archetypal pattern of Eastern political behavior had been set. And at the very end of this period, God, who had before let many an Eastern hero die unaided, had for the first time extended His hand and that to the Slavs.

In general the classical Greeks had lacked political ability. Their particularism had kept them disunited. It was only therefore rather late in Greek historical development that any Greek had undertaken to unite the whole people. Philip of Macedon, the first of a series of Eastern heroes (it all sounds more and more Hegelian)[15] of the Eastern question, had made the initial, un-

successful effort. Alexander the Great had done better, but his
effort too had ended in failure. For, though he had united the
Greeks and thus made it possible for them to realize, in the
Alexandria of the Ptolemies, at least their natural, merely Greek
potentialities, he had spread Greek power too far. The empire
had fallen to pieces. Then Constantine, still another hero, had
founded the Byzantine empire. But this great imperial achievement had not proved to be the beginning of the end of history.
The Romans had not been good civilizers; their abilities had been
mainly political. Rome had been a means not an end. The drama
of history had passed on to new episodes with new protagonists,
the Romano-German and the Slavic peoples. The first one had
come at the very end of the period of the preparation of the
Eastern question. At a time when the Slavic peoples had still been
helpless and stateless, Charlemagne had given the peoples of the
West political formation. There had been the terrible danger that,
along with his successors, this great politicizer of Christianity, the
one true religion, adhered to up to this time by Romano-Germans
and Slavs alike, would, by force and example, lead both West
and East into the heresy of Catholicism. But just at this unhappy
juncture, there had taken place the first of a long series of
"historical synchronisms," phenomena that directed the historian
to a belief in the working of Providence in history and especially
in the history of the Slavs. The religious schism had come just
at the moment of the most extreme danger. The East had been
kept apart from the new false Christianity of the West and in
direct touch with the true Orthodoxy.

Now before examining the second period of the problem, it is
important to note that Danilevsky did not here or elsewhere in
this tale of the Eastern question say that the facts *proved* that
Providence had been nurturing the Slavs. He was still as cautious
and as keen on the statistical method as before. All he was sure
of, he tells us, was that there were certain historical, as there were
certain natural facts which seemed to demand some sort of explanation and that this seemed necessarily to involve Providence.

He explained that the student of the phenomena of nature or of history went through a process of arriving at higher and higher generalizations until he reached a class of generalizations beyond which he could not go. "Proceeding by this road of ascent, from the particular to the general, we come to some categories of phenomena . . . which remain . . . not only separated from one another, but, in regard to any further ascent to one general, real cause, even completely unthinkable. We cannot keep ourselves in this state of dividedness. We can either remain obstinately blind to the unavoidable demands for higher unity, denying it, taking refuge in a theory of accident, *or* we can acknowledge the necessity of an ideal unity in which these diverse categories of phenomena are united, even though they have no physical basis for unity." [16] There were many examples in nature of such mysterious phenomena. Most substances contracted under the influence of cold; but water expanded. Why did all four-winged insects with stingers always have these stingers in the back? What was the relationship of insects to plants? Why was there a constant correlation, in animals, of cloven hooves and upper teeth?

In history there were mysterious synchronisms. Why had the fall of Constantinople (and the flight of the Greek scholars), the invention of printing, and the discovery of America come at the same time? The cause was mysterious, but the beneficent historical results gave some hint of its nature. If the Greek scholars had not arrived in the West at this time, there would have been little to print. Without the discovery of America, the combination of printing and classical learning might have made Europe into an imitative and sterile civilization. But that discovery had, beneficently, provided all kinds of new data about nature and peoples. The classical authors had had to be criticized for inaccuracies and fantasies. This had saved European cultural originality. "The causes of the synchronistic link of such diverse events it is impossible to hope to discover except in that plan of world-governing Providence according to which the historical life of mankind is developed." [17] It is worth emphasizing again, then, that Danilev-sky was still thinking of himself only as glimpsing, not really knowing, things that could be known with certainty and completeness only by God. Indeed, I repeat, this specious humility and scientistic caution is, as we shall see, an essential point for understanding the unity and coherence in his philosophy.

Taking up the story of the Eastern question once more, we come to its second period, "the Byzantine-Turkish period." During the time from the schism to Catherine II the state-building aspect of the question had been in abeyance. What had happened, for the most part, was that God had continued to protect the spiritual purity of the Orthodox Slavs from the imperialistic, violent, and heretical Europeans. Providence's second intervention had taken the form of the advent of Turkish "Mohammedanism."

The problem of the historical significance of Mohammedanism was a difficult one. This religion was similar to Christianity in many ways. Was it another version of the true religion, one better adapted to the wildly passionate natures of some peoples? No, some of the greatest Christian saints had come from these peoples. Was Islam then meant to be an intermediary religion, a means of transition, for certain peoples, to Christianity? This could not be either, for Christianity had made perhaps least progress among Moslems. Or had Islam had a cultural mission in history, that of transmitting ancient Greek culture to the West? This *had* been one of its historical roles. But it had not been of great significance, for the Greeks could have done their own preserving and transmitting if they had not been subjected to Islamic control. The "justification" of Islam was not to be found in its inner, cultural results, but rather in its service to certain great ends that were inherently foreign to its nature: the protection of the southeastern Slavs and, in some ways, of Orthodoxy generally from Western imperialism and Catholicism. Without the Turkish conquest, the population of the decrepit Byzantine empire would have been subjected to a growing number of papal-dominated states. The Catholics would have got possession of the holy places.

Orthodoxy would have been reduced to a sect like Nestorianism or Monophysitism. The Slavs of the area would never have risen from the stage of ethnographic material. In the words of Goethe, the Turkish power had been "Die Kraft die stets das Böse will und stets das Güte schafft," [18] like a Hegelian hero or holy criminal. This could only have been providential.

The third period had begun with Danilevsky's favorite Russian ruler, Catherine II, and was nearly at its end. Here Russia had gradually taken over the Turkish role of protecting the Slavs from the West. This had required nearly the whole of the third period. On the one hand, there had been confusion on Russia's part, for it had sometimes even united with Europe against the Turks. Bitter experience, especially that of the Crimean War, had taught the lesson that Europe was an enemy not a friend. On the other hand, the little Slavic brothers had initially suspected Russia. The emancipation of the serfs and the Great Reforms had, however, removed all doubt of Russia's inherent liberalism. The historical synchronism of 1853 and 1861 had indeed been remarkable; the simultaneous terminal state of Turkish decrepitude made it even more so. Of course, the Russian protectorship differed from the Turkish too. It was increasingly conscious and more and more readily accepted by the Slavs. Presumably, however, as we shall see, Russia remained, in the words of Goethe, "the power that constantly wills evil but constantly creates good." Anyway, the Eastern question was about to leave the state of quietude and Eastern defensiveness that had obtained since Constantine's limited imperial success. The Slavs, led by Russia, were about to take up again that ancient Herculean labor, the open-sesame of history, the building of a great Eastern state. This would be the Panslav Union. Its institution would involve the seizure of its capital, Constantinople, from the decrepit Turks. War between Europe and Slavdom would follow. The "masks" were off. All "our powers" must be girded for the struggle.

Now unfortunately a full, direct exposition of Danilevsky's Panslavist project and of his ideas about the coming war is not possible in the present context. This is because his proposal for a Panslav Union was cast in a dual frame of reference, that of the providentialist historical vision under discussion and that of his theory of cultural-historical types, of *Realpolitik*. Indeed, at just the point where he began to touch upon the Panslav project he undertook also to "plug in" the theory of civilizations and to shift over to the language of political realism and of this-worldly ends that was appropriate to it. This was marvelously consistent of him. As we have noted, the ancient political heroes of the Eastern question and the Turks had not acted upon a vision of the whole, for only God really knew what that was; they had acted on the basis of the narrower but more certain, earthly practicalities of the immediate situation. God had synchronized their actions with His plans. Thus Danilevsky undertook at this point to act out the role of Eastern (and Hegelian) hero himself, shifting the main focus of his discussion from the metaphysical back to the physical and talking by and large as though there was nothing under consideration but *Realpolitik*, limited and worldly aims, and the theory of cultural-historical types. This fact, though of great importance for the understanding of his overall meaning, makes it difficult to explain his doctrine, for it all but becomes necessary to start saying everything at once, such as what he wanted, why he gave two sets of reasons, why his language differed from one point to another. We are confronted with the key to his philosophy and the most important proof of his totalitarianism at the very point at which we try to follow to the end his statement of his real aims.

Continuing the exposition of Danilevsky's ideas (now less clearly discernible) concerning the realization of Slavdom's potentialities, let us again note that he saw the institution of the Panslav Union as a crowning of the efforts of Philip of Macedon, Alexander the Great, and Constantine. Although he shifts his point of view at this point and tries to push his reader back from theological to positivistic thinking, the providentialist frame of reference frequently shows through the utilitarian, making it just barely possible to continue to follow him at the theological-metaphysical level. His strange eschatology comes through especially clearly at points in his discussion of the "inevitable war" between the Slavs and the West, the war that would develop out of the struggle to build the Union. Danilevsky was evidently greatly worried that it would look as though he was preaching war. This seems to have been an important reason for some lengthy and revealing discussion of the war's providential inevitability.

There are two direct statements about this inevitability neither of which more than hints at his larger framework. "Sooner or later, whether we wish it or not, a battle with Europe (or at least a significant part of it) is inevitable — over the Eastern question, that is, over the freedom and independence of the Slavs, over the possession of Tsargrad, over everything that, in the opinion of Europe, constitutes the object of the illegal ambition of Russia. And, in the opinion of every Russian worthy of the name, it is the necessary demand of Russia's historical destiny." [19] The ontologizing purpose of the war is more evident in the second statement. "We consider . . . the very process of this inevitable war and not only its desired results . . . as salvational and beneficial. For only this fight can sober our thought, can raise the popular spirit in all levels of our society . . . Perhaps we will be blamed for preaching enmity and for glorifying war. But such an accusation would be unjust. We are not preaching war; it would be comical for our feeble lips to attempt to do so. We are merely asserting . . . that a struggle is inevitable and we submit that, though war is a great evil, there are much greater evils, for which war can be just the cure, for 'man will not live by bread alone.' " [20]

It is his lengthy discussion of the situation that would precipitate the war, the situation inviting the seizure of Constantinople and the founding of the union, that is really interesting. That that situation was being arranged by God and not by Danilevsky could be seen from the almost unbelievable accumulation of historical synchronisms in the eighteenth and nineteenth centuries. To the already remarkable synchronism, mentioned above, of 1853, 1861, and the final decrepitude of the Ottoman empire could be added that of the termination of Austria's *raison d'être*.

Like the Ottoman empire, the Austrian had never had any inner rationale. It had begun as and had remained a mere bundle of dynastic inheritances. But it had had historical justification, a dual role of protector of disunited Germany against France and of Europe against the Turks. It had performed its task well. Europe and Germany owed Austria (and also the many Slavs who had long constituted a large part of the population) a great historical debt. However, Austrian disintegration had begun as early as the eighteenth century. Accompanying the decline, from the first, had been a whole series of coincidences. In 1740 Charles VI had died and the unsuccessful effort to probate the Pragmatic Sanction had been undertaken. In that year the rise of Prussia, under Frederick the Great, had begun. This had ended in the unification of Germany in the 1860's and thus in the termination of one essential part of Austria's *raison d'être*, that of protecting the helpless Germans against France. The year 1740 had also marked the death of the Russian Empress Anna. After a brief time of troubles, Elizabeth had come to the throne. She had put Russia on a new road of national policy and national life by throwing out the Baltic Germans who had, since Peter's death, usurped power and run Russia along foreign lines. Catherine had brought Elizabeth's policies to full fruition. Her drive to liberate the Balkan Slavs from the Turkish yoke had been particularly important; it had ended the other half of Austria's *raison d'être*, the protection of Europe from the Turks. Meanwhile, the internal disintegration of Austria had been synchronized with the external changes. Maria Theresa had been weak. Joseph II's attempts at Germanization had accelerated the decline by awakening nationalism among subject peoples. The French Revolutionary and Napoleonic wars had sapped Austrian material strength. The whole political complex might have disintegrated had it not been for Metternich. He had been a "first rate genius, in the full sense of the word." He had managed to lull particularistic forces to sleep and thus to prolong the life of a political anomaly. The hollowness of his achievement was patent, however. Against the background of inevitable forces at work he looked like a tragicomic rather than a tragic historical hero: "the essence of comedy is the contrast between great means and little ends." [21] The Metternichean interlude had ended in the storm of 1848. Danilevsky went into great detail to show that all proposed solutions of Austria's internal political problems — centralism, dualism, and federalism — were futile. The whole series of events and God Himself pointed to Panslavism as the only solution.

It seems clear, then, that, though he thought himself nearly blinded by the existential conditions of his stage of history, Danilevsky believed he could glimpse a coming together of many diverse temporal strands. Unmistakably God was calling Russia to seize Constantinople and to accept the fate of a great war. If the imminent events of that seizure, of the institution of the Union, and of the war were framed, as they seemed to be, in a temporal setting that had obviously been transcendentally arranged, then God was preparing a drama, a liturgy for the Slavs. Everything indicated that they would receive the additional intervention needed for the actualization of their remarkable potentialities. Repetition of the ancient, seemingly absurd, archetypal state-building section of the Eastern heroes was the immediate imperative. Such repetition would bring about the ontologizing liturgy of destruction. Further evidence of the same line of warped liturgical thinking is provided by Danilevsky's evocation of a sacred spatial as well as a sacred temporal setting for the coming events. Again, his quasi-Hegelian heroics make our task of exposition difficult. Nevertheless, it is evident that he wanted his readers to think of Constantinople as something very like the ontological center of the world. Constantinople, or Tsargrad, was the Gordian knot of the Eastern question.

"According to a belief widespread among the Russian peoples and probably transmitted to us from the Greeks along with Christianity, Jerusalem is the center of the world or, in popular language, 'the navel of the earth.' And so it is from the highest spiritual point of view, a place whence comes spiritual light to peoples. But, from a more worldly and material point of view, no place on earth can be compared for centrality of position to Constantinople. There is no other such crossroad of world routes." [22] To the west of it opened the Mediterranean bounded by Asia, Africa, and Europe. To the south the isthmus of Suez, now pierced by a canal (it was opened officially in November 1869), led to the Indian Ocean. To the east were the Black, Caspian, and Aral seas, divided by great isthmuses, but now being crossed by railroads leading into the heart of Asia. To the north rivers and railroads led into the heart of Russia and Europe. A magnificent port, Constantinople was the center of great trade routes. Strategically, it was magnificently defensible. It was also the object of great historical memories and had enormous moral significance. Ancient capitals like Thebes, Memphis, Babylon, Nineveh, and Carthage were now mere archaeological curiosities. Athens and Alexandria lived stunted lives and even Rome had been bypassed by history. Such had never been true of Constantinople. Although its Turkish owners were decrepit, it still had a million and a half people. Shifts of trade routes had not bothered Constantinople, while Alexandria, Venice, and the Italian republics had declined. The Suez Canal would put even England on the commercial downgrade. At its height Rome had had to share its glory with Constantinople, which was once the center of the ancient world. Then it had become the center of the Moslem world. Now it was the center of European diplomacy. And it had a great future before it. "This is a city not of the past only, nor of the pitiful present, but also of the future; it is destined always to rise like a phoenix out of the ashes to ever new heights of greatness." [23] It bore four names, therefore, one for each of its great historical phases: Byzantium for the Greek phase; Constantinople for the Roman; Stamboul, a term of contempt used by the Turks and destined to disappear with them; and Tsargrad, a term used prophetically by the Slavs. "It is not surprising that such a city as Constantinople draws to itself the attention of all politicians. The question who will own it after its present owners are by force of necessity removed from the historical scene disturbs all minds that are not indifferent to the great interests of contemporary history. The particular question of Constantinople has just as much weight in contemporary politics as does the rest of the whole enormous Eastern question." [24]

In short, Danilevsky thought that he saw the signs of a preparation by God of a great historical sacred drama. Like some archaic *rite de passage*, it would take place at a point, at an *omphalos*, where the sacred and the profane, both temporally and spatially, intermingled.[25] Participation in the drama would actualize the potentialities of the Slavs, "the chosen people of God." Perhaps too, it would purge evil divisive forces out of mankind generally, inaugurate a Joachite new dispensation, a Heaven on earth, not only for Russians and Slavs, but also for Europeans, everybody.

The contradiction between this and the theory of cultural-historical types with its realistic political action program seems truly stupendous. In that theory Danilevsky had insisted that either a panhuman or a universal civilization was impossible. To think of such a thing was to fall into the error of naive, unscientific, unverifiable immanentism. It amounted to a hiding in foolish, childish dreams from the hard realities of life. And this would rob the Slavs of the only culture, progress, and sense of meaning that was possible to them in this world. But now, in the last chapters, Danilevsky himself seems to perpetrate all the philosophical sins he had inveighed against and to contradict his own elaborate theory of world history. Yet there was no logical contradiction in Danilevsky's outlook. Though flawed here and there by misplaced emphases and minor inconsistencies, his *Russia and Europe* has a remarkable consistency. But it is neither a utilitarian nor an ordinary metaphysical one. It is rather a type of existentialist consistency and that of a particular ("Russian") totalitarian kind. Keeping in mind his shifts of point of view, their Hegel-like context, and the dialectical temper of the language we have just been studying, it is possible to work out an explanation of the unity, coherence, and ultimate meaning of Danilevsky's philosophy. It is only necessary to set his realism and scientism in their proper shamanistic focus.

3

Whether we historians in the modern Western tradition are inclined philosophically to positivism, idealism, relativism, absolutism, or other outlooks, we are nearly all highly subjective in our view of the past. We assume that we must find the past or interpret it or re-enact it; history without the historian is inert and dumb. Though Danilevsky had been heavily exposed to this subject-object way of thinking (he was a professional scientist after all), he knew another way and he made it play a crucial role in his philosophy of the sixties. The author of *Russia and Europe* wanted it believed that he did not work from the familiar, detached, Cartesian position. He thought much more "objectively" and more vitalistically. He envisaged history as a great manlike organism, not past, inert, and dumb, but contemporary, live, purposeful, even articulate. This view of Danilevsky's was very Russian; it turns up frequently (though usually not in totalitarian form) among nineteenth and twentieth century Russian thinkers, in Belinsky, Herzen, Bakunin, Dostoevsky, Soloviev, Lenin, for instance. It may be variously described. In one sense history was, to Danilevsky, objectively alive, "out there," on its own. In another, history rather than the historian was subjective; that is, it was a purposeful subject and the historian was its object. Still better, the historian was an aspect of history's subjectivity, the chosen, organic voice and instrument of its purpose. The task of the historian was to witness concretely the structure of a great drama and the roles that men were playing or were about to play in it. The evidence that *Russia and Europe* was supposed to be taken as an "objective," non-Cartesian work is necessarily circumstantial. To have stated the point openly and directly would have been inconsistent, invalidating the very statement. The point had to be made rhetorically, by acting it out. Nevertheless the evidence is abundant.

Let us recall Danilevsky's discussion of Slavdom's great potentialities and the means for their actualization that History and Providence were preparing. In the center of this were the Goethean-Hegelian protagonists of the Eastern question: Philip, Alexander, Constantine, the Turks, the Russians (and the Panslav movement). Though narrow in their perspective and selfish in motive, each of these was associated with a mysterious archetypal action arranged by Providence, that of building a great state in the East. This action had at first been nonfunctional in the development of History. Philip, Alexander, and Constantine had simply failed. With the Turkish phase it had become functional for the first time but only in a negative fashion: the Turks had built a great Eastern state which had, though unintentionally, protected the Orthodox from the Catholics during a dangerous era. Not until the nineteenth century had history developed and shaped its nodal problem in such a way that the old state-building ritual action, created by Providence, could play a positive role. In the Russian-Panslav phase of the Eastern question, History had caught up with Providence. History's specifically modern inner contradictions were, at this point, such that the consciousness of the Eastern political hero was exactly appropriate in quality and exactly suitable in function to serve as the objective form of world historical consciousness, now at a very late stage of dialectical self-development toward integrity and (perhaps) universality. That world historical consciousness, like that of the Eastern hero, now involved the idea, "will evil" but "create good." It was dialectical like the modern, posttraditional era where men were sunk in egoism, secularism, power and money interests, yet at the same time vaguely discontent — and unable to think about changing their situation except in the very egoistic terms that were its causes. The specific content of modern historical consciousness was Panslavism, a kind of discontented nationalism and egoism, Panslavism with its narrow, selfish, utilitarian, Bismarckian rationale, traditionalism in modern language.

Now just as Danilevsky seems about to underline the direct affiliation of the Panslav movement with the archetypal quest for a solution of the Eastern question, he begins to shift his language and point of view from a metaphysical to a political realist and positivist level. Indeed, he shifts back exactly to the language, presuppositions, and framework of his utilitarian Panslavism and theory of cultural-historical types. Here, like earlier protagonists, he advocated the building of a great Eastern state or Panslav Union and that for utilitarian and pseudo-liberal reasons, which in comparison with what he had just been discussing were narrow, small, egoistic, merely power political reasons. Obviously the reader is supposed to conclude at this point that Danilevsky was putting himself forth as another Eastern hero trying to work out the ancient, blind, political ritual he had described. Similarly, the reader is supposed to see — since the Panslavic idea was the objective form of History's developing but still alienated consciousness — that Danilevsky's thinking was also History's thinking about itself. In short, he wanted to identify himself as a witness and tool at once of History and of his occasionalistic God.

It is clear that Danilevsky did not mean to identify himself this way simply in regard to the later chapters of his book. When he shifted his language and point of view, he did not merely refer his reader back to his early chapters. He reserved until now his detailed proposals regarding the structure and function of the future Panslav Union. In order to explain his Panslav-utilitarian theory I have summarized it (in chapter 6 above). The theory is not presented concisely in *Russia and*

Europe, however, but is found scattered throughout the book. From Danilevsky's point of view it is logically blended with his allusive metaphysical pronouncements, especially in the later chapters. Identifying himself as a Goethean hero in the way just described, he really acts out that role. The abruptness with which he pulled himself away from the speculative and metaphysical tone of much of the latter part of his book is truly startling. He became so dialectical at times that it is almost as though he had forgotten all the cosmic and providential background he had been so painfully sketching in. The reader gets inveigled into the strictly practical discussion of the constitutional arrangements of the union. Realities seem like parts of a dream. Both fantastic and real, for example, are the lengthy ponderings on the roles of non-Slavs, the Rumanians, the Greeks, the Hungarians, and of those "traitors to Slavdom," the Poles, in the future union. The first two were to be included on grounds of close cultural and religious (religion being a strictly cultural phenomenon here) affinity. The Hungarian Kingdom — Danilevsky was "frankly" though apologetically Machiavellian about it — was to be established and included in the union whether the Hungarians liked it or not; this was a geopolitical necessity. Liberal magnanimity demanded that the Poles be given their own kingdom in the union. Danilevsky's reader would be utterly at a loss here did he not connect all this with the theory of cultural historical types and at the same time realize that the whole typal-Panslavist theory, from chapter I on, was supposed to be taken as the false or alienated consciousness of History at a certain advanced stage of its dialectical development. The utilitarian and positivist language is no sign that Danilevsky wanted to be identified as a Cartesian observer, a social scientist, a mere political moralist. The whole design of his book militates decisively against such an interpretation. Regardless of its positivist temper, this was supposed to be taken as historicist, sort of existentialist language.

In the light of Danilevsky's rhetorical position, it is clear that he is not seriously committed to liberalism, utilitarianism, and Panslavism. He knew such doctrines intimately, better probably than people who were honestly committed to them. But to him they were dialectical-historical necessities — and unpleasant ones at that. On the surface he seems very modern, scientific, secular. For instance, he seems at times most liberal. I dare say his proposals regarding the constitution of the Panslav Union were some of the least Panrussian chauvinistic, and, under the circumstances, most fair that were ever made during the political phase of the Russian Panslav movement. Anyone who doubts this should take a careful look at his consideration of the Polish problem (and that only a few years after the Polish revolt of 1863).[26] While he excluded the "Western provinces of Russia," that is, the parts of Poland taken in the first partition, he insisted that Poland be set up as a separate kingdom within the union. He regarded the Poles as traitors to Slavdom because of their Catholicism, their aristocratic individualism, and their revolutionary tradition; but he insisted there be no effort to hold them down by force or to denationalize them. Their cardinal sin, Westernism, *zapadnichestvo*, was as common in Russia as in Poland, he insisted. Russians who criticized Poles should look at the motes in their own eyes, at the "idealism of Granovsky and the nihilism of Dobroliubov and Pisarev and the doctrine of civilized slavery of Russian conservatives; and the apostasy of Father Gagarin." It all sounds very liberal in spirit. But the reader has no theoretical context to which he can refer such discussion but the theory of cultural-historical types, a theory identified by Danilevsky, however indirectly, with falsity, provisionality, historicist dialectics. He was not liberal-Panslavist. He wanted it believed that History was making him talk this language because it wanted to get things moving. Such language would involve people in the Slavic cause for reasons they, in their alienation, could really understand and to which they could commit themselves. And that, in turn, would involve them in a war that would purge out all false consciousness, in History and in its human instruments. From a biographical point of view, it could well be said that Danilevsky was trying to manipulate his readers into a war by appealing to some of their most enlightened ideas and values in a subtly distorted fashion. His historicist claims seem to have been devices for public face-saving, for cultivation of a false self-image, for agitation, and for guiltless release of aggressive feelings. But he claimed not to be responsible. As far as the logic and consistency of his philosophy are concerned, his claim was well, indeed magnificently made.

An important reason for believing that Danilevsky wished to identify himself as an objectivist, a historical witness, is simply that such an interpretation and apparently only such an interpretation allows us to make sense of the contradictions in *Russia and Europe*, especially in its later chapters. Though it is precisely in these chapters that we find his metaphysical theory of world history, there are also here many examples of Danilevsky's curious blanking out, his acting the role of providential witness and instrument, and speaking almost entirely on one side — the realistic side — of the dialectic. Take, for example, his discussion of the likely advantages of the future union to its members. There is appropriately no mention whatever of the things of the spirit. Membership in the union would (strictly in terms of the typal theory) give Russia a stronger sense of merely national identity. Russia would no longer confuse Slavdom with Europe and be hurt by acting the foolish Don Quixote in international politics. The Greeks, by nature a trading people, would have greater and easier access to world trade through the backing of the union which would provide new sources of capital for commercial expansion. The Bulgarians, Serbs, Croats, Slovenes, Czechs, and Slovaks would receive political independence; their native cultures would flower. This same tone was used by Danilevsky in a like discussion of the rightful owners of Constantinople. Indeed, we are told that no one really had any "direct right" to Constantinople. Such questions were foolish and metaphysical. The realistic question was, "for whom can possession of it have true, real use?"[27] Danilevsky decided in favor of the Slavs, strictly on the basis of naval, military, commercial, and prestige advantages. There was not even a hint at this point that "from God's viewpoint" Constantinople was the center of the world, something like Jerusalem, "the navel of the earth." Apparently, if the latter *was* the case, it was not a matter for Danilevsky's "comic," "feeble" competences. All such discussion in the later chapters can only be taken as (dialectically) false, for Danilevsky made it clear, though only rhetorically (it was the only way he could say it logically), that this kind of narrow, utilitarian thinking was not itself valid as far as he was concerned; it was but an instrument of a still nascent, quite different nonutilitarian way of thinking which History was trying dialectically to work out. Given the whole theoretical framework in which Danilevsky used this mode of discourse, no other interpretation seems possible. That we have to use circumstantial evidence to arrive at that framework is but another index of its existence and specific nature. No one who believed that he was the voice of History could have logically said so. He could only have acted it out. The deed was the way of witnessing the spiritual, God-in-History.

Besides this kind of strictly "false" discussion, there is another type of discourse in the later chapters. It too is most puzzling, in fact not at all understandable, unless we posit again that Danilevsky wished to be thought of as a witness to history's developing consciousness. A look at this discourse further corroborates the idea that Danilevsky's realistic Panslavism and its intellectual paraphernalia were supposed to be taken as an epiphenomenon, an ideological instrument, and a dialectical symbol of processes other than the ones to which that doctrine directly referred. His chapter[28] on the war itself ("Borba") is, in the present context, one of the most interesting in *Russia and Europe*. Evident again are his specious practicality and utilitarianism. But in this chapter (and it seems highly significant biographically, in view of the fact that Danilevsky was anxious not to be accused of preaching war, that it is precisely here) there is some reappearance of the other, metaphysical side of the dialectic. The tone is similar to that in his discussion of the ending of Austria's *raison d'être* and of the world geopolitical position of Constantinople. It recalls also (the metaphysical side of the dialectic is even more prominent there) his "statements" of his Slavophilism and of his providential and quasi-Hegelian theory of the history of civilizations: the language of the doctrine of cultural-historical types is used to express something metaphysical, something toward which that language is supposedly negative. In the chapter on the war Danilevsky's factual and pragmatic approach is at once imposed upon the metaphysical and fractured by it. In a uniquely revealing fashion, the metaphysical approach does not entirely disappear as in the discussions of the union, of the rightful possessors of Constantinople, of the Austrian political dilemmas, and of the Polish problem; it can still be seen overcharging the categories in which it is supposedly imprisoned.

On the surface of the discussion the war had nothing to do with God or great historical drama. It was to be fought for the sake of victory. In strictly functional language Danilevsky undertook to examine the chances of a Slavic victory. He discussed at length the military potential of Russia and its new Slavic allies, the improvement of the Russian army since the Crimean War, the new railroads, the advantage of the termination of Russia's distracting war with the Caucasian mountaineers. But on balance, in his view, the material and political potentials of Russia and Slavdom would be insufficient to win the war. Some extra resources were needed. Danilevsky discussed the problem (in his usual detailed, analytical fashion he covered the whole European political situation) and proposed the possibility of an alliance with one European power. Prussia was assigned this future honor. But this would still not be enough. He turned to the question of the resources of spirit and enthusiasm. The attentive reader pricks up his ears at this point. Why is Danilevsky isolating just this question? Could it be related to his belief — on the other side of the dialectic — that the war would ontologize the Slavic soul? It would certainly be appropriate, "providentially" so, if it turned out that the Slavs could not win the war with Europe without the resources of patriotic enthusiasm. Perhaps too one should wonder about the Prussian alliance. Danilevsky did hint at the end of *Russia and Europe* that the war might somehow cleanse both antagonists and lead to a unity of mankind. How appropriate if Teuton and Slav, the ancient enemies, were allied in such a cause! [29] The parallelism between the two sides of Danilevsky's theory is so striking here that one comes to expect even more of a glimpse of the providential. He is not entirely disappointed. For there is of course now a discussion of the possibility of the Slavs' producing the needed resources of spirit and enthusiasm. It was a real problem because, according to Danilevsky, the Slavs, except Russia, had never been noted for these. Indeed, the Slavs had long been a dormant, passive element in history. But *that* was just the point. There was a historical law, "perhaps" providential in origin, about this sort of thing. According to this fittingly dialectical law, historical peoples who had long been dormant entered into the historical scene with unusual and unexpected *élan* as though they had been hoarding their energies. Their performances surpassed all rational expectations. And Danilevsky predicted, though once again in a cautious and statistical way, that the Slavs would behave in this archetypal fashion in accordance with this mysterious law during the coming war.

He did not here really abandon his practical point of view. He simply communicated a sense that there was more to it all than appeared on the surface, though even this was suggested only in obliquely factual language. Fittingly he thought the Slavs would experience their rising enthusiasm, in the first stages of the war, as a mixed psychological and obscurely spiritual feeling. In the coming struggle Europe had nothing inspiring to fight for. The "balance of power" would be a meaningless slogan; the masses would not rally to it. But "Russia, that country of barbarism, stagnation, and absolutism has suddenly acquired a moral weapon whose power is not entirely clear even to ourselves. This force is called — the peasant allotment! The banner on which will be written, 'Orthodoxy, Slavdom, and the Peasant Allotment' — that is, the moral, political, and economic ideal of the peoples of the Slavic cultural-historical type — that banner cannot but become the symbol of victory. It will be a case of *in hoc signo vinces*. It will bring assurance of victory into our ranks and into those of our allies, and fear and confusion into the ranks of our enemies." [30]

Such schizoid discussion of Slavic "military" potential, of the Slavs' material weakness and psychological strength, of the "perhaps" providential, archetypal nature of patriotic enthusiasm's sudden flowering constitutes unusually compelling evidence of the fact that Danilevsky here thought of himself as writing through a certain kind of existential metaphor. That metaphor expressed a sense of existentially, historically necessary, positivistic, realistic, scientistic vision — one absurdly and dialectically challenged, however, in its own most important categories, by a powerful, more essentialistic order. When we remember the tone and methodology of his earlier account of the cultural-historical types, their classification, their naturalistic functioning, together with the fact that this typal theory was supposedly the justification for a political Panslavist program, we cannot but conclude that he had presumed this curious dualistic point of view all along. Indeed, as we have seen, the utilitarian "liberalism" that informed that earlier discussion was a distorted, "frontist" one, apparently designed to destroy its own most basic methodological and value presuppositions. Moreover, Danilevsky had been as concerned with the problem of releasing instinctual drives in his discussion of the typal theory as he later proved to be in that of the Slavic potential for war. The unity and coherence of *Russia and Europe* is entirely dependent, then, upon the shamanistic metaphor through which the work was written. Though apparently Danilevsky was little influenced, at least directly, by Hegel, he envisaged himself very much, from our point of view, like a Hegelian hero. He seems to have believed, in his own original way, that (to quote Engels on Hegel) "evil is the form in which the motive force of historical development presents itself. This . . . contains the two-fold significance that while, on the one hand, each new advance necessarily appears as a sacrilege against things hallowed, as a rebellion against conditions . . . on the other hand, it is precisely the wicked passions of man — greed and lust for power — which . . . serve as levers of historical development." Like Hegel and Engels, Danilevsky appreciated "the historical role of moral evil." [31] Like Marx, the overcommitted classical economist and revolutionary, he undertook to play such a role himself — by advocating, however, a great world war, rather than a limitless revolution.

Understood in this way, Danilevsky's dualistic mode of discourse, which is used in talking about the war in particular, but which also occurs again and again as some of the most characteristic language of his book, is a sign that his utilitarian language was meant to be taken in a dialectical way. It is also a further testimony to the fact that he wanted it believed that his contradictory way of talking was not hypocritical or agitational, but rather the reflection in his sensitive mind of the contradictions of History itself. History was predestined to integrality. But it was now split between the traditional and the modern (perhaps too between the national and the universal, if we are to take seriously the last page of *Russia and Europe*). It felt discontent but could not become conscious or express itself except in terms of the situation in which it was entrapped. It could only transcend that situation in the situation's own egoistic way, by overdoing the egoism, the manipulations, the power politics. It could glimpse something else. But this glimpse could really only serve subtly to distort, to exaggerate the going consciousness and direction of action. Sensitive men like Danilevsky, being the bearers of History's consciousness talked double: mainly of power politics but vaguely otherwise.

In the metaphor or set of metaphors through which he wrote, Danilevsky also reminds one of the character Shatov in Dostoevsky's *The Possessed*. Indeed, I have wondered if Dostoevsky may not even have had *Russia and Europe* in mind when he created the character. He was reading the work with great interest in the year 1869.[32] *The Possessed* was published in 1871–72. Moreover, a key Danilevsky term — "ethnographic material" — appears in one of Shatov's most important philosophical speeches.[33] And, like Danilevsky, Shatov was an ex-socialist turned Slavophil. In any case, the existential senses of the two, the fictional character and the author in the book, are similar. Shatov was a Slavophil who believed in the Russian people — to him, a factual, historical, nationalistic entity — and in their unfactual, metaphysical future, a time when they would achieve ontological integrality. But he held this last belief most vaguely and did not believe in God. When asked if he believed in God, he said he believed in the Russian people. When pressed on the point, he said, "I will believe in God." [34] In other words, he seems to have thought that his capacities for faith in God were almost nil, that he had to become a new man before he could believe. In his present mental and spiritual state he could only be sure that his inner life was in a state of potency exactly analogous to that of the factually defined, national life of the Russian people. In his scheme, his own and Russian inner lives generally were entirely historical and societal products. Mental and spiritual progress toward integrality were therefore wholly dependent upon nationalist achievements. Though Shatov does not in the novel give any such details, this could easily have involved the belief, to which Danilevsky held, that with the passing of the Russian nation to some new and higher state, through reform or, more likely, revolution or war, the men in it would become the "new men" of Christian theology. This curious *mélange* of faith and doubt, Christianity and nationalism, this totalitarianism, rather than Russian Orthodoxy, seems to have been the substance of Danilevsky's "religion" in the 1860's.

It is not easy to state precisely his doctrine and his claims. One must extrapolate from the various facets of his thinking and so reach a set of ideas that supposedly could not be articulated directly. But at least it is possible to capture the spirit of it all.

In the beginning God had arranged that world history would develop from a primitive to a civilized, from an unconscious to a conscious state, without any losses and with great gains in the process. History's unfolding would eventually result in a multicivilized, utopian socialist Heaven on earth, perhaps only in Slavdom, perhaps everywhere. Though owing much to Orthodox culture (one notes especially the idea of the beatification or "deification" of the mundane world), Danilevsky's view of History was emphatically deistic, that is, History developed according to immanent laws set up by God at the start. His God, however, like Newton's, intervened occasionally — perhaps a bow to the idea of continuous creation and to immanentism, on Danilevsky's part. God added ingredients and behavior patterns as time went on, partly because He had planned things that way, partly to make readjustments necessitated by human sinfulness, for even the chosen Slavic people could sin, could worship the false God of *zapadnichestvo*. The process of History's development had been for a long time only blandly dialectical, a process of splitting, specializing, developing in a one-sided way, then reintegrating. The story of the first civilizations and afterwards of the Hebrews, Greeks, Roman, and Europeans had proceeded like that. Division had been the motive force of synthesis, as it were. The whole process, it had been planned, was to be completed by the Slavs. They would develop socialism and also integrate all the previously developed elements. They would end History and the dialectic.

But the chosen people, even with their marvelous character and all the occasionalistic interventions of Providence, had fallen into sin, idolatry, *zapadnichestvo*. Instead of developing their own (and thus History's ultimate) potentialities for civilization, wholeness, and perhaps universality, they had undertaken to worship Europe and its false claims to finality and universality. Copying Europe, they had become egoistic, utilitarian, and liberal. Even their ideas of resisting Europe and of working out their identity in the face of it, their merely secular nationalism and Panslavism, were but subtle further examples of Europeanism. Slavic, especially Russian, consciousness was now warped and unautonomous. It was an alienated consciousness, exclusive and protective toward the self, God, and possibly mankind where it should have been receptive, open, kenotic. This meant too that History's consciousness — for at this advanced stage of affairs Slavic history was but its objective form — was also alienated, outside its true self, internally divided. Concretely, History seemed to itself eternally and finally alone, without context or meaning, vaguely discontent, externally divided up into one-sided civilizations (American, European, Slavic). Among the chosen people Panslavism perhaps indicated a vague aspiration to selfhood, autonomy, and truth; the aspiration was at least geographically in line, though possibly national exclusiveness was ultimately wrong even in metaphysical form. But Panslavism was related to the true only in a vague, distorted way. It was a kind of subtle self-deceptive device, making it possible for the chosen people to persist in their sin. The nineteenth century was the dark night of the Slavic and world historical soul.

But God, who had foreknown though not predestined that all this would happen, had for some centuries been arranging to make everything right. He had been planning the archetypal, ritual, political action of the Eastern hero and his dialectical consciousness. In the nineteenth century God was undertaking one of His occasional interventions in History and melding the big Eastern ritual action with Panslavism, at once the most sinful and the most advanced form of historical consciousness. God had arranged to make use of the materials at hand so that History might reach its end. Panslavism, pursued *à l'outrance* (and that because of glimpses of something tantalizing but not understood), would lead the Slavs into a period of violent suffering, a *rite de passage*. This suffering, caused by their own sins, would burn out those sins and ontologize the Slavic soul. Then the Slavs would build the Heaven on earth, perhaps for all mankind. Alienation, bland and not so bland, would be finished forever; there would ensue — whether in Slavdom alone or everywhere — a permanent diversity-in-unity between God and man, man and nature, man and man, man and himself. Thus in the nineteenth century God was making History's and Slavdom's apparently hopelessly alienated consciousness, that is, Panslavism, into the key to the final, beatifying development — just as in some ordinary Christian theology He would not only forgive but make benevolent use of man's sinfulness, original and otherwise.

This or something in the spirit of this was the main theme in Danilevsky's philosophy. Now things looked different from the Slavic point of view. The Slavs, only a little more zealously than modern men in general, had a rather strictly secular and merely nationalist-Panslavist sense of being in the world. Nations, supernations, imperialism, power politics made up the content of their thinking and also shaped its categories and values. Life was an egoistic, a hard, cold, particularistic, utilitarian affair. The best that could be hoped for was a relatively stable balance of forces, a world equilibrium of powers and civilizations. Panslavism, pursued *à l'outrance* against European imperialism, was the key to the best possible situation for the Slavs and for mankind; it was the political, cultural, and philosophical answer. Yet there was also a vague sense that there was something large and mysterious connected with Panslavism, a contradictory sense of metaphysical hope. Somehow the Panslav movement seemed the outcome of great historical and providential forces, the instrument of some great order, one involving the development of world history, even the completing of a still unfinished creation. Not everybody got this special feeling without some help. Some men had it more definitely than others. They — especially Danilevsky — were witnesses, tools of God. Still closely entrapped in the darkness, they were given invigorating glimpses of the light. Like anarchists, it was their job to bring to the surface, communicating by example where possible, manipulating and agitating where necessary, the latest forces of creative destruction. They were to spread, enhance, help particularize the feeling of entrapment and vague eschatological promise. The idea was to make people tough-minded and action-oriented within Panslavism — so that they would pursue it for its own sake.

God and History would take care of all the larger questions, those of purpose and of morality, that were involved in this exclusive pursuit of deeds. The invisible hand — how permeated was Danilevsky's thinking, like that of Marx, with English habits — had arranged the world and would continue to make sure that everything would have a beatific end and a rationale. To wonder about such ultimate questions was sinful. Only God could really know all this. It would be hubris to seek such knowledge. Accepting his fate, man was not only being a good servant, however. He was also accepting and more than accepting the alienating results of his own sins; and his punishment was, in turn, a way, the only possible way under the circumstances, at once of attaining and of being with the sacred, from which he had distanced himself. Ultimately, Danilevsky was advising his readers, the absurd ritual deed was everything. Violence was the way, the truth, the life. Hence, he kept saying rhetorically, do not worry about goals or about evil, do not hesitate, do not rationalize, do the deed, push zealously and overzealously for the Panslav Union, enjoy the process itself; History and God will take care of everything else. Indeed, it would seem, without the deeds History and God would even have trouble getting their job done, for violence was now the key to the final unfolding of History and to the completion of creation itself. (Like Dostoevsky, though in totalitarian fashion, Danilevsky conceived of man as a cocreator.) Deeds alone would purge out sin and shake History down to its authentic nature. Deeds had no goal really. They would be an ontologizing ritual; they were all but good in themselves.

Such was the gist of Danilevsky's idea. Here was totalitarianism in its essence. Like Marx and especially his Bolshevik followers, Danilevsky wanted to start a cruel and violent process in the world. The more this was done as an end in itself, the better. This being the case, it seems appropriate not to worry about the fact that he called the process war whereas they called it now revolution, now dictatorship. If matters had developed as he wanted, there would not have been an appreciable difference to those who suffered. Optimistic suffering (Danilevsky's interest in it is another sign that his doctrine was derived from Orthodox culture) was more important than the petty details of what was done, let alone the goals.

Danilevsky's was an evil philosophy. He did not exactly claim otherwise. He claimed rather that the evil was not his responsibility. In objective terms he was partly right. His whole doctrine and the evil in it owed much to unfortunate intellectual potentialities in his mixed traditional-modern, romantic-realist cultural inheritance. Yet it was he who actualized these potentialities. He felt entrapped, hateful, and aggressive (that is, "Panslavic") because of his own hypocrisy (that is, *zapadnichestvo*). "History," the conditions of the time, merely encouraged him not to say so in a more honest fashion.

9

CONCLUSION

Previous students of Danilevsky have seen him as significant in relation to one of two important historical strands: Panslavism and speculative philosophy of history. Neither of these views is wholly wrong. It is rather a case of each being based on a partial and superficial understanding of his major work. Some criticism of these interpretations together with an indication of a more useful view is now in order.

In the standard histories of Panslavism Danilevsky's thought has been given an especially prominent place, often on grounds of its supposedly "typically Russian," "power-hungry Russian" quality. It has been viewed as an especially clear and systematic statement of the "ideology" of Russian Panslavism. Such scholars as Fischel, Kohn, Pfalzgraf, Petrovich, and Fadner (the last two, the most objective interpreters) were anticipated in this evaluation by N. N. Strakhov, who called *Russia and Europe* the "codex and catechism" of Panslavism.[1] It is not always clear whether such an interpretation is meant to refer to Danilevsky's doctrine as a systematizing (a codex) of looser intellectual trends or as an important intellectual influence or both. Anyway none of these seems to have been quite the case.

There is, of course, a special sense in which *Russia and Europe* may be regarded as a "codex" of Russian Panslavic currents of the later 1850's and 1860's: Danilevsky meant to center his totalitarian philosophy on what he regarded as the important contemporary form of intellectual consciousness and he tried to systematize (as well as to render more political) Panslavic opinion for this purpose. The parts of his book in which he attempted this may with caution (his theory is unduly political) be used as a useful index to the nature of that opinion. But as a whole his book cannot be regarded as a seriously Panslavic work, for he was not a sincere utilitarian, quasi-liberal, secular, nationalist-Panslavist. Basically he was at least a metaphysical left Slavophil who thought Slavdom alone capable of realizing the greatest universal providential-historical potentials; if we take seriously his last messianic lines and the universalist spirit of many of his intellectual attachments (naturalistic Christianity, rationalism, science, socialism), he was ultimately anti-particularist and even anti-Panslavist. In any case his Panslavism as a secular and utilitarian doctrine was the object of only provisional and oblique commitment on his part. He attempted to use the modernistic Panslav movement for purposes that were on the whole alien to it. He had no intention of encouraging it because he really advocated its narrowly secular, nationalist, realistic political and cultural aims; he would have been averse to codifying Panslavism. His book as a whole is clear enough on these points. It is too much more than a too politically oriented Panslavist work to be regarded as a "codex."

The catechism idea seems even more unsound. If Danilevsky was a guiding intellectual light of the Russian Panslav movement, we might expect to find some evidence that he was much read or listened to by Panslavists. But a look through two historical volumes published by the Petersburg Slavic Welfare Society and covering the years of Danilevsky's membership fails to uncover much evidence.[2] The record of meetings of the society from 1868 to 1883 attests that, in the view of the membership, there were intellectuals who were a continuing source of inspiration, if not of specific doctrine. Indeed, there were two such favorite intellectuals and each was metaphysically oriented. But they were Tiutchev and Dostoevsky. I was able to find only one mention of Danilevsky.[3] The speaker, one T. I. Filippov, weighed the idea — which he attributed to both Ljudevit Shtur and Danilevsky — that the Russian language could best achieve a position "befitting it in the group of Slavic languages" if Slavic political unification preceded rather than followed cultural. He was strongly inclined to reject the idea, however ("already now Pushkin, Lermontov, Gogol, Turgenev, and Tolstoi have won access for the Russian language into remote places of the Slavic world"). Danilevsky *was* elected to the select body of honorary members of the society but only in 1884 — for being "well known to Slavdom for his writing and for his scientific and social services." [4] The publication history of *Russia and Europe* also fails to make a case for catechetical influence.[5] The book called forth little or no comment in the journals, hostile or friendly, in the years following its initial serialized publication in *Zariia*. That magazine was not aided as a business venture by the publication; it failed in 1872, three years after it was started. With the aid of a subsidy (arranged by Strakhov) from the publishers, The Brotherhood of Social Welfare, 1200 copies of the work were published in book form in 1871. It took until 1888 to create a demand for a new and unsubsidized edition, despite the excited Panslavic agitation of the late seventies in which Danilevsky himself was very active as a publicist. Subsequently *Russia and Europe* went through two editions (1889, 1895); it was not reprinted again in Russia. Thus it enjoyed its greatest popularity during the years 1888 to 1895 when the Panslav movement was in a state of eclipse. The discussion of Danilevsky's ideas in the Russian press in the eighties, nineties, and after was largely devoted to philosophical and social scientific issues raised by the theory of cultural-historical types and mostly taken out of context. An earlier press controversy about *Darwinism* apparently had much to do with calling public attention to its author's other big work. Not much attention was paid to the Panslavic program in *Russia and Europe*. Thus if Danilevsky was regarded in his time as an important Panslav theorist, the evidence for this does not turn up in obvious ways. One cannot but conclude that Strakhov and several modern scholars have greatly exaggerated this aspect of Danilevsky's alleged significance. Perhaps too *Russia and Europe* was not regarded as a catechism because it did not strike Panslavists as a very good statement of their aims, since it was not a "codex" either.

Then there have been commentators who have regarded Danilevsky as an important or at least provocative philosopher of history (one of those big speculators about the plurality and the rise and decline of civilizations) or even a rudimentary social scientist. Beginning in Russia in the 1880's and adopted widely over the Western world since, this sort of interpretation has resulted in his famous reputation as a forerunner of Spengler and Toynbee or, in the view of the more scientifically minded, of modern cultural anthropological theorists.[6] Again this is not a wrong interpretation. But it is so partial as to falsify Danilevsky's intellectual makeup, his commanding interests and intentions. It is as though we knew Marx only as a social scientist, a forerunner of Durkheim, Pareto, or Weber. But besides the (only somewhat relativistic) theory of types in *Russia and Europe*, there is a providentialist, linearly progressive theory of world history. There is also a big Panslavist program interestingly connected to both his theories of world history. One of these (the famous typal one) is supposed to be taken as a kind of alienated version of the other. And the whole doctrine is knitted together in a way that makes Danilevsky appear quite a different kind of thinker from Spengler or Toynbee, an activist, a fanatic, a "political," not a contemplative academic.

Danilevsky was a totalitarian philosopher. He sought in his major intellectual work to call men to undertake the solution of the problem of spiritual alienation and salvation, a bridging of the gaps between man and God, man and nature, man and man, man and himself — and that through employment of the apparatus of the modern state, through violence, war, a liturgy of destruction. Like all totalitarian philosophers, he was a crank; that is, he was obsessed by the cosmic significance of things which ordinary men took more as a matter of course. In his case it was the Slavs and Panslavism; in others, it was the proletariat, socialism, the "Aryan race." Also typically his thinking ran to gimmicks, to Gordian knots: the Eastern question, Constantinople, war, *Realpolitik*. Other totalitarian thinkers have been compulsive about business cycles, class frictions, the mythical Jewish problem, the Communist conspiracy — and always about political violence, whether in the form of revolution, war, or the oppressive and terroristic actions of a dictatorship. And Danilevsky was not only compulsive objectively. He wanted it believed that he felt compelled subjectively, that he was a historical shaman without reason, freedom, or responsibility. He wanted it believed that he was voluntaristic for deterministic reasons. This seems the most accurate and useful context in which to understand his major intellectual effort of the sixties and to evaluate his historical significance.

In weighing that significance, it is important to keep in mind his specific intellectual affinities, historical and morphological. He is not easy to classify either in terms of the main currents of nineteenth century thought or more generally. But, on the whole, in regard to the intellectual history of his time, he fits much better with the metaphysical, rationalist, populist, and utopian socialist radicals — among whom Herzen was the greatest intellect and human being — than he does with the intuitional metaphysicians, the idealists and particularists, the proponents of a neomedieval and patriarchal idea of Russia, the Khomiakovs and Kireevskys. Like the former, Danilevsky wanted Russia by and large not to lead men away from a modern way of life but to lead them to realize its true humanistic and spiritual promise. He could not envisage an end of history and a utopia without science, reason, economic and social and cultural development. He recognized the most important sources of these to have been Western European. He criticized "the West" and its Russian imitators less for what they represented, culturally and institutionally, than for failing to realize what he regarded as the ultimate potentials of reason, science, democracy, and progress. He thought Russia uniquely and providentially qualified to correct this unfortunate situation. Something like Chaadaev and very like Herzen he thought Russia's very backwardness a precious guarantee of new spiritual and humanistic perspective in a world that was losing its way. Danilevsky was a "Russian socialist" from the 1840's onward and he thought Russian socialism the gateway to a new and blessed way of life — possibly (*Russia and Europe's* messianism is muted and unclear) for the whole world.

Several things about his intellectual makeup seem previously to have obscured his affinity to the radical populists of metaphysical bent: his Bismarckian nationalism and Panslavism, his "Christianity," and his attitude toward the autocracy. It is worth emphasizing again that none of these really disqualifies him as a Slavophil radical. His Panslavism was a meaningfully alienated and merely instrumental part of his radicalism — as Marx's democratic socialism or modernized capitalism was of his. Of course, there was much "nationalism" and "Panslavism" throughout Danilevsky's doctrine; at all doctrinal levels he insisted that Slavdom (mainly Russia) and Europe were key factors in world history. But the same was true in left, revolutionary Slavophilism generally. As with other bearers of this intellectual tradition, however, nationalist and Panslavic commitments were seriously compromised in Danilevsky by much stronger attachments to local communities, the communes; his basic and dearest idea of community was not nationalist. Even the temper of theory about Russia and the West in the intellectual tradition to which Danilevsky belonged was at most only prenationalist. In left Slavophilism it was as though Russia and the West were at once cultural-geographical entities and parousic natural symbols, respectively, of the sacred and the profane. Just as in Orthodoxy God would ultimately deify the profane nearly in toto rather than (as in many Western Christian views or in Slavophilism proper) purify it and beatify it more selectively, so in left Slavophilism or "Russian socialism," Russia would not reform or cleanse the West and modernity so much as it would bring out their hitherto unrealizable potentials. In Danilevsky, Herzen, and much of the radical populist tradition, everything about nations and civilizations sounds often very traditionalistic, like "Rus" in *The Tale of Igor's Campaign*, like the old epithet "Holy Russia." [7] Omitting totalitarianism from the discussion for a moment the general comparison of Danilevsky with Herzen and other similar thinkers in regard to nationalism is only marred by Danilevsky's insistence on the putrescence of the West and on the idea that Slavdom alone could be saved. Though he hinted the contrary and though the hint was more in line with the spirit of his whole theory than were his explicit xenophobic statements, this was a striking deviation from left Slavophilism (and from the Orthodox tradition from which it seems in important part to have derived). This xenophobia, this fear not so much of the West as of saving the West, is difficult to explain: an intellectual muddle, of which Danilevsky was most capable? a touch of official nationalism? more dialectics? some misplaced hypocrisy? Whatever the explanation of this exclusivist doctrinal touch, it was quite contradictory — as Danilevsky himself seems at least vaguely to have felt — to the spirit of his whole theory and cannot decisively disqualify him as a left Slavophil, a metaphysical radical populist, a Russian socialist. As to his Christianity, though he was Orthodox, what we see of his Orthodoxy is so colored by scientific naturalism and rationalism that it seems closer to his Fourierism and left Hegelianism of the forties than to an authentic spiritual Christianity (however immanentist). Danilevsky was a *homo religiosus* but one almost without a specific religion.

His "loyalty" to the autocracy was also a complicated business, but on balance it should not be used to classify Danilevsky either with bureaucratic conservatives like Katkov or historical ones like Ivan Aksakov. On the one hand, he seems to have favored the system of Alexander II on much the same basis that he did Panslavism. It was an important part of that false modernity which

Danilevsky disliked but which he thought could be used against itself. After all the program in *Russia and Europe* was to have been implemented by the tsar and his foreign minister. This was a curiously ambivalent monarchism. On the other hand, Danilevsky seems to have thought (he is very vague about everything in the future) that the monarchy would go on into the final, utopian period of Slavdom (or mankind perhaps). But that would have been an odd one, some kind of curious democratic and socialist monarchy. Life in those great days would have its center of gravity in decentralized social formations, the new communes. Here, with the human spirit fulfilled, there would not have been much for the monarchy to do. Danilevsky seems to have been a monarchist partly because of the way he saw the current historical situation and its dynamics, partly because of the holistic and kenotic elements in his orientation, partly because there was a heavy streak of political agnosticism in him. Russian radicalism, as I have pointed out before, was basically less a political movement than an attitude toward and a program regarding modernization and Westernization. Social, cultural, and spiritual — not political — revolution was the big interest of the radicals. Logically specific political emphases in radical programs could vary. In the Russian situation of political oppression, however, the monarchy was hated and most radicals were antimonarchical. But this was only a minor compromise with their fundamental agnosticism about forms of government in general. Danilevsky's monarchism was exceptional for a radical but it was hardly an index of conservatism.

   This affiliation between Danilevsky's ideas and the main tradition of Russian socialism and radicalism can only be made if one omits his totalitarianism from consideration. Once this is brought in, his distance from, say, Herzen, is truly stupendous. In *Russia and Europe* his basic interests and goals were humanistic but his ideas about means and his whole attitude were quite the reverse. His doctrine was a dangerous and evil one, typologically similar to the ideas of forerunners of Stalin and Hitler. Within the intellectual historical genus, totalitarian philosophy, Danilevsky's thought belongs to the rationalistic not the irrationalistic species. So he was a forerunner of the Bolsheviks — like Chernyshevsky or Tkachev — not of the Nazis.

Let me stress a few points concerning this matter. First, there can be no doubt that there are important differences of detail between Danilevsky's theory and the ideas of Marx or Lenin or Stalin. I have heard it said that there are interesting similarities between Danilevsky's proposed Panslav Union and the Soviet bloc in Eastern Europe in Stalin's time. This is absurd. How about Greece, Albania, Austria, Germany, the capital at Constantinople? When Russian imperialist movements push forward, unless the situation is utterly unfavorable, they are likely to move into Eastern Europe. Danilevsky's and Stalin's interests in Eastern Europe were quite different: the former's were related to his central doctrinal concerns, the latter's were much more tactical. One might better pursue the question of detailed similarities between Danilevskianism and Bolshevism by looking at the cores of the doctrines. Many analogies may be drawn: of nation with class, of nationalism with capitalism, of Panslavism with democratic socialism, of the Panslav Union with the dictatorship of the proletariat, of panhumanism and universal humanism with communism; of war with revolution. One might even note a parallel of sorts to Danilevsky's ambivalence about saving the West. In Bolshevism too individuals among the damned (here the bourgeoisie) may be saved but as a social group they will have to go — the fruits of their efforts at civilization will be reaped by the proletariat. But such analogies (rather formalistic anyway) can be pushed too far. There are important differences. Danilevsky was less concerned with industrialism than with a whole range of modern phenomena, science, secularism, nationalism, positivism, liberalism. Manifest and latent doctrinal elements are not so separated and contradictory in Marx and his followers as in Danilevsky. Danilevsky was a kind of *narodnik*, an agrarian socialist, much under Slavophil influence; Bolshevism, though indebted to *narodnichestvo* in many ways, is more directly affiliated to the Russian Westernist than it is to the Slavophil heritage. After all, the Bolsheviks quarreled with the populist tradition. One should be similarly cautious in drawing detailed comparisons between Danilevsky and some of the (marginally and fragmentarily) totalitarian forerunners of Lenin; Pisarev, for instance, was not a *narodnik*.

It is better to view Danilevsky's major theory as an instance of an ideal type of doctrine — Russian totalitarianism — which includes Bolshevism and its various causally affiliated forerunners and which is strikingly different from the Western type to which Nazism, Fascism, and their forerunners belong. All totalitarian philosophies exhibit a significant number of characteristics of a unique intellectual syndrome; there are in such doctrines ends which are ultimately spiritual and humanistic; they are only vaguely stated and are combined with inhuman means; there is deterministic historicism applied to the philosopher and to his audience; there is fixation upon and a liturgical attitude toward some large, existential process of violence; there are prominent "frontist" programs ("socialism," "nationalism") dialectically and mystically related to the true aims. Some totalitarian philosophers (the "Russian type") have a progressive, rationalistic, scientistic, universalist temper, others (the "Western type") are reactionary, much more anti-modern, exclusivist, and irrationalistic. In this scheme there can be no question but that Danilevsky's philosophy was totalitarian and that it was of the Russian type. Just as he was (in a sense) a Herzen not a Khomiakov, so he was a Marx or Lenin not a Carlyle (whom he admired but thought sentimental and romantic because of his hero worship and irrationalism), a Gobineau, or a Hitler. Danilevsky's intellectuality and his attitude toward modernity were progressive, scientistic, democratic, rationalistic. He wanted modernity reshaped without much simplification or purification. He wanted to proceed not regress to an idealized and vastly improved past.

The question of Danilevsky's historical significance should, of course, be considered on the basis of an accurate appraisal of his intellectual position. But, since a misunderstood theory can also be historically significant (Marx's influence has been felt in many curious ways), it is important in weighing its significance to keep the whole picture in mind. There seem to be two possibilities. First, it is possible that Danilevsky was causally significant, that, either understood or misunderstood, his *Russia and Europe* or some other of his intellectual efforts helped appreciably to define the course of Russian thought. The second possibility is that his thought was morphologically significant, that is, that its nature, typological affiliations, and development give us some unusually good insight into the history of modernizing Russian (or other) consciousness. Let us begin with the causal possibility.

Fortunately Danilevsky the totalitarian seems to have had no influence. As far as I have been able to tell few have even understood his doctrine. He provided no mass movement, incipiently totalitarian, with an integrating theory, no ideology with a philosophy. He never provided even an auxiliary rationale for any totalitarian political system. He is highly devaluated and utterly neglected in the Soviet Union. The influence of the partially understood Danilevsky has been minor. As a Panslav theorist he probably contributed *something* to the Russian Panslav movement, but, as pointed out earlier, there is no evidence that his doctrine was the object of any great attention. The theory of cultural historical types had perhaps greater influence than had Panslavism. N. N. Strakhov greatly admired it together with Danilevsky's book *Darwinism*.[8] Constantine Leontiev used the idea of a plurality of civilizations in his philosophy of history.[9] This seems to have been merely a matter of borrowing one idea rather than of being deeply influenced by Danilevsky's work, however. Leontiev's pessimistic and hyperconservative *Byzantinism and Slavdom* is quite dissimilar in intention and spirit from *Russia and Europe*. (Leontiev hated Panslavism in any form; it was modern and therefore bad. It was democratic and vulgar.) The historian K. Bestuzhev-Riumin noted a debt to Danilevsky in his *Russian History*.[10] I found passing mention of Danilevsky in V. V. Rozanov and M. M. Sokolov, the "Eurasian" intellectual.[11] Mikhailovsky says that Professor A. A. Potebnia gave a course of lectures based on *Russia and Europe* at the University of Kharkov.[12] The Soviet historian Pokrovsky tried to show that Danilevsky influenced Pobedonostsev and Alexander III, but the manner of influence is not clear from his account and it is unsatisfactorily documented.[13] In the Western world at large Danilevsky, the philosopher of civilizations, has had some influence on the rise of modern relativistic historical consciousness. But that influence, it must be noted, would not have been felt without Spengler and Toynbee, for the discovery of Danilevsky outside Russia was largely a function of the vogue of those historical theorists. It is notable that a German translation by Karl Nötzel of the parts of *Russia and Europe* dealing with civilizations appeared in Stuttgart in 1920, at the height of Spengler's fame. The discovery of Danilevsky helped amplify but did not help initiate the historical relativist movement.[14] On the whole, further research would probably only uncover other stray items of influence. In the causal sense, it cannot be said that the Danilevsky of *Russia and Europe*, understood wholly, in part, or erroneously (as has usually been the case even in regard to his typal theory)[15] had any appreciable causal historical significance. He had more causal influence in shaping Russian Fourierism and the Russian Darwinian controversy; but I am not inclined to make much of this either. Indeed, except perhaps for his work on the fisheries, modern Russian (to say nothing of European) history would scarcely have missed Danilevsky at all; it would have been much the same without him.

A consideration of his significance is better directed to morphological questions. There is something to his being a forerunner of Spengler and Toynbee. I warn the reader unfamiliar with *Russia and Europe* first hand, however, not to believe that it is anything as ambitious, detailed, sophisticated, or striking as *The Decline of the West* or *A Study of History*. The typal theory of Danilevsky is a contribution to human culture but it is brief, fragmentary, and most amateurish. On the whole, I think Danilevsky's significance in this context has been exaggerated also. He was really a very ordinary intellectual. The main reason historians might read his work *is* morphological rather than causal. But he was a forerunner of Lenin and Stalin not of Spengler or Toynbee.

One of the really big problems of modern Russian historiography is that of the connection of Bolshevism with earlier, native Russian intellectual strands. Gustav Wetter, for instance (to take a most accomplished student of the problem), finds many similarities between Bolshevism and dominant old Russian philosophical traditions. In *Dialectical Materialism* he writes,

At those very points where Lenin has exercised a decisive influence on Soviet philosophy, there are striking points of contact between dialectical materialism and non-Marxist tendencies in Russian philosophy . . . We are thinking of the fact that even in the Soviet ideology, for all its materialist and levelling tendencies, there are certain aspirations still surviving, which animated the minds of many other Russian thinkers in the nineteenth and early twentieth centuries. These contacts . . . are above all concerned with that movement . . . in which, perhaps, a certain peculiar quality of Russian philosophy is most clearly exhibited: with the Slavophil movement in its religious and theological phase . . . and with the powerful school of Russian religious thought which grew out of it and which leads, through V. Soloviev, to such modern Russian philosophers as S. Bulgakov, N. Berdaiev, S. Frank, P. Florensky, L. Karsavin and others.[16]

In the historical part of his book Wetter also indicates links between Bolshevism and the Slavophil movement in its nontheological phase, that is, radical populism. Other scholars have brought up the same problems. The Bolsheviks themselves have defined their heritage in a way that includes Herzen, Chernyshevsky, and company. They have not, of course, embraced Soloviev or Dostoevsky, quite the contrary; they have not seen and do not care to see their own or the radicals' affinities to the kenotic and modern-minded wing of the Slavophil tradition. Yet there is clearly an as yet insufficiently examined problem of the roots of Bolshevism in Russian religious, cultural, social, historical, and intellectual traditions.

It is in throwing light on key aspects of this problem that Danilevsky's thought has its chief significance. On the one hand, his philosophy can help us appreciate the similarities of Russian religious thought to Russian radicalism. Leaving aside totalitarianism, a more authentic Orthodox Christianity and some not great readjustments in his national and monarchical ideas would have made the base of Danilevsky's thought (or Herzen's) very like Dostoevsky's or Fedorov's — without displacing his Russian socialism, his Joachism, his leftism, and (if he really meant it) his messianism. On the other hand, his doctrine suggests how like Bolshevism in general temper Russian modernistic religious thought or Russian metaphysical radicalism could be when given a kind of totalitarian twist such as he gave radicalism. Related morphologically at once obliquely to a progressive version of theological Slavophilism (Dostoevsky, Fedorov, Soloviev, Berdaiev), more directly to radical populism (Russian socialism or revolutionary Slavophilism), and finally to Bolshevism, Danilevsky's doctrine can be pondered with considerable profit by historians interested in the Russian roots of Soviet intellectual totalitarianism.

Such study not only contributes to further appreciation of the Bolshevik heritage. It can also help to widen the scope of the whole historical investigation, which has hitherto often been painfully narrow, largely devoted to showing formal and causal affinities between trivia: Chernyshevsky's "voluntarism" and Lenin's; Tkachev's Jacobinism and Lenin's — as though in a very real sense dialectical and historical materialism themselves were not "made in Russia," that is, as though men (especially modally Russian ones) ever believed anything very deeply and lived by it without profound human, cultural, and spiritual reasons. Herzen, Dostoevsky, Danilevsky, and Lenin were all adherents of a certain kind of materialism.[17] They all

believed in a close relationship between nature and history, action
and thought, in the existence of a huge, dialectical, spiritual-ma-
terial medium operating according to immanent or relatively immanent laws of its own. Each was a modern man, endowed like
Ivan Karamazov, with a "Euclidean mind." But each also con-
templated a non-Euclidean cosmic order and felt an ambivalence
between the real and the symbolic, the empirical and the mythical,
the naturalistic fact and the metaphysical or supernatural.[18] This
teleological materialism, clearly derivative of Orthodox culture
and Russian naturalistic paganism, dominated and crucially informed both Russian radicalism and (making allowances for exceptional though influential idealistic Slavophils and for Tolstoi
and other relatively untypical, "Western" thinkers) Russian religious thought in the nineteenth century. Bolshevism, of course,
owes a huge debt to Marx. He gave it its formal linguistic and
conceptual apparatus. But its all important spiritual, cultural, and
emotional base is hardly more than the main Russian intellectual
tradition given a demonic turn. The nature and affiliations of
Danilevsky's thought, together with the fact of his intellectual
pilgrimage from Fourier to K. E. von Baer, open up a large vista
on the whole of modern Russian intellectual and cultural history.

But it is not only the morphology of this thought that is important. His story, though strictly personal in many ways, is
equally interesting. There are two major facets of interest. First,
he was a professional scientist, well employed, interested in his
work, finding plenty of scope in it. Yet all the time he felt discontented and expressed his discontent intellectually in the form
of a chiliastic utopian socialism. Danilevsky was a radical who
had little practical, let alone political reason for his subversiveness.
His reasons were spiritual, cultural, humanistic, closely related to
his own close experience with change, cultural and institutional,
from traditionalism to modernity. This aspect of his life history
highlights the true nature of the origins of Russian radicalism. It
was not fundamentally a response to oppressive political conditions but a response to the challenge of modernization, an adjust-

ment and a quest for adjustment to modernity and Western culture in a rapidly changing traditional society. His story illustrates the thesis that Russian radicals were not frustrated liberals. They were traditional humanists, societally oriented as much by reason of their Orthodox and gentry-peasant cultural backgrounds and pragmatic educational experiences as by reason of the difficult practical problems of the time. They were very sensitive to the feeling that the usual puritanical and functionalistic version of modernity frustrated and dehumanized. They sought a way of developing another kind of modernity, and the record of their efforts, however funny and amateurish, continues to make denizens of industrial society today wonder if there might not be some other way.

The second interesting aspect of Danilevsky's story concerns the fact that he who had been a humanistic radical turned himself into a totalitarian radical, without *decisive* change in his concepts of being, history, and ends. In this aspect of his story it is as though we see in microcosm the whole tragic intellectual history of Russia in the past century. Though the data are maddeningly sparse, we can see that he did not make his totalitarianism out of whole cloth. It is not that he was influenced by some thinker in a superficial academic way and that this casts light on the "dangers" of Hegelianism or Benthamism or Darwinism or science or religion. It is rather that his totalitarianism was made possible by the whole changing, mixed traditional-modern and romantic-realist cultural situation (which included all kinds of formal schools of thought) of his time and by his Orthodox cultural perspective on it. As the process of modernization accelerated in Russia in the 1850's and 1860's and as its cultural influence deepened, humanistic response became more difficult. The language and values of the spirit were muddled in the sour atmosphere of realism, positivism, secularism, pragmatism, nationalism, and sectarian liberalism. But the feelings that had once found expression in that language and importance under those values were still strong. There arose the possibility of expressing them in the new language, the very one that was antagonistic to them. *Homo religiosus* in loss of a specifically religious faith gave his worship, like Kafka's heroes, to mundane matters and became an idolater. In the sixties Danilevsky seized on this kind of possibility and created one of the earliest and, among the earliest, one of the most complete totalitarian philosophies known to history. The obviously close relationship between his situation and his fanaticism, together with the fact that a similar situation came to be experienced more and more by Russian intellectuals with the onset of the industrial revolution at the end of the nineteenth century, also opens up a large historical vista on modern Russian history.

Moreover it is also clear from this aspect of Danilevsky's story that his intellectual totalitarianism was not an inevitable development. The changing situation understood on an intellectual level and in, for the sixties, an advanced milieu made it possible. But there is no evidence that Danilevsky had to take this path. Other men similarly placed and of similar backgrounds did not make a totalitarian mixture of romanticism and realism. Later Danilevsky himself changed intellectually under much the same circumstances. There is too much suggestion in *Russia and Europe* of hypocrisy and *ressentiment* in the intellectual development that led to his main doctrine to warrant any deterministic conclusions. The evidence is only sufficient to suggest what may have happened to Danilevsky between 1849 and the 1860's, that gave rise to the fund of rancor and deceit without which it seems impossible to conceive the making of his theory. It would seem that again the changing cultural situation, experienced existentially rather than intellectually, contributed greatly. Danilevsky probably forced himself to conform in his modernistic milieu in order to achieve and maintain his success, to avoid more trouble with the police, and to harden his heart in advance to the unexpected blows of life. The articulation of his totalitarian philosophy, itself an autonomous act, was perhaps part of an effort to turn away from an unauthentic state of mind without undertaking the

necessary struggle and painful self-evaluation involved. This is
my theoretical construction. If it is worth considering, it implies
that circumstances, such as the oppressive political regime jittery
in face of change it had itself triggered, and the changing status
implications of traditionalism and modernism played an important role in the existential development that underlay the intellectual. Danilevsky, the totalitarian, would appear to have been, not
a frustrated liberal but a frustrated (partly self-frustrated) romantic radical. So sparse are the data that this part of his story, as I
have told it, may be little more than a fictional illustration of a
philosophical-psychological theory. Even so, it fits so well that I
wonder if it might not be useful to ask similar questions about
the development of other Russian totalitarian intellectuals on
whom there is more evidence.

    History is a spacious discipline. Its vast and complicated sub-
ject matter make it appropriate that it be so. We need all kinds
of history, of events, of institutions, of systems of ideas, of science, agriculture, industry, the arts, and history itself. We need
biographies to detail and show the human side of the stories of
impersonal forces. But there is another possible kind of history
which may be called biographical history. It is not biography if
that is understood as the study of a man's life within a framework
of rather well-set parameters. Biography helps us appreciate that
there *were* people in history but it fails to bring out the more
significant face that there is nothing but people in history. As a
genre, ordinary biography is one of the useful but in some ways
misleading methods of studying history in the large. It
posits a given background, a kind of container in which
its subject must operate and to which he makes some contribution.
Here institutions, ideas, and all the rest are supposed to have lives
of their own. But how they came to life or how they maintain
it is a mystery. Biographical history helps us better to appreciate
the methodological relativity of many of our presuppositions
about the relationship of men to forces and backgrounds, helps

us avoid philosophically an absurd, business-oriented, "bourgeois idealist," secularized providentialism. It has a different intention from ordinary biography and it is a separate genre. Its intention, which is much more radical and ambitious, is to indicate the human meaning of the historical parameters that are so often taken as matters apart from an individual's subjectivity. It is a way of focusing and synthesizing history humanistically. Biographical history is based on the presupposition that human beings and history are one. History does not simply have a human side; it is all human. A biographical history does not create human illustrations for an ahuman story. It creates natural symbols, life histories that are unique instances of the bigger things they also symbolize. This kind of history calls forth witnesses who show how human beings, free and purposeful, live in an era or an important aspect of one. It thus brings out that men and only men make history. Traditions, institutions, and the like have no lives of their own. They are figments (useful ones) of the practices of historical and social scientific disciplines. They would not exist at all if men did not — by purposive commission or omission — continuously create, make and remake them.

Not just anyone will make a good subject for biographical history. The subject has to be of such a kind that he personifies significant phenomena and their interactions over a long stretch of time even beyond his own life span. Because he was a Russian scientist in an age when Russia was still rather a traditional society, because he was a radical who worked for the government for a living and did it well, because he was close to being a good Orthodox Christian as well as a radical, because he turned totalitarian fanatic of a leftist kind in mid-career for reasons connected with the dichotomies of his life experience, because he passed through that fanatical phase — and because of the nature of an important aspect of modern Russian intellectual and cultural history from the forties to the revolution — Danilevsky, ordinary, muddled, determined and free, without any great causal influence, makes an extraordinarily good subject for a biographical history of the intellectual, cultural, social, and existential base of modern Russia's tragedy. He wanted it believed he was a historical witness. In a way he was. That was his real historical significance.

Danilevsky's Writings

Notes

Index

Danilevsky's Writings

Note: all items marked with an asterisk (*) have been inaccessible to me.

* "Literaturnyia zametki" (Literary notices), *Otechestvennyia Zapiski*, vol. 28 (1843); signed D -i. A letter to the editor pointing out that the story "Padenia shirvanskago tsarstva" (The fall of the Shirvan Empire) which appeared in the *Biblioteka Dlia Chteniia*, vol. 52 (1842), was not, except for the first hundred pages, the original work of O. I. Senkovsky but a translation of Morier, "History of Mobarek Shah and the Magician."

* *Kavkaz i ego gorskie zhiteli nyneshnem ikh polozhenii. S obiasneniem istorii, religii, iazyka, oblika, odezhdy, stroenii, vospitaniia, pravleniia, zakonov, korennykh obychaev, nravov, obraza zhizni, pishchi, obrazovaniia i torgovli khishchnykh Gortsev Kavkaza* (The Caucasus and its mountain inhabitants in their present state. With explanation of the history, religion, language, appearance, clothing, housing, child rearing, administration, laws, basic habits, morals, way of life, nutriment, education and trade of the predatory highlanders of the Caucasus; Moscow, Universitetskoi Tip, 1846, 136 pp.) A German translation appeared in Leipzig in 1847: *Der Kaukasus, Physisch — Geographisch, Statistisch, Etnographisch und Strategisch.*

"Dutrochet," *Otechestvennyia Zapiski*, vol. LVIII, sec. II (1848), pp. 1–47, 99–127.

"Kosmos Al. Gumboldta. Perevod N. Frolova. Ch. I," *Otechestvennyia Zapiski*, vol. LVIII, sec. V (1848), pp. 13f; vol. LIX, sec. V (1848), pp. 1–24, 25–62. The three articles are unsigned. I have not seen the first article.

"Uchenie Fourier" (The doctrine of Fourier) in P. E. Shchegolev, ed., *Petrashevtsy, sbornik materialov* (Moscow, 1928), pp. 118–149; or in V. A. Desnitsky, ed., *Delo Petrashevtsev*, II (Moscow, 1941), 290–319.

* "Statisticheskiia izsledovaniia o raspredelenii i dvizhenii narodonaseleniia v Rossii za 1846 god" (Statistical studies of the distribution and movement of population in Russia in 1846), *Zhurnal Ministerstva Vnutrennikh Del*, pts. 34 and 35 (1851). Six articles.

* "O vremeni i kolichestve teploty, nuzhnykh dlia sozrevaniia iachmenia v Ustsysolske (On the duration and degree of heat necessary for the ripening of barley in Ustsysolsk), *Vologodskiia Gubernskiia Vedomosti*, no. 14 (1851).

* "Otryvok iz statisticheskago opisaniia Vologodskoi gubernii" (Extract from a statistical description of Vologda province), *Vologodskiia Gubernskiia Vedomosti*, nos. 1, 2, 11, 12 (1851).

* "Vysota gorodov Vologdy i Totmy nad urovnem okeana" (The elevation of the cities of Vologda and Totma above sea level), *Vologodskiia Gubernskiia Vedomosti*, no. 19 (1851).

* "Prakticheskoe zamechanie o vesennei temperature v Vologde" (A practical observation on spring temperature in Vologda), *Vologodskiia Gubernskiia Vedomosti*, no. 45 (1851).

* "Gidrografiia Vologodskoi gubernii" (The hydrography of Vologda province), *Vologodskiia Gubernskiia Vedomosti*, nos. 45–49 (1852).

* "Klimat Vologodskoi gubernii" (The climate of Vologda province), *Zapiski Russkago Geograficheskago Oshchestva*, 9 (1853): 1–226.

* "O Kaspiiskom rybolovstve" (On the Caspian fishery), *Zhurnal Ministerstva Gosudarstvennykh Imushchestv*, pt. L (1854); pts. LV, LVII (1855); pt. LVII (1856). Translations of articles by Baer.

"Uchenyia zametki o Kaspiiskom more i ego okrestnostiakh" (Scientific notices on the Caspian Sea and vicinity), *Zapiski Russkago Geograficheskago Obshchestva*, bk. XI (1856), pp. 181–227.

* "O rybovodnom zavedenii Vrasskago" (On the piscicultural enterprise of Vrassky), *Zemledelcheskaia Gazeta*, no. 6 (1863). V. P. Vrassky founded one of the first centers of Russian pisciculture on his estate in Novgorod province in 1857.

* *Ueber das Vorkommen von Kropf und Cretinismus im Russischen Reiche* (St. Petersburg, 1858). Translation of an article by Baer. The Russian title is unknown. On goiter and cretinism in Russia.

* "Otvet ekonomicheskomu ukazateliu" (A reply to an economic index), *Vestnik Russkago Geograficheskago Obshchestva*, vol. XXII (1858). A reply to an article by I. V. Vernadsky.

"Kratkii ocherk uralskago rybnago khoziaistva" (A short sketch of the Ural fishing economy), *Vestnik Russkago Geograficheskago Obshchestva*, vol. XXII (1858). Printed in *Sbornik statei*, pp. 452–500.

* "O klimat Rossii. Sochinenie K. S. Veselovskago" (On the climate of Russia. The work of K. S. Veselovsky), *Vestnik Russkago Geograficheskago Obshchestva*, vol. XXV (1859).

"Izvestiia o sobranii cherepov raznykh narodov v Sanktpeterburg-skoi Akademii Nauk" (News about the collection of crania of various peoples in the St. Petersburg Academy of Sciences), *Russkii Vestnik*, May 1859, pp. 3–28. Translation of an article by Baer.

* "Otchet ekspeditsii dlia izsledovaniia Kaspiiskago rybolovstva za 1855 god" (Report on the expedition for the study of the Caspian fishery in 1855), *Zhurnal Ministerstva Gosudarstvennykh Imushchestv*, vols. LXX, LXXI (1859). Translation of an article by Baer.

K. E. von Baer, ed., *Rybolovstvo v Kaspiiskom more i v ego pritokakh* (Fishing in the Caspian Sea and in the rivers flowing into it), St. Petersburg, 1860. Danilevsky probably assisted in the preparation and translation of parts of this volume. It is vol. II of *Izsledovaniia o sostoianii rybolovstva v Rossii* (Studies of the state of the fishery in Russia), published by the Ministry of State Domains.

Opisanie uralskago rybolovstva (Description of the Ural fishery), St. Petersburg, 1860. This is vol. III of the Ministry of State Domains fisheries series. Danilevsky *edited* this.

* "Otchet Vysochaishe utverzhdennoi ekspeditsii dlia izsledovaniia rybnago i zverinago promyslov v Belom i Ledovitom moriakh za 1859 god" (Report on the expedition appointed by his Highness for the study of the fish and trapping enteprises on the White and Arctic Seas in 1859), *Zhurnal Ministerstva Gosudarstvennykh Imushchestv*, vol. LXXIV (1860).

* "Otchet Vysochaishe utverzhdennoi ekspeditsii dlia izsledovaniia rybnago i zverinago pomyslov v Belom i Ledovitom moriakh za 1860 god" (*Zhurnal Ministerstva Gosudarstvennykh Imushchestv*, vol. LXXVII (1860). See previous item for translation of title.

* "Izsledovaniia . . . ekspeditsii v Norvegii v techenie zimy i vesny 1861 goda" ("Studies from [the same] expedition in Norway in the winter and spring of 1861), *ibid.*, vol. LXXVIII (1861).

* "Dopolnitelnyi otchet . . . ekspeditsii" (Supplementary report on [the same] expedition), *ibid.*, vol. LXXX (1862).

* *Razbor proekta Karazina ob ustroistve rybolovstva v Kaspiiskom more i izlozhenie nachal, kotoryia dolzhny byt polozheny v osnovanie* (An analysis of Karazin's project for the organization of the Caspian fishery and a consideration of the factors which should be taken into account in implementing it), Astrakhan, 1862.

Rybnye i zverinye promysly na Belom i Ledovitom moriakh (Fishing and trapping enterprises on the White and Arctic seas), St. Petersburg, 1862. Vol. VI of the Ministry of State Domains fisheries series. Danilevsky *edited* this.

* "*Teoriia lednikovago perioda*" (A theory of the ice age). This was never published. It was read before a general meeting of the Geographical Society on Jan. 9, 1863. There is a summary of the events at the meeting in *Zapiski Russkago Geograficheskago Obshchestva*, bk. 1, 1863.

Statistika Kaspiiskago rybolovstva (Statistics of the Caspian fishery), St. Petersburg, 1863. This is vol. V of the Ministry of State Domains fisheries series. Danilevsky *edited* this.

* "Vzgliad na rybovolstvo v Rossii" (A survey of fishing in Russia), *Selskoe Khoziaistvo i Lesovodstvo*, vol. I (1865). An extract from a report made to the Department of Agriculture on the fishing regulations on Lakes Pskov and Chud.

Coup d'œil sur les pêcheries en Russie, Paris, 1867. Prepared for the Paris World Exposition of 1867. The author's name is erroneously printed "C. Danilewsky." For the original Russian version see *Sbornik statei*, pp. 406–451 ("Vzgliad na rybolovstvo v Rossii").

"Neskolko myslei po povodu upadka tsennosti kreditnago rublia, torgovago balansa i pokrovitelstva promyshlennosti" (Some thoughts in regard to the decline of the paper ruble, the trade balance, and the protection of industry), *Torgovyi Sbornik*, no. 4, 5, 11, 13, 18, 20, 22 (1867). The articles were unsigned. See *Sbornik statei*, pp. 313–405.

"O merakh k obezpecheniiu narodnago podovolstviia na krainem severe Rossii" (On measures for securing the popular welfare in the far north of Russia, *Pravitelstvennyi Vestnik*, no. 90–93 (1868). Printed in *Sbornik statei*, pp. 501–623, dated 1869 (*sic*).

"Rossiia i Evropa," *Zariia*, nos. 1–6, 8–10 (1869). This is called the "first edition."

* "Izsledovaniia o Kubanskoi delte" (Studies of the Kuban delta), *Zapiski Russkago Geograficheskago Obshchestva*, vol. II (1869).

* "Izvlechenie iz pisma N. Ia. Danilevskago o resultatakh poezdki ego na Manych" (Extract from a letter of N. Ia. Danilevsky about the results of his trip to the Manych), *Zapiski Russkago Geograficheskago Obshchestva*, vol. II (1869).

* Neskolko myslei o russkoi geograficheskoi terminologii po povodu slov: liman i ilmen" (Some thoughts on Russian geographical terminology with reference to the words: *liman* and *ilmen*), *Zapiski Russkago Geograficheskago Obshchestva*, vol. II (1869).

* "Dopolnenie k Opytu oblastnago veliko — russkago slovaria," *Sbornik otdeleniia russkago iazyka i slovennesti Imperatorskoi Academii Nauk*, vol. VII (1869). This title means that the article is

a supplement to an "attempt at" a regional Great Russian dictionary. "Rossiia i franko — germanskaia voina (dopolnenie k predshest-vuiushchemu sochineniiu)" (Russia and the Franco-German War; supplement to the previous work), *Zariia*, no. 1 (1871). A supplement to *Russia and Europe*. Printed in *Sbornik statei*, pp. 1–30.

* *Rossiia i Evropa. Vzgliad na kulturnyia i politicheskiia otnosheniia Slavianskago mira k Germano-Romanskomu* (Russia and Europe. Survey of the Cultural and Political Relationships of the Slavic to the Germano-Roman World), St. Petersburg, 1871. This is the "second" edition. The publisher was the Brotherhood of Social Welfare (Tovarishchestvo Obshchestvennoi Polzy), which subsidized the enterprise, evidently planning on "no sale."

Opisanie rybolovstva v Chernom i Azovskom moriakh (Description of fishing on the Black and Azov seas), St. Petersburg, 1871. Vol. VIII of the Ministry of State Domains fisheries series. He *edited* this.

* "Bozmozhnoe vliianie parakhodstva na rybolovstvo v reke Kure" (Possible influence of steamshipping on fishing on the Kura River), *Sbornik Svedenii o Kavkaze*, vol. II, Tiflis, 1872.

Opisanie rybolovstva v severo-zapadnykh ozerakh (Description of fishing on the northwest lakes), St. Petersburg, 1875. Vol. IX of the Ministry of State Domains fisheries series. He *edited* this.

"O nastoiashchei voine, ocherk" (On the present war, a sketch), *Russkii Mir*, no. 207 (1877). See *Sbornik statei*, pp. 31–41 (entitled "Chego my v prave blagorasumno zhelat ot izkhoda nastoiashchei voiny?" — What can we reasonably expect from the outcome of the present war?). One of a series of articles entitled "Voina za Bolgariiu" (The war for Bulgaria).

"Kak otneslas Evropa k Russko — Turetskoi raspre" (How Europe is related to the Russo-Turkish quarrel), *Russkii Mir*, no. 279 (1877). See *Sbornik statei*, pp. 42–52. One of a series of articles called "Voina za Bolgariiu."

"Prolivy" (The Straits), *Russkii Mir*, no. 289–290 (1877). See *Sbornik statei*, pp. 53–70. In the "Voina za Bolgariiu" series.

"Konstantinopol," *Russkii Mir*, no. 308–309 (1877). See *Sbornik statei*, pp. 71–84 ("Voina za Bolgariiu").

"Konferentsiia ili dazhe kongress" (Conference or even congress), *Russkii Mir*, nos. 74–75, 92, 99, 101 (1878). See *Sbornik statei*, pp. 85–138 ("Voina za Bolgariiu").

"Rossiia i vostochnyi vopros" (Russia and the Eastern question), *Russkaia Rech*, no. 1–2 (1879). See *Sbornik statei*, pp. 139–219, where the article is entitled "Gore Pobediteliam!" (Woe to the victors!).

*Filloksera na iuzhnom beregu Kryma i sredstvo borby s neiu (Phylloxera on the south shore of the Crimea and the method of combatting them), Theodocia, 1880.

* "Otchet o resultatakh poezdki za granitsu predsedatelia filloksernoi kommissii" (Report on the results of the trip abroad by the president of the Phylloxera Commission), *Selskoe Khoziaistvo i Lesovodstvo*, Feb. 1881.

* *Sravnenie metodov borby s fillokseroi* (A comparison of methods of fighting phylloxera), Simpheropol, 1881.

* "Otvet na korrespondentsiiu iz Kryma v No. 50 *Moskovskikh Vedomostei*" (An answer to correspondence from the Crimea in no. 50 of the *Moskovskie Vedomosti*), *Moskovskie Vedomosti*, no. 102 (1881). On phylloxera.

"O sposobakh borby s fillokseroi" (On methods of fighting phylloxera), *Selskoe Khoziaistvo i Lesovodstvo*, May 1882. See *Sbornik statei*, pp. 624–671.

"Neskolko slov po povodu konstitutsionnykh vozhdelenii nashei 'liberalnoi pressy' " (Some words on the constitutionalist agitation in our "liberal press"), *Moskovskie Vedomosti*, no. 138 (1882). See *Sbornik statei*, pp. 220–230.

* "Otchet predsedatelia filloksernoi kommissii" (Report of the president of the Phylloxera Commission), no place of publication available (Strakhov lists the title), 1882.

"Neskolko myslei po povodu nizkago kursa nashikh bumazhnykh deneg i nekotorykh drugikh ekonomicheskikh iavlenii i voprosov" (Some thoughts in regard to the low value of our paper money and several other economic phenomena and questions), *Russkii Vestnik*, 8–9, pp. 473–533, 137–198, respectively (1882).

"O puti Madiar s Urala v Lebediiu" (On the route of the Magyars from the Urals to Lebedia), *Izvestiia Russkago Geograficheskago Obshchestva*, 14 (1883): 220–246. This consists of the following: (1) a short section by "L. M." explaining that Danilevsky and K. Ia. Grot, whose book *Moraviia i Madiary s poloviny IX do nachala x veka* (Moravia and the Magyars from the middle of the ninth to the beginning of the tenth centuries), St. Petersburg, 1881, had dealt with this subject, were in disagreement about the route of the Magyars. Danilevsky had written a letter to Grot setting forth his objections. Grot had sent an extract from this letter to the editor of the *Izvestiia* together with his own reply; (2) an extract from Grot's book dealing with the route of Magyars; (3) the extract from Danilevsky's letter; (4) Grot's reply. The section by Danilevsky consists of twelve pages.

P. A. Sorokin in *Social Philosophies of an Age of Crisis* (Boston, 1950), refers erroneously to this as a "historical monograph."

"Proizkhozhdenie nashego nigilizma" (The origin of our nihilism), *Rus*, nos. 22–23 (1884). See *Sbornik statei*, pp. 231–271.

Darvinism. Kriticheskoe izsledovanie, vol. I, 2 pts., St. Petersburg, 1885; Vol. II (one posthumous chapter and indexes), St. Petersburg, 1889.

"G. Vladimir Soloviev o pravoslavii i katolitsizme" (Mr. Vladimir Soloviev on Orthodoxy and Catholicism), *Izvestiia Spb. Slavianskago Blagotvoritelnago Obshchestva*, nos. 2–3 (1885). See *Sbornik statei*, pp. 272–312.

* O nizkom kurse nashikh deneg i novykh istochnikakh gosydarstvennykh dokhodov (On the low value of our currency and of the new sources of state income), St. Petersburg, 1886.

"Ekspressiia ili vyrazhenie chuvstva u cheloveka i zhivotnykh" (Expression of feeling by man and by animals), *Russkii Vestnik*, 5–6, pp. 5–54, 493–534, respectively (1887). This is the same as the chapter in vol. II of *Darwinism*.

Rossiia i Evropa, St. Petersburg, 1888. N. N. Strakhov, editor. This and the two subsequent editions also contain posthumous footnotes inserted by Strakhov. The "third" edition.

* *Rossiia i Evropa*, St. Petersburg, 1889. The "fourth" edition.

Sbornik politicheskikh i ekonomicheskikh statei, N. N. Strakhov, ed., St. Petersburg, 1890. Contains a very useful bibliography based on Danilevsky's private papers. I have used it as a basis for the present list, adding only a few new items.

Rossiia i Evropa, St. Petersburg, 1895. The "fifth" edition.

Russland und Europa; eine Untersuchung über die kulturellen und politischen Beziehungen der Slawischen zur germanisch-romanischen Welt, Karl Nötzel, ed. and trans., Berlin and Stuttgart, 1920. Contains about half the work. Nötzel omitted the crucial chapter on the history of science.

"The Slav Role in World Civilization," an abridged translation by Mark Field of the last chapter of *Russia and Europe* in Hans Kohn, ed., *The Mind of Modern Russia, History and Political Thought of Russia's Great Age*, New Brunswick, 1955, pp. 195–214.

Rossiia i Evropa (New York, 1966). A reprint of the fifth (1895) edition. Edited with a new introduction ("Filosofiia istorii Danilevskago v knige Rossiia i Evropa") by Iury Ivask. This is a splendid edition.

Notes

Chapter 1. Introduction

1. As indicated both in and by the chapter on ideology in the ambitious typological study of Carl J. Friedrich and Zbigniew K. Brzezinski, *Totalitarian Dictatorship and Autocracy* (New York, 1956), intellectual totalitarianism is difficult to characterize. Moreover, there is considerable disagreement among students of the subject because of their varying philosophical orientations. The scheme in this chapter is my own but it owes something to the following works: Hannah Arendt, "Ideology and Terror: a Novel Form of Government," *The Review of Politics*, July 1953, pp. 303–327; Ernst Cassirer, *The Myth of the State* (New Haven, 1946), pp. 189–298 — a neo-Kantian view; Henri de Lubac, *The Drama of Atheist Humanism*, Edith M. Riley, trans. (New York, 1949) — good emphasis by a Jesuit on the confusion of sacred and profane; K. R. Popper, *The Open Society and Its Enemies*, vol. II (London, 1949) — modern positivist stress on fact versus value. Studies of the totalitarian mind helpful to the student of ideology are: Arendt, *The Origins of Totalitarianism* (New York, 1951), pp. 301–439 — on "realism" as fantasy; Zevedei Barbu, *Democracy and Dictatorship, Their Psychology and Patterns of Life* (London, 1956) — especially useful on the two types of totalitarian mind, "Western" and "Russian," as I call them; Erik H. Erikson, "Wholeness and Totality — a Psychiatric Contribution," and Alex Inkeles, "The Totalitarian Mystique: Some Impressions of the Dynamics of a Totalitarian Society" — both in C. J. Friedrich, ed., *Totalitarianism* (Cambridge, Mass., 1954); E. Fromm, *Escape from Freedom* (New York, 1941), points up the regressive aspect; Jules Monnerot, *The Sociology and Psychology of Communism*, Jane Degras and Richard Rees, trans. (Boston, 1953), works out some of the religious background.

2. Good studies of intellectual forerunners are Cassirer, *The Myth of the State*; Carlton J. H. Hayes, *The Historical Evolution of Modern Nationalism* (New York, 1948), chap. 6; Michael Karpovich, "A Forerunner of Lenin: P. N. Tkachev," *The Review of Politics*, July 1944, pp. 336–350; Rufus W. Matthewson, *The Positive Hero in Russian Literature* (New York, 1958); Michael Prawdin, *The Unmentionable Nechaiev; a Key to Bolshevism* (London, 1961); Fritz Stern, *The Politics of Cultural Despair, A Study in the Rise of the Germanic*

Ideology (Los Angeles, 1961); Robert C. Tucker, *Philosophy and Myth in Karl Marx* (Cambridge, 1961); J. L. Talmon, *The Origins of Totalitarian Democracy* (New York, 1960) and *Political Messianism: the Romantic Phase* (New York, 1961); N. Valentinov, *Vstrechi s Leninym* (New York, 1953); Franco Venturi, *Roots of Revolution, a History of the Populist and Socialist Movements in Nineteenth Century Russia*, Francis Haskell, trans. (New York, 1960), chaps. 15–16; Peter Viereck, *Metapolitics from the Romantics to Hitler* (New York, 1941); Gustav Wetter, *Dialectical Materialism, a Historical and Systematic Survey of Philosophy in the Soviet Union*, Peter Heath, trans. (New York, 1958), chap. 13.

3. Any examination of Russian intellectual totalitarianism gets one involved in the difficult problems of interpreting Marxism and Bolshevism and of finding his way in the vast literature about them. Here I can do little more than cite those works which seem to me best and indicate briefly why I find others less useful. The best studies I have read are Joseph M. Bochenski, Emil G. Walter, and Gerhart Niemeyer, "The Philosophical, Sociological, and Economic Doctrines of Communism," in Bochenski and Niemeyer, eds., *Handbook on Communism* (New York, 1962), pp. 15–63; Henri Chambre, *From Karl Marx to Mao Tse-Tung*, Robert J. Olsen, trans. (New York, 1963); George Lichtheim, *Marxism, an Historical and Critical Study* (New York, 1961)—exaggerates the gap between Marx and Lenin, however; the chapter on Marx in De Lubac, *The Drama of Atheist Humanism;* Maurice Merleau-Ponty, *Les Aventures de la dialectique* (Paris, 1955) — very keen; Tucker, *Philosophy and Myth; Wetter, Dialectical Materialism.* Other well-known studies appear to me to overemphasize the rational and ethical (as against the mythical, the "humanist," and the neo-Hegelian) dimension of *mature* Marxism and, because of this, to misunderstand the historical line from Marx to Lenin to Stalin: R. M. Carew Hunt, *The Theory and Practice of Communism* (New York, 1951); Alfred G. Meyer, *Marxism: The Unity of Theory and Practice* (Cambridge, Mass., 1954) and *Leninism* (Cambridge, Mass., 1957); John Plamenatz, *German Marxism and Russian Communism* (New York, 1954); M. Rubel, *Karl Marx: essai de biographie intellectuel* (Paris, 1957). In a different category is Nathan C. Leites, *A Study of Bolshevism* (Glencoe, 1953). This is phenomenologically weak. Leites imposes an objective scheme on Bolshevism which tends to obscure its human meaning.

4. For striking examples of the operation of this pattern, see Alan Bullock, *Hitler, A Study in Tyranny* (New York, 1960), chaps. 13 and 14 — Hitler himself grew more totalitarian at the end; Leonard Shapiro, *The Communist Party of the Soviet Union* (New York, 1960), chaps. 12–16 — on Stalin and Trotsky.

5. See Robert V. Daniels, *The Nature of Communism* (New York, 1962); Leopold Haimson, *The Russian Marxists and the Origins of*

Bolshevism (Cambridge, Mass., 1955); Herbert Marcuse, *Soviet Marxism, a Critical Analysis* (New York, 1958); Valentinov, *Vstrechi s Leninym.*

6. Mircea Eliade, *Myths, Dreams, and Mysteries*, Philip Maigret, trans. (New York, 1960), pp. 25–26; Barbu, *Democracy and Dictatorship*, contains analogous comparison from a psychological point of view.

7. On Orthodox belief, culture, and mentality, see Ernst Benz, *The Eastern Orthodox Church, Its Thought and Life*, Richard and Clara Winston, trans. (New York, 1963); G. P. Fedotov, *The Russian Religious Mind, Kievan Christianity* (Cambridge, Mass., 1946); George Florovsky, *Puti russkago bogosloviia* (Paris, 1937); R. M. French, *The Eastern Orthodox Church* (London, 1961); Jon Gregerson, *The Transfigured Cosmos* (New York, 1960); V. Lossky, *The Mystical Theology of the Eastern Church* (London, 1957); John Meyendorff, *The Orthodox Church, Its Past and Its Role in the World Today*, John Chapin, trans. (New York, 1962); Alexander Schmemann, *The Historical Road of Eastern Orthodoxy*, Lydia W. Kesich, trans. (New York, 1963); Timothy Ware, *The Orthodox Church* (Baltimore, 1963).

8. George L. Kline, "Darwinism and the Russian Orthodox Church" in Ernest J. Simmons, ed., *Continuity and Change in Russian and Soviet Thought* (Cambridge, Mass., 1955), pp. 307–328.

This idea that there was a less severe conflict between science and religion in Russia would seem to be contradicted by Alexander Vucinich, *Science in Russian Culture, A History to 1860* (Stanford, 1963). In this generally excellent and thorough study Vucinich emphasizes over and over that the Orthodox religion was bigoted and reactionary in its view of science and frequently impeded its progress. But his analysis of the situation is crude. He is appallingly ignorant of Orthodox beliefs. Even assuming that Orthodox clergymen were on the whole as hostile to science as he says they were, one wonders why. Was it because of fear for their institutional power or of fear for what they regarded as the truth? If partly the latter, what was that fear like? And what happened to the priests' attitudes after science was established? Then too, Orthodoxy was not the concern only of priests and monks. What is shown about the relation of science and religion by the attitudes of lay Orthodox (even Peter the Great was one of these) or of nonreligious, even antireligious humanistic intellectuals whose philosophic convictions and intellectual psychology owed great cultural debts to Orthodoxy? Vucinich does in fact have much to say that is related to this last question, though he seems not to appreciate the significance of his own findings. He points up nicely a peculiarly Russian strand of holistic, pro-science, humanistic intellectuality, now authentically Christian, now not, running from the eighteenth century (Prokopovich, Lomonosov,

Tatishchev, Boltin, Kozelsky, Novikov) into the nineteenth (Herzen, Dostoevsky). He rightly views this strand as being of great intellectual-historical and cultural significance. He rightly assigns science and scientific culture a great role in its development. But he never notes its obviously enormous debt to Orthodoxy and Orthodox culture. On balance Vucinich's study, despite its explicit thesis regarding science and religion, strengthens my own convictions about the peculiarity of the history of science and religion, of scientific and Orthodox culture in Russia.

9. See N. F. Fedorov, *Filosofiia obshchego dela*, vol. I (Kharbin, 1928), introductory articles by A. Ostromirov, V. A. Kozhevnikov, N. P. Peterson; II (Moscow, 1913), 247–279 (characteristic attitudes toward science). Soloviev's attitude toward the modern age can be studied in K. V. Mochulsky, *Vladimir Soloviev, Zhizn i uchenie* (Paris, 1951) and E. Munzer, *Solovyev, Prophet of Russian-Western Unity* (London, 1956). Dostoevsky's case is less clear. His strictures against "Euclidean" minds and his association with Pobedonostsev can be overinterpreted, however. On the progressive nature of his outlook, see J. van der Eng, *Dostoevskij romancier, rapports entre sa vision du monde et ses procédés littéraires* (The Hague, 1957), chaps. 1–3; Nicholas Berdaiev, *Dostoevsky*, Donald Attwater, trans. (New York, 1957). Proper interpretation of *The Possessed* and *The Brothers Karamazov* also indicates that he was trying to *redefine* modernity: see the discussion of these novels in Mochculsky, *Dostoevsky, zhizn i tvorchestvo* (Paris, 1947).

10. See Henry V. Dicks, "Observations on Contemporary Russian Behaviour," *Human Relations*, vol. V, no. 2 (1952), pp. 111–175; Alex Inkeles, Eugenia Hanfmann, and Helen Beier, "Modal Personality and Adjustment to the Soviet Socio-Political System," *ibid.*, vol. XI, no. 1 (1958) pp. 3–22; Geoffrey Gorer and John Rickman, *The People of Great Russia, a Psychological Study*, 2nd ed. (New York, 1962); Erik H. Erikson, *Childhood and Society*, 2nd ed. (New York, 1963), chap. 10; good general discussion of character and peasant society is E. E. Hagen, *On the Theory of Social Change, How Economic Growth Begins* (Homewood, Ill., 1962), pp. 55–182.

11. For instance, Konrad Pfalzgraf, "Die Politisierung und Radikalisierung des Problems Russland und Europa bei Danilevskij," *Forschungen zur Osteuropäischen Geschichte*, I (Berlin, 1954), 55–204.

12. The best modern scholars of Slavophilism consistently regard Danilevsky as deviating from the original doctrine: Nikolai Berdaiev, *Aleksei Stepanovich Khomiakov* (Moscow, 1912), A Gratieux, *A. S. Khomiakov et le mouvement Slavophile*, vol. II (Paris, 1939); Nicholas V. Riasanovsky, *Russia and the West in the Teaching of the Slavophils, A Study of a Romantic Ideology* (Cambridge, Mass., 1952).

13. An excellent discussion of the idea of the rotting West and its Western sources is P. B. Struve, "S. P. Shevyrev i zapadnyia vnusheniia i istochniki teorii-aforisma o 'gnilom ili gniiushchem Zapade,'" Belgrade, 1940, a reprint from *Zapisok Russkago Nauchnago Instituta v Belgrade*.

14. Alexander von Schelting, *Russland und Europa im Russischen Geschichtsdenken* (Bern, 1948), pp. 238–247, is a perceptive comparison of Herzen and Danilevsky.

15. See Benoit P. Hepner, *Bakounine et le panslavisme revolutionnaire* (Paris, 1950); Scheltung; Venturi, *Roots of Revolution*, pp. 559f.

16. For discussion and references regarding Danilevsky's reputation, see chap. 9 below.

17. Quoted in Sidney Monas, *The Third Section, Police and Society in Russia under Nicholas I* (Cambridge, Mass., 1961), p. 126.

18. *Rossiia i Evropa*, chap. XVII, pp. 122–123 (*Zariia*, no. 10, 1869).

19. See, for example, Raymond Williams, *Culture and Society, 1780–1950* (New York, 1960) — a discussion of Great Britain.

20. Schelting, *Russland und Europa*, contains most useful discussion of the relationship between thought and situation. E. Lampert, *Studies in Rebellion* (New York, 1957), makes a bit too much of the political aspects of the situation but is excellent on the deeply philosophical and "existentialist" nature of Russian radicalism. Edward Shils, *The Intellectual between Tradition and Modernity: the Indian Situation* (The Hague, 1961) is conceptually most sophisticated and the study itself is helpful for comparative study with Russia.

21. The introductory pages of Berdaiev, *Khomiakov*, are interesting on how "Western" Slavophilism was.

22. Nicholas V. Riasanovsky, *Nicholas I and Official Nationality in Russia, 1825–1855* (Berkeley, 1959), is the best study.

Chapter 2. Youth

1. Prerevolutionary dates in this study are Old Style, on the Julian calendar. To obtain equivalent Gregorian dates for the nineteenth century, add twelve days.

2. This chapter is largely based on N. N. Strakhov, "Zhizn i trudy N. Ia. Danilevskago," pp. ix–xxxi of Danilevsky, *Rossiia i Evropa*, 5th ed. (St. Petersburg, 1895) — this same sketch also makes up the introduction of the 3rd and 4th eds.; P. P. Semenov-Tian-Shansky, *Memuary*, I (Petrograd, 1917), 173–219; V. A. Desnitsky, ed., *Delo Petrashevtsev*, II (Moscow, 1941), 285–334 — Danilevsky's testimony at his trial.

3. With regard to Orthodoxy and other Russian phenomena, I shall be assuming the importance of this period throughout this study. On

its importance in general, see Erik H. Erikson, *Childhood and Society*, 2nd ed. (New York, 1963). Occasionally in this study I shall also try to reconstruct aspects of Danilevsky's personality and even of his life history from evidence in his formal thought. For an example and discussion of this procedure (from a more Freudian and less phenomenalist point of view than mine, however), see Walter A. Weisskopf, *The Psychology of Economics* (Chicago, 1955), esp. pp. 107–157, which deal in part with Engels.

4. A storehouse of information about the Lyceum in Danilevsky's time is I. Seleznev, ed., *Istoricheskii ocherk Imperatorskago byvshago tsarskoselskago nyne Aleksandrovskago Litseia za pervoe ego piatidesiatiletie s 1811 po 1861 god* (St. Petersburg, 1861), pp. 182–414.

5. Danilevsky left the Lyceum in December 1842. Though he was given credit for the full curriculum, this indicates some irregularity in his attendance, for the regular curriculum ran six years and began in the summer.

6. On student reactions to Goltgoer, to his successor (after 1841), Major General D. B. Bronevsky, who also used corporal punishment, and to the Lyceum in general, see A. H. Iakhontev, "Vospominaniia tsarskoselskago litseista," *Russkaia Starina*, 60 (1888): 101–124; D. F. Kobeko, *Imperatorskii tsarskoselskii litsei, nastavniki i pitomtsy, 1811-1843* (St. Petersburg, 1911); K. S. Veselovsky, "Vospominaniia o tsarskoselskom litsee, 1837–1839," *Russkaia Starina*, 104 (1900): 3–29; V. R. Zotov, "Peterburg v sorokovykh godakh," *Istoricheskii Vestnik*, 40 (June 1890): 536–539; A. M. Skabichevsky, *Istoriia noveishei russkoi literatury, 1848–1892 gg.* (St. Petersburg, 1897), pp. 272–273; N. Strelsky, *Saltykov and the Russian Squire* (New York, 1940), pp. 21–22; M. Gershenzon and M. Kogan, *M. E. Saltykov-Shchedrin* (Moscow, 1939), pp. 14–17.

7. Danilevsky had a job in the chancery of the Ministry of War from April 1843 to January 1847 when he "retired." He seems not to have actually worked at this much, for he had continuous time off to attend the university. It was probably merely a prerequisite to free auditing.

8. Lyceum graduates, according to their performances, were assigned ranks in the civil service. The ninth rank was the highest possible, the fourteenth, the lowest. Danilevsky was assigned the tenth upon graduation; and he was first in the group receiving this.

9. On Petrashevsky and his friends at the Lyceum, see V. I. Semevsky, *M. V. Butashevich-Petrashevsky*, pt. I (Moscow, 1922; no more published), pp. 25f. Danilevsky seems to have been a reader of romantic literature and of the liberal journal *Otechestvennye Zapiski* (Annals of the Fatherland) while at the Lyceum. At least right after he left, in 1843, he sent a letter to the editor of the Annals complaining that a story that had appeared in another magazine (also a Lyceum favorite), *Biblioteka dlia Chteniia* (Library for reading),

was largely plagiarized by its alleged author, one Senkovsky, from J. J. Morier, "History of Mobarek Shah and the Magician"; see Danilevsky, *Sbornik statei* (St. Petersburg, 1890), p. 673.

10. On courses and professors in the Physico-Mathematical Faculty at this time, see V. V. Grigoriev, ed., *Imperatorskii S. Peterburgskii Universitet v techenie pervykh piatidesiati let ego sushchestvovaniia* (St. Petersburg, 1870), pp. 177–213. Semenov, *Memuary*, I, 173–177, is also useful here because he and Danilevsky took similar curricula. For good general discussion of Russian education in this period, particularly at the university level, see P. Miliukov, *Ocherki po istorii russkoi kultury*, vol. II, pt. II (Paris, 1931), pp. 768–798, and the pertinent section of William H. E. Johnson, *Russia's Educational Heritage* (Pittsburgh, 1950). See also Alexander Vucinich, *Science in Russian Culture, A History to 1860* (Stanford, 1963), pt. III.

11. On Buniakovsky, see B. G. Kuznetsov, *Ocherki istorii russkoi nauki* (Moscow, 1940), pp. 57f; V. A. Riasanovsky, *Razvitie russkoi nauchnoi mysli v XVIII–XX st. st.* (New York, 1949), pp. 41–42.

12. On his long and distinguished career in the society, see L. S. Berg, *Vsesoiuznoe geograficheskoe obshchestvo za sto let* (Moscow, 1946), pp. 57–76.

13. Founded by Catherine II in 1765, the Free Economic Society was Russia's oldest learned society. Its activities included the study of agricultural problems, the dissemination of technical information, sponsoring expeditions for gathering statistics, and sometimes recommendations to the government on economic matters.

14. Basic modern studies are Lewis B. Namier, *1848: The Revolution of the Intellectuals* (London, 1950); Priscilla Robertson, *The Revolutions of 1848, a Social History* (Princeton, 1952); Eric J. Hobsbawm, *The Age of Revolution: Europe 1789–1848* (London, 1962). The review article on the last by J. L. Talmon in *Encounter*, September 1963, raises the issue of the nature and motives behind radicalism in an especially perceptive fashion.

15. The point is hard to document. The best study I know of is Adam B. Ulam, *The Unfinished Revolution, an Essay on the Sources and Influence of Marxism and Communism* (New York, 1960), esp. chap. 3. In the long introductory section of the book he edited, *Marx's Concept of Man* (New York, 1961), E. Fromm raises some interesting points about motivation; but his interest in this essay is more philosophical than historical. Frank E. Manuel, *The Prophets of Paris* (Cambridge, Mass., 1962), chaps. 3–5, is very good on the nature of radicalism and contains some commentary on motivation, although with too exclusive reference to unconscious or quite personal motives. Alexander Gray's sprightly book *The Socialist Tradition* (London, 1947) is also a good guide to the nature of romantic radicalism. The question of motivation comes down in part, of course, to one's presuppositions about the nature of man and his

relation to society. But good historical and social scientific reasons have been developed for presuppositions similar to mine. Relevant conceptual and general historical background on radicalism, intellectual and popular, is to be found in Norman R. C. Cohn, *The Pursuit of the Millennium* (Fairlawn, 1957); Karl Mannheim, *Ideology and Utopia, an Introduction to the Sociology of Knowledge,* Louis Wirth and Edward Shils, trans. (New York, 1936), pp. 192–263; Robert A. Nisbet, *The Quest for Community* (Oxford, 1953), chaps. 4–8; Charles Tilly, "The Analysis of a Counter-Revolution," *History and Theory,* vol. III, no. 1 (1963), pp. 30–58; Michael Walzer, "Puritanism as a Revolutionary Ideology," *ibid.,* pp. 59–90. The evidence presented in Eric J. Hobsbawm, *Social Bandits and Primitive Rebels, Studies in Archaic Forms of Social Movement in the Nineteenth and Twentieth Centuries* (Glencoe, 1960), is most useful, though it seems not to substantiate the author's economic-sociological thesis.

16. There is a large bibliography on the subject. Particularly good recent studies are E. Lampert, *Studies in Rebellion* (New York, 1957); Martin E. Malia, *Alexander Herzen and the Birth of Russian Socialism* (Cambridge, Mass., 1961); James H. Billington, *Mikhailovsky and Russian Populism* (London, 1958); F. Venturi, *Roots of Revolution,* F. Haskell, trans. (New York, 1960). None of these works supports my thesis directly. Only Malia works hard at the motivation problem. His thesis is that radicalism was the result of political frustration under tsarist oppression. Hugh Seton-Watson, "The Russian Intellectuals" in George B. de Huszar, ed., *The Intellectuals* (Glencoe, 1960), pp. 41–50, contains some better suggestions.

17. On the classical temper of Russian romanticism, see Victor Erlich, *Russian Formalism, History-Doctrine* (The Hague, 1955), pp. 229f; D. S. Mirsky, *A History of Russian Literature,* Francis J. Whitfield, ed. (New York, 1949), pp. 71f. On the romantic or traditionalist temper of realism, see Erich Auerbach, *Mimesis, The Representation of Reality in Western Literature,* Willard Trask, trans. (Princeton, 1953), pp. 521f; George Steiner, *Dostoevsky or Tolstoi, an Essay in the Old Criticism* (New York, 1959), pp. 30f.

18. Still the best work on the circle is Semevsky, *Butashevich-Petrashevsky.* Leonid Raisky, *Sotzialnye vozzreniia Petrashevtsev* (Leningrad, 1927) is an interesting Marxist (Pokrovsky vintage) account. Desnitsky, ed., *Delo Petrashevtsev,* 3 vols. and P. E. Shchegolev, ed., *Petrashevtsy, sbornik materialov* (Moscow, 1928) contain rich collections of memoirs and documents.

19. On the content of the discussions, see Semevsky, pp. 101–131; Raisky, pp. 19–90; D. Akhsharumov, *Zapiski Petrashevtsa* (Moscow, 1930); Boris Jakovenko, *Untersuchungen zur Geschichte des Hegelianismus in Russland* (Prague, 1937), pp. 28–32; D. I. Chizhevsky, *Gegel v Rossii* (Paris, 1939), p. 221. Other perceptive discussions of the

circle are Sidney Monas, *The Third Section, Police and Society in Russia under Nicholas I* (Cambridge, Mass., 1961), pp. 248–260; Avrahm Yarmolinsky, *Road to Revolution, a Century of Russian Radicalism* (London, 1957), pp. 69–78.

Another index to the nature of the interests of the Petrashevskians is the fact that one of their major activities was the collecting and reading of books, often "forbidden" ones. On the main library, see Semevsky, pp. 166f; Shchegolev, *Petrashevtsky*, III, 368–372, gives a list of the personal books of some members. Of particular interest to them among the main library holdings were works by the following (the titles are not always known). (a) French liberals, radicals, and utopian socialists: Voltaire, Condorcet, D'Holbach, Benjamin Constant, Michelet, Saint-Simon, Fourier, Cabet, Leroux, Considérant, Blanc, George Sand, Proudhon, Auguste Comte (*Cours de philosophie positive*), Tocqueville (*De la démocratie en Amérique*); (b) German left Hegelian and post-Hegelian works were next in quantity: Feuerbach, Strauss (*Das Leben Jesu*), Marx (*Misère de la philosophie*), Engels (*Die Lage der arbeitenden Klasse in England*), Max Stirner, Karl Biederman (*Die Deutsche Philosophie von Kant bis auf unsere Zeit*), Haxthausen; (c) England was represented by Bentham and Owen; (d) Nicholas Turgenev, the Decembrist, seems to have been the sole Russian representative.

20. Quoted in Yarmolinsky, *Road to Revolution*, p. 71; on Petrashevsky and suicide, see Semevsky, *Butashevich-Petrashevsky*, pp. 38–39 (Petrashevsky quoted). Periods of depression and temptations to suicide were not uncommon among Western utopians—see Manuel, *Prophets of Paris*.

21. See Vladimir C. Nahirny, "The Russian Intelligentsia: from Men of Ideas to Men of Convictions," *Comparative Studies in Society and History*, IV (1961–1962): 403–435. This is a brilliant study, though I disagree with the adverse view of Belinsky and of the Petrashevsky circle. For the conceptual framework used by Nahirny, see Edward Shils, "The Intellectuals and the Powers: Some Perspectives for Comparative Analysis," *ibid.*, I (1958–1959): pp. 5–22.

22. Quoted in Shchegolev, *Petrashevtsy*, II, 46.

23. For Herzen's view and an interesting discussion in favor of it, see Frederick J. Kaplan, "Russian Fourierism in the 1840's: A Contrast to Herzen's Westernism," *The American Slavic and East European Review*, April 1958, pp. 161–172. Shigalev is a character in *The Possessed*.

24. Desnitsky, *Delo Petrashevtsev*, II, 285–334.

25. *Ibid.*, p. 320.

26. *Ibid.*, p. 324.

27. P. Maikov, "Victor Stepanovich Poroshin," *Russkii biograficheskii slovar*, XIV (St. Petersburg, 1905), 577–580; Semevsky, *Butashevich-Petrashevsky*, pp. 34–35, discusses his influence on

Petrashevsky. Poroshin's precocious interest in modern statistics could also have attracted Danilevsky's interest.

28. Monas, *Third Section*, p. 193.

29. Desnitsky, *Delo Petrashevtsev*, II, 287–288.

30. *Ibid.*; Semevsky, *Butashevich-Petrashevsky*, p. 115.

31. Desnitsky, pp. 287–88 (collected extracts of testimony about Danilevsky); Semevsky; Raisky, *Sotzialnye vozzreniia Petrashevtsev;* Akhsharumov, *Zapiski*, p. 27; Shchegolev, *Petrashevtsy*, p. 63.

32. The story is told in Strakhov's introduction to *Rossiia i Evropa*, 5th ed.

33. Desnitsky, p. 324.

34. He never received this degree probably because, having been arrested, he was unable to defend his dissertation.

35. Desnitsky, *Delo Petrashevtsev*, p. 325.

36. Semenov, *Memuary*, I, 212.

37. Akhsharumov, *Zapiski*, p. 27.

38. Monas, *Third Section*, pp. 258–259.

39. Alexander Gershenkron, "The Problem of Economic Development in Russian Intellectual History in the Nineteenth Century," in Ernest J. Simmons, ed., *Continuity and Change in Russian and Soviet Thought* (Cambridge, Mass., 1955), pp. 11–39; Leonard Shapiro, "The Prerevolutionary Intelligentsia and the Legal Order" in Richard Pipes, ed., *The Russian Intelligentsia* (New York, 1961), pp. 19–31. Both articles are excellent on the nonpractical nature of radicalism, however.

Chapter 3. Early Ideas: Science and Utopia

1. "Dutrochet," *Otechestvennye Zapiski*, vol. LVIII, sec. II (1848), pp. 1–47, 99–127; "Kosmos Al. Humboldta. Perevod N. Frolova Ch. I," *Otech. Zap.*, vol. LVIII, sec. V (1848), pp. 13f, and vol. LIX, sec. V (1848), pp. 1–24, 25–62; *Uchenie Fourier* (P. E. Schchegolev, ed., *Petrashevtsy, sbornik materialov* [Moscow, 1928], pp. 118–149). From this same period there is *Kavkas i ego gorskie zhiteli v nyneshnem ikh polozhenii. S obiasneniem istorii, religii, iazyka, oblika, odezhdy, stroenii, vospitaniia, pravleniia, zakonov, korennykh obychaev, nravov, obraza zhizni, pishchi, obrazovaniia i torgovli khishchnykh Gortsev Kavkaza* (Moscow, Universitetskoi Tip, 1846). This contained 136 pages. A German edition, apparently of the same work, was published in Leipzig in 1847. The reviewer of the original panned it. He said that the war against the mountaineers had created a market for such books. He decried publishers' practice of collecting materials, holding them for such moments, and then putting out books *ad hoc*. (*Otech. Zap.*, vol. LVIII, sec. II, 1848, pp. 96–97). I have been unable to locate a copy either of this or of the first of the Humboldt articles.

2. Shchegolev, *Petrashevtsy*, II, 120.

3. A good study is A. R. Rich, "The Place of R. J. H. Dutrochet in the Development of the Cell Theory," *Bulletin of the Johns Hopkins Hospital*, 39 (1927): 330–365. See Danilevsky, "Dutrochet," 2nd article, pp. 119–120, on cell theory.

4. "Dutrochet," 2nd article, pp. 126–127.

5. See Maurice Merleau-Ponty, *Les aventures de la dialectique* (Paris, 1955), pp. 81f.

6. Thus Danilevsky was first a "man of the forties," then a "man of the sixties." On relevant aspects of the larger story see Alexandre Koyré, *Etudes sur l'histoire de la pensée philosophique en Russie* (Paris, 1950), especially the chapters on Hegelianism and on Herzen; Isaiah Berlin, "A Marvellous Decade," *Encounter*, June 1955, pp. 27–39, November 1955, pp. 21–28, and December 1955, pp. 20–34; Herbert Bowman, "Art and Reality in Russian 'Realist' Criticism," *The Journal of Aesthetics and Art Criticism*, March 1954; Bowman, "Revolutionary Elitism in Chernyshevsky," *The American Slavic and East European Review*, April 1954.

7. "Dutrochet," 1st article, p. 4.

8. George de Santillana, "Aspects of Scientific Rationalism in the Nineteenth Century," in Santillana and Edgar Zilsel, *The Development of Rationalism and Empiricism* (Chicago, 1941), pp. 4–5. On the general story, see also Aram Vartanian, *Diderot and Descartes, a Study of Scientific Naturalism in the Enlightenment* (Princeton, 1955); Johannes Strohl, *Lorenz Oken und Georg Büchner* (Zurich, 1936); the chapter on *Naturphilosophie* in Karl Viëtor, *Georg Büchner* (Leipzig, 1934).

9. Danilevsky, "Kosmos," 3rd article, pp. 60–61.

10. On Humboldt's outlook, see Franz Schnabel, *Deutsche Geschichte im neunzehnten Jahrhundert*, III (Freiburg, 1950), 199–206; Erwin H. Ackerknecht, "George Forster, Alexander von Humboldt and Ethnology," *Isis*, June 1955, pp. 83–95. Helmut de Terra, *Humboldt: the Life and Times of Alexander von Humboldt* (New York, 1955), is a useful biography.

11. Alexander von Humboldt, *Cosmos, A Sketch of a Physical Description of the Universe*, I, E. C. Otté, trans. (London, 1864), 36.

12. Danilevsky, "Kosmos," 2nd article, p. 16.

13. *Ibid.*, pp. 15–16.

14. *Ibid.*, pp. 16–23.

15. *Ibid.*, 3rd article, pp. 19–21.

16. *Ibid.*, p. 21.

17. *Ibid.*, 2nd article, pp. 21–23.

18. See Alexander Gray, *The Socialist Tradition* (London, 1947), pp. 136–196, 230–256; Karl Löwith, *Meaning in History, the Theological Implications of the Philosophy of History* (Chicago, 1949), pp. 208–209 (also a reference to Schelling's Joachism here).

19. Shchegolev, *Petrashevtsy*, II, 119, 121.

20. *Ibid.*, p. 130.

21. *Ibid.*, pp. 122–123.

22. See George P. Fedotov, *The Russian Religious Mind, Kievan Christianity* (Cambridge, Mass., 1946), pp. 88f, 380f; Ernst Benz, *The Eastern Orthodox Church, Its Thought and Life,* Richard and Clara Winston, trans. (New York, 1963), pp. 149f. On the "existentialist" quality of modern Russian thought and the relation of this to Orthodoxy see R. E. MacMaster, "In the Russian Manner: Thought as Incipient Action," *Harvard Slavic Studies,* 4 (The Hague, 1957): 281–300; cf. also Klaus Mehnert, *Peking and Moscow,* Leila Vennewitz, trans. (New York, 1963), p. 180.

23. Shchegolev, *Petrashevtsy,* p. 130.

24. Cf. Karl Polanyi, *The Great Transformation, the Political and Economic Origins of Our Time* (New York, 1944), chaps. 4–5.

25. Shchegolev, pp. 134f.

26. Franco Venturi, *Roots of Revolution,* Francis Haskell, trans. (New York, 1960), pp. 85, 88; a similar point is made in Raoul Labry, *Alexandre Ivanovitch Herzen, 1812–1870* (Paris, 1928), pp. 299f.

Chapter 4. The Making of a Totalitarian Philosopher

1. N. N. Strakhov, "Zhizn i trudy N. Ia. Danilevskago," pp. ix–xxxi of *Rossiia i Evropa,* 5th ed. (St. Petersburg, 1895), provides the outline of Danilevsky's life history for this period and down into the seventies. It is a basic source for this chapter.

2. For the titles, see above, the chronological list of Danilevsky's writings.

3. Wilhelm Haacke, *Karl Ernst von Baer* (Leipzig, 1905), is a good introductory study.

4. The basic source on the fisheries expeditions is the series of volumes called *Izsledovaniia rybolovstva v Rossii* published by the Ministry of State Domains. There are nine volumes in all. Pertinent to Danilevsky are: vol. II, *Rybolovstvo v Kaspiiskom more i v ego pritokakh* (St. Petersburg, 1860), probably compiled by Baer; vol. III, *Opisanie Uralskago rybolovstva* (St. Petersburg, 1860), probably compiled by Danilevsky; vol. IV, *Tekhnicheskoe opisanie Kaspiiskago rybolovstva* (St. Petersburg, 1861); vol. V, *Statistika Kaspiiskago rybolovstva* (St. Petersburg, 1863), compiled by Danilevsky; vol. VI, *Rybnye i zverinye promysly na Belom i Ledovitom moriakh* (St. Petersburg, 1867), probably compiled by Danilevsky; vol. VIII, *Opisanie rybolovstva na Chernom i Azovskom moriakh* (St. Petersburg, 1871), compiled by Danilevsky; vol. IX, *Opisanie rybolovstva v severo-zapadnykh ozerakh* (St. Petersburg, 1875), compiled by Danilevsky. See also above, the list of Danilevsky's writings. There were some articles that grew out of the expeditions. I. D. Kusnetzow, *Fischerei und Thiererbeutung in den Gewässern Russlands* (St. Peters-

burg, 1898), pp. 105–114, is a detailed summary of the fisheries legislation written by Danilevsky.

The story of the Geographical Society's interest in the Caspian and Black Sea expeditions is given in P. P. Semenov, *Istoriia poluvekovoi deiatelnosti Imperatorskago Russkago Geograficheskago Obshchestva*, pt. I (St. Petersburg, 1896), pp. 136–139, 343–356. The best picture of the informal aspects is given in Baer, *Selbstbiographie* (St. Petersburg, 1866), pp. 414–436. It deals only with the Caspian expedition but may be taken as typical.

5. The best study is Helen M. Walker, *Studies in the History of the Statistical Method* (Baltimore, 1929), pp. 4–65. See also H. G. Funkhouser, "Historical Development of the Graphical Representation of Statistical Data," *Osiris*, 3 (1938): 269–404, and H. H. Schoen, "Prince Albert and the Application of Statistics to Problems of Government," *Osiris*, 5 (1938): 276–318.

A full and valuable history of statistics in Russia to the mid-nineteenth century is M. V. Ptukha, *Ocherki po istorii statistiki v SSSR*, 2 vols. (Moscow 1955 and 1959). Ptukha, *Ocherki po istorii statistiki XVII–XVIII vekov* (Moscow, 1945), pp. 275–347 is a brief sketch of the early history. I. Miklashevsky, "Statistika" (*Entsiklopedicheskii slovar*, Brockhaus-Efron. vol. XXXI, pp. 476–505) contains some material. On Russian official statistics in the nineteenth century, see (besides Ptukha) August Meitzen, *Geschichte, Theorie, und Technik der Statistik* (Stuttgart, 1903), pp. 45–46 and especially A. Kaufman, "The History and Development of Official Russian Statistics," in John Koren, ed., *The History of Statistics* (New York, 1918), pp. 469–534.

6. Frank H. Hankins, *Adolphe Quetelet as Statistician* (New York, 1908), is a fair account of his life and work. Ptukha, *Ocherki po istorii statistiki*, vol. II, provides thorough evidence of the enormous influence of "Queteletism" in Russia.

I have never seen mention of Quetelet in Danilevsky's writings. But he could hardly have missed contact with Russian Queteletism. For instance, while a student at the University of St. Petersburg, he might have attended lectures by Victor S. Poroshin, who was an extraordinarily popular teacher. He was called the "Granovsky of the University of St. Petersburg." He lectured on economics, economic theories (including, during the 1840's, Fourier's), and statistics. In 1838 he had written a criticism of the descriptive type of statistics in Quetelet's terms as his thesis for the degree of doctor of philosophy: *Kriticheskoe izsledovanie ob osnovanii statistiki* (St. Petersburg, 1838). I have mentioned Danilevsky's even more probable contact with Buniakovsky. The Statistical Section of the Geographical Society was perhaps the most important force for statistical reform in Russia in the fifties and sixties. It was permeated with Queteletism. In the mid-fifties this section drew the attention of the Council of the

Society to Quetelet's work for commendation, which the Council gave. He was elected an honorary member of the Geographical Society in the early sixties. In the fall of 1857 E. I. Lamansky, a former Petrashevskian and at that time a civil servant in the Ministry of Finance, was sent to the International Statistical Congress in Vienna by the Statistical Section. Besides imbibing Quetelet's ideas at the Congress, he also visited the great man himself in Brussels ("Iz vospominanii Evgeniia Ivanovicha Lamanskago (1840–1890 gg.)," *Russkaia Starina*, Feb. 1915, pp. 367–375. Quetelet himself attended the International Statistical Congress in St. Petersburg in 1872 and received a great ovation.

7. V. Buniakovsky, "O vozmoshnosti vvedeniia opredelennykh mer doveriia k resultatam nekotorykh nauk nabliudatelnykh i prei-mushchestvenno statistiki," *Sovremennik*, vol. III, sec. II (1848), pp. 36–49. See also his "Mysli o dvizhenii narodonaselenii voobshche," *Zhurnal Ministerstva Narodnago Prosveshcheniia*, 66 (April 1850): 46–60.

8. One parallel case of interest both in statistics and in the comparative study of civilizations and the courses of their developments is that of Quetelet himself. In *Style and Civilizations* (Ithaca, 1957), A. L. Kroeber writes, "Definitely symptomatic of a positivist approach to our subject is an attempt by Quetelet, the Belgian founder of the formal statistical approach in science. In his *Social System and its Laws*, 1848, he calculates (on pages 158–164) the average duration of five ancient 'empires' according to the chronologies then available to him. Thus 'Assyria' lasted from Assur, 'grandson' of Noah, in B.C. 2347 to the fall of Nineveh in 767 (*sic*), or 1580 years; the 'empire' of the Jews ran from Joshua, 1451 B.C. to A.D. 71, or 1522 years; that of Greece from the Athenian kingdom in B.C. 1556 to 146, or 1410 years. The average of the five cases is 1461 years; which, Quetelet comments, is also the great Sothic year of the Egyptian calendar and the life span of the phoenix. I am inclined to add with a grave face that the standard deviation of the five cases computes to 185 years, or nearly 8 per cent of the mean." Another case is that of Arnold J. Toynbee. See *A Study of History*, I (London, 1934), 178–181. Toynbee speaks here of the similarity between the comparative study of civilizations and the work of statisticians, especially those working "on the business transactions of insurance companies." Statistics in its deterministic aspect had its nineteenth century critics. Dickens was one. Dostoevsky, in *Crime and Punishment*, has Raskolnikov say of a drunken young girl, "Have I not seen cases like that? And how have they been brought to it? Why, they've all come to it like that. Ugh! But what does it matter? That's as it should be, they tell us. A certain percentage, they tell us, must every year go . . . that way . . . to the devil, I suppose, so that the rest may remain chaste, and not be interfered with. A percentage!

What splendid words they are; they are so scientific, so consolatory. . . . Once you've said 'percentage,' there's nothing more to worry about. If we had any other word . . . maybe we might feel more uneasy. . . . But what if Dounia [his sister] were one of the percentage!" (Garnett trans., Modern Library ed., p. 52.)

9. Meitzen, *Geschichte der Statistik*, pp. 45–46; Kaufman, "The History and Development of Official Russian Statistics"; Semenov, *Istoriia geogr. obshch.*, pt. I, pp. 40–47, 123–139.

10. Pages i–ii of vol. II of the Ministry of State Domains series.

11. See Adolf Heydenreich, *Karl Ernst von Baer als Geograph* (Munich, 1908), pp. 71f.

12. O. Grimm, *Fishing and Hunting in Russian Waters* (St. Petersburg, 1883), a small pamphlet, contains this story.

13. Peter Kropotkin, *Memoirs of a Revolutionist* (Boston, 1899), p. 217.

14. Kropotkin, *Mutual Aid, a Factor of Evolution* (Boston, 1955), p. vii and *passim.*

15. "Kratkii ocherk Uralskago rybnago khoziaistva" — Danilevsky, *Sbornik politicheskikh i ekonomicheskikh statei* (St. Petersburg, 1895), pp. 452–499.

16. *Darvinism, kriticheskoe izsledovanie*, vol. I (St. Petersburg, 1885), pt. 1, pp. 468–469. For mention of what seem to be other historical parallels, see James H. Billington, *Mikhailovsky and Russian Populism* (London, 1958), p. 29.

17. D. A. Miliutin, *Dnevnik*, vol. II, 1875–1877 (Moscow, 1949), p. 82.

18. Danilevsky, *Sbornik statei*, p. iii.

19. Like Katkov, Ivan Aksakov, and other Panslav publicists, Danilevsky was a firm public advocate of a high tariff policy during the relatively free trade era of M. K. Reutern, Alexander II's Minister of Finance. B. H. Sumner, in *Russia and the Balkans 1870–1880* (Oxford, 1937), pp. 59–60 (further bibliography here also), has suggested that many "infant industrialists" were interested in Panslavism for economic motives and that Panslav publicists sometimes took up the protective tariff cause because of social connections with them. Danilevsky's continuing interest in the depreciation of the paper ruble and his attempt to connect this with the need for high tariff protection suggests the possibility of social connections in the industrialists' direction also. His articles on the paper ruble were published in 1867, 1882, 1886; titles are to be found in the chronological list of his writings above.

20. *Rossiia i Evropa*, chaps. II and XI (*Zariia*, nos. 1 and 6, 1869).

21. *Pervyia 15 let sushchestvovaniia s peterburgskago slavianskago blagotvoritelnago obshchestva* (St. Petersburg, 1883), p. 843.

22. On the activities of this section in the fifties and sixties, see P. P. Semenov, *Istoriia geogr. obshch.*, pt. I, pp. 37–40, 108–122;

L. S. Berg, *Vsesoiuznoe geograficheskoe obshchestvo za sto let* (Moscow, 1946), pp. 144–172.

23. On Nadezhdin as an ethnographer, see A. N. Pypin, *Istoriia russkoi etnografii*, I (St. Petersburg, 1890), 233–275; Semenov, pt. I, pp. 38–39; Berg, pp. 146–147. N. I. Nadezhdin, "Ob etnograficheskom izuchenii narodnosti russkoi," *Zapiski russkago geograficheskago obshchestva*, bk. II (1847), pp. 61–115, is a good sample of his approach. Nadezhdin was one of the first in Russian ethnography to insist on a "psychic" rather than a physical approach to the study of popular cultures. The physical approach was used by Baer, who wrote the ethnographical article for the handbook of the Geographical Society — see "Ueber den Einfluss der äussern Natur auf die sozialen Verhältnisse der einzelnen Völker und die Geschichte der Menschheit überhaupt" in Baer, *Reden*, II (St. Petersburg, 1889), 3–47. In *Russia and Europe* Danilevsky followed Nadezhdin's way.

On Hilferding, Lamansky, and other lesser Panslavist and Slavophil currents in the section, see Berg, chap. IX. Discussion of the Panslavist activities of Hilferding and Lamansky will be found in Michael Boro Petrovich, *The Emergence of Russian Panslavism, 1856–1870* (New York, 1956), and in Frank Fadner, *Seventy Years of Pan-Slavism in Russia, Karazin to Danilevskii, 1800–1870* (Georgetown, 1962).

24. Semenov, pt. I, pp. 57f; Berg, pp. 49–55.

25. The quotations from Baer and Nadezhdin are on p. 453 of Danilevsky, *Sbornik statei*; see above, note 15, for the title of the article.

26. There is a stimulating interpretative discussion in Hannah Arendt, *The Origins of Totalitarianism* (New York, 1951), pp. 222–265. Still the best general history is Alfred Fischel, *Der Panslavismus bis zum Weltkriege* (Stuttgart, 1919). Hans Kohn, *Panslavism, Its History and Ideology* (Notre Dame, 1953), is better on the ideas and key thinkers. A. N. Pypin, *Panslavism v proshlom i nastoiashchem* (St. Petersburg, 1913), is still a useful account and a good example of the modern quality of the doctrine. On basic intellectual background, see Konrad Bittner, "J. G. Herder's 'Ideen zur Philosophie der Geschichte der Menschheit' und ihre Auswirkung bei den Slavischen Hauptstämmen," *Germanoslavica*, II (1932–33): 453–480; Jerzy Braun, "Die Slavische messianistische Philosophie als Entwicklung und Vollendung des deutschen philosophischen Systeme Kants und seiner Nachfolger," *Germanoslavica*, III (1935): 291–315; D. Chizhevsky, ed., *Hegel bei den Slaven* (Reichenberg, 1934). The best studies of Russian Panslavism in the period under discussion are Petrovich, *Russian Panslavism*, and Fadner, *Seventy Years of Pan-Slavism in Russia*.

27. Ferdinand Tönnies, *Community and Society* (*Gemeinschaft und Gesellschaft*), Charles P. Loomis, trans. (East Lansing, 1957). On the general subject of modernity, community, and nationalism, see Karl W. Deutsch, *Nationalism and Social Communications, an In-*

quiry into the Foundations of Nationality (Cambridge, Mass., 1953); Boyd C. Shafer, *Nationalism, Myth and Reality* (New York, 1955), chaps. 5–10; Edward Shils, *Political Development in the New States* (The Hague, 1962), pp. 32–33. Petrovich, *Russian Panslavism*, chap. 5, contains relevant data on personnel in the movement but there is little sociological analysis and the discussion cannot be said either to confirm or to counter my thesis. The same is true of Fadner, *Seventy Years of Pan-Slavism*, chap. 6. There are more data on personnel in S. A. Nikitin, *Slavianskie komitety v Rossii v 1858–1876 godakh* (Moscow, 1960), pp. 59–81. Nikitin undertakes an analysis in Soviet Marxist terms, attempting to show that "nobles" were the key social group, that there were few "merchants," and that therefore Panslavism was a traditionalist movement. Nikitin fails to convince me because his analytical categories are too crude; after all, there were, for instance, modern-minded bureaucrats of noble origin. He fails to note the vocations of Danilevsky and others.

28. F. M. Istomin, ed., *Kratkii ocherk deiatelnosti s-peterburgskago slavianskago obshchestva za 25 let ego sushchestvovaniia 1868–1892 gg.* (St. Petersburg, 1893), p. 11.

29. *Darvinism*, vol. I, pt. 1, pp. 20–21.

30. On conflicting senses of time in *Russia and Europe* see chaps. 6–8 below. On theories of time and the relationship of the sense of time to the sense of order and meaning, see Karl Löwith, *Meaning in History* (Chicago, 1949); Mircea Eliade, *The Myth of the Eternal Return*, W. R. Trask, trans. (New York, 1954); Hans Meyerhoff, *Time in Literature* (Berkeley, 1955); Helmuth Plessner, "On the Relation of Time to Death," *Man and Time, Papers from the Eranos Yearbooks* (New York, 1957), pp. 233–263; G. van der Leeuw, "Primordial Time and Final Time," *ibid.,* pp. 324–350. On the figure of the man without a sense of meaning in Russian and general European thought, see Walter Rehm, *Experimentum Medietatis* (Munich, 1947); Romano Guardini, *Vom Sinn der Schwermut* (Zürich, 1949); Wilhelm J. Revers, *Psychologie der Langenweile* (Meisenheim am Glan, 1949); V. O. Kliuchevsky, "Grust. Pamiati M. Ia. Lermontova," *Ocherki i rechi*, 2nd collection (Petrograd, 1918), pp. 115–136.

31. Valuable discussions of the changing climate of opinion in this period are Nestor Kotliarevsky, *Kanun osvobozhdeniia, 1855–1861* (Petrograd, 1916); Armand Coquart, *Dmitri Pisarev (1840–1868) et l'idéologie du nihilisme russe* (Paris, 1946); Billington, *Mikhailovsky*, pp. 11–52.

32. See Max Scheler, *Ressentiment*, Lewis A. Coser, ed., William W. Holdheim, trans. (New York, 1961), and Helen Lynd, *On Shame and the Search for Identity* (New York, 1958).

33. Scheler, pp. 69–70.

34. *Ibid.,* pp. 67–68.

35. For Herzen's observations on the new intellectuals see *My Past and Thoughts, The Memoirs of Alexander Herzen*, Constance Garnett, trans. (New York, 1928), VI, 99–112, 191–209. See also K. Leontiev, *Analiz, stil, i veianie; o romanakh Gr. L. N. Tolstogo* (reprint, Providence, 1965), p. 79f.

36. A good discussion of the proper use by the historian of knowledge of such forces is Leon Edel, *Literary Biography* (Toronto, 1957). See also Bruce Mazlish, ed., *Psychoanalysis and History* (Englewood Cliffs, N. J., 1963). Karl Menninger, *Man Against Himself* (New York, 1938) is a good psychoanalytic essay on hate and destructiveness. A persuasive discussion of relationships between existential and behavioral psychological factors is M. Merleau-Ponty, *Phénoménologie de la perception* (Paris, 1945), pp. 180–202.

37. Konrad Onasch, *Dostojewski-Biographie, Materialsammlung* (Zürich, 1960), p. 96. Danilevsky came to Dostoevsky's attention again as early as the winter of 1869: see F. M. Dostoevsky, *Pisma*, II, 1867–1871 (A. S. Dolinin, ed.; Moscow, 1930), pp. 156, 169, 176, 179, 181.

38. See D. I. Chizhevsky, *Gegel v Rossii* (Paris, 1939), pp. 266–283.

39. For accurate interpretation of Shatov (he is not to be taken as Dostoevsky's spokesman) see Romano Guardini, *Der Mensch und der Glaube, Versuche über die religiöse Existenz in Dostojewskijs grossen Romanen* (Leipzig, 1933), pp. 21–33 and *passim* and also K. V. Mochulsky, *Dostoevsky, zhizn i tvorchestvo* (Paris, 1947), chap. 18.

Chapter 5. Later Years

1. Again the basic source for this chapter is N. N. Strakhov, "Zhizn i trudy N. Ia. Danilevskago," in *Rossiia i Evropa*, 5th ed. (St. Petersburg, 1895), pp. ix–xxxi.

2. He stayed there during the war of 1877–78 despite the fact that some of his neighbors, fearing another Crimean campaign, moved out. Danilevsky seems to have preferred to take the advice of his friend and neighbor Miliutin, the Minister of War, who had been assured by Alexander II that this time the League of the Three Emperors would keep "Europe" from combining against Russia (D. A. Miliutin, *Dnevnik*, vol. II, Moscow, 1949, pp. 49–50; the League was still secret at this point). It worked out fairly well. Some Turkish "adventurers" disguised as dolphin fishermen made some local raids, at one point doing a little plundering at Mshatka. This provoked an angry letter from Danilevsky to Miliutin about the ineptitude of the local administration (*ibid.*, pp. 60–61). It was the only incident.

3. Founded by Alexander I in 1811.

4. For Danilevsky's writings on phylloxera, see above, the list of his works.

5. Strakhov mentions the revision in his biographical sketch and the

fifth edition of *Russia and Europe* contains a few footnotes, inserted from Danilevsky's notes, which revise some minor substantive points.

6. On the Balkan crisis and the war, see B. H. Sumner, *Russia and the Balkans, 1870–1880* (Oxford, 1937).

7. N. Ia. Danilevsky, *Sbornik politicheskikh i ekonomicheskikh statei*, N. N. Strakhov, ed. (St. Petersburg, 1890), pp. 31–138, "Voina za Bolgariiu," and pp. 139–219, "Gore pobediteliam!"

8. *Ibid.*, pp. 1–30, "Rossiia i Franko-Germanskaia voina." Danilevsky said that the changed European balance made France rather than Prussia (his candidate in *Russia and Europe*) the power in Europe which Russia should seek to attach diplomatically to her camp in order to split Europe in the coming struggle.

9. *Ibid.*, p. 32.

10. *Ibid.*, p. 32.

11. *Ibid.*, p. 180.

12. *Ibid.*, p. 105.

13. *Ibid.*, p. 84.

14. *Ibid.*, pp. 201–202.

15. *Ibid.*, pp. 208–209.

16. *Ibid.*, p. 44.

17. *Ibid.*, pp. 137–138.

18. *Ibid.*, pp. 220–230, "Neskolko slov po povodu konstitutsionnykh vozhdelenii nashei 'liberalnoi pressy'"; pp. 231–271, "Proiskozhdenie nashego nigilizma"; pp. 272–312, "G. Vladimir Soloviev o Pravoslavii i Katolitsizme."

19. *Ibid.*, pp. 274–275.

20. *Ibid.*, pp. 104–105.

21. *Ibid.*, p. 256.

22. N. Ia. Danilevsky, *Darvinism, kriticheskoe izsledovanie*, vol. I (St. Petersburg, 1885). Volume I of this two-volume work has two parts (actually two bound volumes of about 500 pages each) and comprises the main portion of the work. Volume II (St. Petersburg, 1889) consists of one posthumous chapter, an introduction by Strakhov, a bibliography and indices. I shall have occasion here to cite only the two parts of the first volume.

Danilevsky submitted the work to the Academy of Sciences for a prize. It received honorable mention.

Darvinism has more than biographical significance. It played an important role in the general Darwinian controversy in Russia. George L. Kline, "Darwinism and the Russian Orthodox Church," in Ernest J. Simmons, ed., *Continuity and Change in Russian and Soviet Thought* (Cambridge, Mass., 1955), pp. 307–328, is a good account of major aspects of that controversy, including discussion of Danilevsky. The following articles constitute the elements of a press controversy about Danilevsky's *Darvinism*. Pro-Danilevsky: N. N. Strakhov, "Polnoe oproverzhenie Darvinisma" (1887); "Vsegdashniaia oshibka darvinistov" (1887); "Suzhdenie Andr. S. Famintsyna o 'Darvinisme' N. Ia. Danilevskago" (1889); "Spor iz-za knig N. Ia. Danilevskago" (1889). All these are printed in N. N. Strakhov, *Borba s zapadom v nashei literature*, bk. II (2nd ed., St. Petersburg, 1890); they appeared originally in the *Russkii Vestnik* in the years indicated. Against Danilevsky: K. A. Timiriazev, "Oprovergnut li Darvinism?" (two articles in *Russkaia Mysl*, bk. V, May 1887, pp. 145–180; and bk. VI, June 1887, pp. 1–14); "Bezsilnaia zloba antidarvinisma" (three articles in *Russkaia Mysl*, bk. V, May 1889, pp. 17–52; bk. VI, June 1889, pp. 65–82; bk. VII, July 1889, pp. 58–78); Andr. Famintsyn, "N. Ia. Danilevsky i Darvinism, oprovergnut li Darvinism Danilevskim?" (*Vestnik Evropy*, vol. 24, bk. II, Feb. 1889, pp. 616–643).

Mr. Kline, pp. 317–318, rightly criticizes a statement in my doctoral dissertation (Harvard, 1952) to the effect that this controversy about Danilevsky bears a striking resemblance to the Soviet genetics debate of 1948. He points correctly to important differences in detail between the two. There remains a matter to be emphasized, however. The Lysenkoists did regard Danilevsky as "objectively" belonging to the Mendel-Morgan camp and Timiriazev to theirs. See, for example, V. L. Komarov, N. A. Maksimov, and B. G. Kuznetsov, *Kliment Arkadevich Timiriazev* (Moscow, 1945), chap. III; G. S. Vasetsky, "Filosofskie vozzreniia K. A. Timiriazeva" in *Iz istorii russkoi filosofii, sbornik statei* (Leningrad, 1949), pp. 644–663.

23. *Darvinism*, pt. 1, pp. 9f, 17, 178.
24. *Ibid.*, pt. 1, pp. 3f, 37, 45, 189; pt. 2, p. 467. Pt. 1, pp. 47–196, are very full on all this.
25. *Ibid.*, pt. 1, p. 6; see also pt. 2, pp. 524f.
26. *Ibid.*, pt. 2, pp. 480–484.
27. *Ibid.*, pt. 2, p. 478.
28. *Ibid.*, pt. 2, pp. 529–530.
29. *Ibid.*, pt. 1, pp. 20–21, 23, 27–28, 37.
30. Three vols., Brunswick, 1874.
31. *Darvinism*, pt. 2, pp. 501–502.
32. *Ibid.*, pt. 2, pp. 496–497.
33. *Ibid.*, pt. 1, pp. 430–431.
34. *Ibid.*, pt. 2, chaps. X–XI.
35. *Ibid.*, pt. 2, pp. 468–469, for examples drawn from personal observation.
36. *Ibid.*, pt. 2, pp. 264–265 (also the previous quotation).
37. On the relative validity of the arguments of the morphological critics of Darwin, see Erik Nordenskiöld, *The History of Biology* (New York, 1949), chap. XII; a clear, brief example of this type of argument is Louis Agassiz, "Evolution and Permanence of Type," *Atlantic Monthly*, Jan. 1874, pp. 1–12.
38. See *Darvinism*, pt. 2, pp. 488f, 504–506, 508, 514f, for Danilevsky's views on science and philosophy.

39. *Ibid.*, pt. 2, pp. 505–506.

40. *Ibid.*, pt. 2, pp. 504–505.

41. Baer discovered his affinity to Aristotle after independent intellectual development. See pp. 458–459 of Karl Ernst von Baer, "Ueber Darwin's Lehre" in *Reden*, vol. II (St. Petersburg, 1876). Another modern idealist morphologist with affinities to Aristotle and an outlook remarkably similar to Baer's was J. J. von Uexküll—see Helene Weiss, "Aristotle's Teleology and Uexküll's Theory of Living Matter," *The Classical Quarterly*, Jan.–April 1948, pp. 44–58.
A good account of Baer's general philosophical position is given in E. L. Radlov, "K. M. Baer kak filosof," *Trudy Komissii po Istorii Znanii*, No. 2, *Pervyi sbornik pamiati Baera* (Leningrad, 1927). In Russia, Baer was called Karl Maximovich Baer — hence the "K. M." in Radlov's title.

42. *Darvinism*, pt. 2, p. 479.

43. Baer, *Selbstbiographie* (St. Petersburg, 1866), one of the great works of scientific autobiography, is the best source on this work in embryology. See also George Sarton, "The Discovery of the Mammalian Egg and the Foundation of Modern Embryology," *Isis*, vol. XVI (2), no. 49 (1931), pp. 315–330; Joseph Needham, *A History of Embryology* (Cambridge, Mass., 1934), pp. 190–200; Arthur William Meyer, *The Rise of Embryology* (Stanford, 1939), pp. 54–95, 98–131.

44. On Meckel and Oken, see "Ueber Darwin's Lehre," *Reden*, II, 241f and Ernst Cassirer, *The Problem of Knowledge: Philosophy, Science, and History since Hegel*, William N. Woglom and Charles W. Hendel, trans. (New Haven, 1950), pp. 153–154.

45. I have used the following sources on Baer's thought about evolution: Baer, "Ueber Darwin's Lehre," *Reden*, II, 235–480; Remigius Stöltzle, *Karl Ernst von Baer und seine Weltanschauung* (Regensburg, 1897), pp. 195–289; Wilhelm Haacke, *Karl Ernst von Baer* (Leipzig, 1905), pp. 75–173.

46. This idea of immanent purpose has remained a live issue in our time, though the rise of holism has made it possible for biologists to bypass it to a significant degree: see, for instance, Adrian C. Moulyn, *Structure, Function, and Purpose, an Inquiry into the Concepts and Methods of Biology from the Viewpoint of Time* (New York, 1957), chaps. III and IV; Ernst Cassirer, *The Problem of Knowledge: Philosophy, Science, and History since Hegel*, pp. 205–216.

47. *Darvinism*, pt. 2, pp. 512–514.

48. *Ibid.*, pt. 2, pp. 513–514. See Baer's articles "Ueber den Zweck in den Vorgängen der Natur" and "Ueber Zielstrebigkeit in den organischen Körpern insbesondere," *Reden*, II, 51–105, 173–234. Danilevsky used both these (see Strakhov's bibliography and index to *Darvinism*, vol. II) and "Ueber Darwin's Lehre" as well as Baer's magisterial *Ueber Entwickelungsgeschichte der Tiere*, vol. I (Königsberg, 1828), vol. II (1837).

49. *Darvinism*, pt. 2, pp. 505, 513–514, 510, respectively.

50. Such ideas are evident in his "Ueber den Einfluss der äussern Natur auf die sozialen Verhältnisse der einzelnen Völker und die Geschichte der Menschheit überhaupt," *Reden*, II, 3–47. This is also a clear example of his way of thinking about evolution. This article was first printed in Russian in 1848 in the *Karmannaia knizhka* (handbook) of the Russian Geographical Society.

51. Karl Marx and Friedrich Engels, *The Holy Family or Critique of Critical Critique* (Moscow, 1956), p. 172. A relevant and provocative discussion of spiritualist materialism is R. C. Zaehner, *Matter and Spirit, Their Convergence in Eastern Religions, Marx and Teilhard de Chardin* (New York, 1963).

Chapter 6. Panslavism and Theory of Civilizations

1. The full title of the big work is *Rossiia i Evropa. Vzgliad na kulturniia i politicheskiia otnosheniia Slavianskago mira k Germano-Romanskomu.* It appeared first in serial form in the magazine *Zariia* (*Dawn*) in 1869; numbers 1 (chaps. I, II), 2 (chaps. III, IV), 3 (chaps. V, VI), 4 (chap. VII), 5 (chaps. VIII, IX), 6 (chaps. X, XI), 8 (chaps. XII, XIII), 9 (chaps. XIV, XV), 10 (chaps. XVI, XVII). From now on in this study I shall cite the work by referring first to the chapter number and then the page of the chapter: II, 21; XVI, 82.

There are two summaries of the work: in Konrad Pfalzgraf, "Die Politisierung und Radikalisierung des Problems Russland und Europa bei Danilevskij," *Forschungen zur Osteuropäischen Geschichte*, I (Berlin, 1954), pp. 55–204; J. Skupiewski, *La doctrine panslaviste d'après N. J. Danilevsky, "La Russie et l'Europe"; coup d'oeil sur les rapports politiques entre le monde slave et le monde germano-roman* (Bucharest, 1890).

2. *Russia and Europe* is full of references to the Slavophils: for example, VI, 25–26; VII, 103; VIII, 51, 59–60; IX, 77; XI, 64; XIII, 1. Danilevsky mentioned Khomiakov and Kireevsky most often, Constantine Aksakov only two or three times. He seems to have been influenced especially by Khomiakov's French brochures. But it is possible (the very last lines of *Russia and Europe*, XVII, 130, suggest this) that he knew the latter's *Zapiski* on world history. There were other sources of his Panslav ideas. At one point he referred very favorably to the series of names, Khomiakov, Pogodin, Hanka, Kollar, Shtur (XV, 38). He also quoted from Kollar's famous Panslavist poem "Slavy Dcera" ("The Daughter of Slava," III, 51). Tiutchev was quoted (XIV, 1 — a poem). There is one quotation from a "Galician satirical journal" called *Strakhopud* (VIII, 51). He referred to Pushkin's lines about the Slavic streams flowing into the Russian sea (XIV, 20) but was critical of this idea.

3. The interpretation of Slavophilism that follows is my own. It is based on a reading of the following works: Nikolai Berdaiev, *Aleksei Stepanovich Khomiakov* (Moscow, 1912); Peter K. Christoff, *An Introduction to Nineteenth Century Slavophilism, a Study in Ideas,* Volume I: *A. S. Khomiakov* (The Hague, 1961); Mikhail Gerzhenzon, *Istoricheskie Zapiski* (Moscow, 1910), pp. 3–40; "Uchenie o lichnosti (I. V. Kireevsky)" and pp. 41–86, "Uchenie o prirode soznaniia (Iu. F. Samarin)"; A. Gratieux, *A. S. Khomiakov et le mouvement Slavophile,* 2 vols. (Paris, 1939); Alexandre Koyré, *La philosophie et le problème national en Russie au début du XIXᵉ siècle* (Paris, 1929); Koyré, *Etudes sur l'histoire de la pensée philosophique en Russie* (Paris, 1950), pp. 1–17: "La jeunesse d'Ivan Kireevskii" (which contains important criticisms of Gershenzon's interpretation); Boris Nolde, *Iury Samarin i ego vremiia* (Paris, 1926); Nicholas V. Riasanovsky, *Russia and the West in the Teaching of the Slavophils,* a *Study of a Romantic Ideology* (Cambridge, Mass., 1952); Riasanovsky, "Khomiakov on *Sobornost*," *Continuity and Change in Russian and Soviet Thought,* Ernest J. Simmons, ed. (Cambridge, Mass., 1955), pp. 183–196; Alexander von Schelting, *Russland und Europa in russischen Geschichtsdenken* (Bern, 1948); Nicolas Zernov, *Three Russian Prophets, Khomiakov, Dostoevsky, Soloviev* (London, 1944).

4. See Berdaiev on these concepts. It should be stressed that no thinker used one to the exclusion of the other. Thinkers differed on the kinds of combinations they made. There is further discussion, here and there, in James R. Billington, *Mikhailovsky and Russian Populism* (London, 1958), and Franco Venturi, *Roots of Revolution,* F. Haskell, trans. (New York, 1960).

5. See George P. Fedotov, *The Russian Religious Mind* (Cambridge, Mass., 1946), pp. 110–136, 158–175.

6. See *Rossiia i Evropa*, XIV, pp. 21–28, on the Panslav Union.

7. XIV, 19–20.

8. V, 1–2. This had the status, in Danilevsky's system, of one of five "laws of movement or development" of civilizations.

9. X, 29.

10. XV, 53f. The theme of the United States and Russia (or Slavdom) as new civilizations different from old, declining "Europe" runs all through *Russia and Europe.* Probably this reflects an influence of Tocqueville, whose *Democracy in America* was a favorite in the Petrashevsky library.

11. XV, 58; VI, 34.

12. For an interesting discussion, from a different point of view, about Danilevsky and the messianic theme in Russian thought, see Hans Kohn, "Dostoevsky and Danilevsky: Nationalist Messianism," in Ernest J. Simmons, ed., *Continuity and Change in Russian and Soviet Thought* (Cambridge, Mass., 1955), pp. 500–515.

13. F. M. Dostoevsky, *The Diary of a Writer*, Boris Brasol, trans., II (New York, 1949), 903–904.

14. Chapter III contains a particularly full discussion of Europe's direct and indirect domination of Slavdom. Danilevsky also pointed with alarm to growing English influence in Persia and to possible English influence in the Caucasus.

15. See XV, 46–57, on European imperialism and its fluctuations.

16. Chapter XI, "Europeanism is the Sickness of Russian Life," is the fullest discussion of Westernization.

17. II, 32.

18. Chapter I deals with 1854 and 1864.

19. II, 22–23.

20. II, 51. Chapter II is entitled "Why is Europe hostile to Russia?" It sets forth elaborate "proof" of Europe's hostility and its irrationality.

21. XI, 96.

22. II contains the fullest discussion of Russia's "self-sacrificing" foreign policy.

23. See III.

24. All through his book Danilevsky hit at the ultranationalist periodical *Vest* (The news), as the principal organ of this strand of opinion.

25. VI, 24–25.

26. In XI, 83–84, Danilevsky set forth his conviction that mere editorial writing could not affect the outlook of the public. Only big social scientific works, exercising profound influence over long periods of time could do so. His example of such an influential work was Adam Smith, *The Wealth of Nations*.

27. For further discussion of and citation of literature in the subject, see chapter 9 below and my article "Danilevsky and Spengler: A New Interpretation," *The Journal of Modern History*, June 1954, pp. 154–161.

28. III, 67.

29. An excellent discussion of pertinent aspects of Cuvier's philosophy of science is Ernst Cassirer, *The Problem of Knowledge, Philosophy, Science, and History since Hegel*, William H. Woglom and Charles W. Hendel, trans. (New Haven, 1950), pp. 118–136. See also *Rossiia i Europa*, IV, 88f on Cuvier and the nature and history of taxonomy.

30. IV, 74.

31. IV, 75.

32. IV, 78.

33. IV, 85, 88.

34. IV, 88. The question of the Slavic type was Danilevsky's main interest in *Russia and Europe*. He was not much interested in any types but the Germano-Roman and the Slavic except insofar as they

could throw light on this question. In this sense too (as well as in regard to relativism and totalitarianism), *Russia and Europe* is different from *The Decline of the West* or Toynbee's *A Study of History*.

35. The most probable source of Danilevsky's information was the once widely read *Lehrbuch der Weltgeschichte*, 2 vols. (many editions from 1846 on — for example, Leipzig, 1854 or 1865) by Georg Weber. Then he also used Karl von *Rotteck, Allgemeine Geschichte vom Anfang der historischen Kenntnis bis auf unsere Zeiten*, 9 vols. (many editions from 1812–1818 on to the 1870's). Georg Gervinus was the author of the tendentious, liberal *Geschichte des neunzehnten Jahrhundert seit den Wiener Verträgen*, 8 vols. (Leipzig, 1855–1866). Rotteck was also an extremely tendentious historian. Reading Gervinus and Rotteck, in particular, might have helped give Danilevsky the idea (contrary to the authors' intentions) that Western Europe had a superiority complex and was imperialistic behind its self-congratulatory paeans to progress.

For discussion and bibliography on the Rückert question, see my article "The Question of Heinrich Rückert's Influence on Danilevsky," *The American Slavic and East European Review*, Feb. 1955, pp. 59–66.

36. IV, 89–90. Translated by P. A. Sorokin in his chapter on Danilevsky in *Social Philosophies of an Age of Crisis* (Boston, 1950), pp. 58–59.

The suggestion of racism and of the idea of naturally superior and inferior peopes is unmistakable here and elsewhere in *Russia and Europe*. On the other hand, Danilevsky explicitly attacked the racial theories of the Swedish anatomist Anders Adolf Retzius and of the German historian, Georg Weber (VII, 52f). Evidently he did not think of himself as a racist. Perhaps the racism we see in his philosophy was an unintended consequence of his emphasis on the mysteriousness of God's ways in history.

37. V, 1–2. This had the status of a "law of development" in Danilevsky's system.

38. V, 3–11, is a discussion of types of influence.

39. Danilevsky distinguished between "laws" of more quantitative sciences like physics and the "rules" of more descriptive ones like botany or the social sciences. He thought the English political economists in particular confused rules with laws. This had led them to the erroneous idea that economic institutions in the West were progressive and those in the East backward. But, in Danilevsky's view, progressive economic behavior could take various specific, institutional forms. The Russian agricultural commune was not backward any more than a fish was backward for breathing with gills rather than lungs.

40. Chapter VI is a full-length discussion of the history of science

and is the best source on the treasury idea. See also N. N. Strakhov, *Borba s zapadom v nashei literature,* bk. II, 2nd ed. (St. Petersburg, 1890), pp. 260f, for discussion of this idea.

41. VI, 47.

42. See Herbert Marcuse, *Soviet Marxism, A Critical Analysis* (New York, 1958), chap. 7.

43. Chapter VI, 33–34, discusses the ideas of "universal" and "pan-human" and the dim possibilities of their realization.

44. V, 15.

45. VI, 38.

46. V, 1–2. This also had the status of a "law of development."

47. VII, 99–100.

48. VII, 97. This whole discussion of cycles is a good example of Danilevsky's statisticism.

49. VII, 101–102. Danilevsky devoted a whole chapter (VII, "Is Europe Rotting?") to Europe's decline.

50. VII, 102.

51. XIV, 6–7.

52. V, 17.

53. VI, 68 f.

54. XVII, 117f.

55. Danilevsky criticized Darwin in *Russia and Europe* (VI, 52; XI, 94). But his criticism was like his view of the English political economists: agreement on the form of the theory, disagreement about the content. He seems (like Kropotkin) to have envisaged intra-species cooperation in interspecies struggle for existence — rather than individualistic struggle — as the mechanism of evolution.

His application of Darwinian concepts to the mind was not typical of Russian intellectuals in this period. See James Allen Rogers, "Darwinism, Scientism, and Nihilism," *The Russian Review,* Jan. 1960, pp. 10–23. However, in line with his distinction between private and public or group man, he did object to the tracing of human ancestry to animals. "How can it be possible that an organic being, like a man, could endlessly develop without at the same time changing his very nature, that is, finally ceasing to be human? I know there are those who think — on the basis that, as in *The Thousand and One Nights* or in Ovid's *Metamorphoses,* something similar happened with monkeys (who, not being able to stand the pressure of progress, turned into people) and on the basis that man is nothing but a perfected sponge or infusorian — that it does not seem strange that the human form too, becoming too narrow for progress, will change, by the wave of a wand, into something more perfect" (V, 19).

56. XIII, 54.

57. On the origins of peoples, see V and VIII, *passim;* X, 30f. Chapter X, 26–27, suggests that the trans-Atlantic migrations were an important formative influence on the Americans.

58. So important was language that the historian could identify the emergence of developed language with that of national self-consciousness. Comparative philology could thus serve as comparative psychology. For instance, one people (the Slavs) counted the smallest gradations of time; another did not. One developed the verb "to have," another "to be." Such linguistic differences were both keys to the nature of psychic structure and hints of the fact of its distinctly pragmatic origin (V, 18).

The first of Danilevsky's "laws of development" underlines the importance he attributed to language in the study of cultures. "Every nation or family of peoples, characterized by a separate language or group of languages whose affinity is close enough to be felt directly without deep philological studies, constitutes an independent cultural-historical type, if it is generally capable, according to its spiritual traits, of historical development and if it has already emerged from its period of youth" (V, 1–2).

59. V, 22.

60. V, 1–2. This was one of the "laws of development."

61. V, 17.

62. X, 30–31.

63. X, 28f.

64. X, 29.

65. X, 21.

66. In his scattered observations (see footnote 57 above) on the origins of peoples, it sounds at times as though he thought historical life from the very beginning of the ethnographic period was a sort of alienated life. Perhaps there was an echo of the idea of original sin here. Anyway even the first period of a people's life cycle was not perfect.

67. V, 23.

68. VI, 29–30.

69. *Ibid.*

70. For a stimulating discussion of *The Prince* from this point of view, see Charles S. Singleton, "The Perspective of Art," *The Kenyon Review*, spring 1953. Hans J. Morgenthau, *Politics among Nations*, 3rd ed. (New York, 1963), is a good example of nontotalitarian (indeed, liberal) political realism.

71. Guido de Ruggiero, *The History of European Liberalism*, R. G. Collingwood, trans., 2nd ed. (Boston, 1959), p. 108.

Chapter 7. Europe, Russia, and Metaphysics

1. VIII, 57–58. On the method of citation of *Russia and Europe* see above, Chapter 6, note 1.

2. VIII, 51–52.

3. He was not unfamiliar with the conception. In discussing the

Hebraic type's religious contribution to the common treasury, he said he meant religion only as a societal phenomenon (VI, 40). In regard to ethics, he suggested a similar distinction. Some "virtues" were societal and at least somewhat relative, some individual and universal. There were three virtues: goodness, justice, and purity. The last was individual and not subject to the effects of "national exclusiveness." But, though it was a matter of emphasis only, goodness reigned in the Russian value system, justice in the European (VIII, 76–77). Incidentally, this latter seems a good insight.

4. IX, 77–78. At one point, speaking of Europe's decline, he seems to suggest that Europe was subject to his typal theory but Russia not: "Is there a way out? For individuals eager for the truth — yes; the doors of Orthodoxy are open. For whole peoples there is probably no direct escape. Europe must first traverse all the steps of old age, sickness, death, and disintegration in order for there to be formed a new ethnographic whole, a new cultural-historical type, out of the disintegrated elements. For peoples, as for individuals, there is no fountain of youth" (IX, 98).

5. XVII, 101–102.

6. Throughout the chapters under discussion, however, there are many inconsistencies. The typal theory is dragged in here and there. There are also occasional lapses into a purer version of Slavophilism, one which allowed for a degree of human freedom and responsibility (see notes 4 and 10 of this chapter for examples of these inconsistencies).

7. VIII, 57–58.

8. Danilevsky damned atheistic statism without illustrating sufficiently why he thought it wrong. The only relevant discussion refers to the growing practice of civil marriage in Europe (IX, 89f). Civil marriage was a mere contract. As such it could be as easily dissolved as made. Divorce hurt children. Moreover, the only moral norms governing civil marriages were natural ones. Natural morality, without the control of revelation, was relative: some peoples approved polygamy, incestuous unions, exchanges of husbands and wives. On grounds of natural morality alone, there was no way of distinguishing good from evil marital practices.

9. For instance, Napoleon III had invented the plebiscite. But it was a farce, for peoples were asked to vote on meaningless questions. The people of Savoy were asked if they wanted to be incorporated into France or into Italy, not whether they wanted to be independent.

10. Facing X, 21. Danilevsky ridiculed what he described as efforts toward alleviation of the European problem of socio-economic liberty. Guaranteeing the "right to work" bypassed the much more basic problem of the land monopoly of the upper classes. Instituting popular sovereignty would only lead to a tyranny of majority over minority. The majority were the poor in the cities, a group which

invariably acted in the most selfish interests. Their rule would ultimately lead to communism or military dictatorship.

Danilevsky credited Macaulay with this last idea. But he was also using a really Slavophil conception in his discussion of popular sovereignty, for he saw it as a misguided effort to achieve freedom, misguided because undertaken in a warped spiritual and institutional environment.

11. VIII, 67.

12. On Russian "character" and its manifestations, see VIII, 66f.

13. VIII, 66.

14. VIII, 68.

15. VIII, 74.

16. IX, 78–79.

17. XVI, 80.

18. It was not that a written constitution or a parliament was wanted. A great civilization was about to be born.

Danilevsky was a kind of tsarist. His political theory, however, was Slavophil and Rousseauist: the tsar was the incarnation of the popular will, *narodnaia volia*. The following are the best sources on his political theory: X; XVI, 79f. "Neskolko slov po povodu konstitutsionnykh vozhdelenii nashei 'liberalnoi pressy'" (Danilevsky, *Sbornik statei*, St. Petersburg, 1890, pp. 220–230) and "Proiskhozdenie nashego nigilizma" (*ibid.*, pp. 247f).

19. Here and there throughout chapters 6–8 of this study I refer to Danilevsky's varying views of time. His confusion about the structure of time is a good index to the fact that he was confused in his life orientation, values, and sense of meaning in a more than academic-intellectual, that is, in an existential way. Pointing up this confusion, its nature, and its connection with Danilevsky's cultural and social situation is thus a way of again suggesting the biographical relevance of *Russia and Europe*. For references to works on time used see chapter 4 above, note 30.

20. One striking little example is an observation (II, 31) on the partition of Poland. Danilevsky was describing how Catherine II had set out to recover only former Russian lands, how she, in the light of European humanitarian standards, had felt guilty, and how Austria and Prussia had taken advantage of this to get a share for themselves. Danilevsky's main point was that Catherine should have simply looked out for Russia's interests and Poland would have survived. But he also asked, "Or are there, perhaps, humanitarian heads that say that magnanimity demanded that Russia deny herself what was her right rather than agree to the destruction of Poland? Indeed this is all that Russia could be accused of — from the most Don Quixotic point of view."

21. F. M. Dostoevsky, *The Diary of a Writer*, Boris Brasol, trans., II (New York, 1949), 836.

22. Karl Löwith was reminded of the Westerners and the Slavophils

in discussing the German left Hegelians and the later Schelling. See *From Hegel to Nietzsche, the Revolution in Nineteenth Century Thought*, David E. Green, trans. (New York, 1964), pp. 115f, 141f.

23. Danilevsky was not consistent on Peter. See chapter 6 above: in the typal theory he blamed Peter for "falling in love" with Europe and traced the beginning of *zapadnichestvo* to this. This dualistic view of Peter is an interesting parallel to Danilevsky's "democratic-tsarist" political theory. Unlike the Slavophils he thought it possible to redeem or to transfigure the Petrine heritage, the monarchy, and Westernized Russia in general. Danilevsky thought about reform in terms of rearrangement and reintegration of given factors; the Slavophils had thought of it more in terms of sorting out good and bad factors and eliminating the latter.

Chapter 8. Totalitarianism

1. Historians of modern Western thought in general and modern Russian in particular seem to have paid relatively little attention to the mythological and rhetorical aspects of their subjects' writings. But see Christopher Dawson, "Karl Marx and the Dialectic of History," chapter V of *Religion and the Modern State* (London, 1935), and Kenneth Burke, "The Rhetoric of Hitler's 'Battle,'" in *The Philosophy of Literary Form, Studies in Symbolic Action* (Baton Rouge, 1941), pp. 191–220. In his *Studies in Rebellion* (New York, 1957), E. Lampert highlights many interesting and relevant facets of the thought of Belinsky, Bakunin, and Herzen; but Lampert is a moralist and gives little attention to comparative and developmental historical matters. Classic examples of good mythological and rhetorical study are Carl L. Becker, *The Heavenly City of the Eighteenth Century Philosophers* (New Haven, 1932); F. M. Cornford, *From Religion to Philosophy* (London, 1912), and *The Unwritten Philosophy and other Essays* (Cambridge, 1950).

2. XVII, 92–93. On the method of citation of *Russia and Europe*, see above, chapter 6 above, note 1.

3. Hegel is mentioned here and there in *Russia and Europe* (for example, VI, 70) but always unfavorably — as a typical apriorist German, a mind obsessed with *ein durchgreifendes Princip*. There seems to have been no direct (but possibly much indirect) influence.

4. XVII, 96.

5. XVII, 99.

6. This occasionalism seems an intellectually appropriate extension of the intellecual universe of Adam Smith, Bentham, Darwin.

7. XVII, 99.

8. XVII, 129.

9. The schism of the Russian Old Believers raised no problems for

Danilevsky. In his view they were still really Orthodox and they had long been a constructively critical element, a "loyal opposition" in the Church.

10. XVII, 112–113.

11. See XVI, 86–87, for more discussion of *War and Peace*. Danilevsky thought Tolstoi's philosophy of history substantially correct. He interpreted it as a kind of blind fatalism and liked Tolstoi's suggestion of the weird power of Russia in 1812. Like other critics, however, he thought the philosophy hurt the artistic unity of the novel.

12. XVII, 130; note the kenotic image at the very end.

13. Danilevsky had a fixation on the number four. There were four periods of the Eastern question, four sides to the future Slavic civilization, four possible solutions to the Polish question, four stages of typal development, and (omitting the disfunctional stage of the artificial system) four stages in the history of science. His thinking about the four members in the family of his childhood may have been the origin of this. C. G. Jung found the number 4 symbolizing completeness repeatedly in the mythologies of the world. See *Psyche and Symbol, A Selection from the Writings of C. G. Jung*, Violet S. de Laszlo, ed. (New York, 1958).

14. XII, 1–2.

15. On the Hegelian hero, see the excellent article by Robert C. Tucker, "The Cunning of Reason in Hegel and Marx," *Review of Politics*, July 1956, pp. 269–295.

16. XII, 9–10. Statisticism is a strange business. The "statistician" begins his study with the omission of causal considerations. Then he comes to see regularities, parallels, and the like. In certain cases, he can be tempted, if he forgets that he had decided at the outset to omit causal considerations, to visions of Providence's workings. For discussion of and references regarding other such cases, see George Sarton, "Preface to Volume XXIII of *Isis* (Quetelet)," *Isis*, 1935, pp. 6–24.

17. XII, 12–13.

18. XII, 23.

19. XVI, 54.

20. XVI, 54–55.

21. XII, 45. Danilevsky said (XIII) that he drew much of his information about Austria from the Czech historian, Palacky, though he disliked Palacky's pro-Austrian ideas. He said he used Gervinus as a source on the Turks (XII, 18) and their historical mission.

22. XIV, 1.

23. XIV, 3.

24. XIV, 4.

25. On the temporal and spatial setting of liturgies, see Mircea Eliade, *Patterns of Comparative Religion*, Rosemary Sheed, trans. (New York, 1958). The most likely source (conscious or otherwise)

of Danilevsky's familiarity with such things was the Orthodox Liturgy or Mass.

26. XIV, 22–28.

27. XIV, 9.

28. XVI.

29. He noted the incongruity of Slav-Teuton alliance himself and went on at some length to point out that Providence was at work in the situation (XVI, 68–76). But after the Franco-Prussian War, he changed his proposal, for the balance of forces in "Europe" had shifted. See "Rossiia i franko-germanskaia voina (dopolnenie k predshestvuiushchemu sochineniiu)," *Zariia*, no. 1, 1871, or Danilevsky, *Sbornik statei* (St. Petersburg, 1890), pp. 1–30.

30. XVI, 89.

31. Karl Marx, *Selected Works*, V. Adoratsky, ed., vol. I (New York, no date), pp. 446–447. The lines are from Engels' *Ludwig Feuerbach and the Outcome of Classical German Philosophy*.

32. F. M. Dostoevsky, *Pisma*, II, 1867–1871, A. S. Dolinin, ed. (Moscow, 1930), pp. 156, 169, 176, 179, 181. Dostoevsky was at first very favorably impressed. But then he became critical; for example, "[I am] not convinced that Danilevsky delineates with *full force* the ultimate essence of the Russian mission, which consists in the revelation of the Russian Christ before the world, the Christ *unknown* to the world and whose principle is contained in our kind of Orthodoxy. In my view this is the whole essence of our future role as civilizer and resurrector, as it were, of all Europe and [this is] the whole essence of our future life" (letter to Strakhov from Florence, March 1869).

33. See p. 255 in the Modern Library edition, Constance Garnett, trans. (New York, 1936).

34. *Ibid.*, p. 256.

Chapter 9. Conclusion

1. See the lengthy discussions of Danilevsky in Alfred Fischel, *Der Panslawismus bis zum Weltkriege* (Stuttgart, 1919); Hans Kohn, *Panslavism, its History and Ideology* (Notre Dame, 1953); Michael Boro Petrovich, *The Emergence of Russian Panslavism, 1856–1870* (New York, 1956); Frank Fadner, *Seventy Years of Panslavism in Russia, Karazin to Danilevskii, 1800–1870* (Georgetown, 1962); Konrad Pfalzgraf, "Die Politisierung und Radikalisierung des Problems Russland und Europe bei N. J. Danilevskij," *Forschungen zur Osteuropäischen Geschichte*, I (Berlin, 1954), 55–204, overdoes the affinity of Danilevsky's thought to that of Pogodin, official nationalism, and Russian Panslavism proper. J. Skupiewski, *La doctrine panslaviste d'après N. J. Danilevsky, "La Russie et l'Europe"; coup d'oeil sur les*

rapports politiques entre le monde slave et le monde germano-roman (Bucharest, 1890), is similar, though much more polemical than Pfalzgraf's work.

2. F. M. Istomin, ed., *Kratkii ocherk deiatelnosti s-peterburgskago slavianskago obshchestva za 25 let ego sushchestvovaniia 1868–1892 gg.* (St. Petersburg, 1893) and *Pervyia 15 let sushchestvovaniia s-peterburgskago slavianskago blagotvoritelnago oshchestva* (St. Petersburg, 1883).

3. *Ibid.,* p. 330.

4. Istomin, *Kratkii ocherk,* p. 56.

5. The source of some of this publication history is N. N. Strakhov's life of Danilevsky, pp. ix–xxxi of *Rossiia i Evropa,* 5th ed. (St. Petersburg, 1895). See also above, the list of Danilevsky's writings.

6. The more important items in the early, Russian, pre-Spenglerian discussion are the following: N. K. Mikhailovsky, "Rossiia i Evropa," *Sochineniia,* III (St. Petersburg, 1888), 364–405; V. S. Soloviev, "Rossiia i Evropa" (1888), "O grekakh i bolesniakh" (1889), "Shchastivyia mysli N. N. Strakhova" (1890), *Sobranie Sochinenii,* V (2nd ed., St. Petersburg, 1911–1914), 82–147, 267–286, 287–311, 312–319, 320–351; N. N. Strakhov replied to Soloviev with "Nasha kultura i vsemirnoe edinstvo" (1888), "Poslednii otvet g. Vl. Solovievu" (1889), *Borba s zapadom v nashei literature* (2nd ed., St. Petersburg, 1890), pp. 218–286, 287–304, and with "Istoricheskie vzgliady G. Ruckerta i N. Ia. Danilevskago," *Russkii Vestnik,* Oct. 1894, pp. 154–183; Constantine Leontiev replied to Soloviev with "Vladimir Soloviev protiv Danilevskago," *Sobranie Sochinenii,* VII (St. Petersburg, 1913), 285–379; N. I. Kareev, "Teoriia kulturno-istoricheskikh tipov," *Sobranie Sochinenii,* II (St. Petersburg, 1912), 67–107; P. N. Milioukov, "La Décomposition du Slavophilisme (Danilevski, Léontiev, V. Soloviev)," *Le Mouvement intellectuel russe,* J. W. Bienstock, trans. (Paris, 1918). These writers all misread, or better, underread, *Russia and Europe.* Those "against" Danilevsky (Mikhailovsky, Soloviev, Kareev, Miliukov) accused him of nationalistic isolationism. Those "for" him (Strakhov, Leontiev) sought to meet the attack both by pointing to elements of respect for "mankind" in Danilevsky's theory and by defending nationalism in some form.

On Danilevsky and Spengler, see Arthur Luther, "Ein russischer Vorläufer Oswald Spenglers," in *Alere Flammam* (Leipzig, 1921), pp. 51–59; M. Schwartz, "Spengler i Danilevsky (dva tipa kulturnoi morfologii)," *Sovremennyia Zapiski,* 28 (1926): 436–456; Pitirim A. Sorokin, *Social Philosophies of an Age of Crisis* (Boston, 1950), esp. pp. 49–71, 205–243; H. Stuart Hughes, *Oswald Spengler: A Critical Estimate* (New York, 1952), esp. pp. 44–50; J. G. DeBeus, *The Future of the West* (New York, 1953), esp. pp. 10–16; A. L. Kroeber, *Style and Civilizations* (Ithaca, 1957), esp. pp. 109f.

7. The epithet and its meaning are discussed in Michael Cherniavsky, *Tsar and People, Studies in Russian Myths* (New Haven, 1961), chap. 4.

8. Strakhov, *Borba s zapadom*, 2nd ed.

9. Nicholas Berdaiev, *Leontiev* (London, 1940), chap. 5; Iwan von Kologriwof, *Von Hellas zum Mönchtum, Leben und Denken Konstantin Leontjews (1831–1891)* (Regensburg, 1948), p. 134.

10. K. Bestuzhev-Riumin, *Russkaia istoriia*, I (St. Petersburg, 1872), 4f. See also his "Teoriia kulturno-istoricheskikh tipov," appendix to *Russia and Europe*, 5th ed., pp. 559–610.

11. V. V. Rozanov, "Otvet G. Vladimiru Solovievu" (*Russkii Vestnik*, April 1894, pp. 204–205); M. M. Sokolov, "Rossiia, Evropa, i chelovechestvo," *Russkii Vestnik*, Oct. 1904, pp. 627–696.

12. Mikhailovsky, "Rossiia i Evropa," p. 369. Potebnia the Slavicist.

13. M. N. Pokrovsky, *Diplomatiia i voiny tsarskoi Rossii v XIX stoletii. Sbornik statei* (Moscow, 1923), esp. pp. 230–301.

14. Most commentators (see note 6 above) on Danilevsky and Spengler have used Danilevsky in this way.

15. Robert E. MacMaster, "Danilevsky and Spengler: A New Interpretation," *The Journal of Modern History*, June 1954, pp. 154–161.

16. Peter Heath, trans. (New York, 1958), pp. 552–553.

17. A spiritual materialism such as that found in both Hegel and Marx of whom J. N. Findlay writes, "There is . . . as much materialism in Hegel as in Marx, since matter is for him a *stage* in the 'Idea.' (Just as there is also a strong strain of teleological idealism in the supposedly scientific materialism of Marx)" — *Hegel, a Re-examination* (London, 1958), p. 23.

18. See Renato Poggioli, *The Phoenix and the Spider* (Cambridge, Mass., 1957), pp. 28f. I am here paraphrasing some of Poggioli's remarks about Dostoevsky.

Index

Tartars, 222, 241, 247
Tatishchev, 324
Teleology, in world history: and theories of evolution, 148–149, 170; posited by Danilevsky, 149
Thebes, 272
Thiers, Louis Adolphe, 54
Tilsit, Treaty of, 192
Time, conflicting senses of, 119, 213, 242–243, 337; as linearly progressive, 252–253
Timiriazev, Kliment Arkadevich, 162–163
Timkovsky, K. I., 60
Tiutchev, F. I., 292, 342
Tkachev, Peter, 54; forerunner of Russian totalitarianism, 9, 16, 299, 304
Tocqueville, Alexis de, 92, 122, 329, 343
Tolstoi, Constantine, 157
Tolstoi, D. A., 36
Tolstoi, Leo, 15, 147, 180, 247, 293, 305; *Anna Karenina*, 95; *War and Peace*, 259
Tönnies, Ferdinand, 114–115
Totalitarianism: Danilevsky as forerunner of, 1, 15–17, 127, 161, 286–290, 298, 301, 306; characteristics of, 2–8; of voluntarism and determinism, 6–7; main types of, 8–15, 300; cultural conditions for, 30, 145, 305–306; Danilevsky's early lack of, 121; blend of romanticism and realism, 143; Danilevsky's later trend away from, 149–150; in articles on Russo-Turkish war, 154; of theory of Slavic Union, 245–246; proof of Danilevsky's, 268; Danilevsky as philosopher of, 294–310. See also Bolshevism; Russian totalitarianism
Toynbee, Arnold J., 21, 294, 302, 303, 334, 345
Traditionalism, in Russian radicalism, 44, 48, 305–306
Transcendentalism: in Western totalitarianism, 9; in Panslavism, 180, 249
Treitschke, Heinrich, 9
Trondheim, 100

Tsargrad, *see* Constantinople
Tsarism: Danilevsky's attitude toward, 22–23, 52, 58–59, 156, 297–298, 349; official attitude, 29–30. *See also* Monarchy
Turgenev, Ivan Sergeevich, 61, 224, 293
Turgenev, Nicholas, 329
Turks: and the Russo-Turkish war, 150, 155; control of Slavs by, 188, 222; and Crimean War, 191; and Mohammedanism, 266–267; kept from Europe by Austria, 270; and Slav state, 275. *See also* Eastern question
Typal theory, 198–213; Europe and Russia contrasted, 232–233, 348. *See also* Civilizations, cultural-historical; Cultural-historical types

Uexküll, J. J. von, 341
United States, 343; and balance of world power, 122; as union of states, 184; one of three separate cultures, 185; foreign policy of, 191–192; principle of liberty in, 209; national character of, 217–218
Unitéism, 89–90
Unity of nature, 77–80
Universal: contrasted with national, 195; human civilization as, 208–209
Universality: two concepts of, 210–211, 300; Western dream false, 224
Ural Cossacks, article on, 113
Utilitarianism: Danilevsky's, 122, 123, 136, 162, 276; in Russia in 1850's, 143; rejected in Darwinism, 148, 163–164; attributed to English, 163–164; and Slavophilism, 182, 226; degree of Danilevsky's commitment to, 277–278
Utopian radicalism, 15, 19, 43–44; Danilevsky's, 23, 85–86, 134, 258; expression of romanticism, 47; in *Russia and Europe*, 124–125, 248
Utopian socialism: advocated by Danilevsky, 23, 295, 305; God's aim through History, 286

Values: as objective outside man, 158–159; and distinction between

Russian Research Center Studies

1. *Public Opinion in Soviet Russia: A Study in Mass Persuasion,* by Alex Inkeles
2. *Soviet Politics — The Dilemma of Power: The Role of Ideas in Social Change,* by Barrington Moore, Jr.*
3. *Justice in the U.S.S.R.: An Interpretation of Soviet Law,* by Harold J. Berman. Revised edition
4. *Chinese Communism and the Rise of Mao,* by Benjamin I. Schwartz
5. *Titoism and the Cominform,* by Adam B. Ulam*
6. *A Documentary History of Chinese Communism,* by Conrad Brandt, Benjamin Schwartz, and John K. Fairbank*
7. *The New Man in Soviet Psychology,* by Raymond A. Bauer
8. *Soviet Opposition to Stalin: A Case Study in World War II,* by George Fischer*
9. *Minerals: A Key to Soviet Power,* by Demitri B. Shimkin*
10. *Soviet Law in Action: The Recollected Cases of a Soviet Lawyer,* by Harold J. Berman and Boris A. Konstantinovsky
11. *How Russia is Ruled,* by Merle Fainsod. Revised edition
12. *Terror and Progress USSR: Some Sources of Change and Stability in the Soviet Dictatorship,* by Barrington Moore, Jr.*
13. *The Formation of the Soviet Union: Communism and Nationalism, 1917–1923,* by Richard Pipes. Revised edition
14. *Marxism: The Unity of Theory and Practice,* by Alfred G. Meyer
15. *Soviet Industrial Production, 1928–1951,* by Donald R. Hodgman
16. *Soviet Taxation: The Fiscal and Monetary Problems of a Planned Economy,* by Franklin D. Holzman
17. *Soviet Military Law and Administration,* by Harold J. Berman and Miroslav Kerner
18. *Documents on Soviet Military Law and Administration,* edited and translated by Harold J. Berman and Miroslav Kerner
19. *The Russian Marxists and the Origins of Bolshevism,* by Leopold H. Haimson
20. *The Permanent Purge: Politics in Soviet Totalitariansm,* by Zbigniew K. Brzezinski*
21. *Belorussia: The Making of a Nation,* by Nicholas P. Vakar
22. *A Bibliographical Guide to Belorussia,* by Nicholas P. Vakar*
23. *The Balkans in Our Time,* by Robert Lee Wolff
24. *How the Soviet System Works: Cultural, Psychological, and Social Themes,* by Raymond A. Bauer, Alex Inkeles, and Clyde Kluckhohn†
25. *The Economics of Soviet Steel,* by M. Gardner Clark
26. *Leninism,* by Alfred G. Meyer*
27. *Factory and Manager in the USSR,* by Joseph S. Berliner†
28. *Soviet Transportation Policy,* by Holland Hunter
29. *Doctor and Patient in Soviet Russia,* by Mark G. Field†
30. *Russian Liberalism,* by George Fischer
31. *Stalin's Failure in China, 1924–1927,* by Conrad Brandt
32. *The Communist Party of Poland,* by M. K. Dziewanowski

* Out of print.
† Publications of the Harvard Project on the Soviet Social System.
‡ Published jointly with the Center for International Affairs, Harvard University.